SCHOOL OF AMERICAN RESEARCH
ADVANCED SEMINAR SERIES
Published by Cambridge University Press

Published by the University of New Mexico Press

Chiefdoms: power, economy, and ideology

CHIEFDOMS: POWER, ECONOMY, AND IDEOLOGY

EDITED BY
TIMOTHY EARLE

Department of Anthropology
University of California, Los Angeles

A SCHOOL OF AMERICAN RESEARCH BOOK

CAMBRIDGE
UNIVERSITY PRESS

Published by the Press Syndicate of the University of Cambridge
The Pitt Building, Trumpington Street, Cambridge CB2 1RP
40 West 20th Street, New York, NY 10011–4211, USA
10 Stamford Road, Oakleigh, Melbourne 3166, Australia

First published 1991
Reprinted 1997

British Library cataloguing in publication data

Chiefdoms: power, economy, and ideology. – (School of
   American Research advanced seminar series).
   1. Western world. Social systems. Evolution. Systems
   analysis
   I. Earle, Timothy K.   II. Series
   303.44

Library of Congress cataloguing in publication data

Chiefdoms: power, economy, and ideology / edited by Timothy Earle.
      p.   cm. – (School of American Research advanced seminar series)
      "A School of American Research book."
      Includes bibliographical references and index.
      ISBN 0–521–40190–9
      1. Chiefdoms – Congresses.   2. Political anthropology – Congresses.
      3. Social status – Congresses.   I. Earle, Timothy K.   II. Series. GN492.55.C48   1991
      306.2 – dc20 90 – 43065 CIP

Transferred to digital printing 2000

ISBN 0 521 40190 9

WV

Contents

Contents

Contributors

PROFESSOR RICHARD BRADLEY
Department of Archaeology
University of Reading

PROFESSOR ROBERT DRENNAN
Department of Anthropology
University of Pittsburgh

PROFESSOR TIMOTHY EARLE
Department of Anthropology
University of California,
Los Angeles

PROFESSOR GARY FEINMAN
Department of Anthropology
University of Wisconsin,
Madison

PROFESSOR YALE FERGUSON
Department of Political Science
Rutgers University

PROFESSOR ANTONIO GILMAN
Department of Anthropology
California State University,
Northridge

PROFESSOR PATRICK KIRCH
Department of Anthropology
University of California,
Berkeley

KRISTIAN KRISTIANSEN
Ministry of the Environment
The National Forest and
Nature Agency
Denmark

PROFESSOR CANDELARO SÁENZ
Department of Anthropology
State University of New York,
Purchase

PROFESSOR VINCAS
STEPONAITIS
Research Laboratories of
Anthropology
University of North Carolina,
Chapel Hill

Preface

Chiefdoms are intermediate societies, neither states nor egalitarian societies. The understanding of them and their dynamics lies at the base of recent attempts to study the evolution of complex societies. Earlier concepts of chiefdoms, deriving especially from the work of Service and Sahlins, have been much criticized, and many have advocated abandoning the chiefdom concept and similar evolutionary typologies. This general theoretical dissatisfaction, coupled with extensive new archaeological and historical studies of such societies, made me realize that a reconsideration of chiefdoms was overdue.

In late 1985, I talked over with Jonathan Haas, then director of programs and research, the idea of an Advanced Seminar on chiefdoms at the School of American Research. He was encouraging and helped me develop the seminar proposal and participant list. The goal was to bring together scholars with archaeological, historical, and ethnographic research on chiefdoms from around the world.

The seminar, "Chiefdoms: their evolutionary significance," was held January 18 to 22, 1988, at the School of American Research. Discussions were lively, ranging widely over many intellectual perspectives and geographical areas. Both American and European intellectual traditions were represented, although some bias towards a "Michigan/Columbia school" might be apparent. Most would consider themselves materialists although the diversity was clear in discussions, at times heated, among those whom others might label marxists, structural marxists, and cultural ecologists. Geographically, North

America, Mesoamerica, South America, Europe, and the Pacific were particularly well covered; major gaps, however, were apparent in sub-Saharan Africa and Asia, where the chiefdom concept has been little used. The participants in this seminar were primarily archaeologists, largely because of the recognition broadly within anthropology that evolutionary approaches require a long-term diachronic perspective. Sáenz, the one ethnographer, analyzed the historical sources for the Saharan society with which he works; Ferguson, a political scientist, provided a valuable perspective from outside anthropology in addition to his historical analyses of Greece and Italy.

All of the contributors to the present volume were participants in the seminar. In addition, Jonathan Haas, whose own work on social stratification was a keystone for several arguments at the seminar, sat in on many of our discussions and we tried actively to involve him. Winifred Creamer joined us for several meals and added important insight from her own research on chiefdoms. As can be seen in Chapter 1, which summarizes the seminar discussions, participants came to the seminar with quite divergent views on chiefdoms; at times everyone appeared to be talking at once, or at least trying to be recognized. In the end everyone was heard and we arrived at a degree of agreement that could not have been anticipated in the early discussions.

With only one exception, participants prepared papers before the sessions in Santa Fe and these were circulated to all. Vincas Steponaitis, who was both moving to a new job and becoming a first-time father, agreed to join after considerable cajoling but without written seminar paper. All of the papers included in this volume have evolved significantly from their seminar drafts, enriched from the productive interactions of our week together.

All who have participated in the Advanced Seminars at the School of American Research seem to come away with the memory of a charged intellectual event. Our group melded together for that week into a community of scholars that we will always remember. The School's staff pampered and supported us in such a utopian environment that it spoiled us for the real world. I thank Jonathan Haas, Douglas Schwartz, and the smoothly working team of the SAR for this remarkably productive experience.

1
The evolution of chiefdoms*

TIMOTHY EARLE

This book developed out of a seminar on chiefdoms held at the School for American Research. The seminar sought to understand the processes that underlie the origins and evolution of complex stateless societies. Discussions quickly focused on the nature of power: how chiefs obliged others to follow their direction. The participants in this book deal with the bases of power in chiefdoms; they all argue that a society's economy and ideology stand in different ways as the infrastructure and justification for developing political domination.

A chiefdom was rather loosely defined as a polity that organizes centrally a regional population in the thousands (Carneiro 1981; Earle 1987a). Some degree of heritable social ranking and economic stratification is characteristically associated. The question then becomes how we can understand the evolution of these societies out of a milieu of more simply organized community groupings, the development and cycling of these chiefdoms, and their eventual collapse, stasis or state formation.

Based largely on comparative studies of ethnographic cases, the

---

* Much of this introductory chapter derives from a summary of the chiefdom seminar published in *Current Anthropology* 30: 84–88.

1

accepted theoretical position on the evolution of chiefdoms has been to see central leadership as a social solution to particular ecological and economic problems. Since Malinowski, chiefs have been viewed as tribal bankers who manage their group's economy for the benefit of all (see Steward 1955). For example, redistribution of chiefdoms was thought to handle the need for local specialization when a growing population settled down to farming in an ecologically variable environment (Service 1962; cf. Earle 1977). Population growth was seen by adaptationalists as creating subsistence problems and the need for technological and social solutions (compare Boserup 1965; Johnson and Earle 1987). To understand the evolution of leadership was thus to identify the economic conditions coming out of a society's adaptation which require central management for their effective and efficient operation.

This established consensus has been criticized in a number of studies looking at the evolution of chiefdoms in particular regions of the world (summarized in Earle 1987a). In chiefdoms, redistribution did not seem to integrate specialized subsistence economies; irrigation systems seemed to be too small-scale to require regional organization; and repeatedly population densities were quite low. With a general agreement on the inadequacies of earlier perspectives, the seminar sought a new consensus that would change the way social evolution within chiefdoms is conceived and studied.

An issue that stirred debate was how an evolutionary typology could be constructed (Kristiansen, Chapter 2 below). Chiefdoms as a uniform unilinear stage of evolution was rejected because of the considerable variation within the category. Some advocated developing a refined social typology to break down the variability into structural types. Kristiansen, for example, argued that although important variables might well be the same across a general type such as chiefdom, the way that the variables were structured was fundamentally different. These structural differences then resulted in inherently different dynamic properties. He thus draws the distinction between chiefdoms and stratified societies as based on contrasting structures of the economy and ideology. Others, while accepting the concept of chiefdom as a useful analytic category, emphasized the importance of studying systematically variability in certain critical dimensions.

Within chiefdoms, three schemes for understanding variability were used repeatedly in the seminar:

2

(1) The scale of development, although probably continuous, can be dichotomized as simple vs. complex chiefdoms (Earle 1978; Steponaitis 1978; Wright 1984; Johnson and Earle 1987). Simple chiefdoms have polity sizes in the low thousands, one level in the political hierarchy above the local community, and a system of graduated ranking. Complex chiefdoms have polity sizes in the tens of thousands, two levels in the political hierarchy above the local community, and an emergent stratification.

(2) The basis of finance, although representing admixtures in individual cases, can be characterized as to the medium of payment, staple vs. wealth (D'Altroy and Earle 1985). Staple finance, often in the absence of extensive exchange, involves the mobilization and disbursement of food and technological goods as payment for services. The simplest form of staple finance involves providing feasts, common in virtually all chiefdoms. Wealth finance involves the procurement of items of symbolic value, either through long-distance exchange or patronized craft production, and their bestowal on supporters. The possession of these wealth objects is desired because they define an individual's social position and economic prerogatives.

(3) The structure of chiefdoms may be distinguished as group-oriented vs. individualizing (Renfrew 1974). Group-oriented chiefdoms emphasize the importance of group definition through investment in corporate labor constructions that are so common in chiefdoms. Individualizing chiefdoms rather emphasize the distinguishing of elites by status defining adornment (often items of wealth) and special housing and burial monuments. These schemes to understand variability are of course complicated by the historical conditions that affect individual cases. The point to hold in mind is that variation as seen in the schemes determines the dynamics of societal developments, and it is these dynamics that we wish to disentangle in our analyses.

The seminar also agreed that, to understand evolution, research must focus on sequences of long-term change (Drennan, Chapter 11 below; Kirch 1984; Kristiansen 1982). Despite a utility in developing

evolutionary theory, further cross-cultural studies of ethnographic cases have limited utility. Emphasis on ethnographic cases tends to stress functionalist theories with little possibility for rigorous evaluation. Rather research should now document archaeological and historical sequences and evaluate the similarities and differences in societal change from region to region (Drennan, Chapter 11 below).

With this accord on the importance of variability and diachronic studies, the seminar focused on understanding the dynamics of chiefdoms as political institutions. As the chapters in this book make clear, this perspective departs quite substantially from the established adaptationalist position. Specifically, each author investigates the various economic, political, and ideological means by which rulers try to extend and maintain political control. The unstable and cyclical character of chiefdoms is apparent in our cases; political centralization often fails.

In considering power relationships, discussions frequently returned to the commoners' evaluation of the costs of compliance wth a leader's demands compared to the costs of their refusal (Haas 1982). To construct a complex polity, leaders must bind followers to themselves; the leadership must be able to control the commoners' labor (Feinman and Nicholas 1987). What keeps them from "voting with their feet" and moving away from the centers of power and extraction? Larger groups do not form naturally; technological and social adjustments are necessary to concentrate and coordinate increasing numbers of people (Johnson 1982).

Is it population pressure which is to blame? In contrast to the adaptationalist position, population growth as a prime mover for cultural evolution received little support in the seminar. Drennan, Feinman, and Steponaitis emphasized the very low population densities that have been documented by intensive surveys for the chiefdoms in the Oaxaca Valley of highland Mesoamerica, for the Black Warrior Valley of Alabama, and for the Valle de la Plata in Colombia. Population density appears also to have been low for the early chiefdoms of southern England (Bradley). Population increase, however, certainly was associated with the evolution of political systems in the Marquesas and in Greece. On the Marquesas, population growth and resulting environmental deterioration created a susceptibility to severe drought that bound a local population to its leader and his large central stores of breadfruit (Kirch). In Greece, population growth accompanied

4

Mycenean state formation and, following the precipitous "Dark Age" decline, contributed to the emergence of the polis (Ferguson).

Generally, seminar participants were willing to accept that demographic pressure was a cause for social change, especially where resulting pressure could be demonstrated to intensify circumscription, as in the Marquesan case. However, the largely unspoken consensus favored Cowgill's (1975) argument against population as a prime mover. As Feinman and others emphasized, population growth rates are so highly variable in prehistory that changing rates must themselves be explained. Referring to the basic Darwinian model of natural selection, Gilman reminded the seminar that as far as the family was concerned, population pressure was constant, as family sizes always press against their ability to feed themselves. Any search for ecological and economic prime movers, such as population pressure, seemed in the seminar to meet with the discrediting countercase: "But among the . . ."

Rather, the seminar focused on the nature of the political process responsible for the creation and maintenance of regional polities. Simply phrased by Gilman, what do the bosses do to gain and extend power? A listing of ten potential political strategies included the following:

(1) giving (inflicting debt), feasting, and prestations;
(2) improving infrastructure of subsistence production;
(3) encouraging circumscription;
(4) outright force applied internally;
(5) forging external ties;
(6) expanding the size of the dependent population;
(7) seizing control of existing principles of legitimacy (the past, supernatural, and natural);
(8) creating or appropriating new principles of legitimacy;
(9) seizing control of internal wealth production and distribution;
(10) seizing control of external wealth procurement.

In strategies (1) and (2) leaders attempt to seize economic power derived from control over the means of production and/or distribution. To the degree that a people's subsistence is controlled, options of refusing to abide by central decisions are very limited. This control may result in a system of staple finance in which the surplus generated

as rent was used to support a nonproducing sector of the population. The ownership of the irrigation systems in southeastern Spain (Gilman) is such a circumstance. The development of the field systems in the European Iron Age (Earle) may well represent a land ownership system elaborated and formalized as a means to control subsistence production. In pastoral chiefdoms, such as the African Twareg chiefs (Sáenz) and the European Neolithic and Bronze Age societies (Bradley, Kristiansen), ownership of animals offered another basis for economic control. Alternatively, the chiefs' domination of long-distance exchange with external urban markets may offer control over productive technology and staple foods (Sáenz). Such exchange relationships were certainly important in the Aegean, where an export economy directed at the eastern Mediterranean civilizations contributed significantly to Minoan and Mycenaean state formation (Gilman).

Strategies (3)–(6) may involve an elite who exert control internally and extend control through conquest and external alliances. Warfare has been recognized as a common characteristic of chiefdoms (Carneiro 1981), as warriors were used to conquer new communities (and their tribute base) and to intimidate communities reluctant to give up their full share to the overlord. At the end of the Greek Dark Age, for example, Sparta expanded through conquest (Ferguson). Interestingly, the potential for control based on military force seems quite limited and unstable. In the Iron Age of Europe (Bradley, Kristiansen), the Argaric Bronze Age of southeastern Spain (Gilman), and the Mantaro Valley in Peru (Earle), warfare was prevalent but local chiefdoms were apparently unable to expand spatially to incorporate sizeable regional populations. Many of the small Greek poleis remained politically independent for a long period and were not incorporated into the expanding states. The naked force of warriors would appear to be difficult to marshal, such that a likely trajectory was for local groups to retain political autonomy by defending themselves in fortified locations virtually unassailable with the tactics of war characterizing chiefdoms.

Strategies (7)–(10) depend primarily on power derived from an ideology that strengthens the legitimate position of leaders as necessary to maintain the "natural" order of the world. In many cases this involves the leaders securely connecting themselves to the past. For the English Neolithic and early Bronze Age monuments, burial

6

mounds seem to plant a community's leadership line on a hill or ridge that dominates the landscape (Bradley 1984). Equally important is competition for external ties to a new ideology, often associated with an "international style," which is used to set the ruling elites as a people apart (see Flannery 1968; Helms 1979). For example, the warrior elite of northern Europe identified themselves with such symbols as the war chariots and stools from the distant Mediterranean (Kristiansen 1987a). The increasing control of long-distance wealth exchange and the use of that exotic wealth to attract and control local labor appear important facets of chiefdom development in highland Mesoamerica (Feinman); a similar pattern would appear to exist for the Mississippian chiefdoms (Steponaitis). Elites justified their position with reference to external sources of power inaccessible to others. The special wealth objects were often associated with powers that both symbolized and encapsulated the elites' divinity or at least nonlocal legitimacy.

The importance of ideology as a source of chiefly power has several historical examples. In the emergence of the polis, the myth of a Golden Age served as a ruling ideology; each polis held myths of heroes and patron gods important for creating the group's political identity (Ferguson). The Saharan nomadic chiefs likewise used the external Islamic state ideology in their political maneuverings (Sáenz).

The use of esoteric wealth, with associated external ideologies, can serve as status defining markers and as political currency used to materialize political relationships. The importance of controlling the distribution of foreign objects can thus be used to draw in a local population and reward their participation. An ideology derived from the external relations is, however, vulnerable to changing international conditions of trade and exchange. As such it is inherently less stable than a staple finance system. The different character of this finance system may thus give distinct dynamics to the chiefdoms in terms of scale of integration and stability of control.

Some stability may be gained by linking these esoteric objects to local ceremonies, as seen clearly in their association with ceremonial architecture in the Formative cultures of highland Mesoamerica (Feinman) and in the Mississippian culture (Steponaitis). As in the Wessex case, these ceremonial places may have been tied to land ownership. It likely was not coincidental that the first ceremonial architecture was probably for activities creating and reinforcing com-

7

munity bonds, rather than stressing status differences (Drennan). Many early chiefdoms appear to fit comfortably within Renfrew's model of a group-oriented chiefdom (Kristiansen).

Perhaps the most heated discussions in the seminar focused on the question of the priorities of power. Drennan, Feinman, and Steponaitis argued strongly that in the Mesoamerican and Mississippian chiefdoms, no convincing argument could be made for strict economic control, as would be seen in ownership of land or central storage. Rather, populations seem to have been drawn into sociopolitical systems in part through manipulated "smoke and mirrors," an ideology of religiously sanctioned centrality symbolized by the ceremonial constructions and exchanges in foreign objects of sacred significance. Those in the seminar who remained skeptical of this position were quieted by the argument that in simple chiefdoms the actual amount of labor and goods being mobilized from a dependent population was sufficiently small to present a low cost of compliance; the question of any necessary economic coercive power became mute as the cost of refusal need be only minimal and could be ideologically based.

On the other side, both Gilman and Earle kept returning to the position that power differential, although ceremonially sanctioned, must lie in the control over labor through control over subsistence. At least in some circumstances, as in the Polynesian cases and those from southeastern Spain, evidence for this economic control through ownership of land, productive technology, and storage is evident.

Earle argued that the development of complex political systems relies not simply on having access to a source of power but on the ability to control that power. Multiple sources for power certainly exist in the economy, military, and ideology (Mann 1986b), but the establishment of a social hierarchy would seem to depend more on being able to exclude others from power than simply on the existence of the power sources. One must ask whether a source of power is open to all or only to a select few; for example, what is it in a group that restricts access to the supernatural powers important to establish legitimacy? Political systems based on sources of power that cannot be easily controlled will be unstable. It was asserted by Earle that political stability ultimately depended on the ability to tie alternative sources for power to controllable aspects of the economy.

This position became somewhat grudgingly accepted, but with an

8

important caveat – what after all is "real economic control?" Kristiansen argued that, prior to true class formation, ideology penetrated social life as a cosmology of natural order and therefore served as a necessary element in control of labor and production. For example in Mesoamerica, economic power seems to have derived from a complex and interdependent system of ceremony, esoteric wealth obtained from long distances, craft production and local markets (Drennan, Feinman). Several participants felt that the strict economic controls discussed by Earle and Gilman were inappropriate for understanding the origins of chiefdoms but became important only in more complex chiefdoms where a class system existed.

The resolution of this debate was based on a recognition by all participants that the three components of power (i.e. control over the economy, war, and ideology) to some degree present alternative strategies. Ferguson emphasized how polities contain overlapping, layered and linked authority patterns with different factions and institutions competing for power (compare Mann 1986). These different factions within a single chiefdom or between competing chiefdoms may opt for different strategies to attempt to dominate each other. The Marquesan case (Kirch) illustrates how chiefs, warriors and inspirational priests with their different power bases competed with each other without an ability for any sector to dominate. The complexity of the political dynamics of the Marquesan chiefdom, rather than representing an odd exception, may characterize many chiefdoms. Effective domination would seem to depend on interlocking the different strategies so as to concentrate power and overcome the limiting characteristics of the individual power sources.

As an example, considerable attention was given to the European Neolithic and Bronze Ages. An important source of power was certainly the society's ideology which involved both elaborate local ceremonies of place and status identification with foreign symbols. At the end of the Neolithic period, these two forms of ideology appear to have been at odds, each used by competing groups in Wessex (Bradley). Both forms of ideology were strongly grounded on economic control. The elaborate ceremonial constructions, associated with both funerary and cosmic ritual, would seem to have grounded the ideology in the economy through the use of the monuments to define productive territories controlled by the chiefs (Earle). Elites could retain leadership by affirming their necessary roles in maintaining local sub-

9

sistence economy through ritual. Essentially the monuments materialized a social and ritual landscape that could be owned by those maintaining and defending rights to the monuments. The land over which ownership was proclaimed was largely open pasturage for animals. These animal herds contributed significantly to the society's subsistence, but more importantly the animals would have served as a concentratable and productive form of wealth used to finance elite strategies for control. The animals appear repeatedly as the foods for feasts, in which leaders would have compensated followers for their support (Bradley). At the end of the Neolithic period, the ideology became based more on the use of wealth (especially the metal) obtained from a distance. Chiefs were identified by an elite international style and ideology that both legitimized their distinguished status and, in the case of the metals, created a technology of warrior domination through force (Kristiansen). Most importantly, though, access to this new ideology could be controlled by the fact that it was economically based. The wealth objects had to be obtained through long-distance exchange open only to elites (Helms 1979), and then had to be worked by a few craftsmen who could be controlled through elite patronage (Brumfiel and Earle 1987).

The success or failure of the various political strategies (and ultimately the success of the chiefly institutions on which they are based) would appear to be in part determined by the ecological and social conditions. The nine "environmental" conditions most responsible for differences in successful trajectory of political development are listed below:

(1) natural productivity and potential for intensification;
(2) regional population density;
(3) existence of external markets;
(4) natural circumscription;
(5) concentration of productive resources;
(6) proximity to needed nonfood resources;
(7) proximity to avenues of trade and communication;
(8) social circumscription;
(9) structural preconditions of hierarchy.

As Steponaitis emphasized when making up this list, these conditions are certainly not sufficient cause for chiefly development. Cases exist

in which social complexity failed to develop despite the presence of some critical conditions.

It is convenient to recognize two aspects of these environmental conditions that especially affect the development of chiefdoms. First are the conditions that permit the generation and extraction of a surplus. This surplus, on which the new institutions of chiefdoms depend, is the product of the productive potential of the land (condition (1)), the human labor to make it fruitful (condition (2)), and external markets (condition (3)) that offer alternative sources of energy. Second are the potential conditions that circumscribe a people's options and thus permit a surplus to be mobilized and channeled toward a center. Circumscription, as articulated by Carneiro (1970), essentially limits the opportunities available to a human population; it increases the cost of refusal by limiting the options. To some degree environments differ in their relative circumscription (condition (4)), as of course is evident when contrasting the isolated islands of the Pacific with the broad continental areas of Europe or Mesoamerica. This circumscription is locally a product of how concentrated, and thus easily controlled, are the most productive lands (condition (5)), necessary nonfood resources (condition (6)), and trading opportunities (condition (7)). Beyond these are the external political environment (condition (8)) including antagonistic groups whose control of land in effect circumscribes socially the group.

The internal sociopolitical structure (condition (9)) may also exclude much of the population as political actors, as in the case of the Polynesian chiefdoms where the existing social structure of the colonizing populations apparently affected the course of social development. An inherent and accepted principle of social inequality continued to structure political behavior in Europe well after the fall of the Roman empire and its effective economic basis for power (Ferguson).

A critical point reached by the seminar was that environmental conditions are not something simply presented to a human population. Rather environments are dynamic sets of cultural and natural conditions that are constantly modified and created by human intervention (Bargatzky 1984). For example, in the Valley of Oaxaca, the early concentration of social and economic activities including ceremonies, craft specialization, and the like created a positive draw to local population that apparently brought them in close to the center

11

and made the control of labor possible (Feinman). Or more simply, although the concentration of natural productivity is initially derived from soil, rainfall, vegetative cover, and the like, the resource base quickly becomes altered through human intervention. Humans act to improve the resource base through such projects as irrigation, terracing, and drainage; they also act to degrade the resources through overuse and induced erosion. In Hawaii, and in Europe as well, the two processes together had the effect of concentrating the productive resource into limited zones that came to be owned by the elites. This action may be part of purposeful political strategies to increase economic control, as in the Hawaiian case (Earle 1978), or part of unforeseen consequences of individual household and community action to improve their lot, as in the Danish case (Kristiansen). In either situation, the effect was largely the same, i.e. the creation of conditions permitting elite control through exercising powers of land ownership.

Other examples of changing conditions have to do with circumscription. Natural circumscription may be quite low, as for example in a continental area like Europe, but the opportunities available to a local population become circumscribed as the landscape fills in and is divided up as owned territories. Ferguson made the interesting suggestion that warfare between polities in the Aegean Dark Age may have been encouraged at times as a political strategy to increase social circumscription. Thus the regional extension of a chiefdom could actually weaken it by eliminating an external threat. In a similar vein, the fortification walls of a European hill fort could act as much to enclose (circumscribe) a population as to protect it from an enemy.

It can probably be demonstrated how different environments present different opportunities for control and finance. These different conditions and how they create quite different trajectories for development may affect profoundly the successes of alternative political strategies. Therefore the potential to develop intense irrigation, as in Hawaii or southeastern Spain, gives a potential for strong local control over the staple resource production, but in the absence of a movable wealth tends to remain limited in spatial scale. The development of a wealth finance system as articulated to an external justifying ideology and/or a military superiority can overcome this localism to create an expanding political system. However, the trade-off is to make the system dependent on external relations that can disrupt local patterns of domination.

12

The evolution of chiefdoms

When studying the dynamics of chiefdoms, as discussed above, researchers have studied the dynamics of the polity itself. Although the regional organization of chiefdoms is normally taken as one of their most fundamental characteristics (Carneiro 1981), an understanding of the operation of chiefdoms should also consider different scales of analysis. The four scales discussed most frequently are the household, the community, the chiefly polity, and the interpolity region (Johnson and Earle 1987). To understand the evolution of chiefdoms requires understanding the household and community as semi-autonomous units that may exist in competition with each other and in opposition to the overarching polity. Thus the centralization of the chiefdom should always be seen as a fragile, negotiated institution that is held together by an economic interdependence, a justifying ideology, and a concentration of force.

The cycling of chiefdoms received considerable attention in our discussions. Centers of power shift through a region and the extent of integration builds up only to collapse. The reasons for this cycling would appear to be multifaceted. First, and most fundamental, the ability to sustain political integration requires the polity leadership to maintain the balance between the compliance and refusal costs. Given constantly changing local and regional conditions, this must have been a continual juggle. Second, and not discussed at any length, chiefdoms, with their limited high-status positions, are inherently competitive in their political dynamics (Earle 1978). What this means is that individuals are constantly vying for controlling position. Two opposing forces are thus created: one a centralizing tendency as individuals seek to concentrate power and eliminate the opportunities for rebellion, and the other a fragmenting tendency as local leaders seek to pull themselves apart from overarching rule and establish their independent authority. It is perhaps more surprising that some chiefdoms are able to sustain themselves than that others disintegrate. Here the importance of close economic control would seem of paramount importance.

Chiefdoms, however, must not be understood in isolation but as broadly interacting polities linked into regional interaction spheres (peer polity interaction [Renfrew 1982a]) and into world economic systems (core–periphery relations [Rowlands, Larsen, and Kristiansen 1987a]). Thus the dynamics of evolution and collapse can often be understood only by the external relationships involving political com-

13

petition, long-distance exchange, and international ideologies that act to bind elites more to each other than to the local groups they dominate (Kristiansen).

Our discussions could be seen as both exciting and discouraging. Much progress has been made in understanding chiefdom development, but each attempt at simple synthesis was met with criticism. Drennan, cast in the role of spoiler, was especially critical of the formulations offered. Drawing evidence from six prehistoric sequences in Mesoamerica, Panama, and Colombia, he argued convincingly that differences between sequences had not been adequately explained. Some of these differences appeared early in the respective sequences and conditioned later developments, such that any explanation for state formation must ultimately consider the dynamics of preceding chiefdoms. This understanding led Drennan to stress differences as opposed to similarities. A frequent joke was that we could speak confidently of cause and consequence only where we knew little. Problems identifying the economic basis of social complexity in the well-documented archaeological record for Oaxaca and the Big Black kept being referred to, and Kristiansen stressed the need to overcome such problems by seeking generating structural principles behind the apparent contrasting archaeological sequences.

The synthesis that emerged from the seminar discussions is ultimately more powerful because it recognizes the extreme complexity and interdependence of the sources of power and control within society and the forces of instability and division that constantly threaten to tear it apart. Of particular interest is the long-term cycling of chiefdoms that creates local and regional patterns of expansion and collapse (devolution).

The basis of the emerging consensus is that chiefdoms must be understood as political systems. To do this, attention must focus on political power and how it is generated and itself controlled. Especially important in this regard is how the subsistence economy becomes redirected to finance the emerging regional institutions of the chiefdoms. Control over the political economy is maintained by a combination of military and ideological activity. Part of the mobilized surplus may be used to develop the economic base as well as to support a warrior class to defend and conquer lands and to support ceremonies which establish the legitimacy of the rulers. The combination of economic control, military might, and ceremonial legitimacy is a repeated

14

theme of the cases developed in this book. Many options are available for the control on which chiefdoms depend, but these options are not infinite and are not equal in their stability and growth potential. The choice among the options depends on particular conditions of the environment, technology, and individual case history; the outcome is significant variation in the speed and extent of evolutionary development. The recognition that political processes of chiefdoms are linked to available options for power and control should carry us a long way towards explicating the variable character of evolutionary change that underlies the evolution of social complexity.

Chiefdoms, states, and systems of social evolution

KRISTIAN KRISTIANSEN

INTRODUCTION: CHIEFDOMS AND STATES, A CRITICAL ASSESSMENT

In this chapter, I will clarify the diverse evolutionary terms that have been applied to intermediate-level societies. My concern is to identify basic structural contrasts and large-scale processes that together help explain social change in northern European prehistory during the Bronze and Iron Ages. Although the societies of these times have often been called chiefdoms, I want to emphasize that such a gloss term obscures the critical transformation that characterized European society at the end of the Bronze Age. It is the nature and the reasons for this transformation that I wish to illuminate in this paper.

Several recent works stress the inadequacy of our present evolutionary typology and emphasize that an individual type, such as chiefdom, spans too broad a range of variation (Feinman and Neitzel 1984; Upham 1987; Spencer 1987). Although some might propose abandoning evolutionary theory (Hodder 1986; Shanks and Tilley 1987, ch. 6), it remains the most persuasive explanatory framework in archaeology and we are probably well advised to continue to use a refined evolutionary perspective. Attempts which have been made to redefine evolutionary typologies specify and define variants in terms of scale

(Steponaitis 1978), in terms of organizing principles of the political economy (D'Altroy and Earle 1985; Earle 1987b), in terms of ecological conditions (Sanders and Webster 1978), and in terms of underlying structural dynamics (Friedman and Rowlands 1977).

Although each redefinition has introduced important new concerns, we are quickly becoming mired in a proliferation of terms without much attempt to relate these terms systematically to each other. For example, how do tribal prestige goods systems, as defined by Friedman and Rowlands (1977), relate to wealth finance in chiefdoms, as defined by D'Altroy and Earle (1985)? How should we compare alternative types such as stratified society, defined by Fried (1960, 1967), or *militärische Demokratie*, originating in the work of Engels (1977 [1891])? In addition, the chiefdom concept has been applied to a range that many would see running the gamut from tribal to state societies. Has the chiefdom type lost its heuristic value?

In my opinion, the reason for this state of affairs is that a few variables have been studied without due consideration of their implications for the organization of production in the societies under study. Thus cross-cultural studies, such as Peebles and Kus (1977), Claessen (1978), or Feinman and Neitzel (1984), use correlations between variables, such as population size, levels of decision making, settlement hierarchy, or status distinctions to define levels of social complexity. Their focus on correlation between variables overlooks, however, significant differences in structure, such as the nature of tribute/taxation, ownership, labor mobilization and social classes. Often, such structural relationships cannot be directly observed, but can only be inferred through interpretation of the cultural whole. What may look like a continuum without clear dividing lines can reveal sharp structural transformations in key relationships of economic and social control. Organizational properties cannot be treated as separate variables (traits), because their cultural meaning and material functions depend on their place and function in society. Particularly the articulation between the organization of the economy and the polity must be stressed for developing a comprehensive evolutionary typology.

The above critique calls for a reassessment of the organizational properties and their articulation in intermediate societies. What I will argue, unlike other contributors to this volume, is that a fundamental organizational divide exists between tribal societies, of which the chiefdom is a variant, and state societies.

17

To Fried, the transition to a state form of organization was a fundamental one. In an incipient phase, termed *stratified society*, "man enters a completely new arena of social life" (Fried 1960: 721). Most authors have overlooked the fundamental character of this change by focusing on the feature that "stratified society is distinguished by differential relationships between the members of society and its subsistence means" (Fried 1960: 721) and de-emphasizing the social and political changes in organization and exploitation that accompanied this transformation (see Fried 1978). The transformation to stratified society must be recognized as the structural change that underlies the evolution of states (Sanders and Webster 1978; Haas 1982).

I believe that, between chiefdoms and fully developed states, stratified societies were an archaic form of state organization, a genuine phase on the road to full-fledged states (see Claessen and Skalník 1978). In order to highlight the qualitative differences represented by this phase, I will discuss in more detail some of the characteristics and variability of such incipient states in prehistory.

Stratified societies comprise the basic features of state organization, such as strong social and economic divisions and an emphasis on territory (rather than kinship), but they lack developed bureaucracies.

The decisive significance of stratification is not that it sees differential amounts of wealth in different hands, but that it sees two kinds of access to strategic resources. One of these is privileged and unimpeded; the other is impaired, depending on complexes of permission which frequently require the payment of dues, rents, or taxes in labor or in kind. The existence of such distinctions enables the growth of exploitation, whether of a relatively simple kind based upon drudge slavery or of a more complex type associated with involved divisions of labor and intricate class systems. (FRIED 1960: 722)

The emergence of new power relations cross-cutting traditional, communal networks is redefined in terms of economic obligations; the requirement to pay tribute or tax replaces traditional social rights and obligations. Economic exploitation is formalized, enforced by military power, and sanctioned legally as well as ritually. Complexity, scale, and other institutional and political traits are secondary and variable traits to these structural transformations (discussion in Claessen 1978; Johnson and Earle 1987).

Variants of stratification have been recognized by Fried (1960) and others (e.g. Claessen and Skalník 1978; Haas 1982). I have chosen two

18

variants of stratified society that seem to cover a majority of cases, which, for convenience, I call decentralized stratified society and the centralized archaic state. These general terms replace older euro-centric or more historically specific terms such as the "Asiatic state," "*militärische Demokratie,*" or the "Germanic mode of production." This is to stress the general significance of stratified society in world history.

The decentralized stratified society

In his classical work, *The origins of the family, private property and the state,* Engels (1977 [1891]) developed a historical case of decentralized stratified society under the name, "*militärische Demokratie*" or the "Germanic mode of production." He saw *militärische Demokratie* as the highest level of barbarism, where contradictions between the traditional community-based society and a new social and economic order were played out. In *militärische Demokratie,* military leaders sustained themselves through plunder and territorial conquest. Herrmann (1982) has elaborated on this formulation in the light of modern research.

The decentralized stratified society as a general type can be described in the following way. Subsistence production is decentralized, with village communities or individual farms scattered across the landscape. Chiefs and kings set themselves apart from the agrarian substrait and rule through a retinue of warriors. Freed from kinship obligations, the warrior chiefs and king control, undermine, and exploit the farming communities through tribute and taxation. Ownership of land is formalized, and a landless peasant class develops. Regional and local vassal chiefs provide warriors and ships for warfare. Similar social structures may develop in pastoral societies in their interaction with state societies or under internal contradictions of blocked expansion (Bonte 1977, 1979; Irons 1979; Krader 1979; Sáenz, Chapter 5 below).

Towns are absent. Instead trading communities, or ports of trade, are controlled by the central government (Hodges 1982). Specialized craft production is performed by both slaves and free specialists. Centers for craft production may coexist with local settlements, but the craftsmen are attached to elite patrons. Such trading and production centers may develop into towns of small size, and the control and

19

taxation of long-distance trade may play a significant economic role in development.

In Europe, but also in historical cases in Africa and Asia, the ritual, legitimizing role of kinship is replaced by secular and ideological functions, corresponding to the new forms of social and economic control (Mair 1977; Wallace-Hadrill 1971).

Central to the new social form of stratification must be formalized ways to extract tribute, tax, and labor. This income then can support territorial conquest to create the larger polities of kingdoms. Although bureaucracies are not institutionalized, written scripts may be employed by specialists to record transactions. The interaction between conquest warfare and plunder, the control of trade, the formalizing of landholding, and taxation leads to decentralized stratified society.

I see particularly in the European sequence a development from more generalized to more specific ways of surplus extraction linked to emerging markets and private landholding, allowing increasingly formalized taxation and rent collection to develop. Without private landholding and taxation linked to it, the state cannot be permanently sustained in a decentralized economic setting. In the decentralized stratified society, the basic features of the feudal state are gradually formalized.

Centralized archaic state

The "Asiatic state" was coined by Marx, although as a concept its theoretical importance was not elaborated in his works. In this initial model, a centralized, ritually sanctioned government is based on state ownership of land administered to generate tribute. For example, see the temple economies discussed fully by Sofri (1975 [1969]). The historical implications of the Asiatic state have been widely discussed and criticized (Bailey and Llobera 1981; Wickham 1985), and it is now clear that an interaction always exists between a private and a public sector in these societies (see Bintliff 1982). On the other hand, general features of this type recur in initial state formation as the principles of theocratic chiefdoms are formalized (Webb 1975, 1987). The formulation of the Asiatic state by Friedman and Rowlands (1977) may be used as a second, alternative path to state society, in contrast to decentralized stratified society.

The centralized archaic state formalizes the tribal structure of the conical clan into a ruling elite, legitimized by controlled ritual access to the supernatural. The centralized archaic state develops in regions of high productivity where surplus can be generated and controlled. Through a formalized system of tribute, surplus production is converted into large-scale ritual activities, building of ceremonial centers, organization of craft production, and centralized trade. Slave labor and a division of labor along lines of kinship evolve into new classes performing special activities.

The internal economic structure consists of a tribute or corvée relation between local lines and their chiefs, and between the chiefs and their paramount, and chiefly and royal estates maintained by debt slaves and captives.

The centralized archaic state formalized the basic components of a developed bureaucracy to administrate production, trade, and religious activities. In its further development, both warfare for control of essential resources and commercialization of production for trade play important roles (see Gilman, Chapter 7 below; Ferguson, Chapter 8 below). In comparison with the decentralized stratified society, the major difference lies in the centralized economy with its potential for sustaining a state apparatus and the ritualized genealogical structure of the ruling class.

Evolutionary antecedents to stratified societies

Contrasting to my characterization of stratified organization, chiefdoms should be considered as a tribal form of social organization. Economic and political processes are organized along kinship lines (or kinship relations are defined along lines of production and exchange [cf. Earle, Chapter 4 below]). Control, embedded in kinship, has not transformed social groups into classes. Nevertheless, even within tribal structures, hierarchy and exploitation may still be a major factor. By gradually eroding traditional rights and increasing exploitation, the road may be paved for state reorganization. We are dealing with a progression in which the state represents a formalizing of hierarchy and exploitation, a process, if not irreversible, then hardly reversible to a tribal level. Thus a state-class structure rarely disappears entirely in periods of political fragmentation. We should rather speak of state systems that may cycle through a number of organizational forms,

21

such as centralization vs. decentralization, feudalism vs. commercialism, empire vs. city states, etc. (see Ferguson, Chapter 8 below).

The above redefinition of chiefdoms and stratified society has implications for the category of complex chiefdoms, some of which are archaic states, while others may belong to chiefdoms. But how do we differentiate these types? One of the most important points to consider is how the labor crews that built the ceremonial centers of Stonehenge or platform mounds in Peru were recruited. The significance of such constructions depends less on the total scale of labor involved than on its *organization* (see Bradley, Chapter 3 below). Was it based upon occasional mobilization through social obligations and rewarded by reciprocal feasting, or was it based upon formalized control of communities through land ownership? Only in the latter case are we dealing with a state form of organization (for an interesting debate, see Haas 1982: 183ff.). To recognize the probable organization of labor requires a consideration of such aspects as the size of individual work parties and the overall design integrity of the monuments.

In Fig. 2.1, I indicate two evolutionary trajectories which can evolve from the tribal systems structured on kinship and community. Following Renfrew (1974) and Earle (Chapter 4; D'Altroy and Earle 1985), I have defined two types of chiefdoms – collective and individualizing, based respectively on staple finance and its control over subsistence production and on wealth finance with its control over valuables (Kristiansen 1982, 1984). Wealth finance as defined by Earle has much in common with prestige goods economies as defined by Friedman and Rowlands, just as staple finance and tributary systems represent another, if not opposing, strategy of economic control (see Earle, Chapter 4 below). In both cases wealth is considered to be the basic economic operator. Staple finance, however, is dominated by vertical relations of production and exchange, prestige goods being a dependent variable; whereas in prestige goods systems, horizontal relations are dominating and sufficient to establish control of labor and production. These two principles are not mutually exclusive and may be combined in various forms of social organization, although in prestate societies prestige goods economies are mostly linked to individualizing, segmentary, "pastoral" societies, while staple finance is rather linked to collective, territorial and "agricultural" societies. In essence, it seems reasonable that different sources of income used to support emerging elites will result in very different internal and devel-

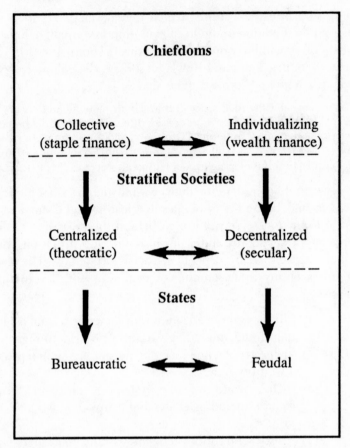

Fig. 2.1   A temporal model of alternative evolutionary trajectories

opmental characteristics in stratified societies. Thus chiefdoms based on staple finance may develop into centralized archaic states and those based on wealth finance, into decentralized stratified societies (Fig. 2.1).

EVOLUTIONARY TRAJECTORIES AND SYSTEMS OF SOCIAL EVOLUTION AND DEVOLUTION

In the preceding section I have considered the internal structure and articulation of two ideal types of social organization without discussing

23

the historical contexts under which they develop. To do so we must give up the traditional notion of evolution as a unidirectional process taking place within bounded social units (Ekholm 1980, 1981; Friedman 1976; Friedman and Rowlands 1977). Evolution is a *spatial*, as well as a temporal, process. This demands

that we consider the total space within which reproduction occurs as a process. Within that space we must consider the social structured properties that determine the nature and intensity of flows and thus the rate of reproduction in the larger system. Finally we must deal with society not as consisting of actual societies, but of structures of temporal processes. (FRIEDMAN 1976)

If we are to consider chiefdoms within such a spatial framework we need to understand the principles that lead to and distinguish various social formations. We need to go behind the prevailing evolutionary typology of chiefdoms and states to define the structuring principles which create spatially dependent social formations. The theoretical premises of my understanding of evolution and devolution are as follows:

(1) tribal social organization may generate several evolutionary trajectories, including variants of chiefdom organization;
(2) their direction and potential depend upon their place within a world system;
(3) such a world system can be very large and structurally diverse, including center and periphery relations from states to tribes;
(4) consequently tribes, chiefdoms, and states may be understood as parts of a contiguous structure defined in space; and
(5) from this understanding it follows that chiefdoms more often than not are dependent in some way upon their place in larger historical cycles of evolution and devolution.

Such an approach has several theoretical implications (Rowlands 1987). The dichotomy between internal evolution and external domination dissolves, and the traditional polarization of production and exchange can no longer be maintained. The complexity of such world systems – whether based on core–periphery relations (Wallerstein 1974; Friedman and Rowlands 1977) or on interacting regional systems (Renfrew and Cherry 1987) – has yet to be explained. Fig. 2.2 gives a schematic outline of such a world system. In the center, city states and empires have evolved. They are then linked economically

24

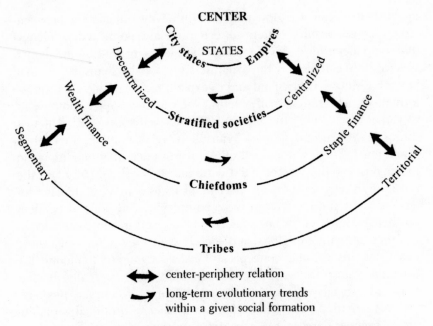

CENTER

Fig. 2.2   A spatial model of center/periphery relationships among evolutionary types

and politically to peripheries at increasing distance (P1, P2, P3) where societies can be graded by evolutionary complexity. Cross-cutting this spatial structure is a long-term evolutionary trend towards increasing political centrality and economic control. After the emergence of state systems, it is no longer possible to talk about independent developments. This does not deny autonomous developments, but, as interlocked regional exchange systems have been in existence since the Neolithic, we have to consider processes of change on a larger scale than the local and regional system. Chiefdoms are in many cases, perhaps in most cases, a secondary development. Such an approach naturally has consequences for understanding the ethnographic present. Many "autonomous" chiefdoms and tribes may simply be devolved societies, temporarily cut off from the larger system of which they had historically been a part (Cohen 1978: 54; Ekholm and Friedman 1979).

Within such a world system, the regional systems maintain a degree of autonomy, despite their dependency on remote regions for supplies of metal, prestige goods, and ritual information. Long-term trends

established within a region may determine the interaction between regions by establishing patterns of economic and political dependency that help determine the course of development within the larger system. If we can identify the dynamics of regional systems, we are in a better position to understand and to explain major changes and transformations of interregional systems, such as the Lapita complex in Oceania (Kirch 1987), the Midwestern Hopewellian in North America (Braun 1986), or the Corded-Ware/Bell-Beaker complex in Europe (Shennan 1986b). The crucial question is: under what conditions do regional interactions become a driving force? We should also face the possibility that less complex, peripheral regions may be decisive for development and collapse in more complex core regions, dependent on their peripheries for raw material, labor, and in some cases food.

When applying this global approach to concrete studies, one should avoid rigid institutional concepts and instead should try to identify the underlying organizational properties spatially and temporally. Institutions, like social types, always are an outcome of complex processes creating variation in time and space. Whether institutional variations are to be considered along a continuum or divided by abrupt, even catastrophical, changes will be discussed in the last section of this paper.

Is it possible to identify and come to terms with such large-scale processes in archaeological terms? Since archaeologists are dealing with changing distributions of material culture, we may be in a better position than historians and social anthropologists to deal with processes of large-scale change. A major task is to study the way material culture is employed in social strategies to define processes of expansion and resistance and to form local, regional, and international identities (Gailey and Patterson 1987). The consumption of wealth in time and space should give important clues to identifying processes of centralization and ranking when compared with the organization of production. This should be linked to studies of the way values are established and employed as a means to create power and dependency (Earle 1982). This way of establishing value is often linked to cosmologies where power resides in chiefs' ability to travel and create alliances with distant chiefdoms and centers of ritual superiority (see Helms 1986, 1988a, 1988b). Exchange and political power are linked to one another in creating and reproducing local and regional power structures.

ARCHAEOLOGICAL CASE STUDIES

In the following, I will demonstrate how apparently similar configurations in the archaeological record, reflecting rather similar strategies in the development of ruling elites, are based on different systems of production and social organization. I shall proceed by summarizing aspects of social organization, followed by a discussion of ritual depositions and monument construction, and the underlying processes of change.

The Bronze Age

Both the emergence of tribal elites and long-term changes in the nordic Bronze Age have been described in recent works (Jensen 1987; Kristiansen 1978, 1987a, 1987b; Levy 1982; Larsson 1986; Randsborg 1974; Sørensen 1987; Welinder 1976). The following section summarizes some of the major trends as reflected in material culture, settlement, and ecology. Comparison should be made to the Late Neolithic and Early Bronze Age of England where similar patterns emerge (Bradley, Chapter 3 below; Earle, Chapter 4 below).

Leadership during the Bronze Age was ritualized. Chiefs acted as both war leaders and ritual leaders; chiefly women also had ritual or priestly functions. A dual chiefly organization, with two male chiefs, was not uncommon and is reflected in recurrent double-male burials. The ritual chiefs had a following of high ranking warriors, although the nature of this following cannot be specified. War parties seem to have been small, and no major territorial conquest is documented; no defense works existed. Chiefdoms, or rather clusters of chiefdoms, are reflected in localized style variations and in metalwork (Rønne 1987, fig. 24; Larsson 1986, fig. 71 and fig. 88). These stylistic regions are approximately 500–1,000 km², 20–40 km across, normally with one or a few central places (Larsson 1986, fig. 106). Within this region, local settlement units (individual chiefdoms) are defined by clusters of barrows typically only a few kilometers across. Paramount chiefs were in control of long-distance elite exchange in metals, prestige goods, and related exotic knowledge. The rise of chiefdoms around 1500 B.C. was linked to an ideological and military complex of aristocratic warriors that spread from the Mycenaean area and Asia Minor through central Europe and Scandinavia. It was characterized by new chiefly regalia

27

including war chariots, stools, swords, razors, and tweezers (Kristiansen 1987b).

At the local level, groups of impressive long houses, 30 m long and 8 m wide, housed extended families divided into two to three domestic units. To each settlement belonged one or more barrows. Each settlement compound apparently represented a small population whose leader was the local representative of a chiefly lineage; only these chiefs, who represented perhaps ten to fifteen percent of the population, were apparently buried in the barrows. It is assumed that the local branches of the chiefly lineage formed a conical clan with one or a few leading paramount chiefs, normally represented by barrows and settlements of outstanding wealth. The overall ranked structure of the chiefs is reflected by differential access to metal work. Burials have distinct levels of wealth; elite goods, with chiefly swords, were at the top, and common tools, at the bottom. Social diversification was, however, likely based on kinship without real social classes. Both burial customs and material culture were homogeneous, and status distinctions were linked to variations within a common cultural and social framework. This pattern of a common elite style over a broad region is what has been called an international style (see Earle 1989).

Land use was extensive, based on husbandry of free grazing herds and rotating fields in an open landscape. No fixed field boundaries occur, indicating an unstructured land-tenure system, but the landscape was highly structured by barrows and settlements forming a social and ritual landscape that remained stable for a thousand years (Earle, Chapter 4 below).

During the Late Bronze Age, 1000–500 B.C., regional identities emerged, most clearly in areas of economic decline. Stress and competition were apparently increasing, but the overall cultural framework was still intact. A small group of large chiefly settlements and barrows appeared in some areas, suggesting new, regional aristocracies (Thrane 1984; Jensen 1981). At ordinary settlements, houses became smaller and more numerous, apparently a trend towards smaller family groups. Sheep and pigs were most frequent at the commoner settlements, but cattle were dominant at the chiefly settlements (Hedeager and Kristiansen 1988: 86). As some settlements became larger, local and regional groupings of settlements became clear. The landscape was heavily exploited, and open secondary forests for grazing and leaf foddering were reduced or eliminated. Agriculture was intensified as a

28

response to the ecological degradation and population agglomerations. Also harvesting of weeds may reflect an economic crisis that ultimately culminated in the reorganization of agriculture, settlement, and social organization with the advent of the Iron Age.

Let us consider some of the long-term dynamics of a chiefdom structure, as reflected in the employment and consumption of wealth and in the construction of monuments (Fig. 2.3). Three phases will be used as follows: an *initial phase*, when bronze is introduced, and social and economic changes are being prepared; an *expansion phase*, when new ruling elites emerge, employing bronze in prestige building and conspicuous consumption; and finally a *consolidation phase*, when continuity is the dominant theme in burials and ritual, followed by a social decline.

The initial phase

The Late Neolithic was a final period of settlement expansion, just as the landscape was generally becoming more open. During the last part of the Neolithic, imported and locally produced bronze axes were numerous and gradually took over the role as prestige items from the flint dagger. The axes were not yet employed as grave goods, but were hoarded. As a prestige object, they replaced the traditional status objects rather than breaking new ground. Around 1700 B.C., with the

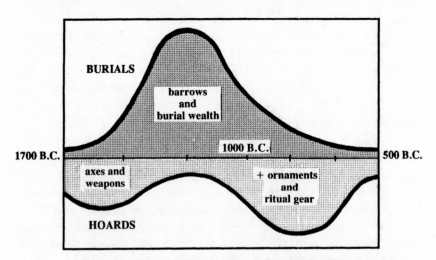

Fig. 2.3   Patterns of investment in wealth deposition and in monument construction during the Bronze Age.

advent of the Bronze Age, both imported and locally manufactured metal objects became more numerous and diverse. Spears, daggers, and finally swords were introduced. At this point, the traditional value system of the Neolithic was undermined. New status positions were gradually built up, linked to control over exchange in bronze, metallurgy, and new efficient weapons. The first burials with weapons appeared at the end of this phase.

Expansion phase

Suddenly, within a generation at about 1500 B.C., the fully fledged chiefdom structure emerged in northern Europe. The new culture was characterized by the original nordic style and mastery in metal work, and by the construction of thousands of monumental barrows. At the same time, ritual hoarding became scarce. This period of conspicuous wealth lasted, with some ups and downs, from 1500 to 1100 B.C., but, already in the later part, the erection of new monumental barrows and wealth consumption in burials declined and was replaced by the continued use of the old family barrows and more symbolic grave goods. Although burial practice changed from inhumation to cremation, this change does not explain the beginning reduction in grave goods, since it was still common practice to have a full-length coffin or stone cist with grave goods. It was apparently not necessary to boast chiefly wealth and superiority as before. The new order had become established. In economic terms, the intensive exploitation of the landscape gradually transformed a productive mixed forest with shrub and grassland to a less productive landscape dominated by grass and heath. Thus from about 1000 B.C., the open landscape, dominated by commons, existed; such a landscape is particularly vulnerable to overexploitation and degradation.

Consolidation and decline

During the consolidation and decline phase, wealth consumption was increasingly directed towards ritual hoarding of valuables, especially female ornaments and ritual gear. Burials were reduced in wealth, the most commonly employed burial type being the urn with cremated bones and a few personal belongings. Razor and tweezer became the standard equipment of high ranking males, and secondary burials in the old family barrows testify to tradition and continuity. In some

regions, especially in eastern Denmark, new ruling elites emerged and demonstrated their power and wealth by constructing monumental barrows, but the overall impression is one of continuity and consolidation.

Behind the façade of cultural continuity, economic stability was being undermined by ecological degradation and declining productivity. Already by 1000 B.C., some regions experienced declining supplies of bronze. The ornamental bronze objects were kept in circulation longer, and tool forms were increasingly produced in stone, bone or antler.

During the same period communal ritual for both male and female chiefs became more complex. Wealth was channeled into ritual gear, such as lures, golden drinking vessels, ritual helmets, and shields. This shift from display to ritual objects can be seen as a reflection of consolidation and crisis; the ruling elites no longer boasted their superiority in terms of personal wealth and status, but they rather acted as mediators to the gods, thereby controlling the destiny and well-being of society. In ritual hoarding, the gods were offered gifts in return for their help and support. This hoarding may also reflect a crisis of legitimation during a period of declining production.

Late in the Bronze Age, the hoarding of costly ritual gear, such as lures, suddenly stopped. Supplies of metal contracted, and the whole chiefdom organization, including its cultural and ritual framework, appears to collapse. Virtually no traditions continued into the Iron Age, except some hoarding of heavy neck rings. In conclusion, during this thousand-year cycle, burials, rituals, and wealth were employed in changing ways to reproduce the social order of chiefdoms. On Fig. 2.4, I have summarized in abbreviated form the major system parameters and their interaction to demonstrate the complexity or multi-causality of change. Despite profound changes, chiefdom organization persisted without the evolution of states.

Wealth finance, in the form of prestige goods, employed a new international value system to differentiate a warrior aristocracy. Wealth finance was used to establish political dominance and economic control; when the international prestige goods system collapsed, the chiefly structure collapsed with it. In that respect the Bronze Age differed from the Iron Age that was to follow.

31

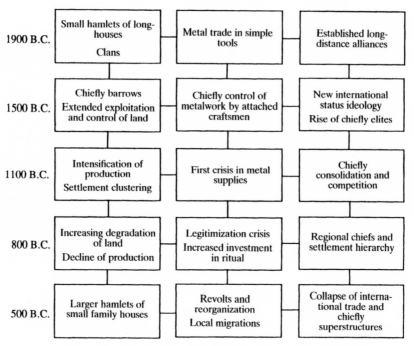

Fig. 2.4   Basic components and their interaction in the development and transformation of Bronze Age society

The Iron Age

The work of Hedeager (1987a, 1987b, 1988) provides the rich and diverse archaeological data from the Danish Iron Age summarized briefly here. Unlike the Bronze Age, the Iron Age is not characterized by a homogeneous cultural tradition in time or space; however, the long-term dynamics of wealth consumption in burials and hoards reveal a pattern similar to the Bronze Age. Since some marked changes in social organization take place during this sequence, I shall outline the basic organizational properties of Iron Age society.

As a response to the economic and ecological crisis at the end of the Bronze Age, production was reorganized with the family farm as the basic unit. In the classic Iron Age farm house, cattle were held at one end and the family at the other. Cattle, kept in stalls, produced manure for the fields that were fixed in a permanent system clearly marked by field boundaries. Although use rights were probably granted

32

to individual farms, the farms of nearly equal size were organized into villages that would have determined crop rotation. The stalled cattle demanded more labor than before to collect winter fodder, and prepare and manure the fields. Meadows were created to produce hay, replacing leaf-fodder from the cleared forests.

The new social relations of production suggest a break-up of the kinship-based community. Land as the basis of production became a defined and limited resource that could be accumulated; like the Greek polis (Ferguson, Chapter 8 below), although the village organization favored an egalitarian ideology, the economic conditions existed for emerging stratification. Such contradictions could be neutralized as long as new land could be cleared for expanding settlements; and the village organization offered an ideal collective framework for such work. The first centuries of the Iron Age saw a major settlement expansion into heavy clay soils covered by forest. This expansion was also made possible by new, more efficient iron tools, and, since iron could be obtained locally, central chiefly settlements lost the control that they had once held by manipulating long-distance exchange.

From around 150 B.C., as the forest had been cleared and settled, expansion came to a halt. From the first century B.C., a new warrior elite became distinguished in burials, and large chiefly farms appeared at some villages. The processes of social and economic differentiation continued for the next two centuries, and, by A.D. 200, settlements were reorganized into fewer, but much larger, individual farms. Land was redivided and granted to individual farms in an infield/outfield system of production; the village had disappeared as an organizational framework of production. The many smallholders had evidently become serfs or craft specialists on the big farms. As settlement concentrated, some grassland commons reverted to forest for timber production and forest grazing. The reorganization resulted in increased production; large barn and store houses appear together with small huts for craft production. Also the first gateway settlements appear to serve long-distance trade for royal estates.

During the first centuries of the Iron Age (500–150 B.C.) stratification is invisible. On the contrary, cemeteries demonstrate an egalitarian ideology. Regional diversification, however, was strong, reflecting tribal identities. The rise of a new warrior elite after 150 B.C. conforms with the reopening of international trade with the

southern Celtic world, as external prestige goods were used to mark diverse statuses. From the birth of Christ, these processes accelerated as the Roman empire took over international trade with the Germanic world.

In opposition to the Bronze Age, social differentiation was based on institutionalized, differential access to land. Local and regional chiefs not only possessed large farms; they also controlled the other farms in the village and other villages. By A.D. 200, taxation and property relations were formalized through the reorganization of land; villages and farms, in the hand of a free class of big farmers, provided military service and paid tribute to the king through his vassals. This system reached its climax in the Viking period when internal territorial conquest was replaced by external conquest and colonization.

The chiefs used revenues from their estates to support a retinue of young warriors, who, freed from kinship obligations, fought for their lord. Regional war chiefs joined in under the leadership of regional kings when territorial battles were taking place. The army, professionalized with a command hierarchy, fought for territory and trade gateways. This whole organization could only be supported by a system of tribute, although spoils of warfare made their contribution.

The reorganization around A.D. 200 formalized for the first time social classes based on property rights. Serfs, or perhaps thralls (slaves), were defined as landless and obligated to pay rent to the landowners.

This whole process towards state formation is reflected in material culture and ritual. The new elites demonstrated social distance not only through burial equipment, but also through selected burial grounds and exclusive burial customs. Some regions, such as northern Jutland, demonstrated their resistance to the new developments by maintaining archaic regional identities in material culture and egalitarian traditions in burial customs. The transformation of Iron Age societies into an archaic state organization represents a laboratory for testing hypotheses about the employment of material culture in social strategies; evidently the processes differ from those of the Bronze Age. But if we consider patterns of wealth consumption in burials and hoards they are nearly identical, comprising the same three phases (Fig. 2.5).

Initial phase
During the initial phase, ritual consumption was collective, exempli-

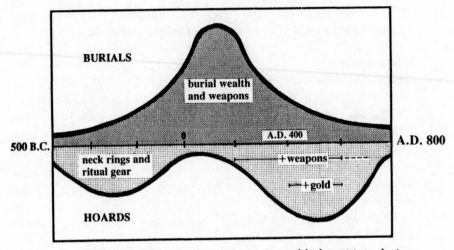

Fig. 2.5 Patterns of investment in wealth depositions during the Iron Age

fied in the hoarding of neck rings and ritual gear; some of these traditions represented continuation from the Bronze Age, relicts that gave feelings of continuity with the past during time of profound change. Otherwise little or no consumption existed in burials. Barrows were no longer employed; instead new cemeteries for the whole village reflected a distinct break with the hierarchical traditions of the Bronze Age. Burial equipment was modest and reflected the same egalitarian traditions as the village itself.

Expansion phase
About 150 B.C., internal processes of social diversification linked to external access to prestige goods, weapons, and status information, led to a radical change in wealth consumption and the emergence of a warrior elite. The new elites employed Celtic and later Roman prestige goods, for establishing and maintaining political power. Roman prestige goods especially were employed in a competitive spiral of consumption to boast and legitimize new ruling elites. As in the Bronze Age, the first period was characterized by rich male burials with weapons, while the later part was characterized by rich female burials indicating a beginning consolidation with less need to boast military superiority. This corresponded to the introduction of a state

organization after A.D. 200. Weapons were then hoarded in large quantities after victorious battles of territorial conquests.

Consolidation

The consolidation phase started around A.D. 400, when wealth consumption in burials nearly halted and hoarding soon reached a climax. Weapons were now in the minority; most hoards consisted of gold in various forms – ornaments, exchange tokens, and coins. The elites were sufficiently consolidated that wealth was no longer deposited in burials. Instead, valuable golden neck rings and ornaments were offered to the gods in return for their support and protection, a ritual gift-giving of kingship.

Hoarding of exchange valuables represented a new element linked to the development of economic transactions, tax, and tribute. The hoards should be considered hidden treasures that were never recovered. Or they could, in the word of the sagas, be considered as treasures hidden to be recollected in the afterlife at Valhalla, where the war heroes met in eternal drinking and war parties.

Although the consolidation phase had much in common with the Bronze Age, and is also characterized by some climatic and economic recession, this did not lead to economic crisis; on the contrary, farms continued to grow and prosper into the Viking period. Quite evidently the new stratified society that was based on staple finance was less vulnerable to external factors. This stability is demonstrated by the fact that after the fall of the Roman empire, the Germanic kingdoms developed new lines of international trade. Another indication of their ideological consolidation was the development of an original Germanic art style to be employed on elite weapons and ornaments, stressing Germanic identity.

By comparison with the Bronze Age, both similarities and differences can be noted. Perhaps the most significant difference is that the social organization of the Iron Age was able to cope with crisis and use that to consolidate the elite, due to the fact that land and production were controlled by individual families and could be exchanged and taxed. But also warfare and military organization had reached a correspondingly higher level. This expanding process of economic and social diversification and political centralization is illustrated in Fig. 2.6. Although a stratified society, it was still heavily reliant on a prestige goods economy of wealth finance, especially during the

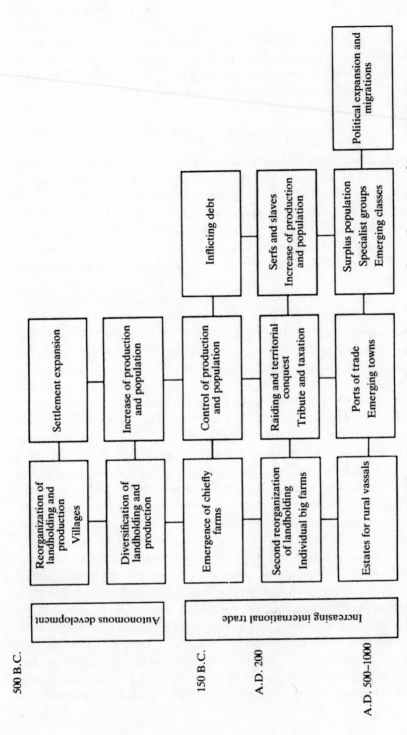

Fig. 2.6 Basic components and their interaction in the development and transformation of Iron Age society

expansion phase. After that, staple finance increasingly took over. Thus neither wealth nor staple finance are linked to a specific level of social organization; the different financial bases, however, strongly affect the system's stability and potential for growth.

CONCLUDING PERSPECTIVES

The two case studies from northern European prehistory demonstrate trends of wealth consumption, monumental works, and symbolic behavior in the rise and consolidation of ruling elites. Without due consideration of the full cultural and social context of these processes, they could easily have been misinterpreted as representing similar organizational structures. Thus, in several works on social evolution, the Bronze and the Iron Age are lumped together in the chiefdom category.

The case studies also contribute to the wider understanding of some of the processes involved in the emergence of elites, centralization, and political control. In conclusion I shall discuss some of the general implications as to the following: the conditions for the rise and fall of ruling elites; the significance of long-term history for understanding processes of evolution and devolution; and the significance of this study for evolutionary theory as discussed in the first section.

The employment of valuables in ritual depositions showed rather similar patterns in both the Bronze and the Iron Ages. In both cases during the expansion phase, weapons or symbols of warfare played a decisive role; during the consolidation phase, less emphasis was placed on symbols of warfare and ritual investment in burial; and then, during the decline phase, votive offerings were given to the gods. I am inclined to believe that actual warfare played a decisive role in sustaining new power relations, but the ideology of warfare, in much the same way as nuclear weapons, also would have served as a deterrent (see Earle 1987a). It would, however, be wrong to single out one or a few prime movers, such as warfare, in the formation of ruling elites and the state in northern Europe (cf. Carneiro 1970; Flannery 1972). The evidence rather suggests a complex interaction of new ideologies (legitimation and information monopoly), warfare (including new weapons and strategies), and the manipulation or take-over of production through tribute and taxation (Figs. 2.4 and 2.6). In that process, which has much in common with the IEMP model of Michael Mann

(1986b: 28ff.), traditional rights and value systems were redefined to serve new interests and classes. What has to be determined, then, are the conditions that allow such structural linkages to be established.

In both periods, adopting external value systems linked to foreign wealth objects was decisive. The new productive system based on the permanent field systems existed for several centuries prior to the take-off in stratification in the Iron Age; it did not unfold until linked to new ritual and social practices. Both cases also saw an introduction of new elite weapons, and, we may assume, new tactics of warfare.

In structural terms the emergence of a new elite was a rapid process that coincided with the establishment of networks and alliances with more complex societies and their value systems and cosmologies that could be used to legitimize emerging power positions. But this would probably not have been effective if some means of economic control had not already existed (see Earle, Chapter 4 below, and Gilman, Chapter 7 below, for comparative evidence). In the Bronze Age, the transmission of international value systems took place through inter-locked regional systems of exchange, whereas in the Iron Age it was a center/periphery relationship with the Roman empire and the Celtic world.

At the transition to the Iron Age, the internal processes of evolution and devolution can be further specified. Social organization did not revert back to a Neolithic tribal level with shifting agriculture; rather, land use during the Bronze Age was transformed into a permanent pattern of landholding that was strong enough to survive the collapse of the elite ideology of tribal aristocracies. The core components of Iron Age social organization were developed during the late Bronze Age, but their potential was constrained by the tribal rationality of Bronze Age society. The new economic basis for differentiation could only be formalized in a new structure after the collapse of Bronze Age social organization.

If we consider the relationship between wealth and staples in the rise and decline of elites, a long-term tendency from wealth finance towards staple finance could be observed, which was linked to changed conditions of political power and legitimacy from expansion to con-solidation. These processes not only transformed social relations of production, but were also linked to ecological change.

In the long-term perspective, staple finance and control of land and resources were increasingly formalized from the Bronze Age to the

mediaeval period. This formalization of the land-tenure system increased the society's stability and its ability to cope with crisis. Only a major ecological crisis and the Black Death during the fourteenth and fifteenth centuries created a temporary halt in the processes of social and economic evolution.

Despite the fact that social differentiation at the beginning of both the Bronze and Iron Ages was based on economic control, legitimation was still massive, demonstrating that resistance to change seethed within the established social order. Tradition and stability were apparently inherent to the tribal and Germanic systems. Even during the early mediaeval period, after A.D. 1100, peasants unwilling to accept the new social order rebelled until the nobility finally gained full control and had their rights universally sanctioned during the sixteenth century as an endogamous high nobility. It is remarkable how drawn-out was the whole progression towards state formation; the basic structure of Bronze Age society persisted for more than a thousand years. Although changing configurations of alliances and regional trajectories of expansion and collapse created temporal and spatial fluctuations, prehistoric evidence contradicts Service's (1972: 142) observation that chiefdoms are fragile and short-lived.

Since the communal life characteristic of the Bronze Age chiefdom is evidently resistant to exploitation, what factors finally create the conditions for internal change and transformation? In both cases, a long-term accumulation of unintended economic and ecological consequences of the dominant social strategies could be observed that gradually transformed the productive basis and potential. During the transition from the Bronze Age to the Iron Age the entire structure collapsed, and this devolution created a completely new society and economy based on land holding and family farms within the collective framework of villages. Once introduced, it became permanent and, in periods of crisis, reinforced the unequal access to land.

The resistance towards change illuminates another characteristic of long-term change and subsequent transformation. During the Bronze Age, both settlement structure and social organization apparently remained intact even when the ecological and economic carrying capacity of a region was exceeded. If we are to explain the persistence of the traditional settlement pattern, we have to consider its social rationality. Social organization of the Bronze Age was inscribed on the landscape (see Earle, Chapter 4). Here were the ancestral barrows and

ritual places, monumentally situated as landmarks in the landscape. Here resided the power of both living and dead chiefs, and the settlement pattern formed a network that gave access to trade and alliances. Here was a familiar ecology of pastoral farming that produced the animals that were a major source of the society's wealth. Since Bronze Age society was built upon the circulation of prestige goods and the participation in alliances, the importance of pastoralism was a crucial constraint. Although such social circumscription clearly tended to accelerate hierarchy, centralization, and a more formalized land-use, such processes were constrained by the inherent tribal rationality. The ecological degradation and economic decline could only be met with new and more efficient technologies and farming practices after the breakdown of Bronze Age social organization. So in a paradoxical way, the unintended economic consequences of long-term social strategies created the basis for intentional change. This implies that the material conditions for change are unpredictable to the social actors themselves; they can only be constructed retrospectively. The historical moments with opportunities for change are very rare indeed.

Long-term changes, hardly visible in a lifetime, contrast with rapid social transformation, which (when triggered) took place within a generation. Resistance and competition were obviously important factors at this time (compare Bradley, Chapter 3 below), but, since archaeology only records the successful, we cannot describe the many individual opponents and attempts to change these basic conditions. Only during the Iron Age, when such attempts became so strongly organized, can we document resistance to the formation of new systems of power.

In recent years, several authors (Ekholm and Friedman 1979; Mann 1986) emphasize a distinct borderline at the earliest pristine state formations. Afterwards, a world system developed that advanced the frontier of civilization, interrupted by cycles of collapse and resistance. As a consequence of such macro-structural transformations during economic expansion, a spatial hierarchy of dependent social formations was created. Fig. 2.2 represents an ideal model of this spatial system. Although it would demand a major research project to apply such a model to Europe, the Near East, and northern Africa in prehistory, the spatial structure of Fig. 2.2 resulted in an evolutionary differentiation between centers and peripheries. This spatial differentiation, however, does not mean that we can apply a traditional evolu-

tionary perspective of time-delayed diffusion; rather the long-distance relationships of center to periphery create an evolutionary gradient representing patterns of development and underdevelopment. The traditional societies at the periphery cannot be characterized solely in terms of their internal organization, since they were both linked to and borrowed structural and ideological features, although transformed, from the center. The developments in European prehistory, claimed by some (see Renfrew 1973a) to be autonomous, could have resulted from the dynamics of larger interacting systems, representing periods of collapse, cultural closure, and break-down of international exchange networks. Center/periphery relationships, based on the exploitation of raw materials, can also lead to technological development on the periphery; could this explain the apparent chronological priority of Europe in metallurgic know-how? Before accepting the autonomous version of European prehistory, such perspectives have to be explored fully.

In remote regions, such as Denmark and northern Europe, I contend that the rise of new ruling elites was linked to external contacts, rooted in the ancient world system (Rowlands, Larsen, and Kristiansen 1987). Denmark was part of international networks where production and exchange of prestige goods were the dominant economic operators, directing flows of wealth and power (Kristiansen 1987b). This interregional dependency created a rather unified social and ritual superstructure stretching from the Aegean to Scandinavia. On the other hand it is also clear that internal processes of demographic, ecological, and economic change were decisive for the developmental potential of the region. The time trajectories of regional cycles therefore were decisive for when and how interaction within the larger system took place.

How do these results relate to the recent critiques of evolutionary theory? Is prediction (or rather postdiction) possible? The answer to these questions obviously depends upon scale and complexity. When restricting ourselves to parameters, such as ecology and demography within defined regions, long-term trends and possible transformations of a specific social strategy can be predicted. But when local and regional sequences are viewed as part of the operation of an ancient world system, the picture becomes much more complex. Its direction has to be determined by the dominant regional trends, defining both constraints and potentialities, allowing us to predict a range of evolu-

tionary options. They also depend upon the range of technological, military, and economic opportunity for political control and resistance that characterized the various world historical periods (Mann 1986b).

Within any regional social organization and interregional system, a number of evolutionary options exist, but the range in options certainly is limited. These choices are the result of multiple actions and interactions beyond the consciousness of any single individual. Cultural and structural parameters defined limits to what was possible at any given moment in history. This was most clearly demonstrated by the thousand-year Bronze Age sequence unconsciously moving towards its final destiny and transformation, while still living within and constrained by the cultural and social framework of Bronze Age chiefly society.

The pattern of change in British prehistory

RICHARD BRADLEY

INTRODUCTION

The study of chiefdoms has changed from analysis of their formal characteristics to a concern with the processes by which they were created and maintained. That is why the study of British prehistory has a distinctive contribution to make. It exhibits a sequence extending over four thousand years, from the adoption of domesticates to the eve of the Roman Conquest, and throughout this period society showed at least some of the characteristics of chiefdoms. At the same time, the archaeological record provides indications of almost continuous change.

On the other hand, it would be a truism to assert that the formal characteristics of chiefdoms conceal a variety of different processes at work. The complexity of the archaeological record in Britain poses its challenges for the prehistorian, but in itself it would offer little to a comparative study of such societies. It is more important to emphasize a broader theme which crosscuts this variation. Contributors to the seminar took quite different approaches to the relationship between ideological and economic factors in the operation of chiefdoms, and an anonymous reviewer of an earlier draft of this paper complained

44

that it failed to commit itself to either a materialist or an ideological interpretation of the British sequence. That comment was perceptive, but the criticism was misplaced, for I shall argue that such a choice should not be made. The division between "culture" and "practical reason" is a peculiarly modern one (Sahlins 1976), and may have little application to nonmarket societies in which, as Friedman says, religion can function as economy and economy as religion (Friedman 1975; cf. Godelier 1977). Our case studies will show how ideological factors may provide the motive force for socioeconomic changes, even when they issue in ecological disaster; as so often, the environment sets limits to developments that it does nothing to determine. Similarly, we shall see how more "rational" or predictable relationships between a population and its natural resources can be maintained quite effectively through the conventions of ritual activity.

To summarize the argument, this paper traces two successive sequences in the archaeology of southern England, the earlier driven by the demands of ritual and ceremony, and the later by the dictates of food production. During the first of these sequences, the demands imposed by ceremonial activity became so severe that they seem to have outstripped the productive capacity of the environment. Only at that stage do adaptationist approaches make much contribution to the argument. During the second sequence of change, a concerted attempt was made to maximize agricultural production, but as part of that process a new ideology was adopted, which emphasized the links between the fertility of the land and its population.

At the same time, it would be mistaken to treat these developments in isolation. A number of contributors to the seminar emphasized the ways in which neighboring polities might compete with one another through time, in particular for access to prestige goods from outside the local system. The decline of one group might accompany the rise of its competitors. For this reason the well-documented sequence in Wessex, already described by Renfrew (1973b) and Cunliffe (1978b), is contrasted with developments in an adjacent area, the Thames Valley. The striking contrasts in the ecology of these two study areas will also make it easier to distinguish between changes that could be rooted in environmental factors and those that were influenced more powerfully by ideology.

The paper is in three sections. The first introduces the two archaeological sequences, their treatment in earlier discussions of chiefdoms,

45

and the nature of both our study areas. The second section provides a summary of current interpretations of the archaeological sequences in Wessex and the Thames Valley, with a particular emphasis on questions of ideology and economy. At this stage the emphasis is on contrasts: those between earlier and later prehistory and those between these two regions. This section is essentially descriptive, and limitations of space preclude detailed argument. This is reserved for the concluding discussion, which cuts across these regional and chronological divisions to consider how far the course of events as a whole had been determined by six of the factors discussed by the participants in the seminar: subsistence and settlement; ritual and ideology; territorial organization; conspicuous consumption; warfare; and long-distance trade.

1 THE CHIEFDOM IN BRITISH PREHISTORY

It was Colin Renfrew who introduced the chiefdom concept into British archaeology. In 1973 he published an analysis of society in central southern England (Wessex) between the fourth and second millennia B.C. (see C. Renfrew 1973b). This was one of the most influential contributions to the development of a "social archaeology," but also introduced some of the British evidence to a wider audience. It is the obvious starting point for this account.

Although Renfrew was careful to discuss the *sequence* in his study area, he also relied on a list of twenty characteristics of chiefdoms drawn from the work of Elman Service. He was able to recognize no fewer than twelve of these in Wessex. Since 1973 the same model has been used in more general reconstructions of earlier prehistoric society in Britain (eg. Burgess 1980).

It has had an equally powerful influence in studies of later prehistory, although the model has not been applied with the same attention to detail. Iron Age societies have also been described as chiefdoms, and interest has been shown in the role of redistribution in the development of hill forts (Cunliffe 1978a). Of the twenty elements discussed in Renfrew's paper, at least thirteen can be recognized in Wessex during the Iron Age, and yet the archaeology of these two periods seems to have little in common. Why is it that these societies,

both described as chiefdoms, differ so completely from one another? My task is to describe some of these differences, before considering how they came about.

In earlier prehistory the evidence for settlements is elusive and residential structures are rare. There is little sign of intensive food production. Instead numerous monuments were associated with the dead. Equally important is the development of a whole series of public monuments, only a few of which could have fulfilled any residential functions. Renfrew suggested that the increasing scale of such constructions evidences the harnessing of growing amounts of human labor and that their spacing in Neolithic Wessex shows the development of a series of distinct polities.

The later prehistoric sequence offers a total contrast. Here the priorities are reversed. Settlements dominate the archaeological record, evidence of food production is widespread, and field systems and land boundaries survive to the present day. By contrast, there is more limited evidence for the disposal of the dead. Elaborate artifacts continued to be made, but now they were deposited mainly in bogs and rivers. The ceremonial centers of the earlier sequence went out of use, and instead we find a series of defended enclosures. A small number of these provide evidence of warfare, but more of these hill forts contain groups of storehouses. Only in southeastern England did more complex polities develop, most probably as a result of contact with the Roman world.

A more subtle contrast exists between the evidence from Wessex and developments in a neighboring region, the Thames Valley. In earlier prehistory the Thames Valley contains a range of monuments similar to that of Wessex, but throughout the sequence these were executed on a smaller scale. Moreover, whilst the burial record echoes that in Wessex, the grave assemblage is rarely so elaborate. A still sharper contrast can be found during later prehistory. It seems possible that Wessex lost its dominant position and that the Thames Valley now played a more important role, with a group of high status settlements and evidence for the large-scale consumption of bronze metalwork. Despite a phase of disruption accompanying the first adoption of iron, this region maintained its importance through the first millennium B.C., so that the Thames estuary is the region which sees the most striking political changes during the period of contact with the Roman

world. Iron Age Wessex, on the other hand, was characterized by a less centralized society, dominated for a long period by the fortified sites known as hill forts.

For these reasons it is insufficient to look at Wessex in isolation, even though it has played such an influential role in the discussions mentioned earlier. We must contrast this well-known evidence with developments in the Thames valley, if we are to understand the larger structures of which these areas formed a part. In order to do so, however, we must appreciate not only the character of these areas today, but also the ways in which their natural environment would have responded to human exploitation.

Most of Wessex is occupied by an extensive chalk plateau, between 70 m and 300 m high and about 6,500 square kilometers in extent. This is dissected by a series of streams and rivers, most of which flow southwards into the English Channel. Although this plateau supports a fairly thin soil cover today, it was originally mantled by a deposit of loess, the windblown silt so much favored by the first farmers in northwest Europe (Catt 1978). Loess is well drained and extremely fertile, but it is also vulnerable to erosion. Whilst it was certainly present in Wessex during the Neolithic period, much of this covering may have been lost by later prehistory (Fig. 3.1).

The Thames Valley, on the other hand, is less extensive. It runs for roughly 180 km and is flanked by terraces of Pleistocene gravel. The valley is rarely more than 5 km wide. This area would also have provided favorable conditions for arable and pastoral farming, although the soils which flank the valley seem to have undergone episodes of erosion which contributed considerable material to the floodplain (Robinson and Lambrick 1984). In this case the process of soil erosion led to a significant *improvement* in the agricultural potential of the river valley. This may have happened from the Later Bronze Age onwards.

Lastly, both these areas are flanked by still less stable soils which now support tracts of heathland. Again this has not always been the case, and there is evidence that these soils experienced a fairly short period of colonization before the pressures of human exploitation caused a drastic decline in their agricultural potential (Bradley 1978a). They have been regarded as marginal land ever since.

The following section presents a more detailed account of the archaeological sequences in Wessex and the Thames Valley. At this stage the

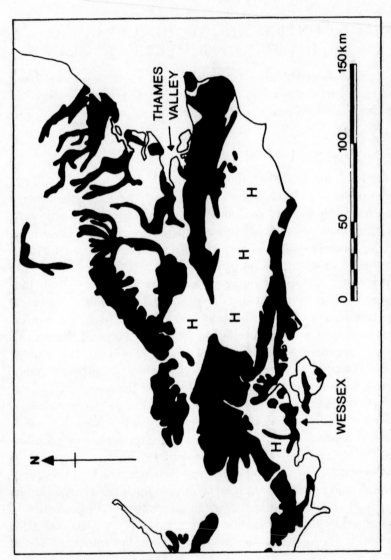

Fig. 3.1   Central southern England, showing the location of the study areas in relation to the main distribution of soils containing loess (after Catt 1978). H indicates the major areas with evidence of heathland formation during prehistory
(Drawing: Simon Smithson)

emphasis is on the detailed patterning observed in the archaeological record. Beneath its surface, however, it conceals the broader processes considered in Section 3 of this paper.

2 CONTRASTING SEQUENCES IN THE PREHISTORY OF SOUTHERN ENGLAND

We can consider the archaeological record in terms of two basic sequences, here described as "earlier" and "later" prehistory. Together they can be divided into five separate phases.

Earlier prehistory

Earlier Neolithic (ca. 4000–3000 B.C.)

Earlier prehistoric developments went through three separate phases. In the first, little suggests a sedentary pattern of settlement. Cattle were more important than crops, and the major demands on labor were made by funerary monuments – elongated mounds or cairns, the more elaborate of which are found in regional clusters. These monuments provide clues to the beginning of a process of differentiation that became more pronounced in later periods. The number of human remains on these sites is too low for them to have housed the entire population, and it seems likely that successive stages in the rites of passage were increasingly selective (Bradley 1984: 21–5). It was usual for the bones of men, women, and children to be mixed together beneath these mounds after they had lost their flesh.

Over the same period, a series of earthwork ("causewayed") enclosures were erected (Bradley 1984: 26–31). These are found mainly in lowland Britain and sometimes occupy peripheral positions between the regional style zones defined by artifacts. They saw a number of activities, including feasting, exchange, and the exposure of the dead, and are thought to have been used for seasonal aggregations (Burgess et al. 1988). The rather marginal position of the enclosures is emphasized by the fact that they were often built in woodland. *Pace* Renfrew it no longer seems as if they were the *centers* of social territories.

The development of both types of monument has some features in common. Both were apparently constructed in segments, possibly by different work parties. Burial chambers might be subdivided so that

they could house different families, different age or sex groups, or even different body parts, and the same principle underlies the construction of causewayed enclosures, whose ditches were excavated in a series of segments of approximately equal size. Distinctive deposits of artifacts and human or animal bones could be placed against the causeways, and the separate sections might be recut in precisely the same positions after the enclosure ditches had been refilled (Mercer 1980). It seems likely that the forms of both these monuments reflect the participation of separate communities in their construction. It may have been important to emphasize this in the final layout of these sites.

There are signs that social differences were emerging during the Earlier Neolithic. The burials in Wessex show a gradual trend towards the deposition of articulated corpses, usually male and sometimes accompanied by grave goods (Thorpe 1984); in the Thames Valley the development of individual burial could even be emphasized by the construction of circular mounds (Bradley and Holgate 1984). Sometimes funerary monuments were enlarged on a massive scale. Occasionally long mounds were extended into enormous "bank barrows," and rectilinear enclosures with a similar ground plan were embellished until the most massive of these "cursuses" was 10 km long.

The causewayed enclosures saw a still more drastic change. By 3000 B.C. some had assumed a residential role, and a number of the earthworks were reconstructed on a defensive scale. The causeways in the ditches were removed and the ramparts were rebuilt. There seem to be links between these different processes, for a number of the enclosures are associated with burial monuments containing articulated bodies and even grave goods. Some enclosures also seem to have been attacked and destroyed (Bradley 1984: 35). Extraordinary efforts went into these changes. The largest causewayed enclosure complex required an investment of about a million worker hours, whilst the largest cursus is of a similar order of magnitude.

These developments are seen in both our study areas, but the causewayed enclosures and long barrows in the Thames Valley were built on a smaller scale than those in Wessex. Similarly, the enclosures on the river gravels are often found so close to one another that they do not seem to have belonged to large social groups. The same is true of cursus monuments.

On a regional level there is a recognizable link between the size and

density of nonutilitarian monuments and the presence of large areas of loess, but to some extent that relationship is deceptive. Whilst it does suggest that an area like Wessex was capable of sustaining large-scale ceremonial activity, land use may have been extensive rather than intensive. Indeed the high proportion of wild plants among carefully excavated food remains suggests that closer comparisons are to be made with complex hunter-gatherers than with sedentary agricultural communities. Attention seems to have been lavished on the dead, whilst the living remain archaeologically invisible.

Later Neolithic (ca. 3000–2200 B.C.)

The second stage of the sequence saw the expansion of long-distance exchange and growing contrasts in the character of different regions. In the Thames Valley we find more evidence of individual burial, now more often accompanied by grave goods and covered by a circular mound (Bradley and Holgate 1984). In Wessex, on the other hand, more attention was paid to the building of ceremonial monuments. Some features are common to both processes, particularly the presence of non-local objects. The development of long-distance "trade" is best illustrated by the production and distribution of stone axes (Clough and Cummins 1979). These had been made at a number of centers from at least 3700 B.C., but it was with the later development of the causewayed enclosures that we find major extensions in their distribution. During the Later Neolithic there are further changes, and production may have intensified. We also see changes in the distribution of these axes. Originally these had shown a gradual decrease in frequency with distance from the source, but now the products of some workshops seem to be clustered at the outer edges of their distribution. No doubt many are settlement finds, but others seem to have been deposited deliberately, often in or around ceremonial centers. A similar emphasis on exotic objects can be recognized from the contents of Later Neolithic burials (Kinnes 1979). In each case, social networks were apparently becoming more extended.

Similar changes are illustrated by the style of artifacts and monuments. Portable objects no doubt traveled widely, but different mechanisms must be envisaged for the close links between the design of ceremonial monuments in separate areas of Britain (Bradley and Chapman 1986). Some of these share a distinctive style of decorated pottery whose ultimate origin was in northern Scotland. By now par-

ticular groups or individuals may have been capitalizing on their links with distant areas and even their access to specialized knowledge. The extraordinary scale on which Later Neolithic monuments were built also suggests the possibility of competitive emulation. This is particularly true in Wessex.

So far this account offers a different reading of the evidence from Renfrew's interpretation, and so two important points must be emphasized. First, it appears that the building of large Neolithic monuments took place *discontinuously*. There is no evidence for a steady increase in the amount of labor invested in their construction (Startin and Bradley 1981). At the same time, the importance of long-distance relations means that the developments in any one part of Britain can no longer be viewed in isolation. On the other hand, the design of the new ceremonial centers (henge monuments) shows that the work force was being organized on a different basis, and Renfrew is right to detect signs of greater central direction; no longer is there any evidence of the "segmentary" construction of large earthwork monuments.

By 2500 B.C. then, the sequences in different regions of Britain have diverged (Thorpe and Richards 1984). Some, like the Thames Valley, are distinguished by evidence of individual burial, but in others, notably in Wessex, ceremonial centers were built in which the individual's role is by no means evident. A few of these sites could have doubled as high-status settlements and show evidence of large-scale feasting, but in both areas people were acutely aware of the past. The locations of existing features in the landscape profoundly influenced the positioning of later monuments, and even the redundant earthworks of the Earlier Neolithic formed the focus for a series of intentional offerings. It is vital to recognize that a long cultural sequence is involved, and in both of our study areas phases of use and disuse may well be separated by centuries (e.g. Richards 1984). This does not suggest the continuous growth that Renfrew originally postulated, so much as an attempt to legitimize changes in political organization by drawing on the "symbolic capital" provided by monuments of earlier periods. The distribution of such centers of power may no longer owe so much to the distribution of natural resources in the landscape, for the most important element was perhaps the past itself. The astronomical alignments incorporated in some of these monuments may have played a similar role, by making the new system seem part of the

natural order (cf. Bradley 1987a). This phase invites similar comment to the Earlier Neolithic, for in both study areas the evidence for specialized ceremonial sites eclipses any trace of contemporary settlement. The main development was the growth of more extensive social networks. These lay behind the provision of non-local artifacts in graves and henge monuments, and provide a context for the adoption of exotic ritual practices. Although more parts of the landscape may have been used at this time, there is no environmental evidence for economic intensification, even in the vicinity of the largest of the Wessex henges (R. Entwistle pers. comm.).

Earlier Bronze Age (ca. 2200–1400 B.C.)
It is from about 2200 B.C. that we enter the final stage of this sequence, with the extension of long-distance relations to the European mainland. It was through such connections that fine pottery ("Beakers") and metalwork were adopted. Not surprisingly this link is first seen in areas like the Thames Valley in which the accumulation of exotica was already well established, and such connections are chiefly evidenced by burial finds (Thorpe and Richards 1984). Elsewhere, for example in parts of Wessex, the change took place more gradually, and the major henge monuments were recommissioned after an interval of desertion (Bradley 1984: 82). The one monument to see a sustained investment of human labor was Stonehenge. The duality between ceremonial centers and rich burials eventually broke down, and those earthwork complexes became the focus for a dense distribution of cemeteries. Complex burials are found in both our study areas, but those in Wessex stand out through their exceptional richness.

Throughout the earlier prehistoric sequence little is known about the subsistence economy. During the Earlier Neolithic the largest concentrations of surface finds mark the sites of special-purpose enclosures; otherwise domestic activity has left ephemeral traces. During the Later Neolithic flint scatters are denser and more extensive, suggesting that settlement was perhaps less mobile, but in southern England excavation has shown no sign of lasting structures of this date (Bradley 1987b). Flotation and wet sieving never produce the quantity of carbonized cereals known on later prehistoric sites, and the economy may have been based principally on livestock and on wild resources (Keeley 1984, 1987). The one major development during the Later Neolithic and particularly the Earlier Bronze Age was a

significant expansion in the settled area to incorporate tracts of marginal land which often support heathland today. Some of the newly settled land is so close to the regions with the complex burials that its use may have helped to underwrite developments in the latter areas through the production and mobilization of staples (Bradley 1984: 89–91). There is nothing to suggest that political developments were financed by economic intensification, but the same objective could have been met through the exploitation of an ever more *extensive* area. That idea might even explain the course that events were to take, for it was not long before the soils that were the last to be colonized came under serious pressure. They provide evidence of declining fertility and impeded drainage, just as the loess soils on the chalk show the first signs of erosion. Not surprisingly these strains seem to have resulted in a gradual change to the political geography of southern England: Wessex lost its dominance over peripheral areas, and other regions, such as the Thames Valley, assumed a more prominent role, so that in our second sequence we find a much closer relationship between agricultural production and the distribution of portable wealth. One way of reading the later stages of this sequence is to suggest that the requirements of traditional ideology became increasingly incompatible with the realities of earlier prehistoric land use. Although there is no real evidence of intensification in either study area, there are signs that more marginal soils were gradually pressed into service. At the same time, the major foci in the social landscape remained unchanged over two thousand years. The price of that extraordinary respect for the past was a growing mismatch between ambition and achievement. The main monuments of the Earlier Neolithic may have been located in areas with productive tracts of loess, but loess is notoriously susceptible to soil erosion, and by the mid-second millennium B.C. the environment of Bronze Age Wessex was becoming increasingly brittle, and drastic changes were on the way. At the start, ritual and ceremonies had made only moderate demands; now the declining resources of the region as a whole made demands of their own. The entire system gave way.

Later prehistory

The second basic sequence has a different point of departure. From about 1400 B.C. our main concern will be with evidence for food production and the ways in which exotic objects were consumed.

There is also evidence for a different relationship between the living and the dead. Here the archaeological sequence can be divided into two phases.

The Later Bronze Age (ca. 1400–700 B.C.)
The productive base was rapidly transformed and the distribution of exotic objects moved away from Wessex, with its long history of ceremonial activity, and onto the more resilient soils of the Thames Valley (Bradley 1984: 106–27 and fig. 4). From that time onwards there are more weeds of cultivation in the pollen record and more finds of carbonized cereals; we also see the first archaeological evidence for textile production in Britain (Bradley 1978b: 29–53). Important developments took place in the landscape of both study areas, and large tracts of ground were subdivided by field systems, some of considerable size. In Wessex, coherent territories became defined by longer boundary ditches. In some cases these may have divided arable land from pasture, but in others they defined whole "estates," and their creation involved piecemeal reorganization of the landscape. At present their chronology is poorly understood, but the main elements of this system were certainly established by the Iron Age. The size of these land units suggests that they could have operated on a larger scale than the individual settlement.

It is difficult to relate these land divisions to the evidence of contemporary settlements. In each area scattered houses and domestic compounds are known within some of the field systems, but at a few sites this pattern was changed by the establishment of a major enclosure containing one residential unit together with evidence for food preparation and grain storage. The scale of these earthworks made them prominent features of the landscape, but they were not of defensive character (Bradley 1984: 107–9). It is revealing that there seems to be a direct relationship between the size of these enclosures and the productivity of the surrounding land (Ellison 1981).

With the establishment of the larger estates, greater evidence for social distinctions is found. Evidence exists for a wide range of settlement sites, and these may have enjoyed differential access to exotic products. Our best evidence comes from the Thames Valley, where a distinctive class of fortified enclosure has been recognized in areas with large amounts of fine metalwork. These "ringworks" were first thought to be henge monuments, but on excavation they have proved to consist

56

of massive circular earthworks, dominated by one large round house and enclosed by a rampart built in the same manner as hill fort defenses in Europe (Bradley 1984: 120–1). Some of these sites seem to have formed the nucleus of a wider scatter of residential activity. Bronzeworking and large-scale meat consumption took place on some of these sites, which were probably high-status settlements commanding the major routes by which exotic goods were distributed.

By contrast, in Wessex a parallel trend may be represented by the development of hilltop settlements, a number of which produce finds of high-quality metalwork. Many of these later became hill forts, in some cases during the Bronze Age. Such sites can occupy pivotal positions in relation to the territories defined by linear ditches (Bradley 1984: 118–19). The roles of these hilltop sites are poorly understood, but by the Iron Age a number of them provided centralized food storage.

What happened to the monuments of earlier periods? In both areas these were either ignored or destroyed. The use of the great henge monuments ended in the Earlier Bronze Age and few artifacts of first millennium date have been found there. Only limited attempts were made to preserve the less impressive monuments, but some were left intact in islands of unploughed land. Isolated mounds did not fare so well, however, and many more were leveled by cultivation (Bradley 1981a).

Not surprisingly, evidence for the disposal of the dead also changes sharply. Where new burial mounds were built, these were insignificant structures. In both areas burials were often communal and consisted of clusters of cremations, many of them contained in pottery vessels exactly like those used in settlements; no longer was social position reflected by the provision of special types of urn (Ellison 1980). Cemeteries were often located close to the settlements and their fields, as if the ancestors were to be involved in the business of landholding. Despite the lavish production of fine metalwork, elaborate artifacts are virtually absent from these cemeteries.

The distribution of metal deposits also changes. The richest Earlier Bronze Age material occurred in the graves of Wessex, but later finds of metalwork are concentrated in the Thames Valley (Bradley 1984: 106–24), where the most elaborate items were ceremoniously deposited in rivers or wet ground. This area also contains most of the higher-order settlements. Some of the metalwork is of Continental

origin, and much of it is fine weaponry, suggesting that martial symbolism was important.

It seems possible that such lavish consumption had a competitive character, as if the large-scale destruction of wealth was itself a source of prestige (Bradley 1982). At the same time, these deposits seem to take over from the grave goods of the Earlier Bronze Age. This material may have been deposited during rites of passage, for at least some of the metalwork in the Thames had been accompanied by human skulls of the same date (Bradley and Gordon 1988). The recognition of this material does much to redress the impression of an undifferentiated society suggested by the cremation cemeteries. It is also consistent with the discovery of isolated human bones inside Later Bronze Age settlements, especially in the Thames Valley.

In summary, the Later Bronze Age saw a drastic reorganization of the landscape around the needs of food production (see Earle, Chapter 4 below). Access to the most fertile land may have been carefully controlled, and in Wessex a series of "estates" developed, a few of which may be linked with higher-status settlements. Such evidence of social distinctions is echoed by differences in the treatment of the dead. Where the ordinary settlements might be accompanied by undifferentiated cemeteries, the richer sites were often in areas with deliberate deposits of fine bronzes, some of which may have been associated with human remains. These sites also participated in the import of exotic metalwork.

The contrasts with the earlier sequence are extremely striking, but for our purposes certain features stand out. Within the two study areas, occupation sites dominate the archaeological record, and clear signs exist for agricultural intensification. To a large extent we also find a close relationship between the economic potential of different regions and the presence of high-status settlements. Votive deposits of fine metalwork are found in the more productive areas. Few of these features could be identified during earlier prehistory. At the same time, there may be the first indications of a new ideology. Older burial mounds and ceremonial sites were abandoned or destroyed, and now the disposal of the dead was more closely related to the areas selected for settlement. Cremation cemeteries developed close to the houses and their fields, and human bones may have circulated as relics. Such links between the dead and the living were to become more pronounced during the Iron Age.

Iron Age (ca. 700 B.C.–A.D. 43)

By the end of the Later Bronze Age the Thames Valley had assumed a dominant role, even though it was far away from the sources of this metal. The movement of nonlocal artifacts could have been controlled from high-status sites in this area, but the consumption of so much bronze weaponry may have put the metal supply under strain. As a result the raw material was increasingly recycled. What is referred to as the Bronze Age/Iron Age transition seems to have seen an overall shortage of prestige goods (Bradley 1988).

This change in wealth availability had drastic consequences. The declining rate at which fine metalwork was imported could have sapped the power of communities in lowland areas like the Thames Valley. It would also have severed those relationships through which this material was distributed to other regions, including Wessex. This meant that competition for status could no longer be mediated through the consumption of weaponry, and there may be growing evidence that conflicts came into the open (Bradley 1984: 134–6). A substantial number of hilltop settlements were fortified, and a few were destroyed by fire. There is also evidence for political fragmentation as ceramic style zones became smaller and their boundaries more tightly defined.

The power of communities in the Thames Valley was weakened by these changes, and peripheral groups who had been forced into a dependent position by their exclusion from the metal trade were able to make their mark in the new system. Many of the lasting features of the later prehistoric economy developed during this phase – new crops, new agricultural tools and a range of new facilities within the farms themselves. More effort was invested in the land, and more land was brought into commission. Many of the monuments that had survived the Later Bronze Age expansion were now brought under the plough (Bradley 1981b). Although existing estimates are rather subjective, it is clear that the population rose (Cunliffe 1978b).

It is often supposed that such massive food production underwrote major divisions of wealth and power, but evidence for social differentiation is elusive. Hill forts are usually considered in this context. These are much more common in Wessex than in the Thames Valley, and their massive defenses involved a large investment of labor, although this was of a different order of magnitude from the ceremonial centers of the Later Neolithic period, built when the population was much lower. Apart from residential buildings, some of rather temporary

character (Stopford 1987), the main features of the defended sites are above-ground storehouses, which occur in higher proportion than on other sites (Gent 1983); the same is also true of grain storage pits. At the heart of a few extensively excavated hill forts there were also small shrines. In two areas of Wessex, the produce stored in the defended sites must have come from a larger area than the occupants themselves could have farmed (Gent 1983). This may be an example of a staple finance system, but, if so, the sheer number of contemporary defended sites hardly suggests the emergence of polities of much extent (see Earle, Chapter 4).

The intensification of food production was ubiquitous, but it was only on the most fertile soils, well outside the area dominated by hill forts, that this process may have led to lasting differences of wealth. We know all too little about developments in this part of the country, but it appears that in the middle of the Iron Age a major process of nucleation and settlement growth took place, so that what started as self-contained farmsteads became extensive unenclosed settlements (Cunliffe and Rowley 1978). It is possible that sometimes these developed through the amalgamation of previously dispersed groups (Bradley 1984: 140). There is less evidence for the building of defenses in this area, and little sign of the centralized storage that is found in the major hill forts. The Thames Valley is located on one edge of this system.

The dense distribution of hill forts is sometimes thought to reflect the existence of stable territories dominated by a powerful elite, whose authority was reinforced by their control of surplus produce. The open settlements of the river valleys, on the other hand, are rarely considered in detail, so that our impression of Iron Age society is unbalanced. Looking at the sequence as a whole, we might suggest that, far from showing a period of stable social ranking, the early Iron Age witnessed a phase of devolution resulting from the collapse of Later Bronze Age society (Stopford 1987; cf. Kristiansen, Chapter 2). The building of so many defended sites suggests a period of instability, and this may be one reason for the protection of agricultural produce. By contrast, it could have been in areas like the Thames Valley, where there is evidence of nucleation, that there was greater scope for individual advancement. There is no sign that society was equally fragmented, and such a resilient landscape provided more opportunities for agricultural expansion than the chalkland soils.

Links between the living and the dead became even closer at this time, and it is usual to find quantities of human remains within the settlements themselves, where scattered bones and even entire bodies were deposited in corn storage pits. These burials were rarely accompanied by grave goods, but similar pits often contain special deposits, including meat joints, sacrificed animals and agricultural equipment. This link with storage pits is so pervasive that it seems possible that the dead were believed to exert an influence over the agricultural cycle.

The contrasts between Wessex and the Thames Valley became more evident during the period of renewed contact with Europe which preceded the Roman Conquest. Opinion is divided whether the Late Iron Age saw the emergence of the state in southeast England under the influence of Roman diplomacy and Roman trade (Haselgrove 1982). Nonetheless, the distinctive political geography of this period does highlight some of the contrasts evident in Iron Age archaeology as a whole. It seems likely that larger polities developed through a process of federation in the face of Roman colonial ambitions. At the same time, the native social structure was disrupted by the influx of luxury goods from the Continent and the demands of trading partners in the Roman world. The areas which had seen the development of the larger undefended settlements were precisely those in which political change was greatest. They came to form the power base of dynasties whose territories were to be enshrined in the administrative divisions of Roman Britain (Todd 1981: 29–59). The dynastic capitals were in extensive settlements, some of them bounded by enormous linear earthworks, where we find concentrations of imported artifacts, complex burials and evidence for craft production, including the minting of inscribed coins (Collis 1984). One major focus was the Thames Valley, where the deposition of weapons in rivers resumed on a large scale. Outside such areas, however, change was only piecemeal. Society remained fragmented; in some areas the hill forts went out of use, but in others they remained in commission through to the Roman Conquest. Here coinage was adopted only fitfully, suggesting that society lacked the stable structure evidenced in lowland England.

The contrast is never clearer than at the conquest itself. The more centralized societies were rapidly annexed, and a number of their capitals were adopted as the sites of Roman towns. Sometimes their rulers allied themselves with the Roman power, and where they did

not do so, whole polities could be reduced by a single military expedition; but in those areas in which hill forts had played a major role, social territories were probably smaller and the Roman army was forced to reduce a series of different centers of resistance (Cunliffe 1978a: 127–30). What clearer indication could there be of the contrasts in social organization that for so long had distinguished our two study areas?

Lastly, such contrasts extend to the role played by the supernatural. We have emphasized the existence of two quite different systems, but ideology played an important part in both. In Wessex the reorganization of food production may have issued in a system of staple finance, evidenced by the centralized food stores found in some of the hill forts. Given the role that these sites could have played in the political economy, it is not altogether surprising that corn storage pits formed a major focus for the deposition of the dead and the provision of special offerings. Indeed such concentrations of storage facilities are sometimes found together with shrines. In the Thames Valley, where hill forts are much less common, similar deposits are known, but in this area they are almost eclipsed by the evidence for more lavish offerings of river weapons; more occasionally, these finds are again associated with shrines. In this case the locations of these finds are strikingly different, and by the Late Iron Age both the shrines and the river metalwork tend to be discovered along the *boundaries of emerging polities*. There is little to suggest the link with agricultural production so characteristic of ritual deposits in Wessex. In this case ideology seems to have played a part in reinforcing a new political system.

3 COMMON PROCESSES?

Section 2 of this paper describes how the archaeological record of southern England is crosscut by two different sequences of development and also by major changes in the prominence of two neighboring regions. There were significant contrasts in the importance of ideology and food production between "earlier" and "later" prehistory, and the sequence as a whole allowed us to consider the well-known evidence from Wessex in a wider regional perspective. It still remains to consider how far these striking developments can contribute to our wider understanding of the evolution and operation of chiefdoms, and it is at this point that we must be guided less by other studies of the British

Isles than by the approaches considered elsewhere in this volume. Having emphasized the extent of variation to be found among the "chiefdoms" of southern England, we must distance ourselves from the fine detail of the archaeological record and work towards a greater level of abstraction. To what extent were similar processes at work in both sequences or both study areas? Six features are amenable to analysis in the British Isles: subsistence and the pattern of settlement; ideology and the treatment of the dead; territorial organization; warfare and the uses of weaponry; long-distance exchange; and conspicuous consumption.

Subsistence and settlement

These features are at the heart of any sustained analysis, and underlie most of the chronological and regional contrasts noted earlier in this paper. As we have seen, little is known about food production during the earlier prehistoric sequence. No doubt the landscape offered possibilities for expansion and also set limits to growth, but only occasionally have we seen these processes at work. The primacy of Wessex during the Earlier Neolithic period may have owed something to the great tracts of loess occurring in that area, but from then onwards it seems likely that the political system was financed *through the gradual extension of the settled area*, rather than any *intensification* of food production on the chalk. The decline of Wessex in relation to the Thames Valley could be due to the wasting of the more marginal soils first settled as part of that process. On a more local level, however, little obvious relationship exists between the development of social complexity and what is known of the settlement sites of the same period.

A much clearer relationship between food production and social complexity *can* be suggested in the Later Bronze Age, but it would be rash to see this evidence as completely straightforward. The high-status ringworks were located in parts of the Thames Valley with a productive economy, but the formation of more complex societies seems to have depended on their ability to convert differences of economic success into differences of prestige through control of exotic goods, so that when the influx of fine metalwork was curtailed at the beginning of the Iron Age, agricultural expansion alone was not enough to prevent fragmentation.

Relations with the supernatural

As we have seen, ideology may have been equally important. It would be easy to suggest that this was the prime mover in the Neolithic system, whilst food production played the dominant role in later prehistory, but the evidence is rather more complex. Relations with the supernatural do seem to have been important during the first part of the sequence, so that large areas of the landscape were structured around the ceremonial centers and burial places of earlier generations. At times the detailed layout of these monuments incorporated astronomical alignments that served to link activities at these sites to the natural world. The past was a resource as powerful as any identified by settlement archaeology. If those locations had once attracted interest through their exceptional fertility, they may have retained their regional importance into a period of environmental deterioration. Only when the disparities between ideology and food production became too great were major changes instituted.

It is all too easy to overlook the importance of ideology in the later prehistoric period. In our earlier sequence it had a public role, but in subsequent phases it may have been equally important although it was largely integrated into the agricultural cycle (Barrett in press). In both study areas the Later Bronze Age reorganization of the landscape involved the siting of cremation cemeteries alongside some of the farms. This link between the living and the dead is the start of a new development. As these cemeteries went out of use, we find an emphasis on deposits of unburnt bone. At first these were placed on the edges of settlements, but during the Iron Age the deposits were increasingly located *inside* the settlements, and whole bodies are found, as well as groups of animal remains and agricultural tools (Wait 1985). These bodies were generally deposited in corn storage pits, suggesting a close connection between the agricultural cycle and broader concepts of regeneration. Small shrines are also found amidst the storehouses in major hill forts, perhaps indicating an ideology that linked the supernatural and the economic fortunes of the community. This suggests a connection between the increasing role of staples in the political economy and the promotion of ritual practices that stressed the bonds between the ancestors and the food supply. Once the dead had dominated the living, but now they were "domesticated."

64

The pattern of change in British prehistory

Territorial organization

Food production and ideology can be considered together when we turn our attention to territorial organization. How were resources defined at the local level? Here there is yet another contrast, for in earlier prehistory there is little evidence for the enclosure of agricultural land. Rather, access to territory seems to have been controlled by the symbolism of place, expressed so vividly in the location of burial monuments and ceremonial sites (Earle, Chapter 4 below). These were the fixed points in the social landscape, and many types of activity, from the location of settlement areas to the disposal of occupation debris, were carried out with an awareness of these associations. By contrast, the later prehistoric sequence paid scant regard to these symbolic structures, destroying some of the monuments and effectively ignoring others, as the landscape was reorganized around the needs of productive agriculture. In place of the studied continuities created during the earlier sequence, we find a rejection of the past. Now territories were defined in physical form, by extensive systems of fields and, in Wessex, by territorial boundaries. The one feature which still recalls the earlier system is the way in which these boundaries incorporated existing burial mounds. The development of linear earthworks during the closing years of the Bronze Age prefigures the growth of hill forts on the chalk.

When we consider those hill forts, it is all too easy to emphasize their "defensive" character and to forget that the ceremonial centers would have had just as much impact on the landscape. Each must have played a major role in territorial organization. Neither group seems to have been built at times of particular prosperity. They do not mark the culmination of a period of change, but can appear towards its beginning, as if the building of such extraordinary structures enshrined a view of the world that was meant to last – again ideology may have played a major part in the process of change. This observation applies to the scale of Later Neolithic monuments as much as it does to the first Iron Age hill forts. This is especially obvious if we consider the efforts needed to build them (Startin and Bradley 1981). The labor estimates for the ceremonial sites are much higher, even though those monuments were built at a time when subsistence agriculture was apparently less productive. We have also seen changes in work

organization between the successive groups of Neolithic monuments. This entailed more central control of the process of building the large henges. How revealing that the evidence of unfinished *hill forts* suggests a return to the simpler procedures of the Earlier Neolithic. Once again the Early Iron Age is revealed as a period of fragmentation.

Weapons and warfare

Mention of hill fort building also introduces the question of warfare. This is not much in evidence. At the end of the Earlier Neolithic a few of the causewayed enclosures assumed a defensive character and were apparently attacked and burnt, but after that there is nothing similar until the Bronze Age/Iron Age transition, when again we find the building of a series of defended hill forts. Such evidence can be deceptive, however, as few of these sites provide any direct evidence of conflict. By contrast, the final phase of warfare, which seems to have accompanied the political expansion of the Late Iron Age, is known almost entirely from literary sources. If direct evidence of warfare is limited, a broadly consistent picture is provided by finds of weaponry. Earlier Neolithic arrowheads were lethal weapons, well suited for use in warfare, but during the Later Neolithic projectile points changed their nature and seem to have been more appropriate for use in formal combat (Edmonds and Thomas 1987). One specialized type is particularly often found in large earthwork monuments. The use of arrowheads as status objects continued in the Earlier Bronze Age, when archery equipment was commonly buried with the dead. A similar impression is provided by the metal daggers of this period. It is not certain that these were used in warfare, and most examples have been found in graves. Wear analysis suggests that the simpler examples were committed to the ground fairly rapidly, whilst the more complex objects found with rich burials may have been insignia and were kept in circulation over a longer period (Wall 1987).

Again the later prehistoric sequence provides a different impression. In the Later Bronze Age many weapons were deposited in rivers. The martial symbolism is obvious, but the important point is that this is the *first period* when such objects show signs of combat damage; there are also occasional finds of human bones with wounds. The Iron Age evidence is still more clear-cut, and the increased number of skeletons with signs of weapon injuries shows that conflicts were still more

widespread (Dent 1983). Although such evidence is by no means common, it is entirely consistent with interpretations based on the changing character of monuments. The provision of fortified food stores in the Iron Age suggests that some of these conflicts were over agricultural resources.

Trade and exchange

Deliberate deposits of weaponry are especially difficult to interpret. Whether they are found in graves or discovered in rivers, they suggest a warrior ethos, but, as we have seen, not all would have been used in combat. At the same time, many of these objects, or the raw materials from which they were made, originated in far-distant areas. Such discoveries introduce the question of long-distance trade. This is doubly important in British prehistory, for the scale of exchange networks seems gradually to have expanded through time, whilst fluctuations in long-distance relations are reflected in other parts of the archaeological record.

The first sequence shows a straightforward development from the small-scale networks of the Earlier Neolithic, through the nationwide exchange of artifacts and iconography of the Later Neolithic, to the Continental-scale networks of the Earlier Bronze Age. These developments were associated with the steadily more specialized roles of artifacts: in some areas exotic goods may have indicated personal status, and in others more ritualized systems incorporated distinctive symbols drawn from distant areas. In this case some continuity exists between our two sequences, and the exchange of prestigious metalwork is found *throughout* the Bronze Age. Indeed, there was such a deep-rooted emphasis on the consumption of *exotic* materials that as the supply of fine bronzes to the votive sphere declined, communities seem to have been reluctant to use iron objects in the same ways, despite the complex processes needed to make them. At this point deposition decreased (Bradley 1988). It was only when contacts with Europe were renewed, in the century before the Roman Conquest, that links with the outside world again were emphasized by grave goods and river finds.

Not only did long-distance trade change its character, but fluctuations in the intensity and direction of that trade had a profound impact on other parts of the archaeological record (Bradley 1981b). Our

earlier prehistoric sequence traces the steady expansion of long-distance links up to about 1400 B.C. The decisive break between the two sequences comes at a time when we have evidence for fluctuations in these wider networks. Ultimately, they may be due to crises outside the local system altogether, but as the Wessex landscape came under ecological pressure, communities in the Thames Valley took advantage of this period of uncertainty to establish new alliances. This marks the change to another system in which social distinctions were based more directly on differences of food production. Much the same sequence is found again as the metal trade diminished at the Bronze Age/Iron Age transition. Once more we find a rupture in exchange relations, followed by decisive changes in the management of the food supply. This change is mirrored by sudden changes in the archaeology of Wessex, compared with the middle and lower Thames, as if communities in the latter area had usurped the power base of the groups who had been controlling the bronze trade. Such alternating episodes of prestige trade and agricultural renewal have been recognized in other parts of Europe (Bradley 1981b).

Conspicuous consumption

Finally, similar distinctions are apparent when we ask how access to land or portable wealth was transformed into the differences of prestige on which social distinctions depended. An important link in the chain is the evidence for conspicuous consumption. This can refer to consumption of the food supply through feasting or the sacrifice of animals; to the consumption of energy in the building of great monuments; or even to the destruction of wealth as exotic objects were removed from circulation in burials or votive offerings. All three practices are well attested in British prehistory. We have already considered the role of monument building, and there is evidence of large-scale meat eating from Earlier Neolithic enclosures. In the same way pig feasts are strongly evidenced in Later Neolithic henges, as well as some of the settlement sites of the same period. In each case the food remains were deposited ceremoniously, together with fine artifacts. When single burial became firmly established during the Earlier Bronze Age, evidence for feasting disappears, but we still find complex artifacts in the graves.

The changes that transformed the later prehistoric landscape are

mirrored by largely new forms of consumption, in particular by river metalwork. This is poorly understood, but it is likely that the deposition of that material was on a large enough scale to have put serious strains on the metal supply (Bradley 1988). Once that supply had been disrupted, in the earlier part of the Iron Age, emphasis again was placed on differences of food production. Now we find evidence of animal sacrifice from hill forts, settlements, and shrines, although it is only in the Late Iron Age that we see much evidence of large-scale meat consumption; at present this appears to be limited to sites involved in long-distance exchange. During the Late Iron Age we also encounter a new series of rich burials, and once again fine artifacts were deposited in rivers. A notable feature of this system is that now these votive deposits were concentrated around the boundaries of major territories (Bradley 1987c).

Summary

We considered this last example at the end of Section 2, but it is worth recalling here, for it combines the evidence from several sources: food production, conspicuous consumption, and territorial organization. Ideology also plays a part in establishing a "symbolic" boundary around the newly developed polities. Such a complex situation is entirely characteristic of the sequence in prehistoric Britain. At the same time, the basic processes that led to social change are exactly those discussed by other contributors to the seminar. The specific details vary considerably, even within this particular case study, and in the British Isles no one factor appears to dominate the others, although striking differences of emphasis are seen at different times. Many of the processes thought to typify the development of chiefdoms *can* be identified here, and yet they characterize societies which actually had little in common with one another and regions in which the local sequences possessed a distinctive character of their own. If chiefdoms are no longer identified from a checklist of separate elements, we must ensure that the study of *processes* never becomes equally schematic. There is considerable virtue in making use of the time depth provided by the archaeological record, but much of its richness would be lost if comparative studies did not pay due regard for the *specific practices* evidenced in each local sequence, for it is on that level that such processes have to be identified. There would be little point in looking

at this material in such detail if its distinctiveness were to be obscured by overabstraction. Britain provides a provocative case in which the separate elements isolated by writers on chiefdoms fail to capture the reality of the archaeological record in its abundance and sheer variety. If British society was simpler than some of the others discussed in this volume, the task of understanding it is no less complex.

CONCLUSION

This paper has described an extremely long sequence of change in two neighboring areas of southern England. Both have a substantial history of investigation, and Wessex has played a significant part in the discussion of chiefdoms in prehistory. Although this particular account differs from some of the interpretations offered before, its importance for comparative studies is the way in which it allows us to investigate the changing relationship between economy, ideology, and power over a period of four thousand years – the very issues highlighted in the title of this book. I began this account by suggesting that any choice between materialist and ideological interpretations of chiefdoms was likely to prove unsatisfactory, and the same applies to the other "prime movers" discussed in the previous section. Almost without exception, those processes, however important in their own terms, merely emphasized the depth of the divisions between what I have called "earlier" and "later" prehistory. That distinction is not, as one reviewer suggested, the distinction between two different *ways of studying the past*; nor are the societies studied here in any sense different in kind. These case studies illustrate different *relationships* between ideology and economy in the past, not different allegiances among the doctrinal disputes of the present. A narrowing of our perspectives may give us the illusion of clarity, but it can do so only at a price. If the past is simplified too drastically before we feel able to investigate it, it will not be worth studying at all.

Property rights and the evolution of chiefdoms

TIMOTHY EARLE

In this chapter, I will concentrate on the fundamental relationships between the development of chiefs and specific property rights. The evolution of chiefdoms hinges to a large measure on the ability to control or direct the flow of energy and other basic resources through a society as a means to finance new institutions (Earle 1977; D'Altroy and Earle 1985; Johnson and Earle 1987; Price 1978). Chiefdoms with their distinctive nonproducing elite sector depend on the ability to mobilize and direct a "surplus" extracted from the commoner producers. To be sure, control is never a simple procedure; as we discussed at length in the School of American Research Seminar, chiefs can use diverse economic, social, political, and religious strategies; however, control rests first and foremost on dominating labor, the limiting factor in production in nonindustrial societies (Price 1984).

Now control over labor itself is never easy because a tension always exists between social levels over rights to allocate labor (Johnson and Earle 1987). Families do not freely give up labor without either an expectation of direct return or the threat of force. Similarly the leader of a local group is reluctant to deliver up labor to a higher authority in as much as this undercuts his local support base. Labor mobilization depends usually on an explicit reciprocity, a return for service. What

71

the emerging elite has to offer its supporters may be somewhat variable, but the recurrent pattern would appear to be access to land and its productive resources.

The importance of property rights as crucial to the process of social evolution has been recognized by many scholars. Among nineteenth-century theoreticians, private property rights were especially emphasized by Marx and Engels (1965 [1846]; Engels 1972 [1884]), who delineated the key role of private property in developing systems of economic domination and political control. The evolutionary (Marxian) emphasis on private property came under vehement attack by the Boasians (Lowie 1947; Hershkovits 1952), who refused to recognize an evolutionary importance of ownership. Perhaps as a result, in Service's (1962) influential neo-evolutionary synthesis, property rights were not regarded as particularly important. Among anthropologists, Fried (1967) revived an interest in property rights. He focused on the shift from communal to private rights as underlying the differential access to strategic resources, the key economic ingredient for stratification and the evolution of the state. Sahlins (1972: 92–4) reiterated this position by equating the shift from kinship to property as a basis of control with the beginnings of bourgeois states. Among economists, Douglass North emphasized the role of property in state systems: "States attempt to act like a discriminating monopolist, separating each group of constituents and devising property rights so as to maximize state revenues" (1981: 23).

On the basis of the evolutionary framework laid out in Johnson and Earle (1987), it is possible to discuss some changing roles of property rights in the evolution of social complexity. Although certainly not a simple unilinear development, this sketch may help focus attention on how critically important ownership can be in social and political relationships. First, at the family (band) level of organization, land rights are ambiguous and flexible. As described for the San (Lee 1979), for example, lands are not divided into discrete, bounded territories. Rather lands are associated with particular camps on the basis of established patterns of use; these home ranges are not defended territories. Property rights, however, do exist, especially tied to limited and concentrated resources such as the San water holes or Shoshone pine nut groves. Such rights are often associated with particular people or families with long use rights, but others may ask permission to use the specific resource; permission is rarely refused, but it obligates the

visitor to extend reciprocal rights on his own lands. The flexibility and openness of property rights among hunter-gatherers has been explained as a necessary adaptation to local variability in resource yields from place to place and from year to year (Yellen and Harpending 1972). Cashden (1983), however, emphasizes that territoriality exists among such groups, maintained by social boundaries.

At the local group (tribal) level, property rights are radically transformed with the creation of lineage or clan groups associated with specific, demarcated land sections that are defended along their perimeter. Ownership is publicly established during ceremonies, such as when the Tsembaga "plant the rumbim," and the boundaries of clan territories are staked out (Rappaport 1967); participants in such ceremonies then share rights to the land. Collier (1975) has argued that such corporate groups evolve as a response to increasing population density and resulting conflict between groups. Individual families receive land through their clan/lineage; traditional rights to clan lands are sanctioned by history – their ancestors inhabited the lands and their ghosts are thought to persist there. Families clear and improve sections for garden and house sites, but their rights depend on continuing use. Abandoned lands revert to the clan. Collier (1975) points out that individual titles emerge in these societies at high population densities when land is continually used and internal conflict ruptures the corporate groups. In highland New Guinea, for example, individual land ownership is associated with high population densities and intensive agriculture (Podolefsky 1987).

At the level of the regional polity (chiefdoms), considerable discussion was raised in the seminar concerning the role of property rights and resulting political control. Many seem to follow the position originally articulated by Fried that ranked societies (or simple chiefdoms) relied on kinship as the primary mechanism of control. I explicitly argued that land tenure, even at the emergence of social differentiation, could be quite important. In simple chiefdoms, chiefs are local leaders, highly respected members of the clan. Clan lands are spoken of as owned by the chief, who can manipulate his position for significant political advantage. The Trobriand Islanders illustrate how this works. The local sublineage (*dala*) owns agricultural land, but the group's leader, by controlling the annual allocation of subsistence plots, effectively controls access to it (Malinowski 1935). A household can obtain land only from the leader, and he can allocate use rights to

73

non-*dala* members who support him politically. The leader also exercises control through his ownership of the magic that accompanies all major steps in farming. He is thus central to the production process and uses this position to further his political ambitions.

In more complex chiefdoms, the chiefs characteristically become the primary landowners; this clear ownership of land increases the chiefs' economic power reflecting control over subsistence production. For example, among the Hawaiian chiefdoms, the paramount chiefs were the owners of all lands (Earle 1978). They then allocated community territories (*ahupua'a*) to high-ranking chiefs who were their close relatives and supporters in wars of succession and conquest. In turn the community chiefs offered land plots, especially on irrigation systems, to individuals in exchange for their labor on chiefly land and projects.

The preceding evolutionary pattern for land tenure is of course simplified and should not be taken as an invariant unilinear scheme. In fact, the basis of control can be highly variable, as the seminar suggested; however, the evolution of property rights by which chiefs control primary production can be seen as basic to the evolution of many complex stratified societies. To investigate the nature of land tenure in the evolution of chiefdoms, I will review the archaeological literature for two long-term trajectories – the Hawaiian Islands and the Wessex region of southern England. These are historically independent and in many ways contrasting cases of prestate social dynamics, but, as I shall argue, the significance of economic control through varying systems of land tenure is a constant theme. The archaeological recognition of land tenure systems will also be discussed.

CHIEFDOMS OF THE HAWAIIAN ISLANDS

The evolution of complex Hawaiian chiefdoms, from the first Polynesian colonization of the islands in about A.D. 500 to their "discovery" by Captain James Cook in 1778, has become a critical case in the evolution of intermediate level societies. Several important ecological and economic theories (Wittfogel 1957; Sahlins 1958; Service 1962) were developed using Hawaiian data and have since been tested and elaborated there (Hommon 1976; Earle 1978; Cordy

74

1981; Kirch 1984). In many ways Hawaii has become a litmus test for ideas about the evolution of chiefdoms. The extensive historical information that is available puts processual flesh on our archaeological bones. Extensive details for this discussion are to be found in the above references.

Hawaii consists of seven major islands with a combined area of 16,600 km². Isolated from all other major land masses by more than 3,000 km (Kirch, Chapter 6 below: Fig. 6.1), these islands are the peaks of a volcanic mountain range that rises directly from the ocean floor. The geologic age and extent of erosion varies greatly from island to island. To the east, the large island of Hawaii (10,400 km²) is volcanically active, and its broad slopes have few valleys and permanent streams; its population at time of contact has been estimated at 100,000, organized as a single chiefdom. With these data, population density can be estimated at approximately 10/km². To the west, the smaller island of Kaua'i (1,400 km²) is heavily eroded with deep canyons that carry water from the central mountains to the sea; its population at contact was perhaps 30,000, or approximately twenty-one persons per km². Because the productive alluvial soils developed for irrigation agriculture were, however, restricted to the eroded valleys and coastal fringe, the prehistoric population was concentrated here, where densities often reached several hundred persons per square kilometer.

At time of contact, the four complex Hawaiian chiefdoms were each centered on one of the main islands – Kaua'i, O'ahu, Mau'i, and Hawaii. The society was rigidly stratified with a small ruling class owning all productive resources and a commoner mass attached to particular lands which they worked for their subsistence and their chief's income. The chiefs were considered gods and controlled the main ceremonies connected to fertility and war.

Questions of how these complex chiefdoms evolved can be addressed most effectively with the use of the archaeological record recently summarized by Kirch (1984). Using these archaeological data, the ties between population growth, agricultural intensification, settlement, and monumental construction help illustrate how developing systems of institutional finance underwrite the evolution of a centralized, hierarchical, and stratified society.

Population and subsistence

Population estimates are based on the work of Hommon (1976, 1980), Cordy (1981), and Kirch (1984: 104–11), which rely on the number of dated features, usually houses with radiometric or hydration determinations. Earliest dates indicate a colonization of the islands by a small population before A.D. 500. Settlement began on the windward coasts and only gradually expanded leeward to more marginal lands (Cordy 1974). Our best dated evidence comes from a number of archaeological projects along the west coast of the Big Island and a systematic survey of the small island of Kaho'olawe (summarized in Kirch 1984). Both areas have low rainfall and were occupied relatively late (A.D. 1000), they experienced a period of rapid growth up to A.D. 1500–1700 and then a decline. Although evidence has not been so systematically recovered for the optimal windward and alluvial environments, a suggestion of continuing growth (if at a reduced rate) up to contact seems more likely (Kirch 1984: 110). This picture would appear to approximate a single 1,200-year cycle of logistic growth as a colonizing population expanded and intensified resource use and eventually became constrained by available resources. (The multiple cycles of growth and decline described for the Wessex case contrast with this.)

Early settlers along the coast maintained a mixed economy with fishing and agriculture. In the windward Halawa Valley of Molokai for the period A.D. 600–1200, Kirch and Kelly (1975) document a gradual shift to agriculture; pig and dog increased in the diet at the expense of fish. After A.D. 1200, as population expanded, people settled the inland zone, signaling a growing emphasis on agriculture. Burning and heavy erosion have been dated to A.D. 1200, probably associated with shifting cultivation. On the ecologically marginal island of Kaho'olawe (Hommon 1980), up until the fifteenth century, occupation was restricted to a small coastal population; by the sixteenth century, as population nearly doubled, expansion to the interior would have been based on shifting cultivation. The ensuing rapid decline then may represent an ecological crisis in the agricultural regime.

On the alluvial soils of all major islands, intensive irrigation systems were developed during the sixteenth century (Earle 1980; Tuggle and Tomonari-Tuggle 1980; Athens 1983; Kirch 1985b) and regular terraced field systems were developed on the slopes of western Hawaii

(Rosendahl 1972). Both kinds of field systems represented a reorganized landscape with significant investment in infrastructural changes including irrigation, terracing, and dividing walls that created a human patchwork of permanent fields.

Settlement pattern

Throughout the sequence, settlements were small clusters of houses spread out across the landscape. Early on, the houses were along the beach, but, with expansion of agriculture, population spread inland to be immediately associated with agricultural fields (see, for example, Earle 1978). Communities were largely dispersed, with clusters of houses associated with kin groupings of several families. Villages virtually did not exist, except perhaps associated with chiefly residences. Except for some enclosing walls, this dispersed settlement pattern would appear to be nondefensive; however, we know that warfare was both frequent and savage. How can this apparent contradiction be reconciled?

Archaeologically the evidence for warfare is ephemeral (Kirch 1984). A dispersed settlement pattern is normally seen by archaeologists as an indication of peaceful relations. In Hawaii, refuges have occasionally been noted, including some ridges cut by transverse ditches and walled lava tubes. Occasional caches of sling stones have also been described. The historic accounts, however, document frequent and savage warfare that took place between competing chiefs for the paramountcy and between chiefdoms for control of local communities and islands. It is my interpretation that the lack of fortified settlements indicates that warfare, largely the concern of a ruling elite, had relatively little immediate impact on local populations. In fact the large scale of political integration, at the level of full islands, suggests that for all intents and purposes life in the local community was peaceful. In essence chiefdoms in Hawaii maintained, at least at the end of the sequence, a broad regional peace. (This pattern will reappear in the British case for the Age of Stonehenge; see also Drennan, Chapter 11 below.)

Monuments and their construction

Monumental constructions as we are used to for the chiefdoms of Wessex, Mississippian culture (Steponaitis, Chapter 9 below), or

Mesoamerica (Feinman, Chapter 10 below; Drennan, Chapter 11 below), or even the Marquesas (Kirch, Chapter 6 below) did not exist in Hawaii. Constructions are small in scale and probably required relatively small and local work forces. Most important are the *heiau* shrines that can consist of elaborate stone platforms and enclosing walls. For the island of Kaua'i, Bennett (1931) lists 122 *heiau*, of which 28 are considered large and probably related to ceremonies of the ruling chiefs. The large *heiau* frequently consist of multiple paved terraces enclosed by walls; the *heiau* were frequently built on hilltops or slopes, where their prominent location could give an impression of size at the same time that actual expenditure in construction was minimized. These large temples were spaced fairly regularly along the coast, typically in the more important local communities; the residence of the ruling paramount chiefs of Kaua'i had five large *heiau*, while only two other communities had more than one large *heiau*, and those had only two each.

The use of the large *heiau* is well documented in the historic record. Ceremonies of war, when the paramount chief prepared for conquest, were conducted here. They were also used in the Makahiki ceremonies, an annual festival when the paramount chief acted as the god Lono who was thought responsible for the fertility of the lands (Peebles and Kus 1977). The stick figure of the god was paraded around the island where it would stop at each local community's shrine to collect annual contributions (tribute) as part of a mobilization used to support the chiefly institutions (Earle 1977).

What we know about the dating of the *heiau* is sketchy. The only reasonably comprehensive study is that of the Kane'aki *heiau* in the Makaha Valley of Oahu (Ladd 1973; R. C. Green 1980: 63–9). This temple was constructed in six distinct stages, beginning in the sixteenth century; the temple was expanded in size at each rebuilding, was enclosed by wall, and finally, in the last two stages, probably took on the status of a large *heiau* involved in major ceremonies. Smaller *heiau*, several excavated by Ladd, existed in the valley. Dating apparently to the late historic period (seventeenth and eighteenth centuries), these contemporaneous shrines show a regular spacing that Green interprets as documenting a formalized division of the valley's resources among community groups. For Halawa Valley, Kirch and Kelly (1975) describe many small shrines associated with local ceremonies and territorial divisions within the valley. In the

late pre-historic period, a major *heiau* was also constructed in Halawa.

Overall labor investment seems to have increased significantly in the last two hundred years before contact. This is seen in the *heiau*, but in all cases the labor involved was modest. Although no systematic work has been done on this problem, the primary labor investment was evidently in productive resources – the irrigation complexes, terraced fields, and large fish ponds. In all cases these improvements were built mostly late in the sequence, not, strictly speaking, as a direct response to population pressure, which appears to have peaked, but rather to finance the expanding and centralizing chiefdoms. At least some of the irrigation systems, such as the Anahulu systems on Oahu and the Waikoloa system on Hawaii, were apparently developed just at contact by Kamehameha to support his military adventures (Kirch 1985b). The importance of the elaborate irrigation and dryland field complexes as connected to the system of chiefly finance and land tenure will now be explored.

Changing patterns of land tenure

Leading up to what we know of the historic pattern of political economy is a distinctive pattern of changing land use and redefinition of the landscape. The associated conditions of population growth and destructive shifting cultivation created the base economic conditions that required or encouraged a rapid reorganization of subsistence production towards permanent field systems both on the irrigated alluvial soils and on suitable uplands.

This "intensification" in land use was, however, important first and foremost as it affected the nature of land ownership. It seems reasonable to assume that, prior to this reorganization late in prehistory, territories were held as lineage lands managed by chiefs as group leaders. At this time, investment in the construction of monuments of any kind is unknown. Following the reorganization of the subsistence base, the most productive lands became improved and carefully divided up. Considerable labor was invested in these structured changes to the landscape. Individual fields and farms were demarcated by permanent terraced plots and subdividing walls. Where topography did not provide sharp definitions, stone walls were used to define community and subcommunity units.

At this point, the basis for the historic staple finance system would

have been in place; community land, given over to the chiefs, served as their income estates. Use rights to individuals were given in return for household labor on chiefly lands and other projects. In the early historic periods, the boundaries and subdivisions of land units were well known and recited in land claims. Named rocks, ridges, streams, walls, and shrines were all used to delimit the perimeters. In one interesting law case, chiefly ownership of a land segment on Kaua'i was identified explicitly according to whose manager had rights to put its residents to work (Earle 1978: 189).

Certainly the primary basis for finance created in the reorganization of the subsistence economy was also associated with religious monuments. These monuments appear to have marked territorial divisions and to have served to legitimize the existing pattern of land ownership, with the chiefs as earthly gods responsible for the "natural" processes of production. The message seems clear, however, that when land ownership is unambiguously defined, as it was in the field systems and fish ponds, the need to invest labor in complex ceremonial architecture is not great. This suggests that the amount of labor invested in monuments is *not* a straightforward measure of central control but rather reflects one pattern of control, the importance of which we can now investigate with the British evidence.

CHIEFDOMS OF WESSEX

In a seminal article, Colin Renfrew (1973b) argued that chiefdoms evolved in the Wessex region of southern England during the Neolithic and Bronze Ages. On the basis of the distribution of labor invested in burial and ceremonial monuments, he inferred sizeable polities centrally organized and controlled by chiefs. The territorial nature of the Bronze Age barrow cemeteries had earlier been described by Fleming (1971), and Cunliffe (1978a) later argued for a continuing territoriality and chiefly redistribution centered on the Iron Age hill forts of southern Britain.

Wessex encompasses approximately 9,000 km^2. The region has gently rolling relief, low in elevation. Soils vary from the light soils covering the chalks to the heavier clays and alluvial soils along the stream courses. Especially important for prehistoric settlement have been the extensive chalklands of the Salisbury Plain, the Marlborough Downs, Cranborne Chase, and the Dorset Ridgeway, which may have

been covered originally with loess (Bradley, Chapter 3 above). Streams that at times were the focus of settlements include the Upper Kennet, Wylye, Avon, Test, Stour, and Frome. The catchment areas of these streams create a natural zone that is distinct from the gravels of the upper River Thames to the north, the low marshlands of Somerset to the west, and the chalklands of Sussex to the east.

In the summary to follow, I rely heavily on the synthetic work of Richard Bradley (Chapter 3 above, and 1984; Bradley and Hodder 1979; Barrett and Bradley 1980; Bradley and Gardener 1984). Building on his work, my goal is to focus on how growth and decline in population, a shifting subsistence, and social organization are inter-related. Especially important is to show how changes in the socio-political organization of chiefdoms were linked to changing mechanisms of land tenure and finance. Using a chronological scheme adapted from Burgess (1980), three periods are identified:

(1) the Age of Early Farmers (4100–3000 B.C.), equated with the Early Neolithic;
(2) the Age of Stonehenge (3000–1400 B.C.), subdivided into the Late Neolithic (until 2200 B.C.) and the Early Bronze Age (afterwards);
(3) the Age of Hill Forts (1400 B.C.–A.D. 43), subdivided into the Later Bronze Age (until 700 B.C.) and the Iron Age (until the Roman Conquest).

Population and subsistence

Population is a critical variable for models of the evolution of complex society. In ecological models, population represents the basic needs of the human group; in political models, population represents the available labor that must be controlled and directed. Using the English data, population density and distribution have been difficult to measure. In terms of comparability between time periods the best measure that could be devised is the number of sites with radiometric dates (with one standard deviation as calibrated by Stuiver and Reimer [1986]) in each 100-year time block (compare Rick 1987). Although this measure is certainly biased toward monuments which are particularly visible and thus likely to be excavated, both later and earlier components are frequently encountered during excavation such that

81

each excavation represents a sampled locus of potential human activities. In addition, recent public archaeology along highway corridors provides a relatively unbiased sample of archaeological sites with radiometric dates.

For the Age of Early Farmers in Wessex, the earliest dates commence about 4100 B.C. (Fig. 4.1). From 4100 to 3300 B.C. the number of sites with radiocarbon dates increases consistently from three to fifteen as population grew to occupy the more desirable locations in Wessex. After 3300 B.C. population may have declined with a low of eight sites with radiocarbon determinations spanning the time frames from 3000–2800 B.C., early in the Age of Stonehenge. From 2800 to 1700 B.C. the number of sites with radiocarbon dates increases consistently to a second peak of fourteen sites. This is during the Early Bronze Age when burial mounds were constructed ubiquitously through Wessex. Population appears to decline again to a low of only four sites in the tenth century B.C. Then sites increase in number somewhat, but this probably masks a more significant growth suggested by the increasing size of settlement sites through the Age of Hill Forts. A quick inspection of Fig. 4.1 suggests three cycles, each of roughly a thousand years, with population peaks in the Early Neolithic Period, in the Early Bronze Age, and in the Iron Age.

To evaluate the population cycles with independent evidence, I tried to inventory the frequency and distribution of temporally diagnostic artifacts. For the Ages of the Early Farmers and of Stonehenge, the arrowheads are reasonably common and show broad distribution throughout Wessex and England (H. S. Green 1980). The projectile point assemblages from southern and central England seem roughly to support the population trends suggested by the radiocarbon dates for the early parts of the sequence (Bradley 1986a). The leaf-shaped arrow points, diagnostic of the Age of Early Farmers, represent a consistent ten to twenty-five percent of point assemblages; Wessex with its twenty-three percent appears to have been a region of relatively high settlement density. The frequency of transverse arrow points then, indicative of the Late Neolithic, dominates the Wessex assemblage with forty-nine percent; for southern England, this style of point is strongly concentrated in the upper chalklands of the Wessex region and to a lesser degree Sussex. Subsequently – and unexpectedly, based on the radiocarbon date frequencies – the percentage of barbed-and-tanged points, indicative of the Early Bronze Age, drops off substan-

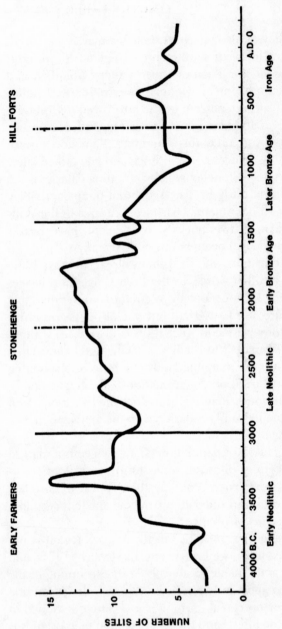

Fig. 4.1 Number of sites with calibrated radiometric determinations for each 100-year time frame. Shown are three cycles of population growth and decline

83

tially in Wessex. Bradley (1986a) suggests that this may represent an early shift in settlement focus in south-central England to the non-chalk, lowland regions of the Thames River Valley, Corallian and Vale, and the Bournemouth area, where barbed-and-tanged points comprise forty-three to seventy percent of the arrowhead assemblage. Alternatively, the drop in abundance in Wessex may reflect less conflict in which the arrows were used; this could reflect a regional peace imposed by the increasing scale of political integration described later.

With regard to the Age of Stonehenge, an intriguing data set is the cultural material *under* the Early Bronze Age burial mounds (Bradley 1978a). Of thirty-one well-documented barrows excavated in the Wiltshire and Dorset chalklands, twenty (sixty-five percent) have Beaker (transitional Early Bronze Age) occupation, eight (twenty-six percent) have Late Neolithic occupation, and six (nineteen percent) have Early Neolithic occupation. In other words, by the Bronze Age most locales with barrows had already been occupied. In contrast, in the marginal heathlands of Hampshire and Dorset, all but one of the twenty-three Early Bronze Age barrows were constructed on land surfaces without earlier occupation. This suggests to Bradley (see Chapter 3 above) that population expanded into the marginal lands at a time corresponding to the second peak in radiocarbon determinations. The fragile conditions of these marginal zones may well have resulted in their rapid depletion and the decline in numbers of sites with the radiocarbon date for the Later Bronze Age.

To summarize, the pattern of population change suggests a marked cyclical growth and decline following some form of economic collapse. Changes in the subsistence economy then appear to correlate with these population cycles in order to provide adequate food and a basis for developing systems of finance.

Evidence for the changing subsistence in the Wessex region is not unambiguous, but has been well reviewed by Evans (1975) and Bradley (1978a, 1984, and Chapter 3 above). At the beginning of the Neolithic, England was apparently forested. Although the expanding population's dependency on cereal farming is presently questioned, a progressive clearing of the forests and the local creation of grasslands is evident. The importance of domesticated animals (cattle, sheep, and pigs) is documented in the faunal remains, and the site catchment areas associated with the causewayed enclosures from the Age of Early

Farmers would appear to favor animal husbandry (Barker and Webley 1978; Smith 1984).

During the Age of Stonehenge, forests continued to be cleared (or were recleared after a regeneration associated with a population decline), and a fairly open environment with extensive grasslands became dominant in much of southern England through the time period of interest. The major henges were located in agriculturally productive valleys in the chalklands. Based on the location of much of the ceremonial architecture in areas of open environments, stock raising was probably an important part of the economy at this time (Fleming 1971). Because of the high energetic costs of pastoralism to support a population of sufficient density to have constructed the major monuments of the Age of Stonehenge, however, it seems unlikely that husbandry would have dominated the subsistence economy.

Rather the animals probably served as movable wealth which could have been dominated by the elites as part of a developing political economy. Certainly husbandry would have produced special meat products that would have been particularly important in ceremonial feasts associated with the monuments that will be described momentarily.

As the Age of Hill Forts commenced, the economy was dramatically transformed. Much of the population, now living more off the chalks, apparently came to rely on intensive farming. Elaborate agricultural field systems were constructed around new settlements, and major settlements contained extensive grain storage buildings. Evidently, for the first time, the subsistence economy depended heavily on cereal crops. This shift in the nature of the subsistence economy was probably mirrored in changing patterns of finance as the central storage and subsequent distribution of the grain staples became important.

Social organization: settlement pattern and monuments

The best evidence for the social organization of chiefdoms is the settlement hierarchy and its associated monumental construction (Renfrew 1972; Earle 1987a). Settlement hierarchy helps identify the scale of integration and the number of levels in the political system; the labor invested in monumental construction helps determine the extent of central control over people.

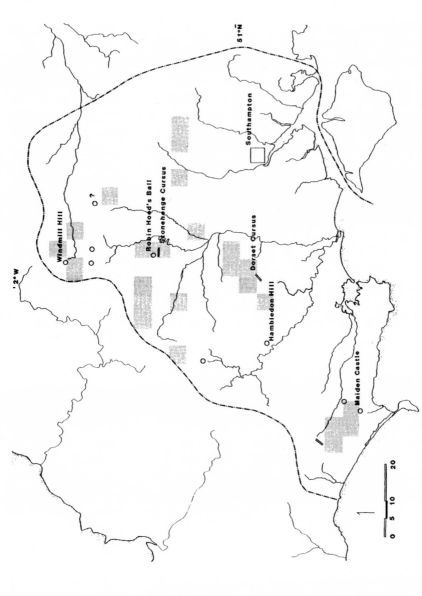

Fig. 4.2 Location of the Early Neolithic monuments in Wessex. Circles are the enclosures, and parallel lines are cursus monuments. The shaded blocks represent RCHM 25 km² survey blocks that contain four or more long barrows. The modern city of Southampton is located for easy reference

Settlements of the Age of Early Farmers were relatively ephemeral, hamlet-sized sites, identified by scattered pits and refuse. In addition were eight (possibly ten) "causewayed" enclosures, the most famous of which is Windmill Hill (I. Smith 1965). These enclosures have one to three encircling earthen banks, at least in some instances revetted, that set off an area of 1.5–7.7 ha. The fill for the banks was obtained from a series of pits excavated around the exterior of the banks. Although internal features are rarely preserved, artifacts and refuse indicate that these sites were often settlements and served for ceremonial feasting probably involving interpolity ceremonies (Bradley, Chapter 3 above). The location of the enclosures on high prominences, often where later hill forts were positioned, and the evidence for burning and concentrated arrowhead finds indicate the probable importance of interpolity conflict at this time. Most importantly the two-tiered settlement system suggests a political arrangement into simple chiefdoms.

Three types of monuments punctuated the landscape of southern England during the Age of Early Farmers. Most important were the long barrows, which were long, wedge-shaped mounds flanked by ditches and with forecourts and façades that lead into chambers used for communal burials. More than 175 long barrows were constructed in Wessex. Out of 376 25 km^2 grid squares in Wessex (as used by the site files of the Royal Commission on Historic Monuments [England]), long barrows appear in forty-seven (twenty-two percent) of the grid blocks. Sixteen grid units have four or more long barrows (maximum eleven) (Fig. 4.2). The labor invested in these barrows was often substantial, with the large West Kennet long barrow representing perhaps 15,700 man-hours (mh) of labor investment (Startin 1982).

The eight to ten causewayed camps were, in addition to settlements, large monuments of this period. All were not equal in size: Hambledon Hill (Mercer 1980) with its extensive outworks stands out as unusually large and complex; others are quite modest. Startin (1982) has estimated 62,760 mh for Windmill Hill, one of the larger enclosures. It is argued that these monuments were constructed by independent teams, each working in one pit around the bank. These teams would have been small, perhaps representing separate kin groups brought together for the undertaking.

When comparing the two types of early monument, the enclosures dominate in size; however, in overall investment, the abundant long

87

barrows were primary. The importance of these monuments was evidently part of an elaborately constructed environment of southern England that emphasized the importance of ancestors (Fleming 1973; Bradley 1984). This point is further strengthened by the fact that at least some of the activities taking place within the enclosures involved burial ritual.

Towards the end of the Age of Early Farmers, the third form of monument documents a major shift in scale of labor investment. Three remarkable cursus monuments were constructed near the heaviest concentrations of long barrows on the Wessex chalklands. Most famous is the Dorset Cursus, the available evidence from which has been summarized by Bradley (1986). The Cursus was a massive rectangular enclosure, 10,000 m long but never more than 100 m wide, demarcated by parallel banks (perhaps revetted to a height of 2 m) and external ditches. Estimates of labor in this monument are conservatively 500,000 mh. The cursuses were carefully aligned with neighboring long barrows, suggesting to Bradley that the cursuses were primarily involved in burial ritual. At least the Dorset Cursus suggests a solar alignment that was to become critically important later for Stonehenge. The overall impression is that the effort invested in the cursus monuments represented a considerable focusing of control over labor at a time when population was quite low, perhaps even declining.

The spatial pattern of the monuments gives a reasonable understanding of the probable political landscape of Wessex at this time. The numerous long barrows are distributed discontinuously with four major concentrations (twenty-two to sixty-one barrows in each) corresponding to the areas with the three cursus monuments and with Windmill Hill. Additionally there are six smaller concentrations, three to six in a local area, further to the east. The relationship of the causewayed enclosures to these concentrations of long barrows is problematic. In some cases, the enclosures are close to the concentrations as around Windmill Hill, Robin Hood's Ball, and Maiden Castle; others, such as Hambledon Hill, Whitesheet, Rybury and Knap Hill, appear marginal. The pattern of causewayed enclosures indicates a fairly regular spacing, with a few clusters as in the northern and southern groups. These patterned distributions of the monuments suggest four relatively enduring polities, probably indicative of chiefdoms,

and a number of smaller polities with less centralized control around the peripheries of Wessex.

The labor investment in the early Wessex monuments substantiates a degree of central control appropriate for simple chiefdoms. Although similar monuments exist elsewhere in England, the scale of Hambledon Hill or the Dorset Cursus is without equal. Startin (1976; 1982, Table 42; Startin and Bradley 1981) has estimated from 11,000 to 63,000 mh (midpoint, 37,000) for the construction of causewayed enclosures and 3,000 to 16,000 mh (midpoint, 9,000) for the long barrows. With the labor estimate for the cursus monuments, these figures can be extrapolated to 3,400,000 mh for fifty-five generations (twenty years each) or 62,000 man-hours per generation (mhpg). Although the tempo of labor investment is possible to judge with present data, variation in labor investment probably existed from generation to generation as individual monuments often appear to have been built relatively quickly and then soon abandoned only to be reused later.

The existence of a settlement hierarchy and its association with monumental construction document that, early in the English Neolithic period, the organization of political life in Wessex was already organized as competing chiefdoms. Each was composed of multiple local corporate groups that worked together to construct larger monuments.

In the Age of Stonehenge, settlements continue to be ephemeral and most probably represented small hamlets spread out in the landscape. At least the possibility exists that settlement mobility, as would be appropriate for husbandry, may have been high. Pits and refuse scatters, which are the main traces, concentrate close to the monuments that consisted especially of henges and barrow cemeteries. At present, little evidence for warfare exists for this period. Although no settlements were fortified, this may simply indicate a broad regional peace maintained within the chiefdom. For the Late Neolithic especially, the high frequency of arrowheads, sometimes concentrated as in the Windmill Hill area, may document regional conflict.

The archaeology for the Age of Stonehenge is dominated by a panoply of different monuments (Fig. 4.3). Most impressive were the henge monuments. Henges are banked enclosures, similar in appearance to the earlier causewayed enclosures, but with continuous

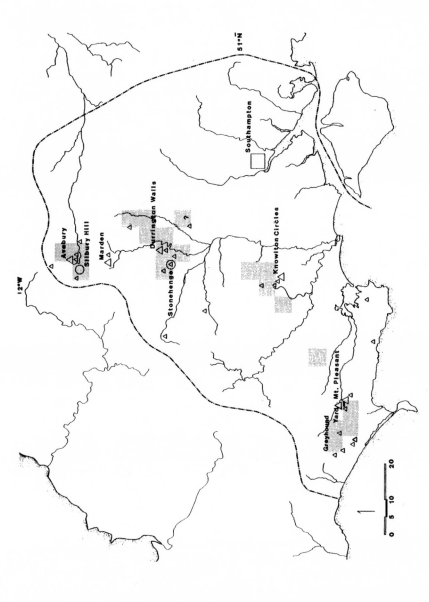

Fig. 4.3 Location of the Late Neolithic and Early Bronze Age monuments in Wessex. The triangles indicate henges, large for the primary monuments which are named. The circles indicate special monuments which are also named. The shaded blocks represent RCHM 25 km² survey blocks that contain fifty or more round barrows

ditches typically inside the bank. The enclosures vary considerably in size from less than 0.1 ha to as large as 12.5 ha for Avebury. Interior constructions included large post buildings, stone circles as at Stonehenge and Avebury, the pit rings of Maumbury Rings and Stonehenge, and the massive timber wall at Mt. Pleasant. Stonehenge and Avebury both had large ritual avenues connecting the main monument to other sites. Near to Avebury was the massive, artificial Silbury Hill, constructed during the same time. The major henges (Mt. Pleasant, Knowlton Circles, Durrington Walls, Marden and Avebury) were all located centrally to their probable polities. Many smaller henges and stone circles dotted the landscape and probably served as focal points for local ceremonies. Evidently these henges varied considerably in importance and represented a hierarchy of ceremonial construction that suggests a strong centrality in political organization.

Somewhat later, while construction ceased at most of the major henges, 8,000 or more round barrow mounds were constructed across the landscape. These mounds, although in most cases considerably smaller than the earlier long barrows, were characteristically designed for single interments, rather than the communal burials of the earlier monuments. The round barrows were typically built in cemetery clusters on prominent positions along ridges or on hilltops. The individual barrows were often arranged in discrete lines or clusters that suggest social or political relationships as would be expected for ruling lineages. Individual burials were associated with special grave goods that varied importantly in richness; the most impressive were the famous Wessex graves which contained wealth objects of gold and bronze that distinguished important leaders. Generally the extensive labor invested in the construction of the henges for chiefly ceremonies became redirected into the construction of the barrow cemeteries that memorialized individuals and their genealogies (compare Renfrew's [1974] distinction between group-oriented and individualizing chiefdoms).

The political organization of the landscape has been well discussed in the seminal papers by Fleming (1971) and Renfrew (1973b). The distribution of the barrows is indeed very broad, occurring in seventy-seven percent of the Wessex grid squares. As mentioned earlier, settlement spread apparently for the first time into the marginal land that became degraded to heath. Despite this broad distribution, distinct

clusterings of barrows existed. Using a minimum density of fifty recorded barrows for a 25 km^2 block, the dominant clusters were the Stonehenge region west of Durrington Walls with 993 barrows in 200 km^2; the Dorset Ridgeway south of Mt. Pleasant and Greyhound Yard, 490 barrows in 100 km^2; Cranborne Chase west from the Knowlton Circles, 273 barrows in 75 km^2; and the downs west of Avebury with 238 barrows in 75 km^2. The association of the barrow concentrations with the major henge monuments is evident, suggesting a continuing division of the region into four major chiefdoms. These chiefdoms were, however, not equal in their control of labor through time. Starting with a basic equality among the four centers in the Late Neolithic, the Stonehenge and Avebury polities seem to have emerged as dominant. Sometime during the Early Bronze Age, the Stonehenge region may have asserted dominion over most of Wessex.

The increasing scale of political integration indicated by the pattern of monuments translates into a significant increase in the overall control of labor during the Age of Stonehenge. Without a more detailed chronology, I will simply consider the aggregate construction for the time period averaged across eighty generations; this calculates as perhaps 191,000 mhpg, a threefold increase over the Age of Early Farmers. Table 4.1 presents the rough calculations.

The important point to be made for the Age of Stonehenge is that the political organization of Wessex continued to be that of multiple competing regional chiefdoms. These chiefdoms apparently consolidated power quite considerably through time and shifted their structural representation from the group-oriented ceremonial monuments to the more individualizing cemeteries. Finance appears to have relied on the production and distribution of cattle as mobile, locally produced wealth and later the additional use of nonlocal metal wealth to demarcate individual status.

At the beginning of the Age of Hill Forts, although the chronology is not yet fully clear, small settlement enclosures are found, often associated with elaborate new field systems and urnfield cemeteries. These enclosures, probably representing hamlet-size defended residences, are broadly distributed in the chalklands and in the lowlands, especially to the east where settlement earlier had been thin. Forty-five percent of the grid units contained enclosures, many dating to the Later Bronze Age. Some concentrations of enclosures exist, as

Table 4.1. *Labor investments in monumental construction during the Age of Stonehenge (3000–1400 B.C.)*

Monument type	Number	Investment per	Total investment
Large henges	6	500,000	3,000,000
Small henges	25	10,000	250,000
Special monuments			
Stonehenge II, III	1	2,000,000	2,000,000
Silbury Hill	1	4,000,000	4,000,000
Round barrows	8000	750	6,000,000
			15,250,000

Investment per generation = 191,000 mh

in Hampshire, but the overall impression is the division of the landscape into many small-scale polities. During the Iron Age, the broad settlement distribution continued as thirty-nine percent of the grid units contain settlements. The most important settlements of this period are the hill forts themselves, recorded in twenty-two percent of the grid squares. Many of the forts were quite small, only a few hectares in area surrounded by a single ditch and bank, but, later on, the sizes of some forts expanded to greater than 5 ha, and were often surrounded by multiple banks and ditches. Within many of the forts, the extensive grain storage structures indicate the probable importance of a new staple finance system.

A regional settlement hierarchy, indicative of competing polities, is clearly documented archaeologically. The multi-walled forts, greater than 4.9 ha, show a tendency towards regular spacing (Hodder and Orton 1976: 46), indicative of inter-fort political competition and independence. Several smaller forts, enclosures, and undefended settlements found within the catchment areas of the larger forts were probably dominated politically by these settlements (Palmer 1984). Size of polities was, however, not large; distances separating the larger forts averaged only 6.5 km. Many independent polities probably existed until just before the Roman conquest, when larger-scale chiefdoms were apparently re-established under the influence of intense external trade with the Roman world (Cunliffe 1984b).

Table 4.2. *Labor investment in fortification during the Age of Hill Forts (1400 B.C. – A.D. 43)*

Type of fortification	Number	Investment per	Total investment
Enclosures	445	2,500	1,112,500
Small hill forts	136	25,000	3,400,000
Large hill forts	23	200,000	4,140,000
			8,652,500

Investment per generation = 124,000 mh

During this period, the construction of monuments per se ceased. Ceremonial sites such as Stonehenge, Avebury and the Mt. Pleasant were abandoned after many hundreds of years of cyclical reuse. Nothing replaced them, except for the considerable labor that went into construction of elaborate field systems and the fortified settlements. Burial practice was transformed with non-monumental cremation cemeteries in the Later Bronze Age and simple interment burials, often in storage pits, during the Iron Age.

The labor invested in the fortifications calculates as 124,000 mhpg, assuming seventy generations, as seen in Table 4.2. This may represent some decrease in the amount of organized construction, but it most obviously represents a major change in the *goals* of construction. The extent to which we are even dealing with monumental construction is in question; certainly no explicit ceremonial or burial monuments were built at this time. The construction of the hill forts and the field systems, however, should not be dismissed as simply utilitarian as it may signal a major transformation in the nature of economic and ideological control as I will argue later.

With the transition to the Age of Hill Forts, social organization changed dramatically. In a good example of devolution (see Kristiansen, Chapter 2 above), the Early Bronze Age chiefdoms fragmented, to be replaced by relatively local polities. During the Iron Age then, the spatial extent of the polities remained small, not because of their simple organizational structure which was most probably that of chiefdoms, but because of the change in the nature of finance from a mobile wealth finance that permitted spatial expansion to a staple

finance system that restricted it. As I will now discuss, associated with this change in finance were necessary changes in how the landscape was structured to demarcate a new system of land tenure.

Changing patterns of land tenure: a suggestion

During the 4,000 years of prehistory just summarized, major transformations are apparent in the nature of political organization. Causes for these political changes were not simply demographic or environmental, but reflected systematic changes in the political economy. Specifically, by changing the system of land tenure as represented by an altered landscape in Wessex, chiefs changed the way in which labor could be controlled so as to finance their regional institutions.

During the Age of Early Farmers, a fairly rapid growth in population and intensification of land use lead to intergroup competition and warfare. The area of Wessex became divided up into polities varying in size and complexity. The construction of long barrows represented the explicit definition of territories associated with local kin-based groups and their ancestors. The construction of these long barrows can, in my estimation, be best interpreted as an elaboration of ceremonies of place; in essence, their construction planted the ancestral lines in the landscape, creating lands owned by corporate groups (Bradley, Chapter 3 above).

These corporate groups were then embedded in a regional system connected to the causewayed enclosures and the major cursus monuments. Essentially the landscape became transformed from an unmarked natural world to one carefully demarcated and associated with corporate kin groups. The role of kinship as seen in the ritual significance of ancestors illustrates the organizing kinship principles that Kristiansen singles out for chiefdoms (Chapter 2 above). It is important to emphasize, however, that these kinship principles were *not* an abstract calculus but were firmly planted through monumental construction in a physical landscape. In other words, it was not the relationship within people that was most important, but the relationships between people and emerging corporate groups that became relevant.

During the Age of Stonehenge, the gradual expansion of population

and of a political economy based on pastoralism resulted in a full clearing of the landscape and movement into ecologically unstable regions. The social outcome was an initial expansion in the number of polities, each centered on a major henge monument similar in labor investment to the cursus monuments.

The main changes during the Age of Stonehenge were ideological but firmly grounded in a manufactured landscape. The major monuments, I suggest, created a sacred space set off for ceremonies that fundamentally separated the rulers from the ruled and identified their legitimacy with universal forces outside the world accessible to commoners. As on the Hawaiian Islands, the ceremonies associated with the major monuments probably involved basic generative rituals conducted by the chiefs. Beginning with the layout of the Dorset Cursus and most notably with the solar alignment of Stonehenge, the monuments took on an internal organization aligned on the movement of the heavenly bodies. "By bringing the sky's cosmic order down to earth, monumental architecture creates sacred space" (Krupp 1983: 229). Thus, in the ceremonies, chiefs became more than local leaders; they would have acted as gods.

By constructing these ceremonial places, the chiefs also created landmarks that visually dominated the open environment of Wessex and would have asserted ownership over the surrounding pastoral lands. As a general principle, resources become owned when they have been improved by an individual. The capital investment in the monument thus would have created ownership resting squarely in the hands of the chief who built them. The close association of the most impressive barrow cemeteries with the existing monuments supports this identification of the chiefs with the henges and their ceremonies.

The development in the political economy during the Age of Stonehenge was predicated on a system of wealth finance. At the monuments, the ceremonies were the sacred gathering places where labor, wealth, and subsistence goods could be concentrated and exchanged (Friedman and Rowlands 1977). Early on, finance was apparently based on the production and distribution of animals, as identified by the location of the monuments in good pasturage area and by evidence for ceremonial consumption of meat at the enclosures. In several cases, an individual barrow burial contained parts of cattle, such as the head, indicating a clear ritual association. Later the wealth finance

shifted to the importation of bronze metals and other esoteric goods used to signal individual status differences in the burials and probably in life. The reason to add the use of esoteric wealth in finance to the use of the cattle might have been the ease of movement and central control over distribution allowed in wealth exchange. Under competitive interaction, chiefs must strive to expand their power base in order to retain their political position (Earle 1978).

The apparent demographic and social dislocation at the transition to the Age of Hill Forts indicates a major economic transformation. I have suggested that this transformation resulted from a cyclical collapse of the chiefly economy; the degraded resource base on the margins undercut animal production and/or a loss of control over the long-distance metal objects of wealth, which shifted the center of political activity to the Thames River Valley (Bradley, Chapter 3). The growth in a wealth finance system can rarely be sustained because of problems of inflation, depletion, and overextension. For whatever particular reason, wealth finance systems are inherently unstable, and periodic collapses occur commonly (D'Altroy and Earle 1985; Earle 1987a).

After the regional chiefdoms broke down, a new form of chiefdom arose based on staple finance indicated so clearly archaeologically by the central storage facilities for grain. This staple finance system would have involved direct control over staple production through carefully delimited ownership of land. It is at this time that the coaxial field systems appear in Wessex. These fields, although surely an indication of capital investment in agricultural development, also represent a regular division of the landscape that does not consider topography and specific local conditions. Fleming (1989) describes the large scale of many of these field systems that can cover hundreds of square kilometers. The regional scope of the planning seen in the fields' layout is evidence for their politically motivated design from the top, rather than for local agronomic design. The new field systems appear as social divisions of the landscape with major boundary markers and regularly laid out local fields (Fleming 1982).

It is my contention that this divided landscape can best be interpreted as a new pattern of ownership in which a natural world has finally become fully used and assigned. The field systems portrayed physically a pattern described for Hawaii where access to carefully

defined land can be traded off for labor and staple materials. The hill forts came to serve as the real and symbolic guarantee of this new system of land ownership.

CONCLUSIONS

The discussions that took place in the chiefdom seminar repeatedly focused on the nature of control as the fundamental process for the evolution of chiefdoms. A split existed between those participants who emphasized economic controls versus those who emphasized ideological controls (see Earle, Chapter 1 above). The Hawaiian and Wessex cases help resolve this split by clarifying how the two forms of control are interdependent. In the seminar, I argued that although alternative sources of power certainly existed, real economic power was basic because only it could be controlled across generations to give the stability on which a polity must be based. Although I stand by this interpretation, I now feel that it is necessary to determine what constitutes "real" economic control. As the two cases reviewed here demonstrate, economic and ideological powers come together: the economic base gives the stability for the control as the ideology gives it legitimacy. For example, in the Wessex case, the tremendous investment of labor in ceremonial architecture can be seen as a means to ground the ideology in a physical reality owned and controlled by the chiefs. The monuments thus became a symbolic capital grafted onto a system of land tenure by which labor could be controlled. In this chapter I have attempted to emphasize the role of resource control and associated land tenure on the development of the political economy. This theoretical position is particularly suited to investigation with archaeological data because the physical restructuring of the landscape in the process of created ownership is often clearly visible in the design and pattern of ritual monuments and field systems.

Acknowledgments

I would like especially to acknowledge the considerable help that I received in preparing the Wessex case while I was a Visiting Fellow at Clare Hall in Cambridge. Professor Colin Renfrew and his staff in the Faculty of Archaeology and Anthropology made my stay in Cambridge both enjoyable and productive. At the Southampton office of the Royal Commission on Historic

Monuments (England), Dr. James Leach, Head, and John Hart, supervisor for computerization, were extremely helpful to me in using the archaeological site files for Wessex. Andrew Lawson, Director of the Trust for Wessex Archaeology, brought together field researchers for several informative seminars on Wessex archaeology. Julian Richards of the Trust introduced me to the region's sites and landscape, and welcomed me into his home and friendship. Tim and Sue Champion, Andrew Fleming, Ian Hodder, Steve Shennan, and Bill Startin shared with me their ideas about Wessex and offered insightful criticisms of my initial formulations. Words are not enough to express my gratitude and warm feelings towards Richard Bradley, whose encouragement and assistance have molded my research and understanding of Wessex prehistory.

Lords of the Waste: predation, pastoral production, and the process of stratification among the Eastern Twaregs

CANDELARIO SÁENZ

On August 18, 1852 a camel caravan from Ghat brought the explorer Heinrich Barth on the first leg of his central African mission through the Sahara. In the northern Air Mountains of present-day Niger the caravan was sacked by a notorious border tribe, the Kel Fadey Twaregs. The attackers, the vanguard of a larger group camped in the area, consisted initially of only two men. Of such aristocratic and martial bearing were these two men that they succeeded in terrorizing the caravaneers into submission (Barth 1857–9, vol. I: 238–55).

These "freebooters," as Barth describes them, were members of the Kel Fadey confederation, the warrior aristocrat *tawshet* (section) called the Ighalgawan. These lords of the waste take their name from an isolated cairn in the northern Air region, Mt. Ighalgawan, "(eyrie of) vultures," astride their customary haunts on the caravan route from Ghat to Agadez and a few days north of Makat tan Iklan where the caravan was first attacked.

The contemporary Ighalgawan have no oral history of their attack on Barth's caravan over 150 years ago, but they enthusiastically retell their traditions of how in earlier times they roamed the region "behind the [Air] mountains" collecting *tawse* (tribute) from caravans and fighting the Kel Awey confederation, which was a Twareg rival for control of the caravan trade. The Ighalgawan were still doing this in 1899;

when the Foureau–Lamy expedition, the harbinger of French domination, entered the northern marches of the Air Mountains, it met resistance from Kel Fadey Twaregs (Foureau 1902).

Winter is the principal caravan season in the central Sahara, and if the Barth caravan raid had occurred at that time the numerous camels of the Kel Fadey might have been grazing nearby on pasture watered by occasional winter rains in the isolated northeastern Air valleys of Imanan in the Fadey range or Agamgam and Faras in the Tamgak range. However, by the mid-August monsoon season the camels of the Kel Fadey – belonging in common to the core families of the suzerain oligarchy of the Ighalgawan warrior aristocracy – were probably being pastured some four hundred kilometers to the west, between In Abangharit and Fagoshiya in the verdant floodplains of the Eghazer wan Agadez. This livestock would have been in the care of the Izelitan, warrior pastoralist slaves of the Kel Fadey, and the Ibergalan, technically *imghad* ("free clients") of the noble Ighalgawan but really de-facto serfs caring for camels owned by Ighalgawan patrons in return for milk rights and the right to own a few goats of their own.

In this brief sketch we see a system of production involving a division of labor between groups of warrior aristocrats, on the one hand, who ply distant caravan routes seeking tribute and, on the other hand, client pastoralists who raise camels belonging to the aristocrats, holding them under conditions of reduced franchise involving rights to the consumable products of pastoral production (milk) but not to capital gains in surplus male offspring, which belong to the warrior aristocrats.

The Twaregs are a stratified society; in precolonial times their principal livelihood was drawn from the trans-Saharan caravan trade with pastoralism acting as a reinvestment opportunity for these revenues. I will argue that Twareg social stratification is largely emergent from this organization of work and from particular characteristics of the Saharan environment and politics.

In a recent article, Philip Burnham (1979) has argued against the possibility of stratification among pastoralists, drawing on the example of the Twaregs. Following in part on Pierre Bonte's (1975) studies of the Kel Gress Twaregs of the Nigerian Sahel Burnham writes: "The political fluidity characterizing mobile pastoral societies is a dominant and conservative structural feature which militates against autonomous tendencies towards centralization and class stratification" (1979: 355).

Burnham explains that under the "heavily stocked conditions that normally obtain in pastoral societies," where competition for demographic strength is severe and where lineage organization is prominent, "slaves are frequently assimilated as freemen via adoption or concubinage" which has the effect of "blurring or even undermining class divisions" (Burnham 1979: 354). Burnham adds, importantly, that where there are conditions favoring the collection of substantial tribute, as is common among central Asian pastoralists, there will be tendencies toward stratification (Burnham 1979: 355).

The Kel Gress Twaregs, writes Burnham, control numerous groups of agricultural serfs and are a stratified society precisely because they are tied to a sedentary economy of agricultural production, as are the central Asian nomads, through their control over external trade links and their collection of tribute. But where pastoralists rely purely on pastoral production, Burnham concludes, there will be a processual bias against stratification (Burnham 1979: 355).

For ecological reasons to be elaborated below I find Burnham's arguments convincing only for the narrow band of parameters involving groups that rely almost exclusively on pastoralism in arid zones with great spatial and temporal variation in rainfall. Such groups lacking outside means of replacing livestock after drought disasters would be likely to rely on formalized animal loans and would probably have a developed lineage system. The Wodaabe Fulani of Niger, cited by Burnham, are indeed purely pastoral and essentially nonstratified and are, therefore, an apt example in Burnham's analysis.

On the whole I find Burnham's argument convincing for such groups as the Wodaabe Fulani, and his theory applies to other pure pastoralists living in arid zones with great spatial and temporal variability in rainfall. In the Saharan Twareg case, however, he has misread the parameters, and his assumptions are incorrect. Saharan herders, like the central Asian pastoralists, are principally tribute collectors and entrepreneurs in the caravan trade and as such they operate under different conditions than those described by Burnham.

Burnham's theory may be inapplicable also to the pastoralism practiced in the high rainfall temperate zones of Scandinavia and the British Isles in prehistoric times. For Late Iron Age Ireland, D. Blair Gibson (1988) has recently written an important article on the possible role of cattle pastoralism in the rise of social stratification. The same has been suggested for Late Neolithic Wessex (Bradley 1972, and

102

Chapter 3) and for Late Neolithic Scandinavia (Kristiansen 1982, and Chapter 2; Randsborg 1982). In these cases the bountiful and reliable annual rainfall leads to a highly productive and relatively risk-free system of pastoral production which requires little mobility and, therefore, has certain functional parallels with high-risk Saharan pastoralism when accompanied by a reliable source of revenue from the caravan trade. We are, however, getting ahead of our analysis at this point.

As noted in the introductory sketch, the Eastern Twaregs who inhabit Saharan Ahaggar and Ajjer regions and the Air Twaregs of Niger are stratified politically, and they rely on extra-market controls over labor and economic distribution in pastoral production. Eastern Twareg confederations, generally consisting of twelve or more sections, include: one or more sections of warrior aristocrats, known as *imajaghan*; several sections of *imghad*, a franchise that ranges from free clienthood to de facto serfdom; and slaves, including a section of relatively autonomous warrior slaves called Izelitan and other categories of slaves varying in autonomy and franchise. Kinship is not a factor in the social organization of a confederation except to the extent that each section is considered nominally an endogamous group.

Each confederation is dominated by a core oligarchy of *imajaghan* defined through proximity of relationship through mother and father to a founding ancestress. Thus in the dominant *imajaghan* section of the Kel Fadey confederation, a core ruling oligarchy of families is considered to be direct descendants of their female noble ancestor Tesiggalet, as well as more peripheral families with less access to power and wealth. Jeremy Keenan has demonstrated this kinship process for Twareg confederations of the Algerian Ahaggar in "Power and wealth are cousins" (Keenan 1977a).

In the Twareg economy, the *imajaghan* sections specialize in extorting revenue from the caravan trade and reinvesting it in pastoral production using the labor of clients, serfs, and slaves. Far from "militating against autonomous tendencies towards stratification," the Twareg economic system actually produces a strong processual bias toward stratification, such that formerly egalitarian groups when involved in this form of production eventually become stratified.

My explanation for this assertion lies in an analysis of the pastoral ecology of the northern Air and central Saharan areas occupied by the Eastern Twaregs. It was Gudrun Dahl and Anders Hjort in their

important work *Having herds* (1976) who brought to general attention the fact that one must consider the demographic parameters associated with different varieties of livestock and their productive potential in terms of milk and surplus (male) offspring in any serious study of pastoral production.

In expanding on Dahl's and Hjort's suggestions, pastoral ecologist Stephen Sandford (1983) has elaborated an optimization model that takes into account spatial and temporal variability of rainfall in terms of reproductive demography of livestock. Sandford begins by describing an ideal (baseline) livestock range in which rainfall is evenly distributed with invariable annual rainfall rates. Such a range would have a definite and well-defined carrying capacity for livestock which could be calculated with precision.

Changing the parameters to maintain the same average rainfall but provide variability in rainfall from year to year, Sandford finds that, the greater the variability in annual rainfall in terms of standard deviations, the greater the opportunity cost of a conservative strategy of maintaining the herd capacity at the minimum carrying capacity of the worst year – a strategy advocated by some pastoral development experts as a hedge against desertification. Sandford, however, convincingly demonstrates for regions where livestock markets are well developed (such as the Air), that by maximizing livestock growth rates in good years – even at the cost of occasional disastrous losses in drought years – production in highly variable rainfall zones can approach the productive levels of our ideal baseline pasture with an identical but completely nonvariable annual rainfall rate (Sandford 1983: 39–43).

The level of allowable strategic opportunism will depend on the livestock being raised. According to Sandford sheep and goats respond best to an opportunistic strategy because of their extremely high growth rates which may be as high as forty-five percent per year. This allows a quick recovery from losses occasioned in drought disasters, the onslaught of which was too rapid to allow liquidation of stock in regional markets. However, under conditions of pure pastoralism, Sandford advises against the use of an opportunistic strategy for camel pastoralists in which the maximum growth rates of one to seven percent per year are too low to allow quick restocking (Sandford 1983: 42).

Like Burnham, Sandford has not considered the possible effects of a guaranteed cash flow on the allowable level of risk-taking in camel

pastoralism in arid zones with highly variable rainfall. Desert-side pastoral production below the 50 mm annual rainfall isohyet is precarious but potentially profitable *if* we combine Stephen Sandford's suggestions for combining movement over a wide area with maximum herd growth *and* the factor Sandford did not consider in his model – guaranteed cash flow from the caravan trade. A possible problem concerns the fact that a strategy of patrolling the central Saharan caravan routes for tribute might not be compatible with the labor requirements of a wide-ranging transhumance required for successful exploitation of substantial spatial and temporal rainfall discontinuities in pre-Saharan pasture zones. This problem can be dealt with, however, through a division of labor, with client and servile pastoralists taking charge of the pastoral aspects of production and warrior aristocrats handling the extortion of revenues from the caravan trade.

When the labor of clients is used (as it is among the Twaregs) – to herd the nobles' livestock under conditions of reduced franchise in which the clients often derive only subsistence (in milk) from these animals, while the nobles cull off the capital gains (in saleable male camels) – a form of production is set into motion in which the owners of the capital become progressively richer while their clients remain a dependent class. The final effect is a bias in favor of accumulation by noble warrior aristocratic Twareg sections such that, in the long run, pastoral polities tend toward strong internal stratification.

I am prepared to argue that the principal factor in Twareg stratification is this organization of production, in which Twareg warrior aristocrats are entrepreneurs in the caravan trade and their clients are involved in wide-ranging pastoral transhumance. Furthermore, the stratificational potential of this form of production can be shown under analysis to be applicable to the rise of stratification in higher rainfall areas, particularly the Early Iron Age in Ireland (D. Blair Gibson 1988), and the Late Neolithic and Early Bronze Age in Wessex (Bradley 1972, and Chapter 3) and in Denmark (Kristiansen 1982; Randsborg 1982).

Ultimately, the key variable is not the availability of outside revenues but rather the productive potential of pastoralism in terms of such ecological variables as the variability of rainfall. Where rainfall is higher, as it certainly is in Ireland and in Wessex, such a mechanism as the Twareg system of cash flow through control over the caravan trade is not necessary since the risks of production are low. Mere

control over livestock by members of a rank elite would be enough to expand the wealth of this elite as they accrued capital gains while their clients earned only their subsistence. Placing surplus livestock among fellow tribesmen of lower rank while maintaining rights to their increase would lead eventually to the emergence of an elite class and a fully stratified society.

ON THE ORIGINS OF TWAREG STRATIFICATION

I have argued in the previous section that a processual bias exists in the Twareg system of pastoral production, such that if at some early period the Twaregs had been egalitarian with respect to control over the resources that sustain life, over time, inequality in control over capital gains in livestock would have crept into the system due to the inexorable loss of camels in Saharan drought and their replacement through the revenues of the emergent warrior oligarchies. These warrior aristocrats, if they had ever been closely tied to their servile pastoral cousins through some overarching segmentary lineage system, were in the long run to become endogamous, exclusive, and encysted elites. As Robert Murphy (1967) has noted, the Eastern Twaregs (excepting the Kel Awey) possess the Iroquois kinship systems often found among segmentary societies with exogamous clans and may, therefore, have once had exogamous clans. Be that as it may, they are everywhere composed of stratified confederation sections with no overarching ideology of kinship in the political organization of their confederations.

In examining the Twaregs in history we should, therefore, begin with the question of the origin of *imghad* or client class. Interestingly, the Berbers, among whom the Twaregs are considered to belong, have a reputation among anthropologists as being highly egalitarian. Thus George Murdock (1959: 405) in his encyclopaedic *Africa: its peoples and their culture history* felt it necessary to explain the origins of Twareg stratification, attributing it to contact with and diffusion from the eleventh century Hilalian Arab invaders who drove the Eastern Twaregs from their original Libyan homeland.

To this unsatisfying explanation we may add the conquest theories that are commonly used by the Twaregs themselves to explain the existence of the *imghad* class. Johannes Nicolaisen, who lived among

106

the Ahaggar Twaregs in the 1950s, describes a local tradition that the first camel-riding Twareg invaders of the Ahaggar found an earlier strata of primitive Berber-speaking people called Isebeten who practiced small ruminent pastoralism and hunting (Nicolaisen 1963: 407–8). Nicolaisen's Ahaggar Twareg informants believed that these Isebeten goat raisers were dominated by the warlike Ihaggaran (pl. of Ahaggar) invaders and form the nucleus of the vassal tribes of the Ahaggar.

Folk traditions that *imghad* descend from benighted and presumably archaic groups of Twaregs who possessed no camels abound in the Air. In one Air folktale a member of the Eddas vassals, a group much ridiculed in the Air, is given one of his patron's camels to care for. Never having seen a camel he does not know how to make it kneel down when he arrives at his camp, bringing consternation to his family and kinsmen who believe him to be up in paradise with God and begin mourning him. He is saved by a wise man of the Eddas who suggests that he jump off into a blanket held taut by the men. Later the camel brings forth an offspring which the Eddas, never having seen a baby camel, believe to be a malevolent *djinn*. At the conclusion of this long story, the bravest Eddas "warrior" attacks the baby camel/*djinn*, having taken the precaution of tying a rope around his waist so that the other Eddas can pull him to safety if the *djinn* begins to devour him. After several "rescues" in which he is pulled to safety by the other men he succeeds in chopping off the baby camel's head with his sword.

Tales of this sort are meant both to amuse and to validate an already existing scheme of social stratification. However, as Morton Fried has noted concerning conquest theories of the origin of stratification, of which this genre of explanation is a part, they explain nothing unless they elucidate the internal processes that give rise to stratification (Fried 1967: 213–16).

A plausible explanation for the origin of Twareg *imghad* is one collected by the ill-fated German explorer, Erwin von Bary, who visited the Air in 1877. A Twareg man named Hadj Iata told Bary that all Twaregs were once autonomous (*libres* in Bary's French text), but groups that migrated in and settled down in a new territory submitted to the Twaregs already in power there and thus became *imghad* (Bary 1898: 180–1).

The most important point in Hadj Iata's explanation, that *imghad* are not conquered subjects, but are rather fallen *imajaghan*, would

107

seem to support our analysis of Twareg kinship practice in which a core group of *imajaghan* concentrate power through closely endogamous marriages, while other members of the group are progressively peripheralized. Robert Murphy has noted in "Tuareg kinship" (1967: 167–8) that Twaregs rarely remember ancestors beyond the third ascending generation. With these shallow genealogies, peripheralized nobles separated from power could in a matter of generations become vassals. It may be seen as support of this assertion that in the post-colonial period several Kel Fadey *imghad* sections – the Kel Tedele, the Ifadeyan, and the Ifarayan – have reasserted their claim to *imajaghan* status, a claim that was vehemently denied by the recently deceased Kel Fadey drum chief Mohammed Ag Sidi.

I thus propose that the most plausible origin of *imghad* clients is from the noble Twaregs themselves. Marceau Gast (1976) and Jeremy Keenan (1977a) have written about the dynamic of concentrating power through endogamous marriages described above. This practice of marrying strategically within the kin group to accumulate property and rights to succession becomes even more effective when it is associated with an economic process in which groups peripheralized through marriage are then rendered economic dependents. When peripheral kin are unable to replace their herds after suffering disastrous losses of livestock through drought or raiding, they may accept substantial loan-gift animals from members of the core oligarchy in order to survive, thus becoming clients. In the long run – calculated in centuries – origins are forgotten and stratification becomes a social fact.

THE TWAREGS IN HISTORY

In the following paragraphs I will briefly describe and analyze four historical Twareg groups involved in the trans-Saharan caravan trade that practiced pastoral production using the labor of slaves, serfs, and clients. These will include the pre-1650 Imanan and the later Kel Ahaggar and Kel Ajjer of the Central Sahara, as well as the polity of Izar of Taggada, a fourteenth-century western Air group. This will be followed by a more detailed ethnohistorical and ecological analysis of the Kel Fadey confederation of the western Air, a group studied by my wife Barbara Worley (1987, 1988, n.d.) and myself (Sáenz 1986, n.d.) in over forty months of field research spanning the last decade.

The "kingdom" of the Imanan

When Heinrich Barth passed through Ghat in 1851 the Imanan were "reduced to extreme poverty and to a very small number" (Barth 1857–9, I: 200). In the centuries before the fall from power of the *amenokal* (supreme chief) Goma around 1650 (Duveyrier 1864: 344), however, the Imanan were the dominant group among the Northern Twaregs of the Ahaggar and Ajjer. Imanan control over the caravan route from Tadamakkat (near Gao and Timbuctu) to the Fezzan extended their power through the western Sudan. The French explorer Henry Duveyrier who visited Ajjer in 1859 notes that his contemporaries among the Kel Ajjer Twareg *imajaghan* nobles patrolled the caravan routes, while the *imghad* vassals took care of their livestock and paid annual tribute (Duveyrier 1863: 335). It would not be unreasonable to assume that the earlier Imanan, operating under similar ecological and economic conditions, reinvested revenues from the caravan trade and used vassal labor in pastoral production, particularly since they maintained – even after their decline – nominal suzerainty over ten vassal tribes (Duveyrier 1868: 347).

One of my major claims in this chapter is drawn from Julian Steward's theory of cultural ecology and food production technology, with its concomitant that the organization of work can strongly influence social and economic organization. This idea is described in Steward's (1955) analysis of the Great Basin Shoshone and developed with his student Robert F. Murphy in "Tappers and trappers" (Murphy and Steward 1956). For the Imanan and the later Kel Ajjer Twaregs, patrolling the caravan routes through the central Sahara of necessity removes them from the valleys where the fugitive Saharan pastures of the Tassili can be found, and places them at a great distance from the rich pre-Saharan pastures of the Eghazer Valley of Agadez and the Adrar n-Ifoghas. In order to exploit these pastures it would be necessary either to divide the group into pastoral and predatory sections or else to use the labor of disenfranchised classes – slaves, serfs, and clients in pastoral production – while the warrior sections patrolled the waste for booty.

For the Imanan, our thin documentary historical materials give no evidence as to where they pastured their animals or who herded them. Our knowledge of macro-regional ecology and caravan trade history can, however, give us some important clues. Imanan control over the

now abandoned market town of Tadamakkat west of the Songhay capital of Gao suggests that they could have used the pastures around the Malian Adrar n-Ifoghas Mountains. But the fact that the Twaregs of the Ahaggar region of Algeria, an area formerly under the suzerainty of the Imanan, use the Tamesna pastures of the northwestern Air to graze their animals also implies that the Imanan who controlled this region before 1650 could have done the same. All this can only be speculative, of course, given the paucity of documentary information which forces us to extrapolate or make inferences from the ecology and the more recent, historically attested, economic practices of the Twaregs.

What is more certain is that the caravan route from the western part of the Songhay empire through the Air and Ghat was the principal itinerary of the gold trade between Gao and Tripoli. Its decline after the conquest of Songhay by Morocco around 1590 greatly impoverished the macro-region from the Niger bend to the Libyan Fezzan (Boville 1968: 341). The Imanan Twareg rulers of the region between Tadamakkat and Ghat must have depended greatly on the revenues of the gold trade. Because the fall of the Imanan took place a mere fifty years after the destruction of the Songhay, it is reasonable to conclude that these were related events.

Izar the Sultan of Taggada: an early stratified Twareg polity

In 1353 Ibn Battuta, a Berber from Tetouan, a jurist and world traveler, passed through the copper ore processing and smelting town of Taggada, identified by recent intensive archaeological fieldwork as the necropolis of Azelik near the contemporary salt evaporation works of Teggida n-Tessumt (Bernus and Gouletquer 1976). After spending a few days in the town, Ibn Battuta decided to visit Izar the "sultan" of Taggada whom he describes as a Berber pastoralist living in a mat tent (as used today in the Air) a day's journey from town. Ibn Battuta (1968 [1929]: 337), ever-sensitive to traditional law, noted that Izar succeeded to his position through his mother, described as an imposing woman who feted Ibn Battuta with bowls of milk. While in Izar's camp, Ibn Battuta's needs were met by the *Yenatiboun* whom he describes as being like the domestic servants of the Moroccan Sultan.

In Ibn Battuta's account, therefore, we see a picture of Berber

110

pastoralists much resembling the contemporary Twaregs in material culture and political practice, and we are offered tantalizing hints of stratification in the *Yenatiboun* who must be clients rather than slaves, since otherwise the astute Ibn Battuta would have called them *Abeyadan*. Ibn Battuta describes the pastoralist Izar as the ruler of the copper smelting town of Taggada from which one can draw a strong inference that Izar was taxing the people of Taggada in some way and perhaps using these revenues in his pastoralist enterprise.

The leisurely pace of life in Izar's camp, as described by Ibn Battuta who spent his days there feasting and conversing with Izar and his aristocratic mother, suggests that the arduous work of animal husbandry was being performed by clients. The present-day Igdalan Twaregs, who live in the vicinity of Teggida n-Tessumt, are surrounded by numerous servile clients who are not Twareg but are rather of the same autochthonous Isawaghan stock as the ancient inhabitants of Taggada. These Isawaghan, among whom I have lived in my field research, do most of the work of herding the camels of their Igdalan patrons.

The Ihaggaran

With the Ihaggaran we are dealing with a group well described and studied in the historical present by, among others, Maurice Benhazera (1908), the Père Charles de Foucauld (1925–30, 1951–2), Henri Lhote (1955), Johannes Nicolaisen (1963), and Jeremy Keenan (1977b). The Ihaggaran preyed on the caravan trade from an early date, as Ibn Battuta complains of their exactions on his return trip to Sijilmassa through the Ahaggar in 1353 (Ibn Battuta 1968 [1929]: 338). Leo Africanus also complains about the Ahaggar Twaregs, and during Barth's trek from Ghat to the Air fear of predatory Kel Ahaggar Twaregs was a subject of continuous concern to the caravaneers. In the pre-seventeenth century period of Ibn Battuta's and Leo Africanus' travels the Ahaggar Mountains were controlled by the Imanan of the Ajjer, and they functioned presumably as a kind of natural fortress and base of operations for the Imanan Twareg "protection" operation.

The Ahaggar is not a complete ecological zone for pastoralism. While we have no direct evidence for the economic practices of the pre-seventeenth century period, by the eighteenth century revenues from the caravan trade were reinvested in the Tamesna region of

northern Niger in camel pastoralism (Bernus 1981: 322–3). These camels were cared for by slaves and vassals, who lived constantly among the camels, moving them among the sparse desert pastures of Tamesna in the dry season and then into the valley of the Eghazer of Agadez in the July through October transhumance season.

Nicolaisen (1963: 405) reports from his own research that *imajaghan* warrior aristocrats could take animals from vassals practically at will, but were careful not to take too many. Nicolaisen cites the claims of the Père de Foucauld (1951–2, II: 534) that in earlier times the vassals owned no camels of their own. He also notes that the nobles had the right to join a vassal camp when they needed milk or take a camel in milk from a vassal returning it when it went dry (Nicolaisen 1963: 404–5). In addition, Nicolaisen writes about the practice of *tiwse* (*tawse* in the Air), or tribute, in which vassal groups pay an annual tribute to the drum chief of the suzerain confederation section. Although these payments may seem small (ranging up to a few camels per group), the small expected annual rate of increase in camel herds may, in fact, render them substantial. Recalling David Ricardo's theory of land rent, in land of low productivity rent must be low enough to allow the tenant to live and reproduce properly.

Conclusion of the background and historical summary

This brief summary demonstrates that Twaregs have been socially stratified for a considerable period and have practiced a form of production with extra market controls over the labor of clients and extensive rights in the capital gains associated with livestock production. It is noteworthy that, by using the labor of clients in their reinvestment of revenues drawn from the caravan trade, the eastern Twaregs effectively insulate themselves from the risks associated with pastoral production, while benefiting in good years from its productive potential.

THE KEL FADEY OF THE AIR: A CASE STUDY OF A STRATIFIED PASTORAL CHIEFDOM

The Kel Fadey entered European historical consciousness as the result of the 1857 attack on Heinrich Barth's caravan described in the introduction. Barth's sketch of the Kel Fadey, although brief, gives us

an excellent introduction to their economic system in the mid-nineteenth century. The ruling Kel Fadey nobles, the Ighalgawan, patrolled the central Sahara between 20′ and 23′ N. latitude, from the desert mountains of Fadey to Mt. Ighalgawan. This zone includes the wells of In Azaoua and the strategic juncture of two caravan routes into the Air (the eastern one from Ghat in Libya, and the western one from Touat in Algeria). The Kel Fadey patrolled the Fadey to Ighalgawan area north of the Air Mountains in search of tribute from passing caravans.

This arid and dangerous desert zone has enormous possibilities for raising revenues by a mobile and warlike group such as the Ighalgawan section of Kel Fadey confederation. Barth notes, in part from experience, that Twareg *imajaghan* warrior aristocrats of the Saharan zones subsist on the tribute they raise from caravans. Barth cites a fifteenth-century passage from Leo Africanus complaining of the same (1857–9, I: 204). Ibn Battuta also complained of the exactions of the Ahaggar Twaregs whom he encountered on his final return to Morocco following the Air-In-Azzouza Touat route (Ibn Battuta 1968 [1929]: 338). Barth, as noted above, ended up paying tribute to the Kel Fadey. The raising of revenues by noble Twareg warrior aristocrat sections inhabiting the central Sahara is documented for a considerable antiquity.

The area between Fadey, In Azzouza, and Mararaba is uninhabited central Saharan waste. But it is not devoid of all vegetation and, although yearly averages are low and inconsistent, occasional summer and winter rains sometimes bring up excellent pastures. Thus in August 1852 Barth encountered summer monsoon rains at Mararaba, just south of Mt. Ighalgawan and the 22′ N. latitude line, and in January 1977 I found that the area around Fadey near 20′ latitude had been drenched by winter rains and was verdant with newly germinated grasses and foliage.

Camels can and have been raised successfully in this arid zone north of the 50 mm isohyet, but only by following a highly extensive and opportunistic form of east-to-west transhumance with a summer bias towards the west. This pattern allows the considerable possibility of extremely rich summer pastures in the northern Eghazer Valley floodplain zones, particularly around In Abangharit, and a winter bias towards the east, where the northern mountains of the Air range sometimes receive winter rains which are then concentrated in their western valleys such as Imanan at Fadey and Agamgam west of

Mt. Tamgak. Such a system has been described by the French human geographer Edmund Bernus for the contemporary Kel Tedele (Bernus 1981: 326), now autonomous but former vassals of the Kel Fadey, who have apparently continued this east–west transhumance scheme long since discontinued by other Kel Fadey.

Such an opportunistic transhumance as described by Bernus for the Kel Tedele can be seen in terms of Stephen Sandford's model (described above) as an efficient means of dealing with spatial and temporal discontinuities in rainfall. However, the organization of work concomitant with this system is inconsistent with an organized patrolling of the caravan routes in search of booty. The solution, reflecting the Stewardian theme of this chapter, is found in the organization of work. To reiterate the main point of this chapter: The solution was found in a distinctive division of labor in which (a) noble *imajaghan* – the Ighalgawan of Kel Fadey – patrolled the dangerous border zone of the trans-Saharan caravan route between the wells of In Azaoua and the eponymous Mt. Ighalghawan, while (b) their serfs, warrior slaves and free clients husbanded the nobles' herds of camels in the annual cycle between the Sudanic monsoon-driven floodplains of In Abangarit and the winter rain-fed desert pastures of the far northeastern Air region. The herdsmen, then, were people of reduced franchise, ranging from outright slavery, through various levels of serfdom, to free clienthood with seignorial rights of eminent domain in livestock and escheat remaining in the hands of the warrior aristocrats.

Heinrich Barth observed this economic system in his Saharan travels, writing:

The ruling race of the Imoshagh [*imajaghan*] subsists entirely on the labor of this depressed class, [their *imghad*] as the old Spartans did upon that of the Lacedaemonians, but still more upon the tribute or gherama which, as I mentioned above, they raise from the caravans – a custom already mentioned by Leo Africanus. Without some such revenue they could not trick themselves out so well as they do. (BARTH 1857–9, VOL. 1: 203–4)

Duveyrier, in *Les Touaregs du nord* (1864: 335), also noted the nobles' role in the caravan trade while the *imghad* pay tribute in livestock and husband the livestock of their noble patrons.

Economic historians Stephen Baier and Paul Lovejoy in their important article "Gradations in servility at the desert's edge" (1977), a study of Twareg economic diversification through reinvestment in agricultural production and trade in the Sahelian region between

Agadez and Kano, were among the first to describe accurately the Twareg economic system as not purely pastoral. Baier and Lovejoy's (1977) study, which focuses on the Damergu region dominated in precolonial times by the Kel Gress and Kel Awey Twaregs, draws on Fredrik Barth's (1973: 12–13) earlier economic analysis which describes pastoral production as a form of investment which can accrue capital gains over time. Fredrik Barth adds that, although pastoral production can accrue capital gains, in contrast to land in traditional agricultural production where the quantity of capital remains fixed, it is yet an inherently unstable investment subject to complete loss of capital in times of drought disaster. Elaborating on Barth's (1973) ideas, Baier (1978: 590) writes that the Sahelian Twaregs "used diversification to cushion the risk of loss from drought by reinvesting the profits of rapid growth in the pastoral sector in farming and commerce in the Savannah."

My study of the Kel Fadey is a further elaboration of Barth's (1973), Baier and Lovejoy's (1977), and Baier's (1980) ideas, extending them to the study of Saharan Twaregs without access to Sahelian markets but with access to cash flow through tribute from the central Saharan sectors of the caravan trade. The Kel Gress and Kel Awey described by Baier and Lovejoy invest the profits of pastoralism and trade in agricultural production. The Kel Fadey and Kel Ahaggar are doing the inverse, reinvesting the revenues of tribute collected from caravan traders in potentially profitable but also highly unstable Saharan pastoral production.

It is this latter, more risky, process that I have described for the Kel Fadey which, I contend, entails social and economic processes leading to the emergence of stratification. Inasmuch as the warrior aristocratic *imajaghan* control the rights to the capital increase in the livestock herds – through outright ownership (in the case of slave herdsmen), through serfdom (in the placing of their herds among favored *imghad*), or through the collecting of tribute in livestock from otherwise free *imghad* clients – the warrior aristocracy are in a position to increase their control over their clients as their wealth increases differentially and in greater proportion to their clients' through the fact of their control over capital gains in livestock.

The Kel Fadey of the mid-nineteenth century during Heinrich Barth's visit apparently prospered at the expense of the Kel Awey, whose control over the Air to Ghat caravan route they were usurping.

Historian Finn Fuglestad (1983: 32) writes that the Kel Awey, after having driven their earlier rivals, the Kel Gress, out of the Air, "came under pressure from the Kel Ferwan and especially the Kel Fadei."

That these Kel Fadey were exerting continuous pressure on the Kel Awey is evident from the tone of the letter that the Sultan of Agadez wrote to the Sultan of Sokoto and consigned to Barth for delivery. In this letter the Kel Fadey problem is acknowledged as one of long standing and the help of the Hausa Fulani sultan is requested in eliminating Kel Fadey predation on trans-Saharan caravans (Barth 1857–9, vol. I: 347).

By the late 1870s, however, the Kel Fadey were apparently in the midst of an economic crisis. This information is gleaned from Kel Fadey oral tradition and corroborated with genealogies collected by Barbara Worley (personal communication). This crisis was perhaps due in part to a general decline in the profitability of the caravan trade in the last quarter of the nineteenth century (Baier 1980) and perhaps in part to the ascendance of El Hadj Bilkhu, a powerful and aggressive war leader of the Kel Awey who, according to oral tradition, applied continuous military pressure on the Kel Fadey and possibly drove them out of the northeastern Air. Genealogical informants among the Ighalgawan Kel Fadey note that numbers of their ancestors in the fifth and sixth ascending generations "went south," never to return.

Around that time a new Kel Fadey leader emerged, the terrible Wan Agoda who led the Kel Fadey south in a war of conquest into the central Azawagh, the pastoral heartland of the western Air region. Wan Agoda was extremely charismatic, claiming invincibility in war through three talismans obtained from the three greatest marabouts of the Air, one of whom he reputedly murdered to prevent any other leader from duplicating his powers. In tales still recounted in the Azawagh, Wan Agoda reputedly had the power to move through different parts of a battlefield instantaneously. Through this sort of image management the Kel Fadey were able in a short period of time to attract new sections such as the Itagan, Ibutkutan, and Ikherkheran into their confederation and to drive the Kel Tamazgida, the former masters of the Azawagh, from the region and install themselves.

From that time in the late 1880s the Kel Fadey were transformed from a pre-Saharan to a Sahelian Twareg group and became, like the Kel Gress and Kel Awey, more involved in the local trade and agri-culture, thus becoming in the process less relevant to the major point

of this study – that Saharan camel pastoralism as a form of reinvestment of revenue obtained from the trans-Saharan caravan trade leads to the emergence of social stratification.

CONCLUSION: THE IMPLICATIONS FOR A POSSIBLE ROLE FOR PASTORAL PRODUCTION IN THE DEVELOPMENT OF PREHISTORIC CHIEFDOMS

Frederick Engels, in *The origin of the family, private property and the state* (1972 [1884]) suggested, drawing on Lewis Henry Morgan's *Ancient society* (1877) that pastoralism could have played a role in the development of a particular kind of state – through the development of a *militärische Demokratie* based on the evolution and concomitant control over private property in livestock (see Kristiansen, Chapter 2 above). Such an emergent class, freed eventually from the obligations of kinship alliances and accumulating wealth through their livestock, would form the nucleus of the first stratified society. In recent decades support for Engels' model by a professional anthropologist would have been considered evidence for either poor judgment or mental deficiency, such was the hegemonic domination of the Near Eastern model for the origin of social complexity through processes related to the development of agricultural technology.

Perhaps it was Morgan's fault for not giving us a clearer picture of how control over livestock might lead to the rise of a warrior aristocracy. Beyond asserting that private property began with the practice of pastoralism, Engels gives us no model for explaining the rise of stratification from pastoral accumulation. Within the last decade or so a number of revisionist studies concerning the apparent lack of intensive agriculture in the Late Neolithic, Bronze, and Early Iron Age of the British Isles (Bradley 1972; Gibson 1988) and Denmark (Kristiansen 1982; Randsborg 1982) have appeared.

Drawing on Fredrik Barth's (1973: 12–13) notion that pastoralism is a natural form of capital which functions as an investment in producing capital gains even in the complete absence of modern financial institutions, we can see that merely by controlling rights in the offspring of herds placed among clients with rights only to the consumable products of pastoralism, the controlling elite can gain in wealth and power over time.

117

In the Saharan case described in this paper, the arid climate and slow reproduction rate of camels in the context of regional resource distribution, spatial and temporal discontinuities in rainfall, and the routing of the trans-Saharan caravan trade introduce a dynamic element which could perhaps – acting alone – bring about the rise of stratification. As animals perish in periodic droughts (under conditions in which average profits are adequate to supply the needs of the pastoral population, but breeding stock for restoring the slowly reproducing herds would be lacking) the warrior aristocrats controlling the source of revenue used in rebuilding the herds would eventually (in the long run) become an elite class.

For more humid temperate zones such as the British Isles, the process is less comprehensive in the sense that there is not a selection process for impoverishing particular elements of the pastoral population while enriching others. Yet, if through some other process – as prestige or charisma associated with ritual, managerial effectiveness or some such – an elite gains control over the rights to surplus animals, that group, like the Saharan Twareg *imajaghan*, would eventually come to dominate access to the resources that sustain life at the expense of its rivals.

6

Chiefship and competitive involution: the Marquesas Islands of eastern Polynesia

PATRICK V. KIRCH

INTRODUCTION: DIVERGENT EVOLUTION OF THE POLYNESIAN CHIEFDOMS

Although the concept of "chiefdom" as a societal type was first defined by Oberg (1955) for certain New World groups, it was Service's (1962) evolutionary paradigm that catapulted the chiefdom to a position of theoretical importance. For Service, Polynesian chiefdoms served as the classic ethnographic model for this evolutionary stage bridging the acephalous tribe with archaic states. The seminal monograph by Sahlins (1958), developing Polanyi's (1944) concept of "redistribution," also provided a focus for research on the origins and structure of prestate, stratified social formations. As Earle (1987a: 281) remarks, the Polynesian case material has continued to occupy something of a privileged status in the chiefdom literature: "The work in Polynesia still leads our understanding of chiefdoms, although increasingly the uniqueness of the Polynesian material is mentioned."

Until recently, ethnographic and ethnohistoric descriptions of late eighteenth- and early nineteenth-century Polynesian chiefdoms provided the primary data to test various models of chiefship. In the last decade a maturing of archaeology in Oceania has begun to correct this

synchronic bias, as developmental sequences for various island groups have been established and refined (Jennings 1979; Davidson 1985; Kirch 1982, 1984, 1985a, 1986a). The emerging archaeological data amplify the significance of Polynesia as a key region for the study of prehistoric chiefdoms, since variations between the contact-era societies may now be placed in long-term historical contexts.

As a geographically dispersed set of cultural isolates settled relatively late in world prehistory, Polynesia offers unparalleled opportunities for controlled comparisons of cultural change. All extant Polynesian societies are descended from an Ancestral Polynesian Society which occupied a "homeland" in the Fiji–Tonga–Samoa area between about 1000–500 B.C. Although some problems of culture-history remain unresolved (Kirch 1986b), sequences of dispersal and diversification of the Polynesian societies from this ancestral group are now reasonably well understood, with confirming data from both archaeology and historical linguistics. Thus it is now feasible to commence an analysis of divergence between Polynesian chiefdoms in the context of a *phylogenetic* model (Kirch and Green 1987), with the possibilities of discriminating between homologous and analogous changes.

It is essential to understand, however, that the *origins* of Polynesian chiefship are external to the region, both in time and space. That is, based on comparative ethnographic, linguistic, and archaeological evidence (Kirch 1984), Ancestral Polynesian Society was already hierarchically structured, probably at the level which Johnson and Earle (1987) have termed the "simple chiefdom." Thus the origins of Polynesian chiefship must be sought in the preceding Lapita cultural complex, marking the Austronesian-speaking colonization (between ca. 1600–500 B.C.) not only of Polynesia but of Melanesia and eastern Micronesia as well (Green 1979; Kirch 1987). Recent investigations of Lapita sites suggest that hierarchy in Lapita society was closely linked to long-distance exchange and to control over the production and distribution of prestige goods (Kirch 1988).

While the origins of social hierarchy cannot be sought within Polynesia, the region provides a marvelous field for the study of variation and diversification in patterns of chiefship and for teasing out the various contexts and causes responsible for a myriad range of sociopolitical structures. In an earlier monograph (Kirch 1984), I sought to isolate some of the key processes underlying chiefdom development in

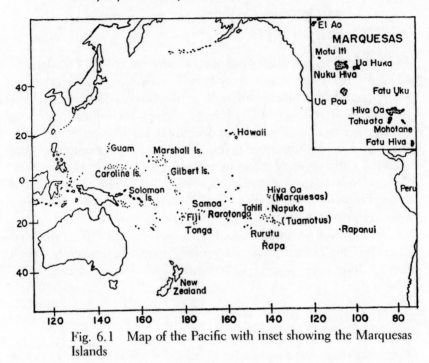

Fig. 6.1   Map of the Pacific with inset showing the Marquesas
Islands

Polynesia. Among the factors emerging from that study were
environmental instability, demographic change, intensification of production, and competition between social groups. Here I extend the
analysis to a specific case, the Marquesas Islands of central eastern
Polynesia (Fig. 6.1). Marquesan society illustrates another form of
structural variation in Polynesian chiefship, in which certain achieved
statuses (priests and warriors) had wrested substantial control of both
ritual and production from the hereditary chiefs. Further, the rich
archaeological record of Marquesan prehistory permits a tentative
model of the temporal development of Marquesan sociopolitical structure. My analysis is divided into two parts, beginning with a review of
the late prehistoric society as reconstructed from ethnographic and
ethnohistorical sources. Once the contact-period "endpoint" of
Marquesan sociopolitical evolution is understood, I turn to the
retrodiction of this system back to its origins in Ancestral Polynesian
Society, through the use of archaeological materials.

121

THE PROTOHISTORIC MARQUESAN CHIEFDOMS

The Marquesas, although "discovered" and named by Mendana in 1595, did not suffer substantially from European contact until about 1800. During the nineteenth century, however, Marquesan society and culture were subjected to intense stresses, including debilitating disease, political subjugation, and cultural suppression by missionaries. Serious ethnographic investigations did not commence until after the collapse of Marquesan society (e.g., E.S.C. Handy 1923; W.C. Handy 1922; von den Steinen 1925, 1928) and thus depended upon the reconstruction of a "memory culture." Fortunately some inaccuracies in these ethnographic treatments have now been corrected by the careful ethnohistorical work of Dening (1974, 1980) and Thomas (1986). I have drawn particularly upon Thomas' study, which goes a long way toward defining the Marquesan sociopolitical structure.

Island setting

The Marquesas comprise an archipelago of ten volcanic islands, of which six have been permanently inhabited in historic times. Geographic isolation between northern and southern groups is reflected both culturally and linguistically. All are "high islands" reaching elevations of 330–1260 m, with original volcanic slopes deeply incised by amphitheater-headed valleys. Rapid subsidence (related to ocean-floor cooling and isostatic adjustment following hot-spot volcanic activity) has led to the drowning of valley mouths, creating deep embayments. The coastlines lack coral reefs because the archipelago is swept by the cold Humboldt current which inhibits polyp growth. Islands range in size from Nuku Hiva and Hivaoa at 335 and 322 km^2 respectively, to Tahuata, Fatuhiva, Uapou, Uahuka, and Eiao in the range of 77 to 52 km^2, down to diminutive Fatuuku at 1.3 km^2. The islands are generally forested, although most of the lowlands are cloaked in an anthropogenic vegetative association (Brown 1931, 1935). The climate is subtropical, with annual rainfall averaging 1200–3000 mm (Adamson 1936: 16). Precipitation varies considerably, both seasonally and yearly, and droughts frequently occur. The leeward sides of islands are also markedly more arid than those to

122

windward. Further details on the Marquesan environment may be found in Chubb (1930), Adamson (1936, 1939), *Cahiers du Pacifique* (1978) and other sources.

From the human perspective, several features of the Marquesan environment are critical:

(1) The islands are fairly small, and relatively isolated from each other by turbulent seaways, thus tightly circumscribing the area potentially controllable by a single polity.

(2) The terrain is rugged, with deep valleys separated by high ridges and impassable headlands. Coastal plains are completely lacking, making communication between valley populations more difficult than in other Polynesian islands. Thus single valleys tended to be the primary territorial units occupied by sociopolitical units. However, the degree of isolation between valley units has often been overemphasized in the ethnographic literature (e.g., E.S.C. Handy 1923: 8–9).

(3) Climatic, topographic, hydrologic, and edaphic conditions were suitable for the cultivation of most Polynesian cultigens, including taro (*Colocasia esculenta*), breadfruit (*Artocarpus altilis*), and bananas (*Musa* cultivars).

(4) Due to the lack of coral reefs and lagoons, the marine fauna (both invertebrates and fishes) is depauperate in comparison with such archipelagoes as the Society and Tuamotu Islands. Nonetheless, molluscs and fish contributed significantly to Marquesan subsistence.

(5) Perhaps most important is the persistent recurrence of drought. Adamson writes: "Periods of several years of abundant rain alternate with periods of prolonged drought; on the leeward sides of the higher islands, and in all parts of the lower islands, the drought may amount to extreme dessication and cause the withering of most of the herbaceous vegetation" (1936: 21). Effects on indigenous cultivation systems were extreme and only partly compensated for by the semianaerobic ensilage of breadfruit paste. The significance of drought as a key ecological pressure on Marquesan populations will be returned to later in this paper.

123

Scale of integration

Accurate information on the population of the Marquesas at the time of initial European contact is unavailable, and reconstructions based on estimates by explorers or early mission censuses vary widely. A figure of 35,000 for the archipelago has often been cited (e.g., Kirch 1984, Table 1). However, archaeological settlement pattern data (Bellwood 1972; Kellum-Ottino 1971; Ottino 1985) reveal a site density suggestive of a somewhat higher population. Suggs (1961: 192) believed that the large island of Nuku Hiva supported "about 30,000" people and speculated that the entire group may have encompassed as many as 100,000. Bellwood (1972: 47), relying on a more empirical method, regards the maximal population as 70,000. A figure of 50,000 for the archipelago at about A.D. 1600 is probably conservative.

Population size is critical if we are to comprehend the *scale of integration* of Marquesan chiefdoms. Unlike Tonga, the Society Islands, or Hawaii, Marquesan polities were not regionally extensive organizations that integrated whole islands or clusters of islands. 'Ua Pou was the only island united under a single paramount chief (Handy 1923: 30–1; Thomas 1986: 84, 148), although there were fragile and temporary alliances between tribal groups on particular islands. The "typical" Marquesan polity, however, consisted of a territorial group occupying a single valley or cluster of adjacent valleys, frequently including several *mata'eina'a* or ramified descent groups. E.S.C. Handy (1923: 25–34) reviews these independent polities as they could be reconstructed in the early twentieth century. The size of such chiefdoms varied from small units that included as few as 500 persons, to large and powerful groups (such as the notorious Taipi, of Herman Melville fame) which certainly numbered as many as 5,000 and possibly as many as 10,000 individuals.

If we compare the Marquesan scale of political (and demographic) integration with that found elsewhere in Polynesia (see Kirch 1984, Table 2), the parallels are closest with such islands as Mangareva, Easter, Mangaia, or 'Uvea. Marquesan polities were certainly larger and more inclusive than those of the atoll societies or of such small high islands as Tikopia or Futuna. Yet, they were also smaller and less integrating than the highly stratified polities of Hawaii, Tonga, the Society Islands, and Samoa.

124

Chiefship and competitive involution

Sociopolitical structure

Marquesan sociopolitical structure, being remarkably fluid and con-
textually based, defies simplistic attempts at description. Indeed, it is
this fluidity, and the overlapping roles of both hereditary and achieved-
status individuals, that render Marquesan chiefship so interesting for
analysis. Here I can merely sketch the key social statuses and point to
their often contradictory and competitive roles.

Haka'iki
These hereditary chiefs (cognate to the general Polynesian term *ariki*),
at least in theory, were the genealogically senior and thus sacred (*tapu*)
leaders of the *mata'eina'a* or ramified descent group (the "tribe" in
most ethnographic descriptions of Marquesan society). The *haka'iki*
were certainly important forces in the community, and substantial
resources and labor were expended in the celebration of chiefly *rites de
passage*. Quite in contrast to other Polynesian societies, however,
there was a "limited belief" in the sanctity of the *haka'iki*, and "the
chief played no active role in the tribal ritual" (E.S.C. Handy 1923:
44, 53). Instead, the ritual prerogatives of the chiefs had been usurped
by the inspirational and shamanistic priests, the *tau'a*.

Tau'a
Shamans, sorcerers, or spirit mediums were found throughout
Polynesia, and the presence of a widespread cognate term (*kaula,
kaura*) suggests that such practices can be traced back to Ancestral
Polynesian Society. The Marquesans, however, developed this particular aspect of ritual to an apogee, with the institution of the *tau'a* or
"inspirational priest," whose power over the *mata'eina'a* rivaled, and
frequently exceeded, that of the hereditary chiefs. By the time of
European contact, *tau'a* had become inherited positions (E.S.C.
Handy 1923: 223) so that the respective roles of chief and shaman were
in some respects inversions of their general Polynesian structure.
Tau'a were charged with "caring for the remains of the dead, presiding
at the tribal ceremonial, and learning and giving utterance to the will
of the tribal god" (Handy 1923: 224). They were greatly feared, resid-
ing in sepulchral temples (*me'ae*) in the isolated recesses of valleys:
". . . a charnel house of past sacrifices, of bones and skulls, of heads of

pigs, of platters of mashed breadfruit, of coconuts and bark cloth"
(Dening 1980: 45).

Toa

The third element in the triumvirate of Marquesan elite was that of the
war leader or *toa*. Warfare pervaded protohistoric Marquesan life, and
not surprisingly warriors and their families occupied positions of property and status. Again, the contrast with other Polynesian societies is
revealing, for in the Marquesas the *toa*, and not the hereditary chief,
led the forces into battle (Handy 1923: 125). (The Marquesan situation
is most closely paralleled by that of Easter Island; see Kirch 1984:
264–78). *Toa* enjoyed various material prerogatives, such as a large
house, special dress and ornament (Fig. 6.2), including extensive
tattooing, and finely carved weapons executed by craft specialists.

Tuhuna

This term, also cognate to a widespread and ancient Polynesian word,
refers to any of several kinds of specialist, including tattooing artists,
wood and stone carvers, canoe makers, and fishermen. According to
E. S. C. Handy (1923: 145–6) the most revered *tuhuna* were the bards
who had memorized the tribal genealogical chants (*tuhuna o'ono*), and
who served as ceremonial attendants to the chiefs. As the services of
tuhuna were compensated for with prestations of food or other valuables, such individuals also constituted the elite of Marquesan society,
and some were evidently under the particular patronage of *haka'iki* and
toa.

E.S.C. Handy (1923: 36) remarked that in the Marquesas "there
were no firmly or definitely established social classes," and although
the positions of *haka'iki* and *tau'a* tended to be hereditary, achievement was also a viable means to power and status (in the case of *toa*,
achievement was essential). Thomas has succinctly captured the key
aspect of Marquesan sociopolitical structure: ". . . there was a lack of
formal unity or coherence in *mata'eina'a* or in their elites; *toa* and
warriors, priestly individuals, 'persons of property,' and the chiefly
families, seem to have been contingently rather than structurally associated" (1986: 32). In short, the protohistoric Marquesan society was
"a dynamic and fluid system in which appeals to legitimacy and highly
structured roles and alliances were not important" (1986: 34).

It would be misleading to leave the impression that all members of

126

Fig. 6.2   A tattooed Marquesan warrior, with ear ornaments,
spear, and trophy skull, sketched during the voyage of
Krusenstern in 1803 (from Kirch 1984)

Marquesan society were organized into one or another of the above
elite statuses, or attached to them as family members. A substantial
part of the population not only lacked such formal status roles, but
were essentially landless, working under a labor–tribute relationship to
an elite household. Such persons (termed *kikino*) had frequently been
dispossessed of their land and property as a result of warfare.

Production

Marquesan subsistence entailed an interrelated complex of agricultural production, animal husbandry (especially pigs), and fishing. The production of farinaceous staples upon which the society depended centered on two crops: breadfruit (*Artocarpus altilis*) and taro (*Colocasia esculenta*). Breadfruit achieved a greater dominance in Marquesan subsistence than elsewhere in Polynesia; Marquesan valleys were vast arboricultural plantations. Because breadfruit yields seasonally (four harvests per year were recognized, although only two of these were substantial), periods of abundance alternated with leaner times. Subterranean storage of breadfruit helped to buffer this temporal variability in food supply. Taro was intensively cultivated in irrigated, terraced pondfields as well as in nonirrigated gardens. Ethnographic accounts have downplayed the role of taro, but archaeological surveys (Kellum-Ottino 1971; Bellwood 1972; Ottino 1985) document the widespread distribution of irrigated field complexes. The breadfruit and taro harvests were supplemented by a wide range of other crops (including bananas, yams, sweet potatoes, coconut, sugar cane, and others), which cannot be described here (see E.S.C. Handy 1923: 181–6; Yen 1974: 140–4).

Vegetable foods were supplemented by fish and shellfish, pigs, chickens, and – at certain ceremonial feasts – human flesh. Faunal analyses of late prehistoric midden deposits (Kirch 1973; Rolett 1987, 1989) suggest that pig was the most frequently consumed animal food. This contrasts with other Polynesian societies in which fish and shellfish generally predominate. That fishing was less important in the Marquesas reflects not only local environmental conditions, but social factors as well. In particular, venturing outside of the immediate inshore waters of one's bay entailed great risk, for this was the zone in which cannibal victims (themselves called "fish," *ika*) were sought by raiding parties from neighboring tribes.

A key component of Marquesan subsistence was the storage of semianaerobically preserved breadfruit in large subterranean pits or silos. The technique of fermenting and storing breadfruit paste, or *ma*, is known throughout much of Oceania (Yen 1975; Cox 1980; Kirch 1984: 132–5), but reached a technological peak in the Marquesas. *Ma* storage pits are frequently part of house platforms (Kellum-Ottino

1971; Bellwood 1972; Ottino 1985), and large communal pits were situated in defensible positions in valley interiors or on ridge-top fortifications (Suggs 1961, fig. 6). While each household had its own smaller *ma* pits, the large reserves were under direct chiefly control, and thus formed one component of economic intensification which could be deployed directly to political ends (Kirch 1984: 134–5).

In the protohistoric period, Marquesan subsistence production, despite its degree of intensity, was periodically unable to provide fully for the caloric needs of the entire population. Thomas (1986: 40) believes that "populations were typically close to a limit," a view supported by archaeological data (see below). Of course, the concept of a *static* limit or "carrying capacity" is false, since limits reflect temporally variable conditions of environment and productive technology. In the Marquesas, despite continued efforts to intensify production and to create buffers of stored food, limit conditions were periodically exceeded due to the onslaught of prolonged drought. Edward Robarts, who lived in the Marquesas from 1797 to 1824, experienced such a drought at Taiohae: "the dreadfull effects of famine was severely felt in all parts of the Island" (Dening 1974: 121). "There died, according to calculation, between 2 and 300 persons in about one year in the Valley I lived in" (1974: 274). However, Robarts' account leaves no doubt that the effects of the famine were not suffered equally among elite and *kikino* persons. Massive stores of ensiled breadfruit controlled by Robarts' own patron chief ensured the survival of that elite family: "For I well Knew a poor man had but little for himself, when the great men had to spare" (quoted in Dening 1974: 274).

The restricted control of the means of production extended beyond agricultural land and *ma* storage, and included the specialized fishing industry. The Marquesan marine environment with its deep bays lacking reefs requires the use of canoes for effective exploitation. These were under the control not of the fishermen themselves, but of the elite chiefs and "persons of property." The early European resident Crook described fishermen as being "under the controul of Persons of Property, who furnish them with Canoes for the purpose of fishing, and barter the fish thus obtained for other needful Articles, out of which they supply the fishermen as they find the occasion" (in Sheahan 1955, app. IV: viii). This expropriation of the fishermen's catch

was confirmed by Thompson: "no sooner is their canoe drawn up . . . than their fish are seized and but a small portion rewards the labours of the fishermen" (1978: 27).

Anthropological discussions of chiefdom economies have variously stressed either managerial or control functions of the elite classes (Earle 1987a: 291–8). In the Marquesan protohistoric chiefdom, elites clearly were responsible for the management of production, but it was their *control* over the means of production, including surplus labor, that gave them their basis of power.

Property appears privatised to an unusual degree, and the control that some "persons of property" exercised over the means of production enabled them to appropriate the surplus labor of people who did not own their own land or canoes . . . The process implies a dissociation of products from their producers which seems foreign to a virtually unstratified small scale society

(THOMAS 1986: 42)

Control of the means of production by chiefs is typical throughout Polynesia; what is unusual about the Marquesas is that such control extended beyond hereditary chiefly establishments to those of competing social statuses: the *tau'a, toa, tuhuna,* and "persons of property."

Mana, ritual, and production

Earle observes that chiefdoms "are states of mind that create justifications for their existence . . . chiefs rule not because of their power but because of their place in a sacredly chartered world order" (1987a: 298). In Polynesia, the sacred (*tapu*) chief is the vessel through which supernatural efficacy (*mana*) flows from the deities to the people at large. Among the Polynesian chief's foremost duties are the "work of the gods," the complex yearly cycle of rituals (closely tied to economic activities) that assure bountiful harvests, successful fishing, and the general productivity of the chiefdom. The chief's control over ritual, conversely, is also the source of his power. Thus, as Thomas observes, "kings are jealous gods; an encompassing chiefly unity does not admit much dispersion or diversion of ritual power" (1986: 95).

As in other aspects of chiefship, the Marquesan case also departs significantly from this Polynesian norm. To a greater degree than in virtually any other society, the ritual prerogatives and power of chiefs were usurped by *tau'a,* and to some degree even by warriors. It was *tau'a* who officiated at virtually all of the critical rituals and

ceremonials of the tribe, who prescribed the times for war, and to whom human sacrifices were offered for "transmittal" to the deities. Although priestly offices were developed in some other Polynesian groups (e.g., the *kahuna* of Hawaii), nowhere else did the power of the priests so thoroughly eclipse that of the hereditary chiefs (the only case which rivals that of the Marquesas is Easter Island). This dispersion of ritual power away from the chiefs is thus a significant departure from the general evolutionary trend in Polynesia, one that points to fundamental contradictions within Marquesan society (see Thomas 1986: 103).

Competition and conflict

To comprehend the dynamic integration of protohistoric Marquesan social structures requires a consideration of competition between social groups, especially the pervasive feasting cycle, cannibalism, and warfare. Although competition occurred between households, it was most marked at the intertribal (*mata'eina'a*) level. Feasts and warfare, while they may appear to be superficially different activities, served the same primary function of competition between *mata'eina'a*. Indeed, a main objective of war was to provide cannibal sacrifices for certain feasts (or to revenge the taking of victims by a rival group). Competition, in whatever form, "was crucial to the pursuit of prestige" not only of chiefs, but of *tau'a* and *toa* (Thomas 1986: 74).

Feasts, *ko'ina*, dominated Marquesan life (see E.S.C. Handy 1923: 203–23). Feasts celebrated victory in war, harvests, the birth of a chiefly heir, betrothal, marriage, and most importantly, the death and memorialization of "great men," particularly *tau'a*. These latter feasts, termed *mau*, required substantial outlays of labor and resources, and also required the sacrifice of human victims. It is a further signal of the power of *tau'a* that their memorial feasts rivaled or exceeded those held for the hereditary chiefs.

The role of feasting in Marquesan society is reflected in settlement pattern and monumental architecture. The Marquesas are unique in Polynesia for the construction of large feasting and dance terraces, called *tohua*, the largest and dominant components of their constructed landscapes. As the archaeological remains of *tohua* provide an index to the temporal development of the competitive feasting cycle, we shall return to these in greater detail later in this paper.

131

Warfare, and the closely integrated cannibal cult, were the ultimate forms of competition between tribal polities. Warfare ranged from simple raiding (usually to obtain sacrificial victims), to forays aimed at the destruction of tribal property (especially food crops, such as by the barking of breadfruit trees), to outright conquest of territory. Thomas (1986: 78) believes that territorial conquest was itself primarily motivated by the competitive, feasting cycle: "Because the Marquesan system . . . revolved around the large scale presentation of food at feasts, there appears to have been a direct emphasis upon the seizure of the means to produce food, land." Certainly, territorial conquest was the ultimate form of competition, for this led to the expulsion of the defeated group, whose members either fled (sometimes desperately putting to sea; E.S.C. Handy 1923: 134), were subjugated by the conquerors, or offered as cannibal sacrifices.

To sum up the fundamental characteristics of Marquesan chiefship, we can do no better than to cite Dening:

> Side by side with legitimating rituals, there was social control by brute force. Together with an all-pervading fear was an almost secular pragmatism. In one respect, the *haka'iki* lay at the centre of all social life; in other respects, there was a dispersal of political, economic, and religious power.   (1980: 92)

To understand the evolution of Marquesan chiefship, and its divergence from other Polynesian polities, requires a departure from the ethnohistoric and ethnographic evidence, and I now turn to Marquesan archaeology in an effort to sketch a model of how this unique form of Polynesian chiefship may have developed over the course of some two millennia.

TEMPORAL DEVELOPMENT OF THE MARQUESAN CHIEFDOMS

The initial study of Marquesan archaeology by Linton (1925) lacked a diachronic perspective, although it did yield a broad survey of stone architecture. It remained for Suggs (1961) to expose the wealth of sub-surface material in Marquesan sites, and to outline a phase sequence that remains a well-argued and insightful analysis of the development of Marquesan society. This has been augmented by Sinoto's important excavations at Hane and other sites (Sinoto 1967, 1979), by settlement pattern surveys (Kellum-Ottino 1971; Bellwood 1972; Ottino 1985),

and other excavations and analyses (Skjolvold 1972; Kirch 1973; Dye 1982; Rolett 1986, 1987, 1989).

Trends in the archaeological record

Demographic change

There has been no explicit attempt to measure empirically the rate of population increase over the course of Marquesan prehistory, although the same techniques applied for this purpose in Hawaii (Cordy 1981; Kirch 1984: 104–11) are certainly possible. Suggs was keenly aware of the importance of demography in Marquesan prehistory, regarding population increase as an underlying factor leading to intense prestige rivalry, and in turn, to the uniquely fluid Marquesan form of chiefship. "The cause of the intense prestige rivalry may be seen in the relation of the population to the habitable land . . . The need to acquire and hold the land necessary for existence and to increase the areas held to accommodate production increases intensified to an extreme the rivalry apparently present in most Polynesian societies" (Suggs 1961: 185–6).

The sequence of population growth in the Marquesas probably approximated a modified logistic curve (see Kirch 1984: 101–4, 120–2). Certainly at European contact the population was large, dense, and under various forms of cultural as well as ecological regulation. Archaeologically, the key questions are: when did the phase of rapid increase and expansion begin; and, how long did it take until high population density and pressure on arable land and on other resources were reached? Based on the frequency of sites from the early Settlement and Developmental Periods, population density remained fairly low until about A.D. 1100, without significant pressure on resources. Beginning in the Expansion Period (A.D. 1100–1400), however, population "suddenly broke out" (Suggs 1961: 182). This rapid upswing in the demographic curve is reflected not only in a major increase in site frequency, but by the appearance of several new settlement components, including fortifications and an early form of *tohua* or feasting platform. By the end of the Expansion and beginning of the Classic Period, population had increased "beyond the point at which all possible ecological niches became filled" (Suggs 1961: 185), with inter-group conflict intense throughout the Classic and succeeding Historic Periods.

133

Environmental changes

Islands were far from stable environments, not only because of natural long-term changes and stochastic perturbations, but due to the impacts of their human colonists. I have already referred to the ethnohistoric evidence for recurrent and often devastating effects of periodic drought, and the relationship between drought and storage. In addition, excavated evidence documents two important human-induced environmental changes:

(1) the depletion and even extinction of a range of wild foods; and

(2) the erosion of arable lands due to clearance and cultivation.

There is faunal evidence from Sinoto's sites for significant reductions in bird, marine turtle, and sea mammals in the Developmental Period (Kirch 1973). Recently, Rolett's excavations on Tahuata have yielded remarkable evidence for faunal extinctions, especially among the avifauna. "The long and continuous occupation of the Hanamiai site allows an unusually clear view of the catastrophic decline of Tahuata's bird populations" (1987: 3; 1989). Among the extinct species represented in the early deposits are rails, pigeons, ground-doves, fruit doves, and lorikeets, as well as large numbers of extant species of sea bird (Steadman 1989). Rolett believes that the decimation and extinction of bird populations reflects not only heavy direct exploitation for food, but habitat destruction. For the human population, however, the net effect was the virtual elimination, by the end of the Developmental Period, of a major source of protein.

Forest clearance, resulting in the destruction of the pre-human vegetation associations and their replacement with an anthropogenic landscape, is also reflected in the Hanamiai sequence (Rolett 1987, 1989). The evidence includes changes in the terrestrial gastropod fauna, and alluvial deposition. "Later evidence of erosion caused by forest clearance occurs simultaneously with an 'explosion' in the frequency of pig bones, suggesting a period of agricultural expansion and intensified animal husbandry" (1987: 6).

In sum, by the end of the Developmental Period the natural environmental stresses periodically resulting from drought would have been exacerbated by human exploitation of the Marquesan environment. These effects included a significant decline in the availability of

wild animal foods and the susceptibility of some arable slopes to erosion.

Intensification of production

Against the background of demographic and ecological trends, the Marquesan archaeological evidence reveals significant changes in production, especially the intensification of arboriculture, pig husbandry, pit storage, and marine mollusc gathering (Kirch 1973; Dye 1982; Rolett 1987, 1989). The general sequence has been summarized elsewhere (Kirch 1984: 156–9), and most of the significant trends are portrayed graphically in Fig. 6.3. Again, change was most pronounced between the beginning of the Developmental Period and the end of the Expansion Period, that is, contemporaneous with the major increase in Marquesan population.

Virtually no archaeological work has been carried out on the field remains of agricultural systems (despite the obvious potential for excavating and dating the taro terrace systems), and thus the intensification of agricultural production must be indirectly inferred from artifactual and faunal evidence. Suggs (1961: 181–2) noted an increased frequency in *Cypraea*-shell breadfruit peelers during the Developmental Period, suggesting that an arboricultural dominance in Marquesan production was established before A.D. 1000. Certainly the increases in pig husbandry are well documented in the faunal suites from Marquesan sites. However, given that pigs were consumed primarily by the elite at feasts (at least in the Historic Period), the increased emphasis on pigs represents a trend toward social competition (on which more below).

The techniques for semi-anaerobic fermentation and pit preservation of breadfruit paste (*ma*) date at least to Ancestral Polynesian Society, and pit storage was likely practiced throughout Marquesan prehistory. However, the unique emphasis on *ma* is again presumed to have developed in the Expansion Period, when both fortifications and residential sites with storage pits begin to dot the landscape. The initial impetus to pit storage was probably the accumulation of starch reserves to buffer the effects of periodic drought and food shortage. Once such reserves were available, however, they could also be put to purely political ends, including use in the competitive feasting cycle.

The faunal suites from Classic Period midden deposits also bear witness to the importance of human flesh in the Marquesan diet.

135

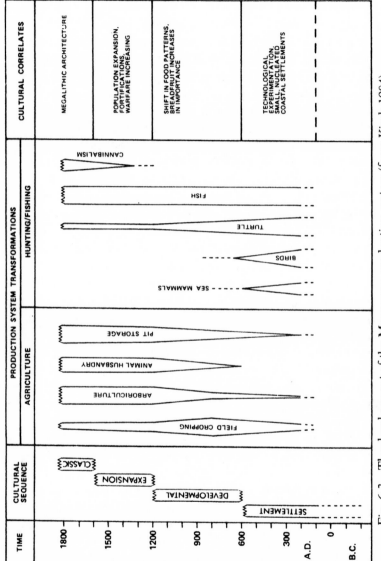

Fig. 6.3   The development of the Marquesan production system (from Kirch 1984)

Although E.S.C. Handy (1923: 219) opined that the consumption of human flesh was largely ceremonial, the evidence of "widely scattered, broken, and often charred" human bones in domestic middens (Kirch 1973: 29) suggests that humans were consumed by a broader range of persons than just the *tau'a* acting on behalf of their gods.

Architecture and settlement patterns

Monumental architecture and settlement patterns provide the clearest archaeological signals of the major changes in Marquesan society and polity that occurred during the Expansion and Classic Periods. Of special importance are the complex structures known as *tohua*, consisting of an artificial terrace (usually supported by a stone retaining wall and filled with earth excavated from surrounding barrow pits) and accompanying special-use structures (house platforms for the chief, priests, and warriors, seating areas for viewers, oven houses, and temples). In the Classic and Historic Periods, these structures reached monumental dimensions; the Tohua Vahangeku'a (Site NT-2) in Taipivai Valley (Fig. 6.4) has an artificial terrace 174 by 26 m, surrounded by a complex array of platforms and features. The labor and resources required to construct these *tohua* reflect significant centralized control, but are not unusual for chiefdom societies (Earle 1987a: 229; Earle, Chapter 4). More noteworthy is that the actual construction of *tohua* constituted a significant part of the inter-tribal competitive cycle. E.S.C. Handy (1923: 205) observed that the construction of a new *tohua* was "always a part of some great festival," while Thomas (1986: 149) opines that "the development of vast *tohua* . . . directly reflects the role of *koina* [feasts] in the pursuit of prestige."

Excavations by Suggs (1961) and others have given some idea of the temporal development of the Marquesan *tohua*. Simple *tohua* lacking the central terrace first appear in the Expansion Period. Suggs (1961: 183) was of the opinion that "the construction of such ceremonial centers by subtribes marks the beginning of the intergroup rivalry" and "a rise in the prestige of the priesthood." (Green [1986: 54] cites linguistic evidence for the antiquity of a council platform, PPN *tafua, from which the concept of the *tohua* was probably initially derived.) The more elaborate form of *tohua* with an artificial terrace appears in the early Classic Period (Suggs 1961: 162–3).

The development of the *tohua* is paralleled by changes in domestic

137

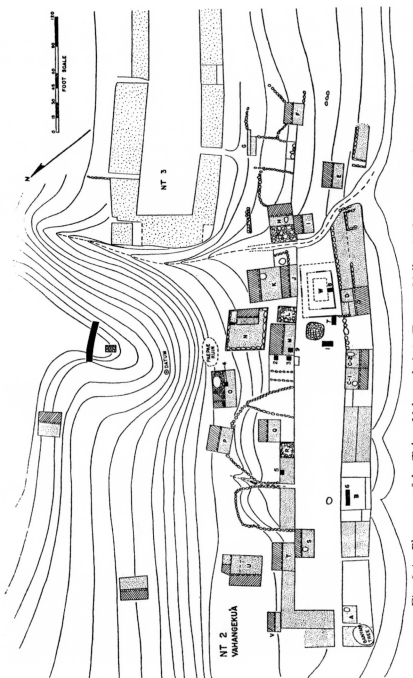

Fig. 6.4 Plan map of the Tohua Vahangeku'a in Taipivai Valley, Nuku Hiva (from Suggs 1961)

architecture. In the Settlement and Developmental Periods, houses were simple affairs associated with single-course stone pavements. From the Expansion to Classic Periods, however, domestic architecture became increasingly elaborate, with substantial energy devoted to constructing high, stone-faced platforms ornamented with risers of cut-and-dressed red scoria and, depending upon the status and resources of the occupants, anthropomorphic images set into façades. Suggs remarks on the use of cut stone: "During the latter portion of the Classic Period cut-tufa slabs for architecture became widespread. The cut slabs served as an index of personal prestige when used in domiciles. The raw material itself attained a quasi-sacred status . . ." (1961: 185).

Another architectural type of substantial importance for understanding Marquesan social change is the *me'ae*, stone platformed temples inhabited by the powerful and feared *tau'a,* rivals of the hereditary chiefs. It is worth quoting Suggs at length on the development of *me'ae*:

There is also a rapid increase [in the Classic Period] of isolated *me'ae* structures of the Megalithic *Paepae* [platform] type, usually found in conjunction with low terrace complexes. These structures often rival or surpass ordinary dwelling structures in size, and generally make lavish use of cut-tufa slabs, so important for prestige. *Me'ae* could be tribal, dedicated to minor or major deities, or familial for use in ancestor cults. The increase in ceremonial architecture is probably linked closely with a rise in prestige of the priesthood. In the discussion of the Historic period, it is shown below how important the *tau'a* were at that time; on the archaeological evidence we may consider their rise to have been a relatively recent phenomenon occurring mainly in the Classic period. (1961: 186)

Competition in late prehistoric Marquesan society is reflected not only in monumental displays of prestige rivalry, but in the settlement pattern evidence for pervasive warfare. Whereas the early periods were characterized by small hamlets situated along the coast at valley mouths, the Expansion and Classic Periods witnessed a population shift into valley interiors, which were more readily defensible. Coastal localities tended to be inhabited only by the specialist fishermen. Further, Marquesan ridgetops were frequently modified – from the Expansion Period onward – by the construction of terraced and ditched fortifications or strongholds.

TOWARDS A MODEL OF MARQUESAN
SOCIOPOLITICAL EVOLUTION

It is now possible to combine the insights from the ethnographic and ethnohistorical analysis, together with the temporal perspective offered by archaeology, to offer a tentative model for the evolution of Marquesan chiefship that had emerged by the Historic Period. Since it is convenient, I will use the four periods of Suggs' sequence to outline this model, although I stress that I am not espousing a unilineal evolutionary process.

Settlement Period

We know extremely little of early Marquesan sociopolitical structure, but we can assume that this did not yet significantly depart from what has been reconstructed for Ancestral Polynesian Society. That is, the society was organized into descent groups, each headed by a hereditary chief in whom both sacred and secular leadership was encapsulated. "An ideology of direct, male descent from the gods, and of associated *mana* and *tapu* was the original mode of legitimation for Polynesian chieftainship" (Kirch 1984: 64). The power of the chief depended critically upon his sacredotal character, and on his key role in the rituals of production.

Early Marquesan chiefs may also have gained some power from the control of long-distance prestige-good exchange, a vestigial remnant of the earlier Lapita system (Kirch 1988). Long-distance exchange has not figured in either ethnographic or archaeological accounts of the Marquesas, but it may formerly have been of some importance. In particular, the presence of substantial quantities of large pearl shell in the early (Settlement and Developmental Periods) sites is noteworthy. Such pearl shell (used primarily for fishhooks and ornaments) is foreign to the Marquesas (which lack coral reefs and lagoons suitable for its growth), and was most likely imported either from the Tuamotu or Society archipelagoes to the southwest. Friedman (1982) has suggested that the early transformation of eastern Polynesian societies reflects the collapse of long-distance exchange, and if my interpretation of the pearl shell complex is correct, archaeological evidence supports his claim.

Developmental Period

Changes that occurred in the Developmental Period were primarily technological adaptations to local Marquesan conditions, and the continued modification of the Marquesan physical and biotic environment. However, these changes helped to fix the environmental, technological, and production system contexts that were critical to the succeeding sociopolitical transformations of the Expansion and Classic Periods.

Expansion Period

Marquesan Society began to assume the outlines of its later structure in the Expansion Period. Population expanded rapidly (the near vertical portion of the logistic growth curve) as marginal areas were brought under settlement, and competition for arable land commenced. The early abundance of wild food resources had been depleted, and terrestrial production (arboriculture and animal husbandry) intensified. Against this environmental, demographic, and production background, the archaeological record provides the first clear signals of competition – both for prestige and of a more violent nature. "Megalithic" architecture, both domestic and community, first appears, as do fortifications.

It cannot be overly stressed that I am *not* identifying a techno-demo-ecological complex as the proximate or even ultimate *cause* leading to a restructuring of Marquesan chiefship. Rather, these changing material conditions provided a dynamic context within which certain inherent and pre-existing structural contradictions in Polynesian sociopolitical organization were played out. Rather than allowing the hereditary chiefs to strengthen their power, the ecological stresses that began to mount in the Expansion Period provided opportunities for chiefly rivals to usurp traditional chiefly status. A contradiction between *hereditary* and *ascribed* status positions is well known for Polynesia as a whole, especially between sacred and secular aspects of power. In the Marquesas, there was competition for *both* the sacred and the secular prerogatives of the chiefs. On the one hand, opportunistic shaman-priests (an achieved, rather than inherited form of priesthood) could seize upon the opportunity presented by an ecological crisis (precipitated, in many instances, by a drought) to claim that the *mana* of the hereditary chiefship was no longer efficacious. Surely,

this was the strategy utilized by early *tau'a* to elevate their positions. On the other hand, the increasing competition over land and other scarce resources gave ample opportunity for warriors (*toa*) to strengthen their particular brand of achieved, secular power.

Thomas (1986) in most respects concurs with the arguments outlined above (although he sees an early tendency towards the evolution of a "more stratified and centralized society" that I am not certain is justified by the archaeological record). Under the emerging ecological pressures of the Expansion Period, "if catastrophic crop failures were frequent, *haka'iki* may well have been blamed, and assassinated or rejected. The longer term result was that the association between chieftainship and prosperity was dissolved" (1986: 147). Chiefs became "disconnected from an essential and fundamental process of ritual social reproduction." *Tau'a*, furthermore, were able to exploit this situation in a manner that the hereditary chiefs could not. "If the work failed, the chief was obviously at fault. *Tau'a*, on the other hand, had an unmediated relationship with *etua* [gods] . . . If production failed, there was no sense in blaming the gods themselves; rather, those who offered sacrifices to the *tau'a* were thought to have been at fault" (1986: 147).

Classic Period
Trends set in the Expansion Period were substantially elaborated in the Classic. Population, having approached the "limit conditions" of the Marquesan environment given Polynesian technology, leveled off as a variety of cultural controls were imposed (including warfare and cannibalism). Terrestrial production was further intensified, although local gains in output were often reversed through the effects of raiding and tree crop destruction. The accumulation of large stored reserves of *ma* occupied significant labor, and as such storage facilities were under elite control, they were increasingly applied to political ends.

During the Classic Period all forms of prestige rivalry and competition were elaborated – perhaps involuted is the better term – into the intermittent cycle of feasts and warfare characteristic of Marquesan society as attested ethnohistorically. This competitive cycle was fed from two directions: by the intertribal competition for scarce land and resources (as well as for *mata'eina'a* prestige), and by the intratribal competition between *haka'iki*, *tau'a*, and *toa* for control over tribal

property and resources.

Suggs has written with insight on the prestige rivalry of the Classic Period:

The intense drive for status may have begun to affect the priests and encourage them to acquire increased secular and economic power through achievement in their own fields, especially in feats of prophecy, magic, and possession . . . During the Classic period the high priests may have been members of the chief's family, often younger brothers . . . if such were the case, there was ample reason for attempts at achieving status, for the tribal chief, under the rule of primogeniture, inherited the title to all the prerogatives and possessions of his father, while younger siblings were inferior. The attempts of the *tau'a* to gain prestige through supernatural means may have been linked in a mutually reenforcing relationship with the efforts of others – warriors, or even chiefs . . . The *tau'a*'s success in gaining prestige may be judged from the fact that they were quite frequently deified as tribal gods.

The condition of acute prestige rivalry that manifests itself in the archaeological record of this period may actually have caused a change in the basis for attainment of chieftainship. Goldman has suggested that a traditional status system was the basis for Polynesian social organization, and that this may have changed to a system in which status could be achieved.   (1961: 186)

By the close of the Classic Period, this involuted competitive cycle had, as Thomas writes, "tended to destroy its own conditions of existence" (1986: 145), through the long-term process of environmental degradation, through repeated attacks on and destruction of the means of production, and through outright social violence. Despite this pervasive destruction, the elite of late Marquesan society controlled sufficient labor and resources to underwrite the construction of some of Polynesia's most impressive architecture and statuary (exceeded only by that of Easter Island), and of a highly stylized tradition of visual arts (especially carving in bone, wood, and stone, and tattooing).

CONCLUSIONS

The Marquesan case, much like that of Easter Island (Kirch 1984: 264–78), is one in which the evolution of chiefship did *not* proceed towards increased and encompassing hierarchy. Unlike Hawaii, Tonga, or Tahiti, Marquesan polities did not achieve a level of stratifi-

cation and complexity that might be said to approach the archaic state. Rather, a dynamic context of rapid population growth, pervasive environmental hazards (especially drought), ecological degradation, and acute competition over productive resources fostered rivalry between inherently contradictory hereditary and achieved status positions. The result was an involuted cycle of prestige rivalry and competition that led as often to the destruction of the very means of production which were the objects of competition. Friedman (1982: 191) recognized these "devolutionary" tendencies in those East Polynesian societies that Goldman (1970) characterized as "open." "They are all characterized by relatively high population density and relatively poor ecological conditions, often themselves the result of overintensification" (Friedman 1982: 191).

Since the Hawaiian case is often cited as representing an "apogee" of sociopolitical evolution within Polynesia, a few key contrasts between Hawaii and the Marquesas will be instructive (see Earle, Chapter 4 above, for a discussion of the Hawaiian evidence; also Kirch 1984, 1985a; Hommon 1986). First, there were major demographic differences: a total population of perhaps 50,000 for the Marquesas compared with at least 250,000 for the Hawaiian archipelago. In Hawaii, this much larger population was integrated at the time of European contact into four major chiefdoms, each encompassing one or more islands. This contrasts markedly with the valley-tribal scale of integration characteristic of the Marquesas. Although the subsistence regimes of both societies were based on a common set of cultigens, domestic animals, and marine exploitation practices, the particular systems of production had evolved along quite different pathways. The Marquesan dominance on arboriculture with pit ensilage, and only minor irrigation in valley bottoms, contrasts with the Hawaiian emphasis on large irrigation works or, in leeward regions, extensive field systems.

Differences between Marquesan and Hawaiian sociopolitical structures have been well documented in the ethnographic literature (e.g., Sahlins 1958; Goldman 1970). The fluidity of Marquesan social structure, and the active competition between *haka'iki*, *tau'a*, and *toa*, differed markedly from the "rigid" hierarchy of the Hawaiian ruling chiefs, whose control of chiefdom ritual was uncontested. These sociopolitical differences are also reflected in the respective archaeological records. The late prehistoric construction of monuments is especially

144

interesting. The *tohua* of the Marquesas are closely equivalent to the larger Hawaiian *heiau* in size and labor investments (although not in function). When we consider that the *tohua* were built by populations of at most a few thousand, whereas the *heiau* were built for chiefs commanding the labor of tens of thousands, it is clear that Marquesan society was investing substantially more per capita in monuments than Hawaiian society. The pervasive cannibalism of late Marquesan prehistory provides another contrast with Hawaii, where human sacrifice was limited to major temple rituals of the paramount chiefs. Thus Hawaiian middens lack the charred and fractured human bones that are common in Marquesan occupation deposits. The emphasis on both monument construction and cannibalism in the Marquesas reflects the involuted cycle of competition that dominated the late prehistoric period.

In the wider field of Polynesian chiefship, the Marquesan case offers a perspective on the evolution of the more highly stratified societies, such as Hawaii and Tonga, that have occasioned the greatest anthropological interest. By revealing the limits and inherent contradictions of Polynesian chiefship under conditions of ecological stress, the Marquesan example illustrates the significance of *material conditions* under which chiefship may develop. In Hawaii, the development of what some have termed an archaic state (e.g., Hommon 1986) out of the identical kind of Ancestral Polynesian Society must in large part be credited to the highly favorable ecological conditions of that extensive and fertile archipelago. Even with high rates of population increase (Kirch 1984: 104–11), the limit conditions to Polynesian economy had not yet been achieved in Hawaii by the time of European contact. What new sociopolitical forms might have developed in Hawaii had the vagaries of history and the "world system" not impinged on the course of change can now only be a matter for speculation.

Trajectories towards social complexity in the later prehistory of the Mediterranean

ANTONIO GILMAN

The specific economic form in which unpaid surplus-labour is pumped out of direct producers determines the relationship of rulers and ruled . . . Upon this . . . is founded the entire formation of the economic community . . . thereby simultaneously its specific political form. It is always the relationship of the owners . . . to the direct producers . . . which reveals the innermost secret, the hidden basis of the entire social structure.

(MARX 1967B [1894]: 791)

INTRODUCTION

Chiefdoms are societies at the threshold of social complexity. Pervasively hierarchical, they have hereditary social inequalities, but not the state institutions which in more complex societies maintain such inequalities. The classic functionalist explanation of such inequalities has been summarized succinctly by the sociologists Kingsley Davis and Wilbert Moore (1966: 48): "Social inequality is . . . an unconsciously evolved device by which societies ensure that the most important positions are conscientiously filled by the most qualified persons." This idea lies at the root of the managerial explanations

146

of the origins of social complexity, and has been taken over by most of the anthropologists who have dealt with this problem. Thus, Marshall Sahlins tells us that "the chief creates a collective good beyond the conception and capacity of the society's domestic groups taken separately. He institutes a public economy greater than the sum of its household parts" (1972: 140). Universally propagated in textbooks of every theoretical orientation, formulated in a diverse spectrum of concrete variants, the notion that bosses are public servants even finds its way into the explanations of anthropologists whose other work clearly indicates that they know better. According to Allen Johnson and Timothy Earle (1987: 209), for example, chiefdoms originate because, "as population increases, there comes a time when the local group or intergroup collectivity can no longer be relied on to handle [certain] life-and-death matters [risk management, technology, warfare, and trade]."

The central difficulty of the managerial account of the development of hierarchical social systems is that it fails to explain why the elites inherit their privilege. Marx points out this difficulty, when he observes that

it is not because he is a leader of industry that a man is a capitalist; on the contrary, he is a leader of industry because he is a capitalist. The leadership of industry is an attribute of capital, just as in feudal times the functions of general and judge were attributes of landed property.

(MARX 1967A [1867]: 332)

To this passage Marx adds a prescient footnote: "Auguste Comte and his school might therefore have shown that feudal lords are an eternal necessity in the same way that they have done in the case of the lords of capital" (ibid.). This, of course, is precisely what functionalist sociologists and anthropologists, the direct intellectual heirs of Comte, have done.

Although the preponderance of anthropological opinion concerning the origins of social complexity remains firmly functionalist, it is perhaps not entirely surprising that the participants in this SAR Advanced Seminar subscribed more to what Haas (1982) has characterized as the conflict position. That is to say, the seminar participants agreed with Earle (1977, 1978; cf. Roscoe 1988) that elites manage the social system in their own self-interest, not for the common good. As Earle (1987: 293–4) points out:

147

Intensification and related changes in the subsistence economy do create problems requiring management, but low-level management would seem in most instances best for the local population. Such management can be expected to be responsive to the needs of the population in contrast to a distant, regional chiefly hierarchy that would be more inaccessible and unaccountable for their actions.

Provision of such low-level administrative services would, of course, be entirely compatible with achieved managerial statuses. However, it is not management that distinguishes "chiefdoms" from "tribes," but rather the nature of superordinate status: in chiefdoms such status is ascribed rather than achieved. Before the development of social stratification leaders had always achieved their positions through service to their followers. The shift to hereditary leadership statuses cannot therefore have come about because of those services. Rather, increasingly complex economies must have given rise to new possibilities for control by leaders. That is, new opportunities for long-term, stable exploitation by leaders of their followers preceded the rise of ascribed superordinate statuses. Focusing on this exploitation involves a marxist rather than a functionalist approach to the problem.

Those of us who work on the later prehistory of the Mediterranean from a marxist perspective might be well advised to use Ste. Croix's (1981) *Class struggle in the ancient Greek world* as a point of departure for our contributions for two reasons. In the first place, it is a very useful example of how to think through the principles of historical materialism when these are to be used outside the primary context of their development. Marx's and Engels' particular insights on the dynamics of precapitalist societies are more than useful, but they depended inevitably on the scholarship of their time. In prehistory, in particular, the landscape of the evidence has been completely transformed over the course of the past century. Just as Morgan's *Ancient society* required Engels to rethink the ideas about the origins of class society which he had sketched out in the *Anti-Dühring*, just so we must go back to the central themes of marxist thinking in order to make sense of the mass of archaeological, historical, and ethnographic evidence which we now have available. Ste. Croix's practice in distilling the essential themes of a marxist orientation to history can serve us as a model of theoretical practice.

In the second place, Ste. Croix's work does for the Mediterranean world from 800 B.C. to A.D. 600 what we would eventually hope to

148

do for the same world for the three preceding millennia. His conclusions can serve, therefore, as a direct historical control on our own. It would be unrealistic, for example, to suppose that forms of exploitation that were significant in prehistoric times were insignificant in later times. A difficult task for prehistorians is to give an appropriate scale to their archaeological reconstructions. Ste. Croix provides us, so to speak, with a useful *terminus sub quo*.

Ste. Croix is manifestly correct in his view that a marxist begins an historical analysis by looking for contrastive relationships of exploitation. Where on a permanent and stable basis one social group can appropriate a portion of what another group produces, those groups belong to opposing superordinate and subordinate classes. Study of the conflict between those classes, of the means by which the superordinate seek to expand and secure their extraction of a surplus and by which the subordinate resist such extraction, is central to a marxist historical analysis. Thus, in a capitalist society it is the superordinate's control over the resources, facilities, and techniques necessary for production and his attendant capacity to deny the subordinate access to the means with which to make a living that is central to class exploitation. Under capitalism the lockout is the quintessential tool of the propertied in the class struggle. As Marx notes in the following paragraph, however, in precapitalist societies, where producers generally retain control of the processes of production, the superordinate extract tribute from the subordinate through more or less forcible means. Ste. Croix's work largely consists of the documentation of the principal means of surplus extraction in the Classical world: direct extractions of labor services and rent from more or less unfree labor (slaves, serfs, tenants, debtors, and so on); indirect, collective extractions of taxes and services from the free. Here the military campaign is the ultimate tool of the propertied in the class struggle. It is worth noting that for Ste. Croix (as for Finley [1973]) the principal source of elite income in the Classical world was ownership of land and other resources and control of the labor to exploit it. Control over commerce was a relatively unimportant source of elite income.

A marxist approach to the prehistory of the Mediterranean must thus deal with two issues: the nature of class divisions where they can be demonstrated to have existed, and the specific form of exploitation that gave rise to those divisions. Dealing with either issue must confront difficult problems of evidence. In part these are due to the

traditional research orientations that have brought the available archaeological evidence to light. Economic matters have been regarded as mundane common denominators of little significance to the prehistory that really mattered and evidence for them has only been developed in some areas for restricted periods. Thus, scholars who have generated the relevant archaeological record have systematically avoided such issues, making it hard to develop Haas's (1982: 91–123) archaeological measures of stratification and class conflict. The difficulties are further compounded by the relatively small scale of social divisions that would have existed in societies at the first emergence of stratification.

Consequently, a less straightforward approach is necessary. We must construct a prehistorical materialism by using (against themselves, as it were) the idealist predilections that most prehistorians have. Although the archaeological record comprises mostly unintentionally deposited remains (i.e., garbage), prehistorians have generally attempted to extract from it the same kinds of information that historians have sought from their written, intentional records. Furthermore, archaeologists have approached prehistory from the normativist theoretical perspectives characteristic of most historians. That is to say, their primary aim has been the recovery and study of materials that embody overt human intentions – stylistically distinctive artifacts, major architectural remains, and burials – in other words, precisely those manifestations that would have required the largest investments of human labor (i.e., "value") and hence have attained the intrinsic qualities sought by normativist prehistorians.

In marxist terms, class must be defined as dependent not on consciousness but on objective exploitation. Ste. Croix (1985: 30) is extremely clear on this point: ". . . if ancient slaves are indeed to be regarded as a class, then neither class consciousness nor political activity in common (both of which were far beyond [their] capacity. . .) can possibly have the right to be considered *necessary* elements in class, in Marx's scheme of things . . ." In any stratified society, however, the ruling class must be a class for itself. They constitute a small minority of the population and obtain disproportionate benefits by extracting a surplus from their far more numerous subjects. If the rulers deceive themselves about their status, if they fail to unite (at least at times) against their followers, they will fail to maintain the social asymmetry from which they benefit. One point of the conspicuous consumption which universally characterizes elite behavior is that

150

through it members of the elite make themselves known to one another. The material remains of elite efforts to maintain their solidarity in the face of their subjects' expectable resistance to giving up tribute are precisely what have attracted the attention of traditionally minded archaeologists. We have, accordingly, a good opportunity to reconstruct the emergence of social stratification by studying the evidence for early ruling-class consciousness.

Given the difficulties of assessing the significance of archaeological evidence in single cases, a comparative approach seems warranted. What I propose, therefore, is to assess the nature of one sequence towards greater complexity with which I am familiar from my own work, the sequence in southeast Spain, with the classic sequence of such development in the Bronze Age of Mediterranean Europe, the Aegean case. There are significant similarities in the two cases. In the past, these have been attributed to diffusion, an approach now discredited on empirical grounds. These similarities are better used to illustrate contrasts susceptible to processual explanation.

SOUTHEAST SPAIN

Southeast Spain (comprising the provinces of Granada, Almería, and Murcia) is a region of strong environmental contrasts (Gilman and Thornes 1985: 10–15). The various mountain chains of the Betic fold system (the Sierra Nevada, Sierra de Segura, and so on) create a strong rain-shadow effect. The uplands of "Alta Andalucía" receive abundant winter precipitation (generally above 400 mm, reaching over 1,000 mm at high elevations), while intermontane basins and the Mediterranean coastal lowlands in the lee of the sierras receive much less rainfall (under 250 mm along the coastal fringe). Being the result of permanent orographic features and general atmospheric circulation patterns, the contrasts between highlands and lowlands would have been stable throughout the Holocene, demanding differing techno-environmental responses by their prehistoric inhabitants.

The Early Neolithic of southeast Spain (6000–4500 B.C.) is a variant of the Impressed Ware complex characteristic of the western Mediterranean as a whole. (For a detailed review of the characteristics of the Neolithic to Bronze Age sequence in southeast Spain, see Molina González [1983]. An analytical summary of its salient features is given in Gilman and Thornes [1985: 15–28] and Gilman [1987a:

151

23–5].) Almost all the known occupations are in caves or rockshelters (hence its name, the "Cultura de las Cuevas"), although ephemeral sites in the open are not unknown. The available paleoeconomic and settlement evidence indicates a nonintensive farming economy; agricultural occupation did not exist in the arid sectors of the southeast.

The Later Neolithic (4500–3500 B.C.) of southeast Spain is poorly known. In the moister sectors, occupation continued at some caves and rockshelters, but the general dearth of evidence is perhaps best explained by a greater use of open-air sites, whose short-term occupations would have left remains of little archaeological salience. In the arid coastal regions some settlement sites and simple megalithic (collective burial) monuments known from early excavations have been assigned to an "Almería Culture" belonging to this time period, but this cultural facies has not been confirmed by more modern, radiocarbon dated discoveries, and may simply group together some of the less elaborated settlements and burial monuments of the following Copper Age.

The Copper Age (3500–2250 B.C.) of southeast Spain, the "Los Millares Culture," sees striking changes in settlement and burial patterns, as well as in artifact and subsistence technology. Large numbers of long-term, open-air, often fortified settlements are known, whose preservation is due to their durable constructional materials. The settlements are generally small villages of less than 1 ha, but the type site of Los Millares (Arribas and Molina 1982) in the arid sector, with an areal extent of 5 ha (one of the largest settlements in Europe at that time), two lines of fortifications and subsidiary forts on the surrounding hills, gives the impression of being a "central place" (although a single exceptional site cannot be adequate evidence for a settlement hierarchy). The prevailing burial rite is collective, with placement in natural or artificial caves or in megalithic chambered tombs (Chapman 1981; Mathers 1984a; Moñita García et al. 1986). The burial places are near settlements and are sometimes grouped in cemeteries, the largest at Los Millares having some eighty megaliths. Grave goods consist of ritual fetishes and utilitarian items, some of which are rendered in valuable raw materials (e.g., ivory or copper). There are significant disparities in the elaboration of tombs and in the wealth of their grave goods between individual tombs within cemeteries and between cemeteries as wholes. Such wealth differentials are more marked in the arid than in the moist sectors of the southeast. As

Hernando Gonzalo (1987) points out, apart from the unique site of Los Millares itself, settlements in the arid and moist sectors of southeast Spain are not clearly differentiated in terms of their size or elaboration. It is, rather, in the funerary monuments and their grave goods that the arid sector's relatively greater complexity is apparent. In terms of artifact technology, the principal new feature of the Copper Age is the (apparently indigenous) development of a simple copper metallurgy. The available paleoeconomic evidence makes it clear that the subsistence base was intensified agriculture, including irrigation in the arid portions of the southeast.

The Bronze Age "El Argar Culture" of the southeast (2250–1500 B.C.) exhibits clear changes in settlement and burial patterns. Occupation sites are generally new, acropolis sites in highly defensive positions. Sites are generally small and the limited range of sizes provides no prima facie evidence for settlement hierarchies. Burials are no longer collective, but individual interments are under the floors of houses. Grave goods consist of the personal finery and possessions of the dead (weapons, ornaments); graves exhibit great wealth differentials. These continue to be more marked in the arid portions of the region. The metallurgical technology is elaborated (tin bronze alloys, silver production, and two-part molds are Argaric novelties). Once again, the available faunal and botanical evidence indicates that the Argaric is characterized by a well-developed Mediterranean farming pattern: remains of all of the principal crops attested to in Roman times have been found on Bronze Age sites in southeast Spain. On the foundation provided by the intensified farming introduced in the Copper Age, the later prehistoric sequence in southeast Spain exhibits increased social differentiation and social conflict.

The changes in southeast Spain in the third millennium B.C. have contemporaneous parallels throughout Europe: the development of metallurgy, an expensive technology for the production of luxury goods; the wide distribution of particular styles of finery; the increase in military activity, both as a practice and as a value; the shift from collective to individualized burial rituals; all point to the development of an upper class whose rule depended, at least in part, on strong-arm tactics and whose recruitment was stable enough to establish wide-ranging, mutually supportive partnerships. The conclusion of the best modern synthesis of the period represents a consensus of Europeanist prehistorians:

During the course of the Bronze Age a number of important changes took place . . . Perhaps the most obvious of these is the rise of the privileged . . . It is hard to think of this process in terms other than those of aggrandizement of the few, the rise of the elite, and the start of social stratification.

(COLES AND HARDING 1979: 535)

The absence of state institutions in third-millennium southeast Spain would, of course, have limited the elite in its self-aggrandizement. Here as elsewhere in prehistoric Europe social stratification developed on the basis of direct, kinship-based patron–client relations. The amount of surplus the emerging elite could take from their followers would be limited by the rationale upon which the claim to surplus was made. Limited as the amount of surplus must have been under conditions of incipient stratification, however, the question of its source remains.

The strictly archaeological record available to us severely limits our ability to approach this problem: there are no records of exchanges of commodities or of collections of rent that would demonstrate the nature of surplus extraction. The best we can hope for is that the theories of exploitation that we develop will be consistent with available archaeological evidence, but the validity of such theories must inevitably be based more on their plausibility than on their empirical support.

For those students of European prehistory who have addressed the question of exploitation, the basis of their thinking has been Engels' treatment of commodity exchange in *The origins of the family*. It is the specialization inherent in elaborate systems of exchange that gives elites the control derived from their positions as middle-men. I would suggest, however, that a more realistic view than Engels' is one that sees the collection of rent from farmers as the source of the elite's wealth.

In prehistoric Europe the emergence of stratified societies coincides with the development of copper and bronze metallurgy. The commodity exchange theory of the emergence of stratification is usually based on the notion that elites controlled the supply of metal. Childe developed the idea that the demand for metal in Near-Eastern civilizations would have generated the rise of compradore elites in those areas of Europe (such as southeast Spain) where metal ore was found. However, radiocarbon dates have demonstrated that social stratification was well under way in Europe before the demand for metal in the

154

Near East could possibly have had any influence on European economy. Childe's core–periphery interpretation of the development of stratification in Europe is therefore untenable. Accordingly, prehistorians have recently concentrated on the role that local development of metallurgy may have played in building exchange networks from the control of which chiefs could extract a surplus. For the El Argar culture of southeast Spain, for example, the explicitly marxist prehistorian Vicente Lull (1983) argues that metallurgy developed distinctions between communities of miners and communities of farmers and that elites arose by exploiting their mutual interdependency.

The development of metallurgy . . . produced a sharp change in . . . production which in turn . . . made necessary other changes in social relations. The original self-supporting communities became communities with complementary production requiring trade. This also caused an improvement in communication and routes of transport; an improvement that fostered a managerial hierarchy, most likely for security reasons. The hierarchy formed in this manner from direct production became concerned in the tasks of organisation and protection of [their] interests. The division of labor . . . produced an emerging trade of products with quite different exchange values. The political classes found in the self-supporting tribal communities were replaced by a new stratification. (LULL 1984: 1,222–3)

Functionalist versions of such views (e.g., Mathers 1984b) commonly see leaders as providing services to their followers in the form of higher-order regulation of exchange systems. Whether or not such relations are seen as exploitative, they face two problems at the level of fact. First, Early Bronze Age metal production was done on an extremely limited scale. At El Argar, the type site of the southeast Spanish Bronze Age and the richest, largest site of that culture to be excavated, the 1,200 burials spanning several centuries yielded a little over 34 kg of copper, the product of only about one ton of ore (Chapman 1984: 1,150). Second, metal was used almost exclusively for nonutilitarian objects such as weapons and jewelry. Eleanor Leacock (1972: 33) has commented that "despite Marx's important discussion of commodity production in the first section of *Capital*, there has been little follow-through by marxist scholars on how the acquisition and exchange of a surplus by early states entrapped urban populations as a lower class . . ." In southeast Spain, where the Copper and Bronze Age communities do not reach more than village size, such follow-through

does not seem possible. Metal-working could easily have been practiced in those villages by the part-time exploitation of nearby ores, without much effect on agricultural production. Thus, both compliance costs and refusal costs (to use the terms developed by Haas [1982: 167–9]) of participating in the network of metal production and exchange would have been minimal.[1]

This is the reason for which I have previously argued (Gilman 1976; Gilman and Thornes 1985) that the emergence of a ruling class in southeast Spain during the Copper and Bronze Ages was based primarily, not on control of metallurgy, but on the extraction of rent from primary agricultural producers (on "staple finance" [D'Altroy and Earle 1985]). The emergence of social stratification in southeast Spain coincides with the introduction of intensified subsistence agriculture characterized most importantly by irrigation, but also associated with the exploitation of animals for their secondary products (traction [horses for transport, oxen for plowing], cheese, wool, and so on), and, perhaps, cultivation of olives and vines. While each of these intensifications would have increased agricultural yields, they all would also have raised the fixed costs of production. Yet, all of them could have been introduced by the agricultural workers themselves, without the help of managers. They constitute, to use Adams' words,

capital investments that enhance the productivity of the tracts and groups they serve but not others. [They] restrict or distort uniformity of access to the primary productive resources of the community and . . . tend to concentrate the potentialities for the production of a surplus of deployable wealth in the hands of a limited social segment . . . They stimulate the concentration of hereditable, alienable wealth in productive resources, and hence also the emergence of a class society. (1966: 54; cf. CHILDE 1951: 89–90)

Agricultural investments made in anticipation of their long-term yield would have created the potential for imbalance, i.e. stratification, in the village society. The assets created by investment of labor can benefit individuals other than the original investors and generate an increased potential for conflict. Under such circumstances, farmers come under a duress which provides lucrative opportunities for those who can mediate such disputes.[2] It is wiser, after all, for a primary producer to relinquish a part of his surplus to a chief against the assurance of collecting more yields in coming years, rather than risk losing his entire investment. This is the logic underlying protection rackets under any circumstances. The grave goods found in Bronze

Age burials clearly testify that, in the absence of state-level authorities, the incipient aristocrats themselves exerted the necessary pressure to develop and maintain social differentiation resulting from such extraction of rent.

That agricultural intensification gave rise to social differentiation in the Millaran and Argaric of southeast Spain becomes clear if we compare those regions to the adjacent areas to the north and west. Southeast Spain is the most arid region, not just of the Iberian Peninsula but of all Europe. Hence, irrigation and concomitant terracing, tree crops, etc., would have been particularly important in order to create a stable and growing yield. By contrast, the moister regions of the southeast such as upland Andalusia and the Spanish Levant, where higher levels of rainfall would have made capital intensification of agriculture less appealing, have yielded contemporaneous archaeological sequences similar to the Millaran and Argaric, but with significantly less accumulation of wealth and hence less social differentiation.

I do not wish to suggest that extraction of rent in an expanding system of staple finance was the only source of income for the Millaran and Argaric elite, but rather, I want to stress the important role such extraction must have played in the emergence of social complexity. This is clearly demonstrated in the increasing presence of luxury items in elite burials during the course of the Copper and Bronze Ages (see D'Altroy and Earle [1985] for the concept of "wealth finance"). Two points are important, however. First, any system of wealth finance must rest on some system of staple finance. Social complexity does not arise from wealth exchange in and of itself – that would be to say, in Carneiro's (1977: 222) apt phrase, that elites "arose by taking in each other's washing" – but rather from the manner in which the surplus that is concentrated into wealth is extracted. Second, the scope of wealth finance operations in Copper and Bronze Age southeast Spain seems to have been very limited. Both production and consumption were local: few objects or materials of specific southeast Spanish origin have been found outside the local region (Gilman 1987a); even within that region, valuables seem only to have circulated over quite short distances. Thus, Lull (1983: 439) notes that tin (as opposed to arsenical) bronzes are much more frequent in Argaric burials of the Cartagena/Mazarrón district (where a source of tin exists) than in contemporaneous burials in the Vera basin, 50 km to the southwest.

Since trade can probably be ruled out as a major source for the expanding wealth noted in the region during the Copper and Bronze Ages, it seems quite clear that the increasing social complexity that wealth connotes rested on the progressive intensification of agricultural production with the concomitant increase in the possibility of rent collection.

The similarities between the interpretation of Argaric social organization and Engels' discussion in the *Origins of the family* of the "military democracy" of the ancient Germans described by Tacitus should be apparent (see Kristiansen, Chapter 2 above). The hereditary leadership nascent in the "Germanic mode of production" (GMP) has nothing to do with the organization of a commonwealth; it originates in the effective concentration of force:

> The military commander who had acquired fame gathered around his person a host of booty-loving young warriors pledged to loyalty to him personally, as he was to them. He fed them, gave them gifts and organised them on hierarchical principles . . . Weak as these retinues must have been . . . they nevertheless served as the germ of decay of the old popular liberties.
>
> (ENGELS 1972 [1884]: 566)

Engels could not, of course, discuss the material basis for the concentration of wealth which would make the pursuit of booty a viable strategy for elite ambitions, but, as Thomas (1987) points out, the "secondary products revolution" (Sherratt 1981), a classic example of capital intensification of farming, is associated with the transition to GMP-like societies at the start of the Bronze Age. These social formations are of particular interest because of their direct historical links to well-documented successors in recent times. As Engels himself notes (1972 [1884]: 558), social formations dominated by the GMP survived in Scotland until 1745 (cf. Fraser's [1972] account of the "reiver economy" of the Anglo-Scottish border tribes of the sixteenth century). Wolf (1981: 51) suggests that "feudal" and "Asiatic" societies are two extremes of a range of "tributary" modes of production. The "Germanic" societies of Europe, both those of the later prehistoric period and of the early modern periphery, would be even further on the small-scale end of the tributary range than their "feudal" successors and contemporaries.

SOUTHEAST SPAIN VS. THE AEGEAN

Colin Renfrew's (1972) great functionalist synthesis of Aegean prehistory, amplified and confirmed by the host of work it has inspired, serves as the starting point for any comparative discussion of the development of social complexity in Mediterranean Europe. It is convenient to review separately how each of the various intertwined characteristics of complexity unfolds over the course of the Early Bronze Age (EB) and Middle Bronze Age (MB) periods in the Aegean (contemporaneous, respectively, to the Los Millares and El Argar phases of the sequence in southeast Spain).

Agriculture

Renfrew has stressed the importance of Mediterranean polyculture in establishing the basis for Minoan/Mycenaean developments. Certainly, plow agriculture and tree crops are present by EB times. Although irrigation may have been practiced by the Late Bronze (LB) Age (Balcer 1974), studies of site locations with respect to agricultural resources suggest it was not an important component in agricultural production (Bintliff 1977: 105). What these studies do make clear is "the priority of self-sufficiency in past settlement location," that "every unit of settlement, from the lowest farmstead to the greatest palace, was placed with an eye to its own subsistence bases, and that trading, defence, communications were an inadequate basis for settlement" (Bintliff 1977: 114).[3] Although the mix of intensifications may differ in detail, autonomous, intensive agricultural production characterizes both Greece and Spain in the later prehistoric period as in recent times (see Forbes 1976). The ethnographic and historic record make it clear that villagers sought such autonomy precisely because assistance from a benevolent managerial authority was unreliable (*contra* Halstead and O'Shea 1982).

The available evidence makes it difficult to assess systematically changes in agricultural practice over the course of the Bronze Age in the Aegean region. It is clear, however, that agriculture is increasingly affected by the differential distribution of power. Thus, the greater importance of cattle (and presumably the plow) in Phylakopi II and III levels (MB and LB, respectively) is the result of the concentration of

the population of Melos into a single settlement (Gamble 1982), a political phenomenon (cf. Adams 1970). Linear B tablets from Knossos document direct palatial control of large-scale wool production (Killen 1964). The much greater number of LB sites with olive remains (J.M. Renfrew 1982) may well be due to elite investments. In neither Copper nor Bronze Age Spain is there any indication of elite intervention in agricultural production.

Metallurgy and other craft production

Metallurgy is the classic example of a high production-cost craft. The metal-working industry of the Aegean is fully developed by EB 2 times. Tin bronze is frequent, cast in two-piece molds or (occasionally) by the lost wax method. Silver and lead production is well documented. (The only elements added to the technical repertoire in the MB and LB are niello work and silver plating.) In comparison, Millaran metal-working is much less sophisticated technologically and shows less typological variety. The quantities put into production in southeast Spain are, furthermore, infinitesimal compared to the Aegean: the single EB 2 hoard from Kythnos contains 7 kg (cf. the amount of metal from El Argar cited above). It is worth noting, however, that although Aegean metalwork is more abundant and elaborate than its Iberian counterparts, the uses to which the metal was put is much the same in the two areas. Even in the LB 1 and 2 times, Mycenaean metalwork consists of "equipment that would follow a king into his grave: mostly weapons, both parade and combat, objects of personal use and adornment, vessels and, once in a while, a tool or two" (Iakovidis 1982: 218).

High production-rate crafts, such as wheel-turned pottery, are also developed by the end of the Early Bronze Age in the Aegean (but are unknown in Copper or Bronze Age southeast Spain). Outside the MB and LB palaces themselves, craft production is combined with subsistence activities: in EB 2 Myrtos, crafts are integrated into domestic production (Whitelaw 1983), and the same pattern continues in MB Palaikastro and LB Gournia (Branigan 1983). This pattern is consistent with the evidence for metal production in southeast Spain, where copper slag is found on a majority of sites, larger and smaller, throughout the Copper/Bronze Age sequence. What is completely absent in Spain is the concentration of specialist activities associated with the Aegean palaces, a concentration attested to not just by the

Linear B records, but by purely archaeological evidence: lapidaries, seal-carvers, bronze smiths, ivory workers, weavers, potters. The palaces supplied raw materials to these specialists and disposed of what they produced. As Brumfiel and Earle (1987: 5) note, such attached specialists result from "the explicit desire of the ruling elites to control the production and distribution of certain politically charged commodities."

Trade

During EB times no materials of clearly Aegean provenance are found outside the Aegean. Imports to the Aegean are all found in Crete and consist of a few Egyptian stone bowls and some ivory. Krzyszkowska (1983) estimates that the extant ivory finds amount to fifteen or twenty tusks' worth and that the total level of imports may have been of the order of three tusks per generation. Within the Aegean during EB 2 the widespread distribution of selected metal and pottery types throughout the region and of Cycladic marble bowls and figurines on Crete and on the Greek mainland suggests regular free-lance commerce and/or gift exchanges. Certainly, in the Aegean, where there are no authenticated tin sources, the very existence of an important tin bronze industry implies widespread exchange of some kind.[4]

Trade in southeast Spain during both the Copper and Bronze Ages exhibits the same general pattern as Aegean EB trade, but on a smaller scale. Some clear imports (also mainly ivory) in Millaran and Argaric contexts, and some clear exports from the Iberian Peninsula – Beakers and metal weapons – are found in North Africa (Harrison and Gilman 1977). Widespread typological similarities in ceramics and metalwork within the Iberian Peninsula in the Copper and Bronze Ages attest to regular prestations between local groups, but, as we have seen, metal production in southeast Spain was localized and did not require extensive commerce.

Certainly nothing in the Millaran and Argaric record resembles the large-scale commerce directed by the palace elites in MB and LB times in Crete and on the Greek mainland (Kopcke 1987). Substantial Minoan and, later, Mycenaean exports make their way east to the Levant and Egypt.[5] Copper, tin, ivory, and other valuables make their way to the Aegean. The recent fourteenth-century B.C. Ulu Burun shipwreck find (Bass 1987) illustrates the volume and nature of LB

trade. The cargo consists of valuable raw materials (tin, six tons of copper, perfumed resins, and so on), the kinds accounted for on Linear B tablets. Indeed, these tablets reveal a particular emphasis on the production of goods with the concentrated value suitable for long-distance trade: perfumes (Foster 1977; Shelmerdine 1985) and textiles (Robkin 1979; Shelmerdine 1981; Killen 1984). The Aegean palace elite's intervention in agricultural and livestock production and its control over specialist production was part of a large-scale system of wealth finance.

Warfare

The development of weaponry and fortifications in both southeast Spain and the Aegean over the course of the later third and earlier second millennia reflects increasing inter-group conflict. In the EB Aegean the variety of daggers and spears is greater than in the Millaran, but the development of fortifications is quite similar. Indeed, the multiple ring walls and forts at Los Millares itself (Arribas and Molina 1982) exceed in elaboration anything in the Aegean. The best comparative measure of defensive preoccupations is the location of settlements with respect to agricultural resources, since the increased transport costs of defensive emplacements will make themselves felt on a daily basis. In the Copper Age of southeast Spain, defensive considerations do not significantly affect convenient access to arable land; in the Argaric Bronze Age, as I have shown (Gilman and Thornes 1985: 180–1), they do. In the Aegean there is no comparable increase in defensive preoccupations. In MB and LB Crete, "the lack of city walls or other defensive works protecting rich palaces has suggested to some . . . a *pax Minoica*" (Cherry 1986: 25). On the Greek mainland, many of the large Mycenaean centers are strongly fortified, but few make significant locational concessions to defense (cf. Bintliff 1977: 115). The contrast between the nondefensive settlement locations and the elaborate weaponry of the Aegean MB and LB can only be explained in terms of the solidity of elite control.

Settlement hierarchies

In southeast Spain during the Copper Age most sites are very small (less than 1 ha). The only possible higher-order center in Los Millares

itself, with a settlement area of 5 ha. In terms of the size of its settlement, the complexity of its megalithic cemetery, and the elaboration of its defenses, Los Millares is altogether exceptional. Nothing known from the Aegean EB compares to it, although the Early Minoan settlement at Knossos approaches it in size (Whitelaw 1983).

In the Argaric of southeast Spain, sites are uniformly quite small: the largest known to me (La Placica de Armas, Caravaca, Murcia) is a little over 1 ha in size. In contrast, the development of the palaces in the MB and LB Aegean leads to some differentiation of site sizes: proto-palatial MB Knossos may cover some 45 ha (Whitelaw 1983; C. Renfrew 1972: 240–4), but the settled area of most of the other major MB and LB centers only reaches about a tenth of that size (the citadel at Mycenae covers less than 4 ha). In short, when later Bronze Age settlements are larger than the 1 to 2 ha range of their larger EB predecessors, this is specifically due to the size of the administrative and residential quarters of the elites (cf. Whitelaw 1983: 340). Only the palace centers stand outside the hamlet–village range of site sizes.

Wealth differentiation in burials

The development of mortuary patterns in Copper and Bronze Age southeast Spain has been reviewed above. The pattern in the Aegean EB is more complex: in the Cyclades and on the mainland the dead are usually placed individually or multiply in cists. Differentiation in grave goods increases over the course of the EB (C. Renfrew 1972: 370–83). By EB 3 the level of differentiation and the kinds of grave goods are comparable to those of the Argaric (so much so that diffusionist explanations of the similarities have been suggested: e.g., Schubart 1973). In Crete, the prevailing EB' burial rite consists of collective interments in round or rectangular tombs. Their prolonged use and the open character of the contexts make assessment of the development of wealth differentiation difficult, but some tombs are certainly much wealthier than others (e.g., the Mochlos II *tholos*). The emergence of an elite social stratum by the end of the EB is beyond doubt.

Funerary practices of EB character continue into later times. In addition, however, there arise much more elaborate burials, for which there are no analogues in the West. These are associated with the developing palace centers. Monuments like the Khrysolakkos tomb at

Mallia and the shaft graves at Mycenae lead into the *tholos* tombs whose distribution defines the LB Mycenaean world. "It was the fusion of the Cretan practice of building large stone tombs with the mainland and Cycladic one of burying only two or three people in each, which yielded the prodigiously expensive construction of the late bronze age tholos tombs" (C. Renfrew 1972: 434). If in earlier times collective burials represented the attachment of lineages to their land, now they represent the separation of elite lineages from the common herd.

DISCUSSION

The comparisons between southeast Spain and the Aegean which we have just reviewed suggest several points. If one considers the situation in each region at around 2100 or 2000 B.C. (the end of the Aegean EB, the beginning of the Argaric), the similarities are striking. Certainly, there was more active trade and craft production in the Aegean and perhaps somewhat greater wealth differentials, but one would have no difficulty placing the two cases in the same ethnological type category. Within a century, the contrasts are immense. The Aegean world has taken off into a higher, more unstable order of complexity; southeast Spain stagnates in a continuation of earlier patterns. Lewthwaite (1983: 179) draws the following conclusion:

The uniqueness and suddenness of the development of the Cretan palace system . . . cannot be explained plausibly in terms of a unique combination of geographic features. No explanation in terms of local adaptation or the local rise of elite groups can be considered adequate which does not predict the non-appearance of such adaptations or political developments in the [western Mediterranean]. It is surely . . . the positive anomaly of Crete which requires explanation, especially since the Minoan system proved itself in the end to be more vulnerable . . . The most striking positive anomaly in geographic terms is the location of Crete with respect to Near Eastern civilization . . .

Developing this line of thinking, Cherry (1984) sees the opportunities of commerce with the Near East as critical in the development of the Minoan palace system. What needs to be added to his analysis is a sense of the dynamic interplay between the opportunities for wealth and staple finance.

The system of land tenure is, of course, critical in this interplay (see Earle, Chapter 4 above). For the last moment of the Aegean Bronze

Age cycle, the tablets of series E (those with the ideogram for wheat) from Pylos provide us with some of the direct evidence lacking in completely prehistoric situations (Bennett 1956). There are 211 series E tablets from Pylos, most of them fairly long (over seventy percent of them with ten characters or more), compared to thirty-one from Knossos and two from Mycenae (most of these having less than ten characters) (Bartonek 1983). In spite of the difficulties of interpretation which this limited, fragmentary corpus presents, Finley (1957: 138–9) points to three conclusions which can be drawn from them: first, the palace regulated access to land. Second, an important juridical distinction existed between land held in "ke-te-me-na" and "ki-ki-me-na," the latter being associated with the "da-mo." The latter term corresponds, of course, to the Classical Greek demos, although its precise gloss is difficult to ascertain. Third, persons covering "the whole range of Mycenaean statuses and occupations, king to 'slave,'" held land in exchange for enumerated products or services, the king holding relatively vast estates (Chadwick 1976: 71). It is tempting to conclude, following Bockisch and Geiss (1973: 116–17), that the palace granted lands to its officials and servants, while commoners (whose tributary obligations are not recorded in the tablets) held land not fully integrated into the palace economy. If so, we would see in the Pylos land tenure system a palace sector oriented to production meeting wealth finance goals existing side-by-side with a relatively independent subsistence sector (cf. Gamble 1981: 221). Such a differentiation between palatial and commoner economic sectors is commonplace in the Near Eastern states Aegean elites would have emulated (Foster 1987).

In the Aegean and southeast Spain, primary producers developed relatively simple intensifications of agricultural production. For reasons which I have discussed, such intensifications open up possibilities for long-term exploitation of primary producers by their (hitherto impermanent) leaders. By the later third millennium such permanent, staple-financed elites are in place in both the Aegean and southeast Spain, and in both areas the elites converted their surplus into valuables. The emergent elites would concentrate their tribute through the production of (and support one another through the exchange of) goods of concentrated value in a process of "competitive emulation" (C. Renfrew 1986a). The whole development of metal-

lurgy is driven by this process. Clearly, Aegean elites by virtue of their geographic position had opportunities for wealth finance which Spanish elites did not: they had at hand Near Eastern potentates to emulate and to engage in exchange. Textile production and scented olive oil would have provided opportunities for Aegean elites to reshape agricultural production in their export interests. Nothing could be further from the redistributive model of palace operations.

Eventually, the Minoan/Mycenaean wealth finance system, a peripheral phenomenon within the Near Eastern world system, collapsed. The systematic surveys carried out in various parts of the Aegean world demonstrate that, when this occurred, not just the palaces, but also most of the villages disappeared. The functionalist view that the palace was a center of redistribution and risk management contributing to the general welfare has the considerable merit that it provides a coherent account of this articulation. Wealth finance would provide a means of acquiring scarce raw materials (especially metals) which would assist the expansion of basic production. The collapse of the exchange network led to the population decline of the post-Mycenaean Dark Age because it caused the disappearance of the institution which had promoted the common wealth. A suggestion that "a general scarcity of bronze" (reflected, perhaps, in the rationing of bronze to smiths at Pylos just before the palace's destruction [Hooker 1982]) "may have contributed to the demise of Mycenaean civilisation" (C. Renfrew 1986b: 155) is accompanied by an account of how an abundance of the material would help overcome the inevitable resistance of peasants to the payment of rent.

Those who see this account as unrealistic, as inconsistent with what we know about the social position of peasantries in general, can easily promote alternative scenarios. When the widespread political instability of the Eastern Mediterranean world system at the end of the Bronze Age caused the Aegean wealth finance bubble to burst and commercial opportunities declined, "all that was left to [the lords of the Mycenaean world] was to rob their neighbors, to live the life of the corsair for as long, but *only* as long, as the amassed wealth lasted among the strongest" (Sandars 1985: 184). While the palace wealth exchange system lasted, the peasantry, sheltered perhaps from greater tributary pressure, would have attained a certain prosperity and a consequent demographic increase, both of which would have been terminated by the elites' predatory involution when their opportunities

166

for mercantile aggrandizement disappeared. The challenge is to find archaeological evidence for any of these scenarios.

Be that as it may, the Minoan/Mycenaean cycle must be understood as the most exaggerated example of the many rises and falls of chiefdoms at various times and places within the world of European barbarians. Once the Minoan/Mycenaean wealth exchange bubble burst, the unintegrated, "Germanic" side of the political economy would once again become the basis of stratification. The post-Mycenaean Dark Age "world . . . of petty kings and nobles, who possessed the best land and considerable flocks, and lived a seignorial existence, in which raids and local wars were frequent" (Finley 1981: 81) resembles the world which was contemporaneous to the Minoan and Mycenaean civilizations in the western Mediterranean. As Finley has noted, the Dark Age memory of the Bronze Age, as reflected in the Homeric tradition, retained no trace of the palatial component of the MB/LB economic system. This must reflect in part the degree to which the development of wealth exchange through the palaces departed from the strategies of elite finance both before and after the MB/LB florescence. As we have noted previously, the dominance of staple finance in the Classical Greek world is unquestionable. The Dark Age was not, however, a return to the state of affairs prior to the Minoan/Mycenaean cycle. The collective burials of Early Minoan Crete must reflect a continuing vertical social integration along kin lines, but in the Dark Age society described in Homer "the fundamental class-line between noble and non-noble is clear" (Finley 1981: 82–3). This was the enduring legacy of MB/LB civilization.

In southeast Spain, the simple systems of exploitation established at the close of the third millennium B.C. lasted until the expansion of the eastern Mediterranean economies in the early first millennium and the introduction of iron technology led to a new basis for the expansion of elite power. In the Argaric, elite ambition found scant outlet in wealth exchange: the Near East was too distant for emulation. Chiefly aggrandizement expressed itself through predation, in internecine warfare, throughout the Bronze Age. The long duration of this social formation should earn it a place in social evolutionary typologies. That place would be a critical one, since it would demonstrate the viability of a class society in which elites are entirely nonmanagerial.

Notes

1. It is sometimes suggested (Childe 1954: 158; Johnson and Earle 1987: 210) that control over metal weapons would have afforded Bronze Age chiefs control over the means of destruction (cf. Goody 1971). In the light of the recent successes of peasant guerrillas in the face of vastly superior armed forces, this seems quite unrealistic. It is the organization, not the technology, of violence that makes it effective.
2. The logic of chiefly extortion is lucidly set forth by Byock (1988: 165–82) in his discussion of the mediaeval Icelandic system of class stratification. See also Gilman (1981, 1987b).
3. Simpson's (1981: 39) strenuous objections to Bintliff's conclusions concerning the primacy of agriculture in determining settlement location are in fact limited to the defensive positions of some (not all) of the palace centers. It seems clear that defensive preoccupations were much more important in determining site placement in the Argaric than in either the Minoan or Mycenaean (see below).
4. Obsidian from Melos is distributed throughout the Aegean region in the EB and earlier. Interestingly, few imports are found on Melos: nothing in EB 1, some northern Cycladic pottery and two marble figurines in EB 2, and (surprisingly) nothing in the earlier MB, the period of political nucleation (C. Renfrew 1982). Torrance (1982: 221) concludes that "the presence of obsidian sources on Melos did not by themselves have important *direct* effects on the culture process of the island." It is clear that obsidian was never part of the system of wealth finance which drove the long-distance exchange system.
5. Compared to the abundant and broad eastern spread of Minoan/Mycenaean materials, their western distribution is much more limited (see T. R. Smith 1987). Most of the Mycenaean pottery in the western Mediterranean is quite late (LB 3) and none of it further west than Sardinia. The direct commercial links traditionally posited by archaeologists to account for similarities between the Bronze Ages in Iberia and the Aegean simply cannot be demonstrated to have existed at any period, let alone during the end of the third millennium (the time of the Argaric's formation).

8

Chiefdoms to city-states: the Greek experience

YALE H. FERGUSON

The only political scientist at the seminar, I was asked for "the political science perspective on chiefdoms," a logical request, except for one lamentable fact: there *is* no such perspective. Most political scientists are preoccupied with twentieth-century states and interstate relations and, except for classical political theory, regard thousands of years of political evolution as largely irrelevant.

Nevertheless, political scientists *should* be interested in chiefdoms, not least because any assumption that the world is essentially one of states is myopic. In fact, the world has long been a crazy-quilt of polities (see Kristiansen, Chapter 2); foci of authority with varying territorial scope, power, and legitimacy; distinct in some respects and overlapping, layered, and linked in others. Chiefdoms have been part of this pattern almost from the outset, and city-states, too, since the third millennium B.C. in Mesopotamia (see Burke 1986).

I did present the main seminar paper on the chiefdom-to-state transition. One or two seminar colleagues suggested that the Greek experience involved mainly more complex societies rather than chiefdoms. This is a completely mistaken point of view, and I have tried to analyze the reasons for it.

I think many analysts are prisoners of ideal types. In their view,

there are "chiefdoms" and there are "states" – and never the twain shall meet: however, much variation exists *within* these categories. Typical of this perspective is the argument of Jonathan Haas (Haas 1982; Haas, S. Pozorski, and T. Pozorski 1987), that the state represents a clear stage in political evolution, characterized by rapid centralization of economic, ideological, and physical power; and by new territorial bounds and more formal institutions of government.

Up to a point, the Greek experience supports distinct categories. Greek political forms during the Dark Age and early Archaic periods are plainly closer to chiefdoms than to anything else. When one compares these periods with succeeding years, significant qualitative and quantitative changes occurred across the regional political land-scape. Many city-states emerged in a relatively short time.

However, the emphasis of this essay is on *variability within* and *continuity across* political forms, which best supports the position of Timothy Earle and others who suggest that political evolution/devolu-tion is best conceived as a process along a continuum of ideal types. We cannot effectively study *either* political evolution *or* devolution if we fail to recognize that *significant aspects of previous political forms persist in later forms and thus account for some of the variability.* "Pure" states do not emerge one step up the evolutionary ladder from chiefdoms, nor do "pure" chiefdoms, one step down from states.

Hybrid polities in the Greek experience merit careful study. During the Dark Age and early Archaic period of chiefdoms, memories of a former Heroic Age of states survived and eventually provided some of the ideological glue both for city-state formation and interstate cooperation. As the Archaic period advanced, kinship patterns of rule (e.g. clans, tribes, artificial kinships), typical of chiefdoms and less complex polities, were only gradually exchanged for territorial patterns of political representation in the "advanced" Greek city-states – and never eliminated entirely. The ethnos stood somewhere between earlier forms and the polis in its degree of common identity, ter-ritoriality, and functional integration. Ritual friendship ties among aristocrats complicated politics within the city-state and, along with tribal identities and the ethnos, continued to be significant in interstate relations.

A second major challenge for ideal types is the problem of "external" relationships. The societies in which political entities are enmeshed typically extend beyond local borders. "Outside" develop-

ments regularly influence those "inside," and the locus of political authority and decision-making shifts over time and by issue. Accordingly, the boundary between "internal" and "external" blurs almost to the vanishing point.

Again, the Greek experience is instructive. For example, during the Dark Age, heads of households on largely self-sufficient estates recognized a local hierarchy, joined in raiding parties for plunder, and participated in far-flung networks of ritualized friendship. Query: Was this a political universe of extended family households, simple chiefdoms, or complex chiefdoms? For production, the pattern was mainly isolated households; however, the tasks of protection, war, and plunder demanded a certain coalescence, a movement toward chiefdoms and complexity.

The analytical challenge increases with the re-emergence of "states" and the appearance of additional political forms generated by state interaction. At one level, states struggled to shake off vestiges of chiefdoms. At other levels, states engaged in intense new peer-polity and center–periphery relationships, and relations with non-Greeks. The contrast between ethnos and polis, for example, was no less than that between subject poleis and hegemons. Center–periphery hegemonies like the Athenian empire had an important institutional foundation. Alliances and protection schemes for shrines and athletic contests also were partially institutionalized. The Delphic oracle was a symbol overarching local polities, with a limited but significant capacity to affect their legitimacy. The Persian empire perennially threatened attack and internal subversion, and eventually acted as a balancer in the Greek system. Query: Was this a political universe of states, unevenly emerging from chiefdoms; states and interstate "regimes"; states, regimes, and "empires"; or some broader "system" involving all the foregoing, including non-Greeks?

The missing conception is that of overlapping, layered, and linked authority patterns – the coexistence and interaction of a great variety of entities which individually might be located at different points along the political evolution continuum.

This essay also speaks to elites' political strategies, especially the issue of the relative importance to control of economic and physical power versus ideology that so enlivened seminar discussions. Dark Age chiefs established their status through surplus generated from herds, estates, and war. Exploitation of slaves and indebted peasants allowed

171

city-state elites leisure for active political participation. Production and trade of commodities played only a limited role. Although taxes other than import and harbor duties were probably hard to collect (see Ste. Croix 1981: 206), war and tribute within hegemonic systems supported public works and state pay.

The Greek case is particularly useful in demonstrating the importance of ideology. Dark Age chiefdoms believed in family, ritual friendship, plunder, and blood revenge; a moral code sanctioned by ancient earth gods. City-state founders had to substitute the idea of loyalty to the city-state community for loyalty to actual and artificial kin. Residents had to be convinced that stealing, blood feuds, and certain gift exchanges ("bribes") were contrary to a new standard of city-state justice. Not surprisingly, this ideological transformation was gradual and often incomplete. Supporters of the city-state posited an "Olympian revolution" among the gods and drew imaginatively upon a Heroic past. The idea of the city-state was reinforced by Delphic pronouncements, the bones of ancient heroes, a major temple to the deity(ies) identified with the community, other impressive monuments, popular assemblies, city religious and secular festivals, theater, athletic contests, and ceremonies for the transfer of power or the pronouncement of laws.

But the most powerful ideological invention of all, properly credited to the Greeks, was the concept of citizenship. As Ian Morris (1987: 2–3) reminds us, in theory and to a substantial extent in fact, in the polis citizens *were* the state. Most were willing, without coercion, to support the state and to defend it with their lives in battle. The negative side, for aristocrats and tyrants, was that citizenship (at least for free males) also seemed to imply a role in political decision-making. Thus, as social complexity increased, the circle of political elites had to expand. Nonetheless, changes in institutions and the degree to which "democracy" was achieved or remained largely symbolic differed greatly from polis to polis.

Greek citizenship sheds a somewhat different light upon a principal concern of the seminar, the commoners' evaluation of the costs of compliance with a leader's demands compared to the costs of their refusal – or "what do the bosses do to gain and extend power?" In the underpopulated Dark Age, peasants were unusually independent, working their own land or for wages on estates. When the city-state emerged, commoners (except slaves) became citizens with presumed

rights in the larger community. Indebted peasantry clamored for relief, and a growing number of non-aristocratic citizens demanded and often received a more direct role in political decision-making. One is reminded of Michael Mann's (1986a: 113–14) observation that power which is less despotic may be more effective. Internal control, like external defense, became a community task. "Leaders" or "bosses" became *ideologically* indistinguishable from the citizenry. The result was wider participation or at least the illusion thereof, although not always greater individual freedom or "better" policies.

CHIEFDOMS TO POLEIS IN DARK-AGE AND ARCHAIC GREECE

Mycenaean civilization in Greece collapsed in stages from about 1400 to 1150 B.C. Proposed reasons for the collapse include grave economic problems, invasion from the north, and/or revolts of Mycenaean subjects; and there were devastating attacks by the mysterious "Sea Peoples" (see especially Sandars 1985).

Mycenaean palaces were the administrative centers of "petty bureaucratic states" (Finley's term, 1981: 53), some larger than later city-states (Chadwick 1976: 12; Gilman, Chapter 7 above). Actually, classification of the Mycenaean entities is difficult, underscoring our previous discussion about inadequate concepts. Renfrew's characterizations, "something more than chiefdoms, something less than states" – or "palace principalities" or "minor states" – seem appropriate. He reserves "chiefdom" for the Early Bronze Age. V.R.d'A. Desborough (1964: 218) insists there was a Mycenaean empire, with Mycenae the capital; however, the balance of opinion is otherwise (Vermeule 1964: 237 sums up pros and cons).

How relevant is the Mycenaean era to subsequent developments? Oswyn Murray (1980: 15) maintains that the centralized palace economy of the Mycenaeans, influenced by the Minoans, resembled the "oriental despotisms" of Mesopotamia and Egypt more than later Greece. Moreover, most physical vestiges of Mycenaean civilization vanished by the ninth century (Snodgrass 1980: 15). From other standpoints the Mycenaean era was critically important. Not everything vanished. For example, the royal citadel at Athens apparently never fell, and Attica received refugees from many areas (see Vermeule 1964: 267 and Sourvinou-Inwood 1974). John Chadwick (1976: 191) sug-

gests that the Greek-speaking population of Crete may have broken up into smaller administrative units which kept written records and re-emerged as the petty city-states of classical times. There was also some continuity in religion.

More important, the Mycenaean past remained heroic in the collective memory. By cultivating their myths, the Greeks were able to revive and advance on a new path with supreme ideological confidence. Gods and heroes provided patrons for the new city-states that eventually emerged. Even tyrants could claim that they were merely reviving the tradition of palace kings. Overarching the city-state there was preserved, as well, a strong pan-Hellenic symbol of identification.

The fall of the Mycenaean civilization ushered in a "Dark Age" period from about 1100 to 800 B.C., concerning which our information – literary (mainly Homer and Hesiod) and archaeological – is extraordinarily limited (see especially Snodgrass 1971). Homer (Ionia ca. 750 B.C.) draws on an older oral tradition and seems to describe primarily the Heroic (Mycenaean) era, although John V.A. Fine (1983: 26) and others argue that much of Homer reflects life in the ninth century.

From limited evidence, what was the Dark Age probably like? "Dorian" tribal peoples moved into Greece or dispersed from former Mycenaean centers and became the dominant mainland population early in the first millennium (cf. Bartonek 1974). Dorians migrated east/southwest, and Aeolians and Ionians eastward. By the ninth century B.C., "Greeks" were living throughout the Peloponnese, the west coast of Asia Minor, and most Aegean islands. The Ionian migrations across dangerous seas, unlike later migrations, were not state-sponsored; most apparently embarked from Athens under the leadership of individual aristocrats (Snodgrass 1971: 373–6).

Migrations did not result from population pressures, for Greece experienced a staggering population decline. Anthony Snodgrass (1980: 20–1 and 1971: 367) estimates that from the thirteenth to eleventh centuries both the *number* and *size* of individual settlements declined to one-eighth of their previous level, less than any time in the previous thousand years or later in antiquity. His is a poignant picture of most Dark Age Greeks living in small settlements, amidst usable but unoccupied land, in a condition of poverty and illiteracy. The western Greek hinterland suffered most, while the more viable settlements faced the Aegean (Snodgrass 1971: 375–6).

174

The key development in the chiefdoms/city-states Dark Age/Archaic Age transition, 800 to 500 B.C., was a shift from group identities based on some form of kinship to those based on locality or territory, the polis. Mann (1986b: 197) notes that Aristotle regarded the polis primarily as *"a community of place." Yet this was only a shift in emphasis, in the primary symbol of identification: there were other competing identities both old and new.* Family and ritual friendship ties from the chiefdom era posed a challenge to the polis, and kinship groups persisted as social and religious entities even after their political role was finally diminished; the ethnos unit was more diffuse than the polis; and other identities continued to be significant in peer-polity and center–periphery relations, and relations with non-Greeks.

Greeks as a whole continued to identify with the names Hellene and Hellas, signifying the entire Greek "race," its territory, language, and culture. With Hellas, Dorians and Ionians each had a similar dialect, cults, and festivals. In all Dorian communities one finds three tribal names – Hylleis, Pamphyloi, and Dymanes – and often others that were probably pre-Dorian. Some uniformity also existed in Ionian tribal names. In Athens four ancient Attic tribes survived, in religious observances, to the fourth century. However, as Antony Andrewes (1967: 85–6) comments, no organization grouped cities of Dorian speech nor did one of the three Dorian tribes in one city necessarily feel solidarity with its counterpart in another Dorian city. Dorians and Ionians were traditional rivals, but so were some Dorian states, like Sparta and Argos.

Tribes (*phylai*) and lesser divisions, including the phratry ("brother-hood"), *genos* ("clan"), and *oikos* ("household"), were obviously important in Greek social and political life; yet scholars disagree about their precise character, role, and origin. Snodgrass (1980: 25–6) observes that the "apparatus of tribal survivals" was more defined in the emerging polis than in more primitive ethnos groupings. This suggests to him that "the system had no ancient pedigree," that Greek city-states invented tribe, phratry, and *genos* as categories for the organization of military affairs and minor religious observances. Similar entities seem to have existed in the Dark Age, but the extent to which they represented real or artificial kinship, and were uniform in character and function throughout Greece is not clear. Fine (1983: 35–6) and Andrewes (1967: 87–8) argue that phratries may have developed in the ninth century when power-seeking aristocrats gathered scattered "kin-

175

ship" groups of common people into "brotherhoods." As Fine notes, it is also debatable whether the *genos* antedated the *oikos*, so that the later significance of the *oikos* involved the disintegration of the clan; or whether the *oikos* had since time immemorial been the fundamental family unit, which later united for political and economic reasons in artificial kinship units called *genē*. The *oikos* was a household, not just family; the more prosperous ones included several generations (four in Athenian inheritance law) and slaves and retainers.

The Dark Age economy was predominately rural and pastoral, with most *oikoi* or estates largely self-sufficient in food and clothing, and this was the setting for evolving political relationships. Metals, luxury items, and female slaves came from raids or foreign traders, usually Phoenicians (Fine 1983: 37). Murray (1980: 49) writes that early Greek society was not "feudal," in that there was no serf class owing obligations to an aristocracy in return for land. Probably, the *oikoi* hired labor to supplement slaves and some peasants worked modest plots of their own land. Mann (1986b: 196–7) posits low status rigidity between aristocracy and free people, "a tension between birth and wealth."

Much of this, however, is uncertain. There were serfs in Laconia, Crete, and Thessaly – and later Sparta. When population eventually rebounded, pressures on the land no doubt increased. Commenting on fifth-century Athens, Moses Finley (1981: 98) cautions that we do not know whether labor was "free or half-free" or "whether such concepts are yet applicable in any meaningful way." Although the lower classes surely had personal and property rights, he suggests, they may have had to surrender some produce or work without pay and may have been tied by law to their land. To complete the picture, one should add to the list of early social groups *demiourgoi* (professionals like bards, doctors, artisans, and craftsmen) and *thetes* (persons without land, trade, or significant kinship ties whose lot was worse than a slave).

Political development had to begin almost anew in the Dark Age. Powerful kings no longer existed after Mycenaean civilization fell, except perhaps in reduced circumstances in Athens. Mycenaean tablets mention a local village official, a *basileus*, and this was the title assumed by leaders of residual and new communities. Murray (1980: 41; see also Snodgrass 1971: 386–8) describes them as "a group of hereditary nobles" identified as much by their lifestyle as by their "wealth, prerogatives or power." Through guest-friendship (*xenia*),

including the gift exchange of goods and services, nobles created a network of mutual obligations. Bands of *hetairoi* supported one another in cattle raiding or piracy (Murray 1980: 50–2). Ritual friendships were similar to actual kinship and hereditary, and often spanned great distances (Herman 1987: 16–34). Nobles' wealth gave them a virtual monopoly in warfare; only they could afford weapons, armor, and horses (Finley 1981: 97). The duties of any *basileus* who rose above his counterparts to the status of petty king or chief (presumably the head of a particularly important household) were probably largely military – to lead the people in battle and organize defense against hostile raids (Fine 1983: 44). Fine (1983: 45) notes that Homer mentions several popular assemblies in peacetime.

The polis emerged against this background in the Archaic Age about the eighth century B.C. and probably first on the mainland. Major contributing factors were apparently a phenomenal increase in population and agricultural surplus, comparable in magnitude to the post-Mycenaean decline. Snodgrass (1980: 24–40; 1971: 378–80) thinks there was less pastoralism and more arable farming. Mann suggests (1986b: 196) that "expansion increased the prosperity and power of the middling-to-large peasant householder as against the aristocracy, who were herders, especially of horses."

According to Snodgrass (1980: 31–4), two additional factors may help account for the polis. The first was a desire to regularize the worship of cult deities at a central sanctuary. Secondly, the Greeks may have been influenced by the Phoenicians, with whom contacts were increasing (cf. Murray 1980: 80–99) and whose independent coastal cities resemble poleis. The Phoenicians were the likely source of the alphabet making writing possible again in Greece, and they may have inspired the trireme warship and Olympic Games (see Boutroz 1981).

Other authors stress the Greeks' remarkable ideological invention of the polis concept itself. Ian Morris argues (1987: 2, drawing on W.G. Runciman) that although it was perhaps predictable that the Greeks would eventually develop state institutions – by emulating earlier advanced societies or through cluster or peer-polity interaction – there was no predicting that states would assume the specific form of the polis. The polis was independent from other poleis and unified with a surrounding tract of countryside; no distinction was normally made between dwellers within and without the city (Snodgrass 1980: 28).

177

Morris maintains (1987: 2–3) that the key is citizenship. The polis "was almost a stateless society, autonomous from all dominant class interests by being isomorphic with the citizen body. The citizens *were* the state." "The source of all authority was . . . the community." "Force was located in the citizen body as a whole, and standing armies or police forces were almost unknown." "We might also say that politics functioned as the relations of production." Similarly, Marxist analyst G.E.M. de Ste. Croix (1981: 286–7) emphasizes that Greeks did not regard the state mainly as a means of preserving property, rather as the instrument of the body of citizens or *politeuma* who had the constitutional right to rule. Hence "class struggle" in this context was an effort by the *demos* to make the state sufficiently democratic to curb exploitation by aristocrats.

According to Morris, the polis was the direct result of "the struggle of Dark Age peasants against a Dark Age aristocracy" (1987: 9), a "social revolution" (1987: 202, 204) – "a sharp, qualitative break in the structure of Greek society" (1987: 3). Morris admits the concept of *politeia* continued to evolve both in theory and institutions, and, in fact, he believes that in Athens and perhaps elsewhere the nobility temporarily managed to reassert their control (1987: 9, 205–8). Nonetheless, he insists "the idea of the polis as a *koinonia* emerged quite suddenly, and from that time on we can speak of the existence of the polis" (1987: 3). Again we are confronted *both* with step-level rapid change à la Haas and considerable variety.

As Fine (1983: 51) stresses, one striking aspect of poleis from Asia Minor to Italy is their small size. Sparta after it absorbed Laconia and Messenia was the largest with $8,300$ km^2; Athens, including Attica and Salamis, had $2,800$ km^2. Other poleis ranged from 80 km^2 to $1,300$ km^2. Populations, too, were small. Athens had only about $10,000$ persons in the eighth century and $35,000$–$40,000$ in 431 B.C., before the Peloponnesian War (Morris 1987: 99–101). Most city-states ranged from $2,000$ to $10,000$ adult male citizens.

Early poleis were hardly the sophisticated cities that many – by no means all – later became. Fine (1983: 56) terms them "straggling agricultural settlements," with citizens living around the foot of a citadel and scattered throughout the polis in isolated houses or small villages. Most cities were not walled until the sixth or even fifth century, and a real marketplace (*agora*) was slow to develop. Ste. Croix (1981: 9) rightly concludes that it is impossible "to give a definition of a

polis that would hold good for all purposes and all periods, and the best we can do is say that a political entity was a *polis* if it was recognized as such."

It is important for our argument about variety and layers of authority that some territorial entities which took shape during the Archaic period, especially in the western half of the mainland, are best classified as ethnos rather than polis. Examples include "canton-like" entities like Locris or Doris; or loose associations of towns and territories like Arcadia, Achaea, or Boeotia (Snodgrass 1980: 44). Snodgrass (1980: 42; see also 1971: 419) speaks to the definitional problem, which, like that of polis, points up the remarkable range of forms in Greek politics: at one extreme the ethnos was "no more than a survival of the tribal system into historical times," a population worshiping a common deity at a single center and assembling periodically for political purposes. Between this and the polis, there were many intermediate forms. If a number of urban centers emerged, "they might attain intermittent autonomy as separate states, and pay only occasional homage to the concept of a unified 'nationality.'" On the other hand, a single city might forcibly establish itself as the political center of a part of the ethnos, making it effectively into a polis. If both processes happened successively, in that order, a very large polis with an impressive resource base might result. Snodgrass (1980: 43–4) explains that the ethnos eventually "provided the basis for a fresh venture in state formation in the autumn of Greek civilization" and (we shall see) a form for interstate alliances.

For several centuries after 800 B.C., the spotlight was on the polis rather than the ethnos, but the polis began to evolve even as it became the dominant political model. Economic growth and changing warfare tactics affected Greek society, profoundly influencing the constitutions of individual poleis. The fact that Greek society itself became more "layered" required a political response. *The city-state symbol of identification had to be strengthened to counter internal diversity; new territorial bases for representation had to be found that would cut across real and fictional kinship ties inherited from the chiefdom era; traditional aristocratic behavior that was inconsistent with the new polis community had to be outlawed; and governmental institutions had to develop more "layers" for representation.*

Several developments together undermined aristocratic rule (cf. Fine 1983: 94–136; Forrest 1978: 45–97; Snodgrass 1980: 85–159;

Finley 1981: 87–105; Hopper 1976: 52–155; Jeffrey 1976: 39–47; Ste. Croix 1981). Continued Greek colonization stimulated trade and manufacturing, swelling the ranks of merchants, shippers, and *demiourgoi* artisans (often the same). Writing, revived about the mid-eighth century, made it easier to keep accounts and to formalize codes of law. The introduction of coinage about the sixth century facilitated exchange and created a new movable wealth. Snodgrass (1980: 131–2) nevertheless warns not to exaggerate the impact of growing commerce and industry, which he regards as still a much less important source of wealth than agriculture, warfare, or religion. In any case, he suggests, many engaged full-time in commerce and industry were slaves or other noncitizens like the Attica metics. Finley (1981: 98) describes Greek society about 650 B.C. as including "'declassed' [aristocrats] and . . . a middle class of relatively prosperous, but non-aristocratic, farmers with a sprinkling of merchants, shippers and craftsmen." Whatever the precise patterns of landholding, we can assume growing population pressures on the land. By the time of Dracon and Solon in Athens (mid-seventh to early-sixth centuries) demands for land redistribution and debt cancellation were reaching dangerous proportions. There was increasing resentment over the aristocracy's control and corruption of the administration of justice.

Another factor undermining aristocratic control was what Finley and most other analysts regard as the most important military innovation in Greek history (about 650 B.C.), the use in close formation (phalanx) of heavily armed infantrymen called hoplites. Hoplites had to provide their own expensive equipment, giving them a financial stake as well as a new role in the defense of the state. This, in turn, engendered what Mann terms (1986b: 200) "an enormous psychic *intensification* of the social relationships of the emerging polis." Commitment to the common good "was not merely a background normative disposition, but an integral part of the battle formation in which the soldier became trapped." Athens and other seapowers carried the military revolution still further by incorporating the lower classes as rowers on warships.

Both the existence of a "hoplite reform" and its political significance are, however, controversial. Morris (1987: 197–201) finds "not a shred of evidence" for change in Greek warfare tactics. He believes that hoplites were used long before the period in question and sees "absolutely no reason to associate a 'hoplite class' with either the rise of

the polis or the rise of the tyrants." (See also especially Snodgrass 1965; Cartledge 1977; and Salmon 1977.)

The emerging polis not only had to widen the circle of governing elites but also had to overcome identities and ritual friendship patterns of behavior associated with Dark Age chiefdoms. We shall shortly see how Athens, for example, forged new representational districts to supplant traditional kinship divisions. No less threatening for the polis were aristocratic ties of ritual friendship. As Gabriel Herman (1987: 6–8) explains, "the ancient world was criss-crossed with an extensive network of personal alliances linking together all sorts of apolitical bodies (households, tribes, bands, etc.)." "The city framework superimposed itself upon this existing network . . . yet did not dissolve it"; "older social groupings and archaic ideals maintained themselves alongside the new ones with remarkable tenacity." Although the city became "the dominant form of organization," guest-friendship overtly and covertly "continued to act as a powerful bond between citizens of different cities and between citizens and members of various apolitical bodies." From time to time "the horizontal ties of solidarity which linked together the elites of separate communities were stronger than the vertical ties which bound them to the inferiors within their own communities." Ritual friendships offered aristocratic citizens "power, prestige and resources," assistance during political struggles, and refuge abroad in time of defeat. The polis thus had difficulty establishing such basic premises as accepting gifts may be bribery, and consorting with enemies of the city-state is treason.

Accompanying the new polis morality was a major religious upheaval, an "Olympian revolution" among the gods. The ancient earth gods, with their code of family and blood revenge, were superseded by an Olympian pantheon headed by Zeus; particular Olympian gods like Athena and Apollo established special relationships with specific cities, along with cult figures from the Heroic past; and these protectors of the city supposedly inspired its new moral codes, laws, and institutions. (Delphi, we shall see, often played a legitimizing role from outside.) In Richard Kuhns's (1962) analysis, the *Oresteia* illustrates some of the changes in thinking. Orestes is beset by advice from two different quarters, the ancestral Erinyes, and Apollo and other Olympians. An Athenian court, which alone can weigh the complicated pros and cons, ultimately rationalizes Orestes' crime of matricide. Orestes learns a central lesson: "The right of action is

181

realized through considerations which go far beyond the individual's impulses and desires; the individual and the family, the house and the clan become subordinate to the city" (Kuhns 1962: 56).

Widespread social conflict ("stasis") led to three major political changes beginning about the middle of the seventh century: the rise of tyrants, the codification of the laws, and the further institutionalization of government to manage demands from a more complex society.

Late in the seventh century, tyrants began to appear, as Finley (1981: 102–3) notes, mainly where urbanization as well as economic and political development were relatively advanced. Hereditary aristocracies could not resolve conflicts within their own ranks and/or involving wealthy commoners, a growing urban population, and indebted peasantry. Tyrants arose in Argos, Corinth, Sicyon, Megara, Epidauros, Pisa, and elsewhere. Solon's constitutional reform in Athens was followed by the Peisistratos tyranny. In one sense, this so-called age of the tyrants was a backward step toward kingship. Few tyrants, however, were able to establish lasting dynasties, and most became increasingly brutal as their power began to erode. In other respects, the tyrants represented a forward step. They bolstered community spirit through impressive public works projects and games and festivals. Most important, they "broke the habit" of aristocratic rule, which paradoxically strengthened the *polis* and its institutions, and in some states led "to government by the *demos*, democracy" (Finley 1981: 104). On the other hand, democracy was never extended to all residents of the polis, permanently implanted, or an entirely unmixed blessing. It is sobering to recall that the next great age of tyrants began with Dionysios I of Syracuse in 405 B.C. – when Greek democracy, weakened by the Peloponnesian War, had self-destructed (see Davies 1978: 147ff.).

Sparta and Athens, in significant respects atypical, nevertheless illustrate two major political trends, codification of the laws and further institutionalization of government. Generalizations about Sparta are difficult because of the paucity of evidence and the Spartan myth of equality and democracy. (Fine 1983: 137–76, from whom we have drawn heavily, casts doubt on some traditional interpretations. See also Forrest 1980.) Legend held that Sparta's way of life derived from an ancient law-giver, Lycurgus, whose constitution created *eunomia* or "the reign of good law." The Great Rhetra, probably a genuinely ancient document (supposedly from the Delphic oracle) preserved by

Plutarch in a very confusing form, purports to distribute the powers of state among kings, council of elders, and an assembly of all the equals. Although Sparta's foundation may have been in the eighth century, its principal features likely date from the latter half of the sixth century – a century or so after the Spartans forcefully extended their control over Laconia and Messenia – and were part of a militarization of the state to insure the continued domination of subject helots (serfs). Also of concern were the *perioeci* ("dwellers round"), other Spartan subjects in surrounding villages with limited rights and obligations, and their own local governments. Thus, Murray's (1980: 153) description of Sparta as "the ideal hoplite state of classical Greece" is accurate, although the hoplite "garrison state" was as much for internal control as for defense against external threats.

The Spartan state was more equal in theory than practice (Fine 1983: 147–51, 155–61). Equality was the prevailing ideology, and all Spartan male citizens were socialized from a very early age into a *state* military "brotherhood" to supersede all other loyalties. Whatever equality prevailed in the barracks did not exist outside. Land was not held in equal portions. Moreover, a nobility of citizens over sixty elected to life terms on the *gerousia* (30-person senate replacing the earlier Council of Elders) dominated the government. Their wealth and influence probably swayed the "popular election" of members of the board of ephors, chief administrative officers during their one-year, nonrenewable terms. Sparta retained a dual kingship, but kings were primarily military leaders. After conflict between them in the sixth century, only one king could lead a military campaign and then only in the company of two ephors. At an elaborate oath exchange ceremony every nine years, the ephors could depose a king. The full assembly of citizens, the *ecclesia*, met about once a month to elect persons to high office and to pass on any legislative questions referred from above. However, debate on such occasions may have been limited to the *gerousia*, ephors, and kings; and the *ecclesia* apparently could be overruled in the event that the people decided "incorrectly."

Athens, although profoundly different from Sparta, also offers an example of a law-giving stage and the elaboration of governmental institutions to accommodate a changing society. (See sections on Athens in works previously cited and Jones 1957, on the fourth century.) Any unity Attica may have had during the Mycenaean era had to be re-established. Thucydides attributed (re)unification or *synoecism* to

183

the national hero, Theseus (a legendary figure like Lycurgus). Presumably one or more kings succeeded in getting various settlements to accept Athens as a political center, brought nobles from them into the royal council, and extended Athenian citizenship to all freeborn native residents of the entire territory. By the early seventh century the king or *basileus* had only religious functions; and the leadership of Athens consisted of a ruler archon, a polemarch or military leader (including jurisdiction over resident aliens), and six other judicial archons. An aristocratic council, eventually known as the Council of the Areopagus, probably held much of the real power, electing the archons directly or nominating them for election by a popular assembly. The aristocratic families who controlled Athenian politics called themselves the *eupatridai* or "well-born." When tyranny was becoming fashionable, ca. 632 B.C., there was an abortive attempt by one Cylon to establish one in Athens. Ca. 621, Dracon codified the laws of Athens, partly to meet criticisms that the administration of justice had become corrupt. The penalties imposed for failure to pay debts and other offenses were extraordinarily harsh (hence "draconian"). Little is known about the precise terms of the code, except the law on homicide, which partly survived in a late fifth-century copy; it was clearly an effort to limit the blood-feuds characteristic of pre-polis society.

In 594 B.C. when Solon became archon, there was a general clamor over debts in Athens. Many small farmers, *hectemoroi* ("sixth-partners"), owed one-sixth of their annual crop to an overlord. Failure to pay this or any debt could result in enslavement of both the offender and his family. Some scholars have looked for crisis conditions that might have increased agitation over debts: economic problems from overcropped land; bad harvests; a foreign invasion; or even the introduction of coined money, which made it easier to lend and borrow. Forrest (1978: 150–6) maintains that the economy may actually have been improving owing to a growth in trade, but Dracon's code itself created resentments. Be that as it may, Solon confronted the problem head-on by abolishing the status of *hectemoros*, cancelling existing debts, forbidding the use of persons as security in future transactions, and allowing debt exiles to return.

Moreover, Solon and, several generations later, Cleisthenes, together removed the last major vestiges of primordial kinship from government. Solon divided the population into four census classes based on wealth rather than birth – *pentakosiomedimnoi* (owners of estates producing

184

500 measures of grain), *hippeis* (cavalrymen), *zeugitai* (hoplites), and *thetes* (those unable to afford hoplite arms). The archonship was limited to the top two census classes, thereby breaking the *eupatrid* monopoly. Solon also created a new Council of 400 (100 from each tribe) to check, exactly how we do not know, the power of the Council of the Areopagus. In addition, he gave the pre-existing popular assembly an extra title, the *Hiliaea*, to express its new function of acting as a court of appeal even against the magistrates themselves. He rewrote the legal code of the state, abolishing the laws of Dracon. Finally, Solon encouraged the rising commercialism of Athens, welcoming foreign craftsmen. The country's economic success exacerbated social tensions. In 561 B.C. Peisistratos established a tyranny, which lasted through his son Hippias to 510 B.C.

In 508 B.C. Cleisthenes, to his own faction's gain, completely reorganized the administrative and electoral system of Attica. He made about 150 small demes (*demos*) the basic state administrative unit, cutting across old local loyalties. (On the old Athenian tribes, phratries, *genē*, and *oikoi*, see Fine 1983: 183–8.) He superimposed over demes ten new artificial tribes, each to elect one military general and fifty members of a Council of 500. Each tribe was further subdivided into three *trittyes*, one from each of the three geographical divisions of Attica – the city, the coast, and the inland. Snodgrass (1980: 196) observes that each new tribe was "a microcosm of the Attic state," undercutting locality and kinship. Moreover, the reforms supposedly gave all citizens equal rights in the election of officials (Hammond 1986: 190). The long-range effect was much more democracy, with an ostracism procedure for unwanted statesmen after 488 B.C., the selection of archons by lot after 487, and the Areopagus declining until it lost its last political powers in 462.

BEYOND THE STATE: GREEK PEER-POLITY, CENTER–PERIPHERY, AND NON-GREEK RELATIONS

Because the polis was so small, "outside" relationships assumed unusual importance. (Original sources include Thucydides, Homer, Herodotus, Xenophon, and Polybius. See also especially Adcock and Mosely 1975; Wight 1977; Burn 1984; Fleiss 1966; and Conner 1984.) Neither Mesopotamian powers nor Egypt posed a major threat, but

Persia did, and the Phoenicians were an important cultural influence. Moreover, the "security dilemma" vis-à-vis other Greeks was acute. Honorable death in battle was seen as heroic, and war was seen as a natural means of augmenting personal, family, and community wealth. Nothing had changed in this respect from the Mycenaean period or the era of chiefdoms. The rise of the polis, however, created a new community for which to fight, and changing military tactics (hoplites and rowers) involved more social strata. Tyrants and later democratic leaders often used real or imagined external threats and war booty to their own political benefit.

Yet for all the violence, most leading and even lesser poleis remained at least nominally independent actors for many years. The physical setting made for economic self-sufficiency. Each canton and many islands have highland, lowland, and coastal habitats; these varying conditions made it possible to raise livestock and also olive trees, grapes, and cereals. As Mann (1986b: 195–6, 201–2, 205) observes, however, Greece was not "particularly privileged" ecologically. The rugged terrain hampered political unification. Few poleis had the resources to incorporate others or to administer them as colonies. Hoplites carried three days' rations, and strategy relied on short battles rather than sieges. Often the city core of the opponent's state might not be overrun. In any event, keeping him subjected was a challenge that few poleis wanted to undertake. Sparta's experience with Messenian helots testified that old identities died hard. The easier course was to settle for slaves or tribute.

Alliances were essential in a system where the units were numerous and vulnerable poleis. Ancient tribal identities, ideology, and historical ties affected the choice of allies, but so, increasingly, did considerations of *Realpolitik*. Thucydides described the shifting alliances during the Peloponnesian War, which pattern grew only more pronounced in subsequent years when more leading actors appeared. Of course, poleis with outsized power in their own subregions perceived that alliances could serve for exploitation as well as for mutual defense and profit. Not for nothing did the Greeks coin the term "hegemon." *In so far as alliances and "empires" were partially institutionalized, with their own rules and decision-making councils, they constituted new political "regimes" or "layers" of authority for certain purposes "above" the polis; which, in turn, regularly impacted upon the polis itself.*

The second of the two centuries from the rise of the Spartan

Alliance circa 560 B.C. to the era of Macedonian intervention saw an intermittent military contest between Sparta and Athens broaden into system-wide instability. Argos, in the seventh century, was the first dominant power to appear. The Spartan Alliance ("the Lacedaemonians and their Allies") began as a sort of Holy Alliance in reverse, ostensibly aimed at Argos and other tyrannical regimes. Sparta arranged it so that pro-Spartan oligarchies came to power. Spartan intervention in 510 B.C. freed the Athenians from the Peisistratid tyranny and set the stage for Cleisthenes. *Thus one cannot understand the development of key poleis without appreciating the fact that their political evolution from the outset was inextricably linked with alliances.*

The Persians' approach precipitated the formation of a Hellenic League around the Spartan Alliance in 480 B.C. Some thirty-one poleis eventually joined, and the League won a narrow victory. Fine (1983: 329) suggests the Greeks were then "almost thinking in terms of a Greek nation." Martin Wight (1977: 59) nonetheless emphasizes that thirty-one "must have been a very small proportion" of all Greek poleis. In any event, unity rapidly dissolved after the victory, partly because some former allies perceived that Athens was attempting to build its own empire through the Delian League. (See especially Rhodes 1985; Hornblower and Greenstock 1984; and Doyle 1986: 54–81.)

Although the Delian League was supposed to seek revenge against the Persians, to gain compensatory booty, and possibly to free some city-states still under Persia, the allies of Athens soon found themselves exploited. Athens became dependent upon cash from allies to maintain its impressive fleet and fund the state pay extended by Pericles and his successors to many lower-class Athenians. In 454–453 B.C. the treasury of the League moved from Delos to Athens. N.G.L. Hammond (1986: 304) comments that the treasury "became a department of Athenian finance" and subsidized the building program at Athens. The number of tribute-paying states increased from 135 to between 155 and 173. Resident Athenians served as outposts of empire throughout the Aegean; and the use of Athenian coins, weights, and measures was obligatory. Athenian warships, in an ancient exercise of gunboat diplomacy, collected any arrears in payment of tribute. In 440 B.C. Athens brutally forced Samos into line regarding its legitimate conflict with Miletus. Then in 428, during the Peloponnesian War,

Mitylene's abortive attempt to leave the League precipitated an Athenian massacre of thousands. As events proved, only the defeat of Athens in the second part of the Peloponnesian War (421–404 B.C.) could end the Empire.

The half-century following the Peloponnesian War (404–354 B.C.), which Hammond (1986) terms "The Period of Transient Hegemonies," was an extremely complex and turbulent era. Adda Bozeman (1960: 69) observes: "During the eighty-five years that divided the Peloponnesian War from the conquest of Greece by Macedon, fifty-five considerable wars were waged by one Greek state against another . . . Every Greek city experienced at least one war, or one internal revolution, every ten years." The first two decades saw the consolidation of the Spartan empire – as autocratic (though not as durable) as the Athenian – with Persian support. Thereafter, Spartan influence declined and the proliferation of "new" major and minor actors was nothing less than astounding: the Boeotian League under Thebes, the Chalcidian League, a second Athenian Alliance, the Arcadian League, the Aetolian League, a League of the Western Locrians, the Thessalian League, and the Achaean League.

The earlier and "lower" political form of the ethnos now served as one model for interstate relations. As Snodgrass (1980: 43–4; see also Larsen 1968) points out, various federations of autonomous entities developed, each one of which might previously have been polis or ethnos, but which now accepted a central political and military authority. He remarks: "The success of this notion is shown by the fact that the Achaean League of the third century B.C. attracted no less than 60 cities into its orbit, including such distinguished former exponents of the polis idea as Argos, Corinth, Sikyon and Megara." Another example, the Chalcidian League, was founded early in the Peloponnesian War and expanded in the fourth century on the initiative of Olynthus. This city was a "simpolity," an ethnos grouping of settlements that formed a single political entity with a common Olynthian citizenship. The city was also an administrative center of a larger group comprising most of the cities in Chalcidice, with a common Chalcidician citizenship and federal government. The latter had "sovereign" powers in its own realm and controlled coinage, while the member cities of the League retained their own citizenships and control over local affairs.

The convulsive transient-hegemonies period in Greece ultimately ushered in the rule of Macedon and "relayering" of the system under

188

the conqueror's auspices. In 362 B.C., during a lull in the fighting, all mainland states except Sparta made a final unsuccessful attempt to revive an all-inclusive League of City-States, with an added collective security dimension. All parties pledged to remain at peace, to settle disputes by negotiation, and to defend one another against aggression. Nonetheless, internecine competition soon resumed.

Alliances were not the only significant interstate regimes with local impact. Others concerned general diplomacy, trade, war, shrines, and games.

Greek diplomacy offers us yet another striking example of continuity, in this instance from Dark Age chiefdoms. *Based in theory on city-state equality, diplomacy made extensive use of the Dark Age social institution of guest-friendship or xenia* (Herman 1987: 130–42). Relationships between communities were facilitated by *proxenia*, a hereditary vice-consulship; an aristocrat with ties to wealthy households in another state might act in his own state on behalf of the other state's citizens. This was a positive dimension of the ritual friendships that persisted after the foundation of the polis. Another institution, isopolity, involved more immediate family. This allowed a man settling in his wife's city to have effective citizenship rights there in matters such as property.

Treaties also guaranteed free trade or fair treatment for traders, heralds, envoys, priests, and/or sojourners. Other agreements concerned peaceful settlement, arms control, or warfare. Treaties of friendship and nonaggression involved arbitration or, more often (see Wight 1977: 52), conciliation. The third party might be a single individual like a tyrant, a board drawn from one or more city-states, or the Delphic oracle. Chalcis and Eretria banned the use of slings and arrows (probably poisoned); and members of the Delphic amphictiony undertook, while battling, not to cut off food, poison wells, or completely destroy one another (on the oath's dubious effectiveness, see Wight 1977: 50). What standards there were degenerated during the Peloponnesian War.

In another realm of functional integration and institutionalization beyond the polis, regional amphictionies arose in the Archaic period to secure the sacred and independent character of worship centers at Delphi, Argos, Delos, Triopium, and elsewhere. Temples were places of sanctuary, rarely violated, but Delphi and other leading shrines had additional functions. Delphi was more important than all the others

combined. The Delphic oracle (Pythia) was a woman over fifty who nine days a year, when the god consented, chewed laurel leaves and muttered incoherently in the Temple of Apollo. Petitioners made a generous gift, ritually sacrificed and purified themselves, and then were ushered in to the oracle. Priests "translated" her pronouncements into suitable verse. Any misinterpretation was the recipient's responsibility. The oracle could be ambiguous or flat wrong, usually (not always) favored the most powerful petitioner, "leaned to conservatism and had aristocratic sympathies" (Wight 1977: 49), and initially displayed an unpatriotic pro-Persian orientation.

Although the Delphic oracle sometimes failed to deliver value for offering and was not incorruptible, she was the principal source of legitimacy in Greece by the eighth century. Wight (1977: 48) terms the oracle "the nearest equivalent in Hellas to the papacy in Christendom." Delphi acquired its early reputation and fortune as the patron of colonization from the far west to Cyrene in Libya and to the Hellespont. Subsequently, many Greek colonies traced their founding directive, however insubstantially, to the oracle. Tyrants, too, sought Delphi's blessing, as later did the leading powers at virtually every critical stage of their political evolution. The *promanteia*, right of first consultation, was an important honor for the polis who received it (although it is not clear who had it when). Sparta attributed its dual kingship to Delphi, and each king was represented by two Spartans elected as "Pythii," who sought the oracle's advice and preserved responses (including the Great Rhetra). In Athens, Solon consulted the oracle prior to his reforms, and each archon and councillor vowed to dedicate a gold statue at Delphi were he to violate a decree of Solon's. In 511–510 B.C. Delphi advocated Sparta's attack on the Peisistratids in Athens, and the new tribal system of Cleisthenes also received Delphic approval.

The Greeks tried to ensure Delphi's inviolability and impartiality, even as they were tempted to subvert the oracle and appropriate Delphi's treasures. (Temples at Delphi and Olympia had the resources to offer loans, but some city-states wanted the bank.) In the seventh century a small amphictiony at Anthela was transferred to the sanctuary of Apollo at Delphi. The amphictiony then placed the sanctuary under its protection and proclaimed Delphi's independence from the neighboring state, Phocis. In principle, the amphictiony consisted of the twelve tribes of Greece rather than city-states. Some adjustment

occurred in actual voting; for example, Athens cast a vote for Ionian colonies and Sicyon had a second Doric vote alongside of Doris. No less than four Sacred Wars were fought over the status of Delphi. The First was in 601 B.C. when the Phocians of Kirrha and Krisa were charged with levying unreasonable fees on pilgrims en route to Delphi; the two towns were laid waste, and their territory was dedicated to Delphi, but Phocis was not permanently deterred. Delphi became a political football between Sparta and Athens and acted as an arbiter of peace treaties punctuating their wars. Philip of Macedon led the Fourth Sacred War in 339 B.C. and went on to conquer the remaining great powers, Thebes and Athens. *Delphi thus was present at the creation and demise of the independent city-state in Greece.*

As with Delphi, the Greeks attempted to preserve their leading games, which had religious and political overtones. Tyrants sponsored games to symbolize their regime, and Athens similarly launched regular Panathenaic festivals after Solon's reforms. Moreover, tyrants and aristocrats with the requisite courage, physical prowess, and wealth (for dedications and equipment like chariots) participated for personal prestige.

We know from a list of victors, our first actual record of interstate significance in Greece, that the Olympic Games were founded in 776 B.C. (see Finley and Pleket 1976). They remained the most important of four major events, including the Pythian Games at Delphi, games at Nemea honoring Zeus, and others at Corinth for Poseidon. The choice of Olympia was partly because it already had a major religious shrine, the Temple of Zeus, second only to Delphi's Temple of Apollo. The Olympic temple, too, received a steady stream of thank-offerings and served as a repository of treaties. Religious activities were prominent in the games themselves.

Finley and Pleket (1976: 23) point out that the selection of the agrarian backwater district of Elis for the Olympic Games was also partly for protection. Games held there would not contribute to the prestige of any powerful host city-state. In addition, during the festival of Olympian Zeus, the entire area was blanketed by a special truce forbidding the carrying of arms, and individual states across Greece allowed athletes safe-conduct to attend the games. Occasionally the truce or games were disrupted, but the record to Roman times is one of surprising stability.

191

CONCLUSIONS

Although city-states in Greece emerged over a relatively short time, our analysis emphasizes both continuity and variability in the chiefdom-to-state transition. Memories of a Heroic Age of states, preserved throughout Dark Age chiefdoms, supported city-state formation and interstate cooperation. The rise of states did not involve the immediate triumph of territorial community identities over those of kinship. The ethnos was less unified than the polis, extensive ritual friendship networks persisted among aristocrats, and tribal identities remained in interstate relations.

Factors apparently influencing the emergence of the city-state were the need for centers for cult worship, a population explosion, transition from pastoralism to agriculture, and the relative independence of Dark Age peasants. While acknowledging the importance of economic and physical power in elites' political strategies of control, stress here is upon the role of ideology: legacies from the past, the invention of the related ideas of the city-state community and citizenship, a reordering of gods and hero cults, and the evolution of new codes of behavior to replace those based on real or artificial kinship.

Even as the polis became the dominant (never exclusive) political identity, local political institutions continued to evolve in response to an increasingly complex society and "external" influences like warfare, trade, and interstate regimes. This essay attributes considerable importance to partially institutionalized peer-polity and center–periphery relations, and relations with non-Greeks.

A central conception is overlapping, layered, and linked authority patterns – the coexistence and interaction of many entities located at different points along the political evolution continuum. Interstate regimes impacted on the polis, and more "primitive" political forms influenced both the polis and interstate relations. The ethnos provided a model for alliances, while an institution reminiscent of Dark Age chiefdoms, guest-friendship, inspired the diplomatic institution of *proxenia*.

9
Contrasting patterns of
Mississippian development

VINCAS P. STEPONAITIS

The Mississippian societies that existed in southeastern North America between A.D. 800 and 1700 are typically described as centralized "chiefdoms" whose economies were based on intensive maize agriculture (e.g., Peebles and Kus 1977; Smith 1978, 1986; Steponaitis 1986a). Although such normative descriptions are adequate for some purposes, they tend to mask the tremendous differences in scale and centralization that existed among these polities. At one extreme were highly stratified, complex chiefdoms, whose political influence extended over large territories with populations numbering in the tens of thousands (e.g., Fowler 1978; Hudson et al. 1985). At the other extreme were smaller, less hierarchical polities; some of these may have been simple chiefdoms, and others – insofar as one can judge from the archaeological record – may not have been chiefdoms at all (e.g., Dickens 1976; Peebles 1987b).

To date, this diversity among Mississippian political forms has not been given sufficient attention as a topic of study in itself. The reasons for this have been many, but two in particular stand out. The first has been a strong tendency over the past fifteen years to portray the origins of Mississippian culture as a unitary phenomenon – a subset of the more general problem of the origins of chiefdoms – thereby focusing

attention on the commonalities, rather than the differences, among Mississippian groups. The second has been a strong, almost dogmatic, preference for explaining Mississippian developments in purely local terms. This emphasis on local process was an understandable reaction against previous explanations that stressed migrations and diffusion, but it had the unfortunate side effect of causing each region to be viewed as a bounded isolate, within which political processes ran their (adaptive) course unhindered by historical events elsewhere. Studies of chiefdoms in other parts of the world suggest that such a view is unrealistic (e.g., Flannery 1968; Frankenstein and Rowlands 1978; Helms 1979; Renfrew and Cherry 1984; Earle 1987a: 296–7; Kristiansen, Chapter 2). Local success in chiefly politics may depend, in no small measure, on access to external knowledge, commodities, and alliances, all of which can be greatly affected by events outside the region of interest. Such external forces may play a pivotal role in either constraining or encouraging political centralization, and must be taken into account if the differences among Mississippian polities and their historical trajectories are to be adequately understood.

My goal in this paper is to compare the Mississippian polities that developed in two different places: the Moundville region of Alabama and the Pocahontas region of Mississippi. Although the two regions are environmentally similar and are known to have been connected by trade relations in late prehistoric times, their political trajectories were markedly different. In the former, an intensely hierarchical polity appeared at ca. A.D. 1200 in which the entire region was unified under the hegemony of a large paramount center (Moundville). In the latter, no paramount center emerged and the polities remained fragmented and relatively simple. Understanding these differences requires that we look not only at local processes, but also at how these regions were articulated in broader networks of alliance and exchange.

THE MOUNDVILLE REGION:
A.D. 900–1650

The first region we shall consider is a 40-km-long segment of the Black Warrior River Valley centered on the site of Moundville in west-central Alabama. The valley, consisting of the active floodplain and adjacent terraces, varies between 5 and 10 km in width and is surrounded by gently rolling hills. During late prehistoric times, much of

the region was covered with hardwood forests (Scarry 1986). The terrace and upland plant communities were especially rich in edible nuts (such as acorn and hickory), while the bottomlands were a plentiful source of fruits, seeds, and tubers. Among the animals that could be hunted in the forests and fields were white-tailed deer, wild turkey, squirrel, racoon, and bear. The backswamps and oxbow lakes that dotted the river's floodplain were ideal habitats for fish, turtles, and waterfowl.

Not only did this region contain a bounty of wild foods, but also it provided an excellent setting for intensive maize agriculture. Arable soils on the river's floodplain and terraces were abundant and fertile; typical maize yields recorded in the early decades of this century (before mechanized farming and fertilizers were commonplace) ranged from 10 to 45 bushels per acre (Peebles 1978: 400–3). Periodic flooding replenished nutrients, making these soils virtually immune to degradation. Nor was farming especially risky: the growing season was comfortably long (averaging more than 200 days), the rainfall well timed and abundant (ca. 120 cm per year), and the water table high enough so that crops planted in floodplain soils were capable of surviving even the worst droughts. Rain shortages serious enough to cause major crop losses on the higher terrace soils were extremely rare events, occurring no more than once or twice a century (Scarry 1986: 119–30).

The Moundville site, after which the region is named, was by far the most important Mississippian settlement in the Black Warrior Valley. Situated on a terrace overlooking the river, the site is nowadays marked by twenty large pyramidal mounds. As is true of Mississippian mounds generally, these earthworks were built in stages and had flat summits that originally supported elite residences, mortuary temples, and other public buildings. Also present at Moundville are extensive midden deposits and archaeological traces of a bastioned palisade that once surrounded the site. All told, the archaeological remains cover more than 100 ha, making it one of the largest Mississippian sites ever built.

No doubt because of its impressive size, Moundville has attracted archaeological attention for well over a century (Steponaitis 1983b). Major excavations there took place from 1905 to 1906, and again from 1927 to 1941 (Moore 1905, 1907; Peebles 1979). These excavations yielded a tremendous corpus of archaeological material, including field records and artifacts from more than 3,000 burials, seventy-five

houses, and countless other proveniences (Peebles et al. 1981). Analyses of this material undertaken over the past twenty years have provided the basis for much of our current understanding of Moundville's society and economy (Peebles 1974; Peebles and Kus 1977; Peebles and Schoeninger 1981; Powell 1988; Welch 1986; Hardin 1981; van der Leeuw 1981; Steponaitis 1983a). Since 1978, additional smaller-scale excavations have produced valuable data on subsistence, craft production, and chronology (Michals 1981; Scarry 1986; Welch 1986; Steponaitis 1983a).

Considerable knowledge has been gained on other late prehistoric sites in the region as well. Surveys of varying intensity have been carried out since the turn of the century (Moore 1905; Nielsen, O'Hear, and Moorehead 1973; Walthall and Coblentz 1977; Peebles 1978; Bozeman 1982; Alexander 1982). A number of outlying sites have also been excavated (DeJarnette and Peebles 1970; Curren 1984; Welch 1986; Mistovich 1987, 1988). It can safely be said that the surveys have located most, if not all, of the Mississippian mound sites, as well as a sample of villages and farmsteads. As a result, we can now draw reasonable inferences concerning the spatial distribution of mound centers and the range of settlement types occupied during any given phase. But it must also be stressed that none of the surveys has been systematic or comprehensive enough to track demographic trends through time; in other words, we still lack data with which to compute reliable estimates of regional population, in either absolute or relative terms.

The late prehistoric chronology consists of five phases, all but the last of which can be subdivided into early and late subphases based on ceramic style (Jenkins and Nielsen 1974; O'Hear 1975; Steponaitis 1983a, 1986b; Curren 1984). From oldest to youngest, the phases and their approximate dates are as follows: West Jefferson, A.D. 900–1050; Moundville I, A.D. 1050–1250; Moundville II, A.D. 1250–1400; Moundville III, A.D. 1400–1550; and Moundville IV (formerly called Alabama River), A.D. 1550–1650. These phases constitute the framework within which the late prehistory of the Moundville region can now be sketched. Trends in settlement and political organization are presented first, followed by the evidence for changes in agriculture, craft production, warfare, and long-distance exchange.

196

Settlement, society, and mortuary ritual

Settlements of the West Jefferson phase sites were distributed throughout the Moundville region and varied considerably in size. The typical village covered 0.2–0.5 ha and may have been inhabited by 50–100 people (Welch 1985). In some parts of the valley, several such villages were spaced closely enough together to form large, almost continuous sherd scatters up to several hectares in extent; whether these large sites represent equally large aggregations of people or simply multiple reoccupations of favored locales is difficult to say (cf. Peebles 1987b: 5–6). Also present were small settlements marked by sherd scatters only 10–30 m in diameter. When excavated, they are typically found to contain one or two small, circular houses and some associated features (Jenkins and Nielsen 1974; Mistovich 1987). Although their role in the settlement system is still far from clear, these small sites may well have been seasonal occupations (O'Hear 1975; Scarry 1986; Welch 1981, 1985).

The evidence for political differentiation among West Jefferson communities is nil. None of the sites exhibit mounds, and none are known to contain elaborate burials. Of course, the latter statement must be tempered by the observation that only a handful of West Jefferson burials have ever been found. The best glimpse of contemporary mortuary patterns comes from the Tombigbee Valley, 50 km to the west, where a number of cemeteries have been excavated. Burials in these cemeteries were typically arranged in loose clusters of ten to twenty individuals, suggestive of kin groups or factions. Differentiation among burials was generally not great; most burials contained no grave goods, and the few that did usually contained shell beads, which in most cases had been sewn onto garments (Welch 1985). The overall situation seems to have been one of autonomous villages and a relatively egalitarian society.

During the Moundville I phase, beginning at ca. A.D. 1050, the social landscape changed dramatically. Single pyramidal mounds were constructed at four of the former villages; these mounds were topped by structures, almost certainly elite residences. None of the mounds was initially very big, but they grew over time as stages of fill were added. The mound at 1Tu50, for example, eventually reached a height of 3 m (Steponaitis 1986b). At least some of these mounds had cemeteries nearby, in which the more elaborate burials were accompanied not

197

only by shell beads, but also by artifacts of copper and other nonlocal materials (Peebles 1983: 188–9, 1987a: 27–9; Steponaitis 1983a). At about the same time these mounds were built, the bulk of the population in the valley abandoned the nucleated villages and began living in dispersed farmsteads. Presumably, each of the mound sites served as the political, economic, and ritual focus for the populace in the surrounding district.

So far as we know, the four local centers that existed early in the Moundville I phase were roughly equivalent in terms of the size and number of their earthworks. The civic-ceremonial center at Moundville, however, differed significantly from the others, in that it had an unusually high number of people living in its immediate vicinity. Recent analyses of sherd collections indicates that most midden deposition at Moundville occurred during the Moundville I phase (Steponaitis 1986b). Although the full extent and distribution of these middens is still unclear (and will remain so until more detailed studies of the pre-1941 excavations are undertaken), they seem to occur in many discrete patches scattered across the terrace on which the site is located, suggesting that an unusually high density of dispersed farmsteads once dotted this area. Based on the surveys that have been done to date, no other district appears to have had as high a concentration of Moundville I phase settlement. It should be stressed that Moundville had no special advantage over the other centers in the fertility or abundance of nearby soils (cf. Peebles 1978: 400–10). Thus, the causes of this centripetal tendency must have been social and political, rather than purely environmental.

Late in the Moundville I phase, at about A.D. 1200–1250, a second major transformation occurred, as Moundville grew to become the dominant political center in the region. What had formerly been a dense residential zone surrounding a small local center was now turned into an enormous civic-ceremonial precinct. The large, rectangular space was laid out, and mound construction commenced along its edges. During the Moundville II phase (A.D. 1250–1400) early stages of at least five mounds, and probably no fewer than ten, were already in use. During the Moundville III phase (A.D. 1400–1550) construction continued until all twenty mounds reached their final form.

Given the regularity of the site's plan, there can be no doubt that the positioning of the mounds had social and religious meaning (Fig. 9.1).

198

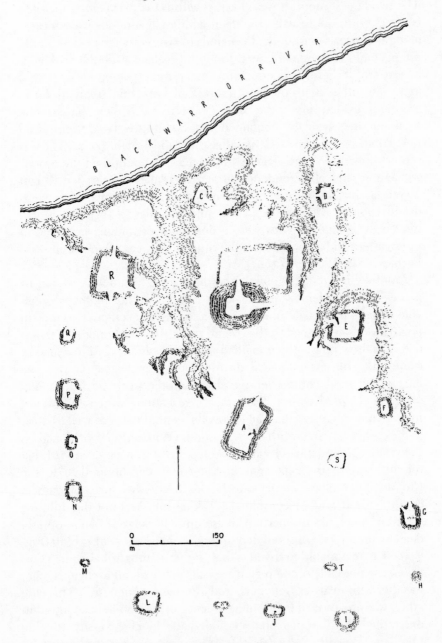

Fig. 9.1   The Moundville site (after Moore 1905)

The two largest mounds were located within the plaza along the site's central, north–south axis. Eighteen additional mounds were located along the plaza's periphery. Two kinds of symmetry are evident in the arrangement of these peripheral mounds (Peebles 1971: 82–3). One is a clear-cut, if slightly imperfect, bilateral symmetry around the central axis. The other is a consistent pairing of large and small mounds, especially evident along the plaza's eastern and western flanks. The small mounds typically contain burials, while the large mounds do not. Based on ethnohistoric parallels, Vernon Knight (personal communication, 1988) has suggested that each pair comprised the mortuary temple and elite residence of a particular clan (also see Knight 1989). He has further suggested that the bilateral symmetry represents the division of Moundville's clans into moieties, a highly plausible model given that moieties were a dominant organizing principle in southeastern Indian societies at the time of European contact (also see Peebles 1983: 190, 1987a: 27).

Moundville's resident population during the Moundville II and III phases was considerably smaller than it had been during the Moundville I phase, prior to its emergence as a paramount center. This drop in population is evidenced by the overall paucity of sheet midden deposits dating to these phases (Steponaitis 1986b) and can best be illustrated by examining the chronological distribution of excavated sherds. The largest and most comprehensive sherd sample ($n = 95,742$) comes from the Depression-era "Roadway" excavation, which followed a long, sinuous transect that cut across the central plaza as well as areas to the east, west, and south of the mounds (Wimberly 1956). Based on the relative abundance of diagnostic types, it has been estimated that roughly seventy-three percent of the recovered sherds date to the Moundville I phase alone; only about twenty-five percent date to Moundville II and III combined.[1] Taking into account the differing spans of the phases in question, these numbers suggest that a fourfold decrease in the rate of sherd deposition occurred after A.D. 1250 (Fig. 9.2). It is reasonable to assume that the remaining inhabitants comprised the pinnacle of the region's social, political, and religious elite, together with relatives, retainers, and assorted functionaries. This elite group was provisioned by tribute, evidence of which has been found in differential distributions of deer body-parts in elite versus nonelite middens (Welch 1986: 74–100). The elite were also capable of

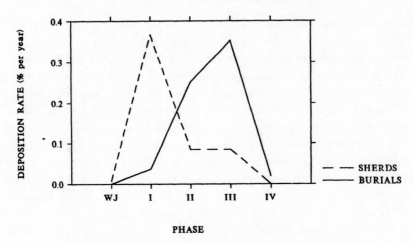

PHASE

Fig. 9.2 The deposition rates of sherds and burials at Moundville. These rates were calculated as the percentage of items assigned to a given phase, divided by the length of the phase in years. The burial percentages are based on Table 9.1. The sherd percentages are based on the published counts from the Roadway excavation, partitioned into phases using the method of Kohler and Blinman (1987; see note 1). Key to phase abbreviations: WJ, West Jefferson; I, Moundville I; II, Moundville II; III, Moundville III; IV, Moundville IV

mobilizing considerable labor, as best indicated by the massive public architecture at Moundville itself.

While Moundville's resident population grew smaller, its *burial* population grew larger (Fig. 9.2). Of the graves that can be securely assigned to a single phase, only eight percent date to Moundville I, and ninety-two percent date to Moundville II and III. These figures strongly suggest that most of the people buried at the paramount center after A.D. 1250 did not actually live there. Clearly, Moundville was not only the political capital, but also an important center of ritual for the region as a whole.

Analysis of the Moundville burials suggests that social differentiation during the Moundville II and III phases was pronounced. Approximately five percent of the burials fall into a group that Peebles has called the "superordinate" segment. These burials were generally interred in or near mounds, and were accompanied by elaborate arti-

201

facts that served as symbols of high rank or political office (Peebles 1974, 1986: 28; Peebles and Kus 1977). Status-related distinctions were evident not only in mortuary ritual, but also in diet and health. Trace elements in human bone indicate that elite males may have consumed more meat than commoners (Peebles and Schoeninger 1981). Although the health (insofar as one can determine from skeletal evidence) of the population in general was quite good, elites showed the lowest incidence of iron-deficiency anemia (Powell 1988: 148). The likelihood of traumatic injury also differed according to social class. Elite males had proportionally fewer broken, cut, and pierced bones than nonelite males, while elite females showed no traces of such injuries at all (Powell 1988: 144–5).

Even while Moundville was at its peak, a number of single-mound centers continued to be occupied. These were presumably used by local chiefs who, though subordinate to the paramount at Moundville, continued to have jurisdiction over their immediate districts. As before, most of the region's inhabitants continued to live in dispersed farmsteads.

Some time after A.D. 1500, the chiefly superstructure that had existed for the previous three centuries began to come apart (Peebles 1986). Initial signs of this crisis were subtle, but unmistakeable in the archaeological record:

- (a) a progressive diminution, during late Moundville III, in the number of burials interred at Moundville, together with the appearance of cemeteries at outlying centers (such as 1Ha7 and 1Tu2; see DeJarnette and Peebles 1970; Welch 1986);
- (b) a burst of late mound construction at these same outlying centers, the largest earthworks being built at the centers farthest away from Moundville (Bozeman 1982; Steponaitis 1978); and
- (c) the reappearance, in late Moundville III, of nucleated villages (Bozeman 1982: 307), presumably for reasons of defense.

Whatever its causes, the dissolution was rapid. By the beginning of the Moundville IV phase in the mid-sixteenth century, Moundville and all the remaining single-mound centers had fallen out of use. The valley's population aggregated in large villages, 1–2 ha in extent (Sheldon 1974; Curren 1984). All evidence of social ranking disap-

peared from burials. Health, too, deteriorated significantly; a severe form of iron-deficiency anemia afflicted twenty-four percent of the burials at one Moundville IV village, and sixty-two percent at another (Powell, 1988: 191). By the mid-seventeenth century, the Black Warrior Valley had become part of a buffer zone between major political alliances to the east (Creek) and to the west (Choctaw), and the region was largely abandoned (Knight 1982).

In sum, the late prehistoric sequence in the Moundville region was marked by several major transformations in political organization. Beginning with relatively egalitarian, autonomous villages at A.D. 900, the region saw the development of small-scale, local centers at about A.D. 1050, followed by the emergence of a paramount center at about A.D. 1200. In the sixteenth century, the chiefly organization collapsed, and the societies in the region once again reverted to a more egalitarian form. Let us now examine some important processes that played a critical role in these developments, beginning with the intensification of food production.

Food production

At the start of the West Jefferson phase, ca. A.D. 900, the region's inhabitants relied for their subsistence on a mixture of hunting, fishing, gathering, and gardening. White-tailed deer was the major source of meat, supplemented by a variety of small mammals, birds, turtles, and fish (Michals 1987). The staple plant foods were nuts – mostly hickory and acorn – that could be gathered in nearby forests. Also eaten were wild fruits (e.g., persimmon, grape, sumac, cherry/plum) and seeds from a variety of starchy-seeded plants (e.g., maygrass, chenopod, knotweed) that were probably cultivated. Maize, a definite cultigen, was present, but only in small amounts (Scarry 1986). Early West Jefferson peoples clearly practiced gardening, but used it only as a minor element in a diversified economy that was based largely on wild foods.

Subsequent centuries saw dramatic changes in the economy as small-scale gardening gave way to intensive agriculture. The process of intensification was remarkably rapid and focused predominantly on maize. Although the percentages of species in paleobotanical assemblages cannot be taken as direct measures of dietary importance, the trend in the archaeological record is clear: the abundance of maize (by

weight) among plant-food remains grew from less than one percent in the early West Jefferson phase, to more than fifty percent in the Moundville I phase (Scarry 1981). Scarry's (1986) exhaustive study of plant remains from finely dated contexts has shown that the intensification of maize production was well underway by late West Jefferson times, and had leveled off by late Moundville I; in other words, the shift from small-scale gardening to intensive farming took place over a span of less than 200 years, perhaps even less than a century. The same trend in maize production, with virtually identical timing, has been documented in the nearby Tombigbee Valley as well (Caddell 1981, 1983).

Studies of wood charcoal suggest that forest clearance progressed in the immediate vicinity of the Moundville site throughout the Moundville I phase, as more and more fields were brought into production (Scarry 1986: 247). Since importance of maize – and presumably the intensity of agriculture – had already increased substantially prior to this time, the additional clearance may well be due to localized population growth (which is known to have occurred at Moundville) or shifting-field cultivation, rather than a further intensification of farming.

Whatever the case, once the fields were cleared and the new economic regime was established, farmers continually manipulated their crops to increase harvests. Two distinct varieties of maize were grown during each phase, yet the phenotypic diversity of cobs steadily decreased through time (Scarry 1986: 360–407). According to Scarry (1986: 405),

both effects could be produced by careful seed selection and diligent field maintenance. Within a cultivar, desirable characteristics can be encouraged and genetic variability can be reduced by saving ears that meet specific standards for seed. Also within a cultivar, phenotypic diversity can be reduced by weeding and other field activities that decrease stress on the growing plants. At the same time, separate cultivars can be maintained by planting the seed for each type in well separated fields so that cross pollination is minimized. Such crop strategies are labor intensive and are generally practiced when maize is produced for high yields.

In short, a dramatic intensification of maize production occurred at about A.D. 1000, just prior to the first obvious signs of political centralization in the region. As time went on and political complexity increased, farmers consistently pushed, or perhaps *were* pushed, to produce even more food from their fields.

Craft production

Let us now turn to the production of socially valued craft items, the so-called "prestige goods," "primitive valuables," or "wealth objects," that invariably play a role in chiefly politics. Such items were generally made of nonlocal or unusual raw materials, and archaeological evidence of their production may consist of

(a) items broken in the process of manufacture,
(b) caches or discarded scraps of raw material, or
(c) specialized tools that can be identified as having been used to make a certain product.

Owing to the vicissitudes of preservation and sampling, such evidence is often difficult to find, and, even when found, its significance often goes unrecognized. Fortunately, in the present instance, production locales have been identified for a number of different craft items, including shell beads, nonlocal-chert bifaces, greenstone celts, mica ornaments, and red-slate gorgets. Although the evidence is uneven, it suggests that craft production changed through time.

West Jefferson phase assemblages typically contain numerous "microdrills" or bit-tools made on small blades or flakes. Wear-pattern studies (Pope 1989) have demonstrated that the vast majority of these tools were used to drill shell beads; a lesser number were used to perforate hide, quite possibly garments onto which these beads were sewn. Such tools are ubiquitous on West Jefferson sites, suggesting that the manufacture of beads and beaded garments was a widespread household activity at this time. The virtual disappearance of these tools in later contexts may indicate either that local bead production declined, or that it became less widespread and therefore less visible in the archaeological record. Whatever the case, it is interesting to note that the tenth and eleventh centuries A.D. represent a peak in the evidence for bead-making not only in the Moundville region, but across much of the southeast as well (Steponaitis 1986a: 392).

The clearest indications of craft production during the Moundville I phase come from local centers, rather than domestic sites. At Moundville, excavations in an elite residential zone yielded an assemblage in which seventy-five percent of the debitage consisted of nonlocal materials, principally Ft. Payne and Bangor cherts (Scarry 1986: 138–74; Welch 1986: 146–71). Significantly, the nature of the non-

local debitage implies that biface manufacture, not just resharpening, took place there. The same midden also contained numerous fragments of greenstone, together with some scraps of mica, copper, and graphite; greenstone was commonly made into celts, mica and copper were used in elite regalia, and graphite was probably employed as a pigment. This unusual concentration of nonlocal materials, some of which may have been manufacturing debris, prompted the excavator to suggest that at least some of Moundville's early residents were "part-time craft specialists" (Scarry 1986: 155).

Relatively few contexts dating to the Moundville II and III phases have been excavated or properly analyzed with questions of craft production in mind. The only detailed information comes from 1Ha7, a local center that dates to the Moundville III phase, at which no direct evidence for production of socially valued artifacts was found, despite a concerted search (Welch 1986). The only known traces of craft activity during these later phases come from Moundville itself, which at this time was the paramount center. These include

(a) a red-slate gorget broken in the process of manufacture (Steponaitis 1983b) and
(b) a cache pit filled with raw mica sheets (Scarry 1986: 163–8).

The dating of these traces is highly uncertain, and the present assignment can only be regarded as a best guess. While the information available for the Moundville II and III phases may be sparse, data pertaining to craft activities during the Moundville IV phase are completely nonexistent.

All in all, present data suggest that the range of sites within which craft activity occurred became ever more restricted with time. From A.D. 900 to roughly A.D. 1050, just prior to the appearance of the first mound sites, the manufacture of shell beads and beaded garments was carried on in virtually every village in the region. From A.D. 1050 to 1250, bead manufacture seemingly declined, and the crafting of artifacts from nonlocal materials – predominantly stone tools and items of regalia – largely occurred at local centers. After A.D. 1250, such craft activity seems to have been restricted primarily to the paramount center (Welch 1986). So far as we know, this pattern persisted until the paramount center declined in the sixteenth century, after which there is simply no information on which to base any inferences.

Warfare

The intensity of warfare in the region at any given time was best reflected by the dominant pattern of settlement. As I have argued elsewhere (Steponaitis 1983a: 172), dispersed settlements could exist only in times of relative peace, or in a situation where hostilities could be reliably anticipated, thereby giving people a chance to retreat to safer surroundings; nucleated settlements, on the other hand, were a response to warfare that was relatively intense or unpredictable. By this measure, the threat of conflict was high during the West Jefferson phase, lessened from Moundville I through early Moundville III, then rose again in late Moundville III and Moundville IV.

Of course, warfare was never totally absent, even in the middle part of the sequence, since weapons and war trophies were prominently depicted in the iconography of chiefship, and Moundville itself was surrounded by a palisade for at least part of that time. But, at the very least, the existence of political centralization seems to have made warfare more controlled, more predictable. This probably stemmed from the ability of chiefs to forge alliances, to adjudicate disputes, and to "rein in" those who would perpetrate unwanted violence against neighboring polities. It also may have stemmed from a fundamental change in the way warfare was waged. Two types of warfare were documented in the southeast by the earliest European explorers (DePratter 1983: 44–67). One was a kind of low-level, "guerrilla" warfare carried on by small raiding parties that would ambush an enemy, kill or capture a few people, then flee. This was the dominant mode of fighting in areas where political centralization was absent, and was often motivated by blood-feuds or other disputes among localized kin groups. The second kind of warfare involved scores and sometimes hundreds of warriors who marched in formation and fought pitched battles under the direct control of a chief. This larger-scale, organized warfare was only waged by centralized polities, and was invariably geared toward political ends, such as the enforcement of tribute demands or the elimination of threats to chiefly power (e.g., Hudson 1988). There can be no doubt that both kinds of warfare occurred prehistorically as well, but, as in historic times, which kind was dominant probably depended on political circumstances. In the Moundville region, I suspect that small-scale raiding took place throughout the sequence, but that large-scale, politically motivated

warfare was confined only to the phases from Moundville I to Moundville III.

It is interesting to note that, in the neighboring Tombigbee Valley, the frequency of skeletal injuries due to human violence was unusually high around A.D. 900–1000, and declined immediately thereafter (Cole, Hill, and Ensor 1982; Welch 1985). Up to thirteen percent of the people in cemeteries contemporary with the early West Jefferson phase showed signs of imbedded projectile points, "parry" fractures, and the like. Only five percent of the population in cemeteries contemporary with Moundville I had similar injuries. At Moundville itself, where most of the burials date to Moundville II and III, less than four percent showed signs of such traumas (Powell 1988: 144–6). Thus, the skeletal evidence from Moundville and surrounding regions is consistent with the interpretation based on settlement patterns, that intercommunity violence peaked in the centuries just prior to the emergence of political centralization.

Long-distance exchange

Patterns of long-distance exchange in the region can best be examined by monitoring the abundance of nonlocal goods in burials. Such goods often took the form of regalia, ornaments, pigments, and "ceremonial" implements, that is, items whose value was principally social and symbolic. While it is not always known where these items were manufactured, the raw materials came from distant sources: marine shell from the Gulf of Mexico; native copper from the Appalachians and Great Lakes (Goad 1978); greenstone, mica, diorite, and other rocks from the "crystalline province" of eastern Alabama (Jones 1939); and galena from Missouri and Wisconsin (Walthall 1981). These sources range from 150 km to well over 1,500 km away.

Nonlocal pottery was also present in the region and often was included in burials. Vessels can be identified on stylistic grounds to have originated in places as far south as the Gulf Coast, as far west as Texas, and as far north as Kentucky (Steponaitis 1983a). Interestingly, almost no pottery entered the region from the east, suggesting that political or household alliances generally did not extend in that direction (Peebles 1987a: 33).[2]

As noted previously, the best information on burials contemporary with the West Jefferson phase comes from the neighboring Tombigbee

Valley. There, the only nonlocal materials that occurred in graves at this time were marine shell and greenstone. The abundance of both materials was relatively small, but seems to have increased significantly between A.D. 900 and 1050 (Welch 1985). For example, the proportion of shell beads made from marine species jumped from only six percent in cemeteries at the early end of this range, to fifty-eight percent in cemeteries at the later end. Similarly, greenstone celts occurred only in the later cemeteries, despite the fact that the number of burials in early and late cemeteries was almost identical.

The incidence of nonlocal materials after A.D. 1050 can best be illustrated with burial data from Moundville itself (Table 9.1; Fig. 9.3). During the Moundville I phase, the intensity of long-distance exchange continued to increase. Marine shell now comprised virtually all the beads found in burials, greenstone celts continued to be present, and a variety of new exotic materials appeared, such as copper, mica, and galena. The total frequency of trade materials peaked around the Moundville I–II transition, then dropped somewhat; in Moundville III, the abundance of most materials was about the same as it had been during Moundville I. By the onset of Moundville IV, exotics had virtually disappeared; none occurred in the small sample burials at Moundville, and only a very few marine shell and greenstone objects have been found in more than a hundred burials excavated at other sites (Sheldon 1974; Curren 1984).

It is interesting to note that nonlocal pottery reached its maximum frequency during Moundville I times, slightly earlier than the other nonlocal categories (Fig. 9.3). This may indicate that nonlocal vessels (or the long-distance contacts they reflected) had greater social value early in the sequence than later, when copper, shell, and other materials became more exclusive tokens of wealth and prestige.

All in all, the observed fluctuations in long-distance exchange correlate strongly with the political developments described previously. Several points bear emphasis in this regard: first, a sudden jump in the importation of marine shell beads and greenstone seems to have occurred at about A.D. 1000, just prior to the construction of the first single-mound centers. Second, foreign materials continued to increase until about A.D. 1200, when Moundville became the paramount center. Third, the century or so immediately following Moundville's emergence to regional dominance saw exotics reach their maximum frequencies in burials. And fourth, a drastic curtailment in

Table 9.1. *Chronological distribution of nonlocal artifacts in dated burials at Moundville*[a]

				Phase[b]			
	I	I/II	II	II/III	III	III/IV	IV
Copper:							
Copper earspool	0	5	7	10	5	0	0
Copper gorget/pendant	1	0	2	4	3	0	0
Copper cutouts[c]	0	1	1	1	0	0	0
Copper ornament (misc.)	0	3	5	4	4	0	0
Copper axe	0	0	1	0	1	0	0
Copper fish hook	0	3	0	0	0	0	0
Total	1	12	16	19	13	0	0
Shell:							
Shell ear plug	0	0	0	1	4	0	0
Shell gorget/pendant	0	2	3	6	3	0	0
Shell beads[c]	2	3	4	23	13	0	0
Shell ornament (misc.)	0	4	1	7	4	0	0
Shell cup	0	0	1	0	0	0	0
Total	2	9	9	37	24	0	0

Other nonlocal stone:							
Metamorphic rock celt	1	1	2	7	4	0	0
Greenstone, worked	0	4	0	0	0	0	0
Mica ornament	0	0	0	2	1	0	0
Limestone effigy pipe	0	0	0	0	1	0	0
Diorite effigy bowl	0	0	0	0	1	0	0
Galena mass	0	1	1	1	3	0	0
Total	1	6	3	10	10	0	0
Total (excluding pottery)	4	27	28	66	47	0	0
Nonlocal pottery vessels	3	5	4	26	10	0	0
Dated burials	17	41	59	222	149	15	2

[a] This table includes data from all burials that can be dated to a span of one or two phases by direct association with diagnostic ceramics; individuals within multiple interments are counted separately. The present figures differ from those presented earlier by Peebles (1987a: Table 2.1) because they are based on a larger sample of burials, including many that could not be dated at the time of Peebles's analysis.

[b] Key: I, Moundville I; I/II, Moundville I or II; II, Moundville II; II/III, Moundville II or III; III, Moundville III; III/IV, Moundville III or IV; IV, Moundville IV (formerly Alabama River).

[c] Multiple items found with the same burial are regarded as a set and counted as a single occurrence.

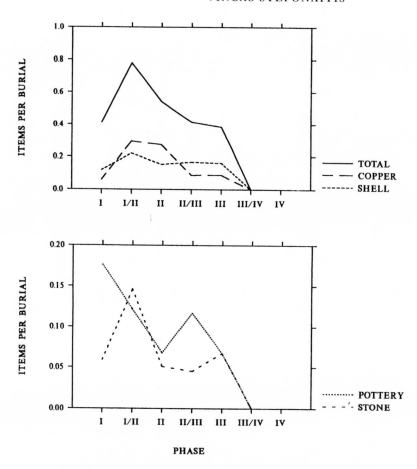

Fig. 9.3 The relative abundance of exotics in Moundville burials. The vertical axis represents the ratio between the number of exotic items and the number of burials that date to each phase, based on Table 9.1. Key to phase abbreviations: I, Moundville I; I/II, Moundville I or II; II, Moundville II; II/III, Moundville II or III; III, Moundville III; III/IV, Moundville III or IV; IV, Moundville IV

long-distance exchange after A.D. 1500 coincided with the region-wide collapse of political centralization. As we shall see, there are good reasons to believe that these correlations were not simply fortuitous, but rather stemmed from the important role that nonlocal goods played in creating and maintaining hierarchical relations.

Discussion

Now that the various lines of evidence have been set out, it remains to draw them together into a historical model that accounts for some of the changes observed. Previous explanations for the appearance of chiefdoms in this region have stressed the functional advantages of political centralization, especially in mitigating the risk of crop failure (e.g., Peebles and Kus 1977; Steponaitis 1983a). Such reasoning, however, has been effectively undermined by Scarry (1986), who has demonstrated that the risk of large-scale crop failure – the kind that might require chiefly intervention – was virtually nil. This case simply highlights the broader realization that managerial and functional explanations of chiefship are generally inadequate, since they take no account of the actual mechanisms by which chiefship was established and maintained (Earle 1987a). Constructing more plausible explanations requires that we focus not on the benefits of chiefship, but rather on the political strategies of emergent elites and the material conditions that helped those strategies to succeed.

The West Jefferson phase appears to have been a time of considerable conflict and competition. Although communities were still basically egalitarian, kin groups and individual leaders vied among themselves for power and prestige. In this context, households throughout the region were led to intensify production. Local manufacture of craft items such as beads and beaded garments greatly increased. I have argued elsewhere that

beads, beaded garments, and other valued craft items probably served as tokens in social transactions. Displayed as possessions, these tokens enhanced personal prestige; presented as gifts, they could be used to build alliances and inflict social debts. Exchanges of such items, especially among budding elites, were instruments of political strategy as much as, if not more than, purely economic activities. (STEPONAITIS 1986a: 392)

Equally important was the sudden shift to maize agriculture that began during this phase. Whether this shift was precipitated by population growth or political demands is difficult to say; some evidence exists for both (cf. Steponaitis 1986a: 389; Scarry 1986: 415–22). Either way, the consequences of this change were profound. The hunting, gathering, and gardening economy of early West Jefferson times probably placed severe constraints on the amount of surplus that could be deployed for political ends.[3] As more fields were cleared and planted in

213

maize, however, these constraints were lifted and a new range of political developments became possible.

The prestige-building transactions fueled by this intensified production were ultimately successful. Around the beginning of the Moundville I phase, social differentiation reached a point at which the elite symbolically split themselves off from the commoners by placing their residences atop mounds. There can be little doubt that Mississippian platform mounds were sacred structures; although the full nexus of meanings originally associated with these earthworks will never be known, linguistic evidence suggests that they were in part metaphors for the earth (Knight 1981). Prototypes of such mounds had been used during the first millennium A.D. across the southeast to delimit sacred areas used in funerary rituals (Steponaitis 1986a: 386). By placing their residences on top of such mounds, elites effectively appropriated this symbol and used it to legitimize their new-found authority. Other ideological manipulations, nowadays invisible, undoubtedly took place as well.

Per capita maize production continued to increase early in the Moundville I phase, but soon reached a plateau. The major economic changes during this phase were in the realm of craft production and exchange, and again seem to have been motivated by political concerns. The manufacture of socially valued, durable goods became ever more restricted to local mound centers, and presumably came more under the control of local chiefs. Indeed, at least some of this craft production took place in the elite households themselves. At the same time, elites expanded their participation in networks of long-distance exchange. The exotic items thereby obtained – copper, marine shell, galena, and the like – were used to further enhance the power and influence of local chiefs. On one hand, differential access to these valued materials served to demonstrate the efficacy of the elite and to mark their special status. On the other, limited redistribution of such items could be used to secure the loyalty of allies and to increase the size of dependent factions. As Peebles (1986, 1987a, 1987b) and Welch (1986) have both cogently argued, by the end of the Moundville I phase, local politics had clearly acquired the characteristics of a "prestige goods economy" (sensu Frankenstein and Rowlands 1978), in which "possession and manipulation of the exotic, the rare, and the valuable served to legitimize the role of the elite and their place in the social order" (Peebles 1987b: 15). The latter set of strategies resulted in

214

further centralization and culminated in the establishment of a paramount center at Moundville.

Of course, none of these political strategies would have succeeded had not certain material conditions been present. Intensification of farming was greatly facilitated by the abundance of fertile land and the ideal climate for growing maize. Similarly, participation in long-distance exchange was made possible by the availability of local surpluses and proximity to trade routes. Yet perhaps the most important factor in all of these strategies was access to labor (Lightfoot 1984; Drennan 1987; Feinman and Nicholas 1987a; Earle, Chapter 4 above). Such access usually entailed maintaining a certain "critical mass" of people close to where the labor was needed. It is not surprising, therefore, that the Moundville I centers all arose in localities that had previously supported dense, West Jefferson phase villages; or that the Moundville II–III paramount center was built on the terrace that had supported the greatest known concentration of Moundville I occupations. The intensity of warfare in West Jefferson times produced a kind of social circumscription (Carneiro 1981) that favored nucleated settlements and limited emigration; such circumscription would have made access to labor relatively easy, even in the absence of political centralization. By Moundville I times, however, warfare had decreased to the point where settlements were mostly small and dispersed. Thus, the concentration of people around the local center at Moundville was probably the result of a conscious attempt by the elites to counteract this centrifugal tendency. One can only guess at how this concentration was achieved, but access to ritual or to nonlocal goods may well have been important incentives (Feinman, Chapter 10 below).

Once it was achieved, the region-wide centralization at Moundville lasted about 300 years; sometime during the first half of the sixteenth century, the Moundville chiefdom collapsed. There are currently two schools of thought concerning why this collapse occurred. Some argue it was brought about, directly or indirectly, by the coming of the Europeans (Curren 1984; Hudson, Smith, and DePratter 1987). These scenarios emphasize the depopulations that were caused by European diseases, which sometimes spread ahead of the Europeans themselves, as well as the cultural and political disruption caused by European presence. Others argue that the collapse was the result of indigenous processes, such as the inability of local farmers to sustain the requisite levels of surplus production, or the severing of long-

distance exchange relationships on which the maintenance of inequality depended (Peebles 1983, 1986, 1987a, 1987b). While we still lack the evidence with which to decide conclusively among these models, it is worth noting that Moundville's decline seems to have begun in the late Moundville III phase, prior to the earliest European incursions in the region. It is also worth noting that when the first Spaniards did arrive, in 1541, they made no specific mention of a large paramount center in the region, suggesting that Moundville had already diminished in importance or been abandoned (cf. Hudson, Smith, and DePratter 1987). Hence, if the Europeans had any effect at all, it may only have been to hasten a process of political fragmentation that was already well underway.

THE POCAHONTAS REGION:
A.D. 1000–1500

The Pocahontas region, named after its largest mound site, is located in the state of Mississippi, about 260 km west of Moundville. The region comprises the area in which the drainage of the Big Black River cross-cuts a physiographic zone called the Jackson Prairie. This portion of the drainage (between the modern towns of Edwards and Canton) is about 60 km long and 35–40 km wide. The river and its larger tributaries are flanked by broad floodplains and terraces, which in turn are surrounded by gently rolling uplands. In late prehistoric times, the region was dominated by hardwood (oak-hickory) forests interspersed with scattered patches of prairie vegetation (Lowe 1919: 219, 238–40). The range and abundance of wild foods would have been virtually identical to those present in the Moundville region. Equally rich was the Pocahontas region's agricultural potential. Early in the twentieth century, it was widely noted that "some of the most desirable lands in the State occur in this area" (Lowe 1919: 241). In terms of soil abundance, fertility, growing season, and rainfall, the conditions for growing maize were essentially the same as, and perhaps even marginally better than, those found at Moundville (see Lowe 1919: 217, 241ff.; Kocher and Goodman 1918; Tharp, Smies, and Musgrave 1920).

The first major archaeological work in the Pocahontas region started in 1927 and lasted through 1929. During those years, James A. Ford and Moreau B. Chambers, a pair of young archaeologists working for

the Mississippi Department of Archives and History, criss-crossed the region recording sites and excavating mounds. Except for a brief summary of some of their excavations (Ford 1936: 115–28), the bulk of this work was never published. Luckily, the fieldwork was of high quality for its time, and recent studies of their notes and collections have provided a wealth of data on late prehistoric chronology and mortuary practices (Shaffer and Steponaitis 1982, 1983). The only modern excavations in the region worth noting took place in 1974, and focused on the peripheries of the platform mound at Pocahontas (Rucker 1976). Although the mound itself was not explored, a large sample of materials was obtained from closely associated middens, which yielded valuable information on the dates and duration of the mound's occupation. Considerable information on settlements in the region also resides in the state's site files (e.g., Neitzel 1968).

The late prehistoric chronology is based on a seriation of ceramic assemblages (consisting of whole vessels) from the burial mounds excavated by Ford and Chambers, and on cross-ties with the well-established ceramic sequence in the Lower Yazoo Basin (Williams and Brain 1983), with which this region shares many stylistic similarities. Three phases have been recognized so far, each named after the site at which it is most clearly represented: the Dupree phase, ca. A.D. 1000–1200; the Chapman phase, ca. A.D. 1200–1350; and the Smith phase, A.D. 1350–1500. In absolute dates, these approximate the Moundville I, Moundville II, and Moundville III phases, respectively. It is interesting to note that the Pocahontas region seems to lack settlements that date between A.D. 700 and 1000, or that postdate A.D. 1500. Whether these gaps in occupation represent accidents of sampling or real abandonments is difficult at this stage of investigations to say.

By comparison with the Moundville region, which has been one of the most intensively studied in North America, the Pocahontas region still remains all-too-poorly known. Studies of faunal remains have been few (Rucker 1976), and studies of plant remains nonexistent. In other words, we lack direct evidence with which to reconstruct subsistence practices and how they changed through time. Given that maize agriculture was intensified virtually everywhere across the interior southeast between A.D. 800 and 1000 (Johannessen 1984; Yarnell and Black 1985; Lynott et al. 1986; Steponaitis 1986a; B. Smith 1986; Scarry 1988), it is safe to assume that the late pre-

historic inhabitants of this region were farmers, but little else can be said. Similarly, no data exist on local patterns of craft production or the intensity of warfare. Hence, the sections that follow will focus principally on settlement, mortuary ritual, and long-distance exchange. Despite the many gaps in our understanding, these lines of evidence make it quite clear that the historical trajectory in this region was different than that at Moundville.

Settlement, society, and mortuary ritual

Late prehistoric sites in the region were of three types: platform-mound centers, burial-mound centers, and hamlets. Platform-mound centers were typically marked by a single, flat-topped earthwork. The best-known example is the Pocahontas site, which is located near the modern town of the same name along the upper reaches of Limekiln Creek, a tributary of the Big Black River. The one platform mound at this site, the largest in the region, stands 6 m high and some 53 m square at the base (Rucker 1976: 7). Judging from the debris that was excavated on its flanks, it was once surmounted by an inhabited structure, presumably an elite residence. Sherd distributions suggest that other residences were scattered in the vicinity of the mound as well. A burial mound is located some 400 m south of the platform mound, but whether these two earthworks were used at the same time is unknown.

The burial mounds were circular, dome-shaped tumuli that served as repositories for the dead. Examples range from 20 to 30 m in diameter and from 1 to 4 m in height. Most often burial mounds occur singly on the landscape; rarely they are found in loosely clustered groups of two or three. Excavations have shown that these mounds were accretional, with burials placed either in shallow pits or directly on the surface then covered with fill. As one might expect in such a case, the number of burials in a mound generally correlates with the mound's overall size; a small mound might contain only a dozen interments, a large one more than fifty. Judging from the inclusive ceramics as well as from the number of burials, it is unlikely that any of these mounds was used for more than a generation or two.

There are no large, dense midden accumulations near any of these mounds or anywhere in the region that would signify the presence of nucleated villages. Rather, it seems that the bulk of the population

during all three phases was dispersed in small hamlets or farmsteads, ranging from 0.1 to 0.8 ha in size (e.g., Lorenz 1986).

At least two dozen mound sites are known to exist in the region; many more earthworks, especially at the smaller end of the size range, probably still remain to be found. Of the known sites, only one platform mound and six burial mounds have thus far yielded excavated collections that can be dated. The platform mound at Pocahontas was first constructed during the Dupree phase, and continued to be occupied well into the Chapman phase (cf. Rucker 1976). The burial mounds sort chronologically as follows: two (Dupree and Sycamore) can be confidently assigned to the Dupree phase; one (Chapman) confidently to the Chapman phase; two (Smith and Gross) confidently and one (Woodbine) tentatively to the Smith phase. Despite the many undated mounds and other uncertainties, three things are abundantly clear: first, platform-mound centers were occupied in all phases except possibly the last; second, burial-mound centers were constructed and used throughout the sequence; and third, no paramount center even remotely approaching the size and complexity of Moundville ever emerged. The largest mound centers were of about the same scale as the subsidiary "local centers" in the Moundville regional system.

Additional insights can be gained from the mortuary ritual manifested in the burial mounds. These mounds contained a diversity of burial types, ranging from primary inhumations to disarticulated bundles of longbones and isolated skulls. The positioning of interments showed little patterning; burials were scattered in seemingly random fashion throughout the fill, and were placed in a wide variety of orientations. The same can be said for the artifacts that accompanied the burials. Typical grave goods included ceramic vessels, greenstone celts, chipped stone tools, pipes, pigments, and ornaments of shell and copper. Many items, by virtue of their placement, did not seem to be associated with any particular burial; it is as though they were placed in the mound as collective rather than individual offerings. Apart from distinctions in burial type, the mounds show little internal differentiation or structure.

An interesting pattern does become apparent, however, when contemporary mounds are compared (Table 9.2). This pattern involves consistent differences in burials and artifacts, and is most clearly evident among the three latest mounds, which date to the Smith

Table 9.2. Distribution of selected artifacts and burial types among burial mounds in the Pocahontas region[a]

	Dupree phase		Chapman phase		Smith phase	
	Dupree	Sycamore	Chapman	Woodbine	Gross	Smith
Total "find" count[b]	94	11	11	18	47	46
Total burial count	42	12	15	30	57	22
Selected artifact counts:						
Copper (misc.)	7	0	0	2	1	0
Ritual bundles[c]	2	0	0	2	4	0
Carapace fragments	0	0	0	1	1	0
Pots	70	5	8	15	38	40
Pot-to-burial ratio	1.67	0.42	0.53	0.50	0.67	1.82
Burial counts:						
Primary	3	6	2	11	13	12
Isolated skull	17	2	6	13	31	0
Disarticulated	1	3	4	2	11	8
Unknown type	21	1	3	1	2	2
Burial proportions:						
Primary	0.07	0.50	0.14	0.36	0.23	0.55
Isolated skull	0.40	0.17	0.40	0.43	0.54	0.00
Disarticulated	0.02	0.25	0.27	0.07	0.19	0.36
Unknown type	0.50	0.08	0.20	0.13	0.04	0.09

[a]Compiled from Shaffer and Steponaitis (1982).
[b]Each "find" is a discrete cluster containing one or more artifacts, as recorded by the excavators in the field.
[c]Each "bundle" comprises a group of small artifacts that were found tightly clumped, as though they originally had been wrapped in a perishable container. Such bundles may contain the following artifacts in varying combinations: clay pipes, quartz crystals, small greenstone celts, flakes, blades, bifaces, bivalve shells, carapace fragments, discoidals, plummets, and sandstone abraders.

phase. These mounds are of two distinct kinds. One kind, represented by Gross and Woodbine, is marked by a predominance of isolated skulls, with primary and bundle burials less common; the consistent presence of copper, ritual bundles, and terrapin carapaces (probably rattles); and about half as many pots as burials. The other kind, represented by the Smith mound, contains mainly primary burials and no isolated skulls; no copper, ritual bundles, or carapace fragments; and about twice as many pots as burials. These distinctions are not simply the result of sampling error: Gross and Smith are radically different despite having similar samples (forty-seven vs. forty-six finds); at the same time, Gross and Woodbine are generally similar despite having different samples (forty-seven vs. eighteen finds). Nor can we attribute these distinctions to geographical variation, since Gross and Smith (dissimilar in content) are only 4 km apart, while Gross and Woodbine (similar in content) are 11 km apart. Analogous contrasts, although not quite so dramatic, can be seen among the earlier mounds as well. Dupree and Sycamore show essentially the same distinctions as the late mounds, except that the pot-to-burial ratios are reversed and carapace fragments are totally absent. Chapman, the only mound that dates to the middle phase in the sequence, has an intermediate pattern, with an artifact assemblage like Sycamore's and a burial assemblage like Dupree's; since no other mounds of this phase have been excavated, how (or if) Chapman differed from them is unknown.

The existence of contemporary yet contrasting mound types may signify the segmentary organization that was common in the southeast at the time of European contact. Ethnographically, different moieties and clans carried different sets of ritual responsibilities, which in this case may be expressed by consistent distinctions in artifacts. The fact that some mounds contain copper, medicine bundles, and rattles while others do not might mean that some social segments had greater rank or preferential access to titles and offices. Even so, the overall pattern in these mounds seems far more expressive of "horizontal" than "vertical" differentiation. Were it not for the (presumably) elite residence atop the platform mound at Pocahontas, there would be little evidence of hierarchy at all.

Thus, in both settlement and mortuary ritual, the dominant pattern in this region is one of stability from A.D. 1000 to 1500. While relatively simple chiefdoms may have existed throughout this span, no paramount centers or pronounced hierarchies ever appeared. In order

to understand the reasons for this trajectory, so different from Mound-ville, we must first look at patterns of long-distance exchange.

Long-distance exchange

The nonlocal materials found in the burial mounds were similar to those at Moundville, but their relative frequencies were different (Table 9.3). The most common exotics were greenstone celts, followed by marine shell ornaments, copper ornaments, galena, and crystals of quartz (the last from sources in the Appalachian Mountains). Foreign pottery was also present, most notably a distinctive terraced vessel of a style that could only have come from Moundville (Ford 1936: fig. 23h). In short, the evidence suggests not only that the two regions were linked into similar exchange networks, but also that these networks overlapped.

When the ratio of exotics to burials in these mounds is plotted through time, an interesting pattern emerges (Fig. 9.4). The two earliest mounds, which date to the Dupree phase, have significantly greater quantities of nonlocal materials than any of the later mounds, which date to the Chapman and Smith phases. Clearly, exotic goods became far less available after A.D. 1200. This, of course, is precisely when the abundance of such commodities at Moundville reached a peak. As we shall see presently, this coincidence may not be spurious, and may help explain certain aspects of the political trajectory just described.

Discussion

Nothing is known of the historical trajectory that led to the emergence of the earliest mound centers in the Pocahontas region at ca. A.D. 1000. But once the mounds appeared, both settlement and mortuary ritual remained remarkably stable for half a millennium, until about A.D. 1500. Earthworks were modest and burials showed little evidence of social ranking. Apparently, late prehistoric chiefdoms in this region stayed relatively simple, and, unlike at Moundville, never coalesced into a strongly centralized regional polity.

The one major change that did take place was a precipitous drop in the abundance of objects made from exotic materials after A.D. 1200. I suggest that it is impossible to understand this change by looking at

Table 9.3. *Chronological distribution of nonlocal artifacts in burial mounds from the Pocahontas region*[a]

	Burial mound[b]					
	Dupree	Sycamore	Chapman	Woodbine	Smith	Gross
Copper:						
Copper earspool	4	0	0	2	0	1
Copper ornament (misc.)	3	0	0	0	0	0
Total	7	0	0	2	0	1
Shell:						
Shell beads[c]	7	2	0	1	1	1
Shell ornament (misc.)	3	0	0	0	0	2
Total	10	2	0	1	1	3
Other nonlocal stone:						
Greenstone celt	18	3	2	2	3	5
Quartz crystal	0	0	0	1	0	1
Galena mass	7	0	0	0	0	0
Total	25	3	2	3	3	6
Total (excluding pottery)	42	5	2	6	4	10
Nonlocal pottery vessels	0	0	0	0	1	0
Total burials	42	12	15	30	22	57

[a]Compiled from Shaffer and Steponaitis (1982).
[b]Arranged from left to right in approximate chronological order. Dupree and Sycamore date to the Dupree phase (ca. A.D. 1000–1200); Chapman dates to the Chapman phase (ca. A.D. 1200–1350); Woodbine, Smith, and Gross date to the Smith phase (ca. A.D. 1350–1500).
[c]Multiple items from the same burial or "find" are regarded as a set and counted as a single occurrence.

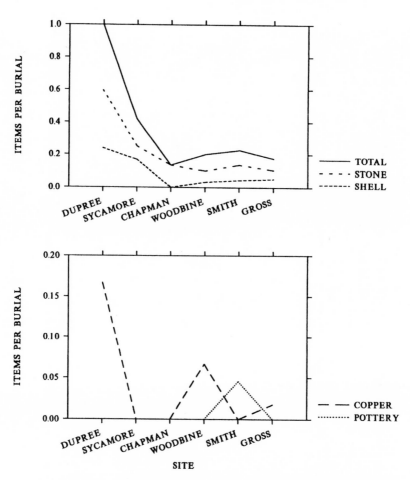

Fig. 9.4 The relative abundance of exotics in burial mounds
of the Pocahontas region. The vertical axis represents the ratio
between the number of exotic items and the number of burials
that date to each phase, based on Table 9.3. The sites are
arranged in approximate chronological order from left to right.
Dupree and Sycamore date to ca. A.D. 1000–1200; Chapman to
ca. A.D. 1200–1350; and Woodbine, Smith, and Gross to ca.
A.D. 1350–1500

events and processes in the Pocahontas region alone. Rather, we must
take a broader perspective and consider contemporary political
developments in neighboring regions.

Between A.D. 1000 and 1200, most groups in the interior Southeast

(from eastern Louisiana to central Alabama) were organized at a similar level of complexity. The dominant pattern was one of relatively small centers and localized settlement hierarchies, presumably indicative of small-scale chiefdoms. At roughly A.D. 1200–1250, however, major political "takeoffs" occurred in a number of places. As we have already discussed, Moundville emerged as a paramount center in the Black Warrior Valley to the east. At the same time, large, multimound centers, such as Lake George and Anna, appeared in the lower Mississippi Valley to the west (Brain 1978; Williams and Brain 1983). In short, A.D. 1200 represents a threshold at which considerably more complex chiefdoms appeared both east and west of the Pocahontas region, but *not* in the Pocahontas region itself.

How would such political developments have affected the local availability of exotics? Prior to A.D. 1200, most polities were similar in scale and centralization; hence, their leaders could mobilize and deploy similar amounts of wealth in the social transactions by which prestige goods were acquired. Potentially, all groups could participate in these exchange transactions on a more-or-less equal footing. With the emergence in some regions of larger and more centralized polities, however, the potential for equal participation no longer held true. The elites in complex chiefdoms could mobilize considerably more wealth than their counterparts in the simpler societies nearby, putting the latter at an economic (and social) disadvantage. Under these circumstances, competition among elites may have caused the "costs" of certain prestige goods to inflate; these costs eventually reached a point at which elites in the less centralized and smaller polities could no longer obtain these items as frequently or consistently as they had once been able. Ultimately, this process might even have led to the appearance of stratified exchange networks, wherein each tier comprised the elites capable of engaging in social transactions involving a certain degree of wealth and prestige. The elites of less centralized groups may have been excluded from transactions at the highest levels, simply because they could not raise the wealth to participate (see Friedman 1975b).

Of course, it is also possible that the Pocahontas region at some point was brought directly under political hegemony of an outside paramount chief. Lake George, one of the largest mound centers in the lower Mississippi Valley, was only 50 km to the northwest, well within the distance from which the most powerful Mississippian chiefs

225

were capable of drawing tribute (Hudson et al. 1985). Such tribute demands, if they occurred, might well have further depressed the wealth that local chiefs could deploy for their own political purposes. While a paramount chief may have distributed prestige goods to local elites in order to help insure their loyalty, the inherent inequality of such tributary relations would have also insured that the local elites never had access to the same range or amount of goods as the paramount (cf. Welch 1986).

No matter which process (or combination of processes) was operating in this case, the effect was the same. Local elites lost much of their access to socially valued nonlocal goods. And, if one accepts the argument made previously that such goods played a key role in the social transactions by which paramount chiefdoms were established, then the prior emergence of paramount centers in neighboring regions may have actively *precluded* the emergence of similar centers in the Pocahontas region, by diminishing the availability of the very tokens that were needed by local leaders to enhance their power and prestige. To put the matter more simply, once Moundville and the lower Mississippi Valley centers "took off," the large-scale political and economic consequences were such that groups in the Pocahontas region could never catch up, at least not while the other centers were still operating. This, more than any other single factor, may account for the "flat" political trajectory that characterized this region's late prehistory.

CONCLUSION

The two regions just examined experienced vastly different political trajectories despite their overall similarity in natural environment. In the Moundville region, a series of small, simple chiefdoms appeared around A.D. 1050; these were consolidated into a single, paramount chiefdom by A.D. 1250. The initial step in this process seems to have been fueled by intensified local production; subsequent centralization was fostered by the development of a "prestige goods economy," which depended on the acquisition and social deployment of craft items made from nonlocal materials. In the Pocahontas region, simple chiefdoms also appeared shortly after A.D. 1000, but no further centralization occurred. I have argued that such centralization was precluded by the prior development of paramount chiefdoms in

neighboring regions to the east and west, chiefdoms whose existence made access to prestige goods more difficult and thereby denied local elites the means by which their own political standing could be enhanced.

Of course, one might wonder why the paramount chiefdom appeared at Moundville first. Natural environment is clearly not the answer, so we are left with several possibilities.

First, a key element in the success of chiefly political strategies is the availability of labor. Other things being equal, a chief with greater access to labor can mobilize larger surpluses that can be deployed for political ends. The Moundville region's population may have been larger, denser, or distributed over the landscape in a way that made it easier to control by emerging elites. Evaluating this possibility will require additional surveys in both regions.

Second, Moundville may have had more direct or easier access to the routes by which prestige goods circulated. Such routes, although somewhat constrained by physical geography, were in no sense determined by it. Rather, their configuration would have depended on the relative locations of, and relations between, inhabited communities. It is also worth noting that socially valued craft items may have been manufactured far from the sources of raw material, and probably changed hands many times before finding their way to the regions with which we are concerned. Hence, reconstructing such routes is no simple matter, and must take the social as well as the physical landscape into consideration.

Finally, it may be that Moundville's priority was essentially a stochastic event, which is to say that the precise reasons for it are now unknowable. For example, the critical factor may have been a particular leader who, by virtue of unusual charisma and political skill, was able to outmanoever rivals in neighboring regions. Archaeologically, this is the alternative one is left with when all other possibilities have been eliminated.

Many aspects of the model I have presented remain speculative and in need of further empirical support. Yet to the extent that these arguments are plausible, they should lead us to realize that particular trajectories of chiefly development may be inexplicable unless they are considered in the context of broader political and economic processes that transcend the boundaries of any single region.

Acknowledgments

Sincere thanks are due to Jeffrey Brain, Ian Brown, Stephen Davis, John House, Charles Hudson, Vernon Knight, John O'Hear, George Milner, Christopher Peebles, Mary Powell, Margaret Scarry, John Shaffer, Laurie Steponaitis, Trawick Ward, Paul Welch, Bruce Winterhalder, Henry Wright, and Richard Yarnell, who offered helpful comments on earlier drafts. But most of all I am grateful to my fellow participants in the seminar that resulted in this volume; many of the ideas presented here took better shape as a result of their insightful discussions and friendly advice.

Notes

1. This estimate was derived by means of the least-squares method of Kohler and Blinman (1987), applied to Wimberly's (1956) sherd counts. A more complete presentation of this analysis is forthcoming.

2. This pattern is remarkably consistent with the political relationships described in the earliest historical records, which come from two Spanish expeditions that took place between 1539 and 1561. Based on these records, Hudson et al. (1989) argue that the mid-sixteenth-century landscape in this area was dominated by a hostile rivalry between two sets of paramount chiefdoms. On one side was a polity called Apafalaya, whose settlements were located in the Moundville region along the Black Warrior River. On the other side were the chiefdoms of Tascaluza and Coosa, whose settlements were found along the Alabama and Coosa rivers to the east. The absence at Moundville of trade pottery from the latter regions fits nicely with this historical model (see Hudson et al. 1989: 43), and further suggests that this social boundary predated the Spaniards' arrival by at least two centuries. The same observations would generally hold true even if one allowed for some uncertainty over exactly where the historically documented chiefdoms were located (cf. Curren 1987; Hudson 1989).

3. Evidence from the nearby Tombigbee Valley suggests that, by A.D. 900–1000, the hunting-gathering-gardening economy was operating close to its productive limits. All the classic indicators of "subsistence stress" were present: the diversity of species being eaten was high, average prey sizes (both within and across taxa) were unusually low, and a large percentage of the burial population showed signs of nutritional deficiency (Woodrick 1981; Cole, Hill, and Ensor 1982; Scott 1983; Welch 1985).

228

10
Demography, surplus, and inequality: early political formations in highland Mesoamerica

GARY M. FEINMAN

The development of permanent positions of leadership and institution-alized forms of inequality are central questions in the social sciences. In twentieth-century anthropology, these related issues traditionally have been framed as the evolution of "chiefdoms" (Service 1962) or "ranked societies" (Fried 1967). For the most part, however, the major research focus has been neither diachronic nor processual, instead concentrating on temporally shallow anthropological or ethnohistoric observations, single reconstructed slices of archaeological time, and, most frequently, cross-cultural compendia of synchronic ethnographic cases. Such studies have provided valuable parameters (and a diversity of classification schemes; see Carneiro 1981; Feinman and Neitzel 1984: 41) for those internally diverse societies which are intermediate in scale and organizational complexity between foraging bands and bureaucratic states. Yet concerning development and change, they can only inspire hypotheses which ultimately must be tested with dia-chronic data.

In a synchronic cross-societal review of nonstate sedentary societies in the Americas, I suggested (Feinman and Neitzel 1984: 78) that more "long-term processual analyses are necessary" since atemporal studies "can only demonstrate correlations and cannot reveal the

historical or causal processes responsible for societal variation." More recently, Drennan and Uribe (1987b: vii–viii) argue in a similar vein.

To a great extent, ethnography has already made what contribution it can to the study of truly long-term change with the kind of cross-cultural comparisons that produced the evolutionary scheme of which chiefdom is a part.

This chapter endeavors to examine the emergence of specialized leaders or "chiefs" from a diachronic perspective. Yet unlike the case-specific contributions to *Chiefdoms in the Americas* (Drennan and Uribe 1987a), the focus here is not on a geographic area where non-state sedentary formations were either especially long-lived or persisted until European contact. Rather, this study is concentrated on the Mexican highlands, an area where nonstate sedentary formations often endured for little more than a millennium prior to developments into more hierarchical urban polities. To understand the variability and change in nonstate sedentary societies, we must consider both those areas where chiefs soon were able to mobilize the resources, connections, and power to establish greater civic-ceremonial complexity (states), as well as regions where chiefly formations were apparently much more resilient.

INTERPRETIVE BACKGROUND

For purposes of this discussion, a "chiefdom" is defined narrowly following Wright (1984: 82), who sees them as a sociopolitical formation in which social control activities are "externally specialized vis-à-vis other activities, but not internally specialized in terms of different aspects of the control process." Thus, chiefly formations should be associated with a supra-household decision-making structure or relatively permanent positions of leadership, but not with the marked internal differentiation of such structures. The most important feature of Wright's working definition (see also Blanton et al. 1981) is that it refers solely to a sociopolitical form and not to a type or class of societies which (by definition) all share the same specified set of societal attributes. This distinction is significant since it recognizes that societies with structurally similar political forms are not *necessarily* equivalent in economic organization, kinship, demographic parameters, or other aspects (see Claessen 1981; Feinman and Neitzel 1984). Furthermore, by defining "chiefdom" in this way, any implica-

tion that sequences of societal change are *uniformly* progressive or linear is avoided.

In Mesoamerica, the earliest archaeological evidence for social differentiation, monumental architecture, and civic-ceremonial centers is found along the coastal plains of the Gulf (Coe and Diehl 1980) and the Pacific (Blake 1987; Clark et al. 1987). Perhaps for this reason, evolutionary studies concerning the *beginnings* of sociopolitical complexity have been somewhat underemphasized in the Mexican highlands in relation to those focused on later state and urban development. Nevertheless, three basic theoretical positions have been advanced to account for the emergence of complexity in the highlands.

Most enduring is the stance which attributes change to direct and sustained contact with the "Olmec" of the Gulf Coast. Although early proponents suggested Gulf Coast trading enclaves (Coe 1965a; Tolstoy and Paradis 1971), militaristic forays (Coe 1965b), and even an empire (Caso 1965) in the highlands, this view has lost significant favor in the wake of two decades of solid archaeological fieldwork on early communities in both the highlands and the lowlands (e.g. Coe and Diehl 1980; Flannery and Marcus 1983a; Grove 1987a). These investigations indicate that sedentary villages with distinct local traditions date rather equivalently to the middle and late second millennium B.C. in many major highland and lowland regions, and that the local traditions were maintained even as the symbols of the "Olmec interaction sphere" (Flannery 1968) were incorporated into regional artifactual assemblages. Thus, an Early Formative (1500–900 B.C.) Gulf Coast presence in the highlands remains archaeologically unsubstantiated, and Drennan's (1984a, 1984b) recent analysis of the high costs of long-distance movement for prehispanic Mesoamerica would seem to cast additional doubt on models which envision major lowland excursions into the highlands for strict economic or military purposes.

A second class of models associates the genesis of highland political development to a suite of local environmental and demographic factors (Sanders 1984a, 1984b). Influenced by Carneiro (1961; see also 1970), Sanders and Price (1968: 128–34) postulated that population density, environmental circumscription, and environmental diversity were essential aspects of this evolutionary process. A decade later, Sanders and Webster (1978: 253, 285–6) reiterated these arguments while also suggesting that environmental risk was a key factor in these

231

political changes. Although the theoretical direction of these arguments is clear (see also Sanders 1972), specific, comparative evolutionary expectations for this process in Mesoamerica's highland regions are
rarely presented. Nevertheless, in the circumscribed valleys of Mexico's highlands, a maintained emphasis seems to be on the presumed
role of population density in the emergence of political complexity.

The third theoretical stance stems from Kent V. Flannery's (1968)
influential model of interregional interaction between the Olmec and
the Valley of Oaxaca in Formative times. From this perspective, highland social differentiation is initiated locally with increasing sedentism
and a greater reliance on agricultural resources, but is then reinforced
and elaborated in part through exchanges of symbolically important
goods and information with the more developed lowlands (Drennan
1976a, 1983a). The limited access to and control of exotic and ritually
charged goods allows emergent leaders to attract and influence potential supporters. As Hirth (1987a: 16) has asserted, elite exchange networks can provide at least three important functions:

(1) They broaden elite control over resource production, (2) they provide
emergency provisioning in times of resource shortfall, and (3) they provide the
jural-political framework within which leaders mediate disputes and maintain
peace between their respective groups.

Nevertheless, as Earle (1982, 1987a: 296) has implied, the mere availability of preciosities or exotic valuables in an exchange sphere does
not in itself promote sociopolitical differentiation.

In a sense, the second and third theoretical positions closely correspond to two hypothetical sequences of development that were
recently characterized more generally and heuristically in a discussion
of regional demography in chiefdoms (Drennan 1987). Drennan's first
alternative views demography as the engine which drives sociopolitical
change. Thus, the advent of decision-making complexity might be
expected to correspond to a particular demographic parameter.

The second sequence begins with the emergence of patterns of economic
inequality in a small autonomous village. Such patterns of differing wealth
would tend to concentrate population in that village as those of greater wealth
take advantage of the opportunities their wealth provides to make others
dependent upon them. Such concentration of dependents would be encouraged by the wealthy since it provides enhanced opportunities for still further
acquisition of wealth. This process would eventually involve the incorpora-
tion of existing small neighboring villages into the system or the founding of

additional small villages by people from the emergent center so as to increase the resource base for wealth accumulation.   (DRENNAN 1987: 313–14)

The remainder of this chapter examines data from the Formative period in highland Mesoamerica (Table 10.1) in relation to the latter two theoretical positions outlined above. In the next section, the results from decades of multiscale, multidisciplinary analyses in the Valley of Oaxaca (Fig. 10.1) are reviewed. Here, the focus is on a program of Formative village excavations by Kent V. Flannery and his colleagues on the Valley of Oaxaca Human Ecology Project (Flannery et al. 1967; Winter 1972; Pires-Ferreira 1975; Drennan 1976b; Flannery 1976a; Flannery and Marcus 1976a, 1976b; Whalen 1981; Flannery, Marcus, and Kowalewski 1981; Flannery and Marcus 1983a; Parry 1987), as well as on the systematic settlement survey of the 2,150 km² region (Blanton et al. 1982; Feinman et al. 1985; Kowalewski et al. 1989). Anne Kirkby's (1973) analysis of *The use of land and water resources in the past and present Valley of Oaxaca, Mexico* also provides a particularly important basis for examining and modeling demographic and human-environmental factors over the long-term in this region.

Subsequently, the Formative era sociopolitical change in ancient Oaxaca is compared to a series of other highland Mexican valleys where regional archaeological programs also have been conducted (Fig. 10.2). In 1972, prior to the availability of systematic archaeological settlement pattern survey data for any region in Mesoamerica outside the Basin of Mexico, William T. Sanders (1972) completed a comparative demographic analysis of many of these same (as well as other) Mesoamerican regions. Now, with the publication of more systematic observations, it is time for a second examination.

Admittedly, the discussion to follow has a strongly regional-scale focus. In part that is because the differential distributions of nonresidential architectural features, especially when conjoined with disparities in settlement size, provide a particularly good foundation for identifying variation and change in sociopolitical complexity. Furthermore, archaeological data at the regional scale are necessary to evaluate prehistoric demographic shifts. While site-specific observations are considered very important to this study and are used whenever possible, such data are placed in a broader spatial perspective. As Drennan and Uribe (1987c: 60) state:

233

Table 10.1. *Highland Mesoamerican chronologies*

MAJOR PERIOD	VALLEY OF OAXACA	EJUTLA VALLEY	BASIN OF MEXICO	E. MORELOS	CUICATLAN CANADA	TAMAZULAPAN
Terminal Formative	Monte Albán II	Monte Albán II	First Intermediate Phase 4	Terminal Formative	Lomas	Ramos
Late Formative	M.A. Late I	M.A. Late I	First Intermediate Phase 3	Late Formative	Perdido	Late Cruz
	M.A. Early I	M.A. Early I	First Intermediate Phase 2	Cantera		
Middle Formative	Rosario	Rosario		Barranca		Middle Cruz
	Guadalupe		First Intermediate Phase 1			
	San José	Early Formative		Amate		Early Cruz
Early Formative	Tierras Largas		Early Horizon			
	Espiridión					

Time scale (left axis): A.D. / B.C. — 200, 0, 200, 400, 600, 800, 1000, 1200, 1400, 1500

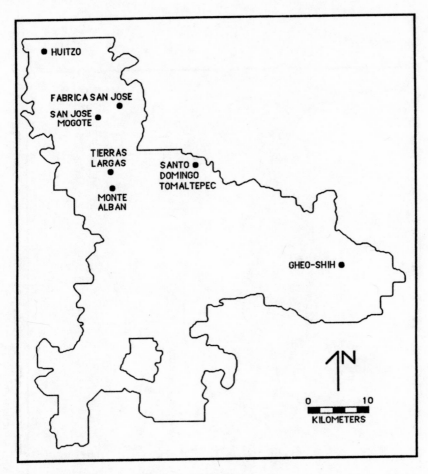

Fig. 10.1   The Valley of Oaxaca

Regional settlement pattern information is especially significant in the study of chiefdoms (or other complex societies) because it is the broadest and most direct approach available to archaeologists for reconstructing patterns of organization at the regional level, and it is the very existence of this regional level of organization that so strongly differentiates chiefdoms from simpler societies.

In sum, the analytical framework adopted here concurs with Earle (1984: 2), who stated: ". . . most important for studying cultural evolution archaeologically has been a reliance on the settlement patterns."

235

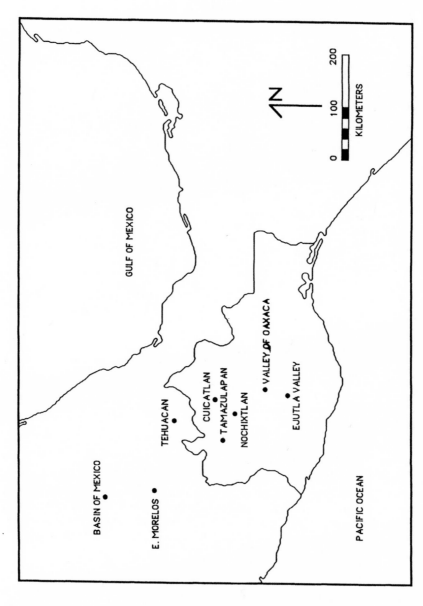

Fig. 10.2   Highland Mesoamerican regions

POLITICAL DIFFERENTIATION IN THE FORMATIVE VALLEY OF OAXACA

In the decades since Flannery established a long pre-Monte Albán (pre-500 B.C.) occupational sequence for the Valley of Oaxaca, numerous books, monographs, and articles have been written concerning the formation and diversification of early village settlements in the region. Hence, this section serves partially as a directed synthesis, specifically focusing the archaeological findings in relation to the two hypothetical trajectories and the factors discussed above. Since the emphasis is on chiefly formation, the discussion is grouped into three parts: the first looks at the region's earliest sedentary communities (ca. 1500–1150 B.C.); the next focuses on the emergence of political differentiation (ca. 1150–600 B.C.); while the third examines the elaboration of those differences, prior to the establishment of the hilltop center of Monte Albán (ca. 600–500 B.C.).

This investigation of early Oaxaca also relies heavily on a diachronic analysis of human–land relations in the region. These discussions compare Kirkby's (1973) observations of land quality and productivity, which were supplemented by the field-by-field observations of archaeological crews who also noted the spatial distribution of land and water resources, with site location and site size information mapped and recorded by the settlement pattern project. Following Kirkby (1973: 124–6), Kowalewski (1980, 1982), and Feinman and Nicholas (1987a: Fig. 4.2), this modeling takes into account (but does not adopt the premise that changes in demography can be explained simply by) the increasing productivity of the maize plant through time. Using formulas, derived from ethnographic studies, that have been employed for settlement pattern research across the Mesoamerican highlands (e.g. Parsons 1971), population estimates are extrapolated from the number and size of recorded settlements. For descriptive purposes, the means of more cautiously derived demographic ranges are utilized in several analyses. While these estimation procedures are not exact, I concur in principle with Sanders' (1972: 101) observation that "this is the only type of archaeological research that can provide reliable data on population history."

The spatial associations of population and agricultural productivity follow the basic research methodology outlined by Kowalewski (1980, 1982). For example, the 4 by 4 km grid system employed here is a

spatial expansion of the analytical structure that he first used (see also Nicholas et al. 1986; Feinman and Nicholas 1987a). The size of the grid corresponds to the amount of land that would be within easy walking distance of sites located in each square. Use of this grid facilitates spatial analyses and cross-phase comparisons. Human-resource relationships also are considered both at the scale of the entire Valley of Oaxaca, and at an intermediate scale that represents the potential "support-zone" or population within a day's round trip (18 km radius) from major regional centers (see Feinman and Nicholas 1987a: 39–44). In ancient Oaxaca where transport was entirely by foot, trips of more than a day would be markedly more costly in time and caloric efficiency (e.g. Lightfoot 1979; Drennan 1984b).

In estimating past patterns of productivity, I assume that the region's earliest farmers had the knowledge and the tools to implement the basic pre-Hispanic water control techniques used in the Valley of Oaxaca (Kowalewski 1982: 150). The irrigation and drainage tech-niques utilized in the region pre-Hispanically were relatively simple (Kirkby 1973; Lees 1973; Flannery 1983), and many of the methods used today were employed by the San José phase (1150–850 B.C.) (Flannery et al. 1967; Drennan and Flannery 1983). Because we do not know the specific cropping practices and rotations employed pre-Hispanically on each field, I have followed Kirkby (1973: 124–6) and Kowalewski (1982: 149–50) in adopting agricultural productivity estimates based entirely on maize. Estimates of prehistoric maize intake are based on Kowalewski's (1982) exhaustive review of ethno-graphic sources in which he found that consumption ranged between 160–290 kg per person per annum.

Before discussing change in Formative Oaxaca, it is important to clarify concepts and hypothetical human–land relationships that have been referred to previously (for more thorough methodological discus-sions see Feinman and Nicholas 1987a; Nicholas 1989). These con-ceptualizations, which are presented both to facilitate cross-phase comparisons and to permit the evaluation of the previously presented models, begin with a specified region's *absolute environmental poten-tial*. That is, given sufficient labor and a specific variety of maize, how many people could be sustained in a region during an average rainfall year. This absolute time-specific ceiling can be distinguished from a second ideal relationship, *maximum production*, which incorporates into the modeling the estimated archaeological population for the

region. Maximum production refers to the amount of maize possibly produced (people sustained) in the region if the estimated population was deployed across the region in the most productive arrangement. In a previous paper (Feinman and Nicholas 1987a), I argued that the observed archaeological settlement pattern in the Valley of Oaxaca never matched this most productive arrangement in any phase, and the goodness-of-fit between the actual and the ideal basically weakened through time.

Potential production, a more realistic indicator of the amount of maize that could have been produced at a particular time, incorporates both the observed archaeological population and its distribution. Thus, potential production is the amount of expected output, assuming that the estimated population farmed only the adjacent terrain (starting with the best land) within the same 4 by 4 km square where each site was situated. Thus, for any spatially defined population (the region, a single arbitrary grid), a *maximum surplus* could be estimated by subtracting that population's required maize consumption from its potential production. Following Johnson's (in press) analysis, I also derived for each phase a rough average indicator of how much maize an individual Oaxacan farmer could have produced above his own maize consumption requirements (see also Feinman and Nicholas 1987b). Here it is necessary to rely on Kirkby's (1973) empirical findings that an Oaxacan farmer, using a *coa* or digging stick, can cultivate only two hectares.

The emergence of sedentary communities

The earliest pottery in the Valley of Oaxaca pertains to the Espiridión complex (1500 B.C.), identified in association with a single house at San José Mogote (Flannery, Marcus, and Kowalewski 1981: 65; Marcus 1983: 42–3). In the subsequent Tierras Largas phase, twenty-six communities have been identified with the total regional population estimated at between 188 and 463 people (Table 10.2). While several sites, including San José Mogote, Tierras Largas, and Santo Domingo Tomaltepec (Fig. 10.1), have been partially excavated, most are known only through settlement pattern survey.

In general, the Tierras Largas phase settlements were small, usually less than one hectare. Only San José Mogote measured more than two hectares. The majority of the region's Tierras Largas phase population

Table 10.2. *Estimated populations by phase for highland Mesoamerican regions*

MAJOR PERIOD	VALLEY OF OAXACA	EJUTLA VALLEY	BASIN OF MEXICO	E. MORELOS	CUICATLAN CANADA	TAMAZULAPAN
Terminal Formative	41,319	2184	120,000	2390	2080	?
Late Formative	50,920	3455	145,000	3127		4500
	14,652	259	80,000	2526	655	
Middle Formative	1835	40	25,000	888		400
	1788	24				
	1942					
Early Formative	327		5000	392		65

Time scale (A.D./B.C.): 200 A.D., 0, B.C. 200, 400, 600, 800, 1000, 1200, 1400, 1500

(roughly fifty percent) was situated in the northern or Etla arm of the valley, with other settlements distributed in the valley's southern arm. For the most part, the Tierras Largas phase occupations were situated near very good, but not necessarily the valley's best or the largest, patches of farm land (Feinman et al. 1985; Nicholas et al. 1986).

At present, San José Mogote is also the only *known* Tierras Largas phase village with nonresidential architectural features. These features include an open danceground as well as a sequence of eight one-room, lime-plastered public buildings (Flannery and Marcus 1976a; Drennan 1983a). While the rituals conducted in these small (4 by 5 m) structures were perhaps more exclusionary than those enacted in the open, these structures, made of the same basic materials used in house construction and built on a level with those residential features, hardly imply a marked degree of status differentiation or decision-making specialization. Nevertheless, San José Mogote, perhaps the area's oldest village, already may have become somewhat different from other communities. The degree of this differential is hard to determine since many of the other Tierras Largas phase communities include Formative period mounded buildings. Yet, without excavations, it is impossible to ascertain whether (or how many of) these mounds overlay Tierras Largas phase public structures like those known at San José Mogote.

The relative autonomy of Tierras Largas phase households is suggested by Winter and Pires-Ferreira's (1976) study of obsidian distributions by source (all exotic to the valley) from a series of excavated household units at the site of Tierras Largas. They argued that the marked household-to-household variability in the obsidian assemblages (by the number and specific sources represented as well as the relative quantity from each source) implied that each household had its own extraregional reciprocal trading relationships. The openness of regional boundaries and household networks of communication also is suggested by the strong similarities between local red-on-buff utilitarian ceramic traditions across Mesoamerica's southern highlands (and beyond) at this time (MacNeish, Peterson, and Flannery 1970; Spores 1972; Zeitlin 1979; Flannery, Marcus, and Kowalewski 1981: 67–8; Winter 1984; see Drennan and Nowack 1984: 152–3 for a parallel argument). Thus, in highland Mesoamerica, as in many other parts of the indigenous New World, the early phases of sedentary

occupation by relatively egalitarian communities are marked by the sharing of basically utilitarian artifact styles over broad regions.

During the Tierras Largas phase, there is no indication of exchange in the rare, highly crafted, or symbolically sanctified items (Drennan 1976a) associated with the later "Olmec horizon" and subsequent San José phase (1150–850 B.C.). Nevertheless, some community inequities in access to exotic goods already may have emerged. Although the excavated samples reported for Tierras Largas phase sites are small and not necessarily equivalent, nine households at Tierras Largas (Winter 1972), situated in the center of the valley just south of San José Mogote, can be compared with two household units from Santo Domingo Tomaltepec in the sparsely inhabited eastern or Tlacolula arm (Whalen 1981). Only a single piece of marine shell was recovered in the latter sample as compared with eleven in the former. Likewise, obsidian made up just over one percent of the total chipped stone at Tomaltepec (Whalen 1981: 30), whereas it comprised between seven to fourteen percent at Tierras Largas (Winter 1972: 172). Whatever actual inequities may have existed, they were probably ephemeral and certainly did not translate into major "public" architecture or other features that we might expect with greater political differentiation.

As I have argued previously (Feinman et al. 1985; Nicholas et al. 1986; Feinman and Nicholas 1987a; see also Nicholas 1989), the estimated valley population was far below the region's absolute agricultural potential. Even in the most heavily settled Etla arm, the estimated population density was lower than one person per km^2 (Table 10.3). It is difficult to see population pressure as a serious causal mechanism at this time. Since most habitations were situated near supplemental sources of water, the great majority could have sustained themselves even in years of low precipitation.

While preliminary demographic-resource modeling indicates that the population within 18 km of San José Mogote could have supported a few households of non-agriculturalists/decision-making specialists even in a dry year, the sparsity of the regional population (labor) and the relatively low productivity of maize suggest that even in an average rainfall year the surplus-producing capacity of the valley populace was not that significant (Table 10.4).

These relationships also can be examined in a second way, in terms of a single farmer or household. Beginning with Kirkby's (1973) estimated productivity of Early Formative maize, a farmer working an

Table 10.3. *Population densities (per km²) in highland Mesoamerica*

MAJOR PERIOD	VALLEY OF OAXACA	EJUTLA VALLEY	BASIN OF MEXICO	E. MORELOS	CUICATLAN CANADA	TAMAZULAPAN
Terminal Formative	19.54	4.23	24.0	5.26	19.44	?
Late Formative	24.09 / 6.93	6.69 / 0.50	29.0 / 16.0	6.89 / 5.56	6.12	17.79
Middle Formative	0.87 / 0.85 / 0.92	0.08 / 0.05	5.0	1.96		1.58
Early Formative	0.15		1.0	0.86		0.26

Time scale (left axis): 200 A.D., 0, B.C., 200, 400, 600, 800, 1000, 1200, 1400, 1500

Table 10.4. *Potential production in an average rainfall year above that required by producing households*

Phase	Within 18 km of San José Mogote	Beyond 18 km of San José Mogote	Total amount
Tierras Largas	18.1*	6.4	24.5
San José	116.3	18.4	134.7
Guadalupe	195.9	24.1	220.0
Rosario	235.9	103.5	339.4

*in metric tons

average plot of valley land in an average precipitation year would require just under a hectare of land for his maize consumption. Consequently, assuming that roughly half the members of each household farm, little extractable surplus would remain. Of course, these figures are estimates, and most Tierras Largas phase settlements were located near better than average farmland that could support more than one person per hectare. But nevertheless, the apparent absence of large-scale mound construction is not surprising.

The emergence of political differentiation

The most dramatic change in the Valley of Oaxaca during the San José and Guadalupe phases (1150–600 B.C.) was the rapid expansion and elaboration of San José Mogote (Flannery, Marcus, and Kowalewski 1981; Flannery and Marcus 1983b). As the site grew to more than 70 ha, the public architecture also increased significantly in scale and diversity (Flannery and Marcus 1976a). At the site, the earliest carved stone monuments in the Valley of Oaxaca were incorporated into public construction dating to the end of the San José phase (Flannery and Marcus 1983b: 54). Increasing status differentials also were evidenced in both burial populations and residential architecture (Flannery and Marcus 1983b: 55; Marcus in press).

The specific relationships that existed between San José Mogote and other valley sites remain uncertain. The remainder of the regional population lived in thirty-eight communities that generally were smaller than three hectares. A number of these settlements had their own public buildings, as well as intra-community status differentials in

residence and burials (e.g. Whalen 1981). Based on Stephen Plog's (1976) analysis of ceramic design elements, even Huitzo, a site at the northern edge of the Etla arm with its own public building, had less interaction and shared fewer designs with San José Mogote than expected by their proximity. Thus, it seems unlikely that San José Mogote had direct administrative control over the entire region. Nevertheless, a degree of political as well as status differential is evident at San José Mogote, where civic-ceremonial structures were raised above the rest of the community on planned and purposefully oriented (8° west of north) stone and adobe platforms.

San José Mogote also had a significant centripetal influence on regional demography (Flannery 1982). Between the Tierras Largas and San José phases, the population of the valley as a whole grew at an estimated rate of 0.59 percent per annum (Table 10.5), while the growth in the Etla arm was more rapid (Feinman et al. 1985: table 2). In both the San José and Guadalupe phases, more than seventy-five percent of the regional population resided in that northern arm. Many of the small communities that were established near to San José Mogote lacked public architecture, and the inhabitants of these communities may have been tied to certain high status individuals at the larger settlement.

During the San José phase, the changes in the valley's political organization were accompanied by significant shifts in interregional exchange and ritual activities (Flannery 1968; Drennan 1976a, 1983). Long-distance networks of communication and exchange were established through which a series of ritual and exotic objects as well as shared symbols were transmitted.

The symbols concerned, which involve figurines and designs on ceramics, have generally been classified as Olmec, although it is now clear that the sharing of symbols in this Formative period interaction was more mutual than has often been pictured. The ritual objects and materials exchanged over long distances included magnetite mirrors, marine shell, fish and stingray spines, shark teeth, and lowland turtle shell.   (DRENNAN 1983: 49)

As Flannery and Marcus (1976b; Flannery 1976b) and others (Drennan 1976a; Grove 1981a, 1987c) have illustrated, many of these objects were linked to high-status and widespread Mesoamerican rituals associated with blood-letting, agricultural production, and leadership. Thus, as Flannery (1968; see also Drennan 1976a) argued two decades ago, the access to these symbolically charged, exotic goods

Table 10.5. Rates of population change in highland Mesoamerica

MAJOR PERIOD	VALLEY OF OAXACA	EJUTLA VALLEY	BASIN OF MEXICO	E. MORELOS	CUICATLAN CANADA	TAMAZULAPAN
Terminal Formative	+0.32%	+0.59%	+0.17%	+0.26%	+0.06%	+0.04%
Late Formative	−0.08%	−0.18%	−0.09%	−0.08%	+0.27%	
	+0.83%	+1.73%	+0.22%	+0.08%		+0.69%
Middle Formative	+1.39%	+0.75%	+0.27%	+0.35%		+0.52%
	+0.02%	+0.11%				
	−0.03%			+0.20%		
Early Formative	+0.59%		+0.39%			

Time scale: 200 A.D., 0 B.C., 200, 400, 600, 800, 1000, 1200, 1400, 1500

may have helped to sanctify the hereditary rights of certain individuals to lead, while the ritual use of these items may also have strengthened the ties between communities, their land, and agrarian production (Kowalewski et al. 1989).

Significantly in the Valley of Oaxaca, access to interregional exchange spheres may have been narrowed by the San José phase. At San José Mogote, the relative uniformity of the obsidian samples from a series of San José phase household units in a single residential ward has led Parry (1987: 22) to suggest that access to this exotic good may have been centrally coordinated, pooled, and redistributed. Likewise, Valley of Oaxaca magnetite, traded as far as San Lorenzo Tenochtitlán on the Gulf Coast (Pires-Ferreira 1975; Flannery 1982), appears to have been worked only in a high-status residential area at San José Mogote (Flannery and Marcus 1983b: 55). The concentration of nonutilitarian craft specialists at specific sites almost certainly enabled particular households and communities to participate more actively in interregional exchange than others. The diversity of exotic goods at San José Mogote far surpasses what is known at other valley sites. Unequal household access to external communications and exchange is indicated by the differential distributions of greenstones, shell, mica, and other rare exotic items in burial and residential contexts (Flannery, Marcus, and Kowalewski 1981: 71–3).

In addition, while the design elements associated with the most elaborately decorated wares were shared with distant areas, utilitarian pottery styles were somewhat more locally distinctive than they were earlier. In other areas of the New World as well, similar changes in the artifactual record are correlated temporally with episodes of increasing social differentiation and political development. Thus, while higher-status households still may have had broad communication links, other families may have had only more parochial networks.

By the San José phase, extraregional (communication and trade) relations may have become more restricted and less open. These shifts in the interregional flow of goods and information may have had important local implications on sociopolitical relations (see Root 1983: 203–4). As Brunton (1975: 556) has theorized for the Trobriands: ". . . where conditions are such that men can act to limit strategic exchange items and pre-empt others from gaining access to them, then the stage is set for the development of rank and chieftainship." Likewise, Helms (1979: 37) argued for Panamanian chiefs that "it must be emphasized

247

that Panamanian participation in such far-flung exchange activities is viewed not simply as an adjunct to chiefly activities, interests, and affairs in Panama but as vital to the sociopolitical dynamics of Panamanian chiefdoms."

This raises the issue of what conditions may have allowed certain households in Oaxaca, particularly those near San José Mogote, to begin to manipulate or control extraregional contacts. While some theorists might clamor for population pressure or environmental circumscription, it is difficult to support such notions with an estimated regional population below 2,000. Even in the Etla arm, there were fewer than five people per km^2, and the regional density was dramatically less (Table 10.3). As my colleagues and I have illustrated elsewhere (Nicholas et al. 1986), during these phases, plenty of top-quality valley farm land remained uninhabited, and the estimated regional population remained only a tiny fraction of the valley's absolute environmental potential (Feinman and Nicholas 1987a).

My inclination is to turn the population pressure argument on its head. The greatest difference in the population–resource equation between the San José phase and the earlier Tierras Largas phase was the more than sixfold increase in the amount of surplus maize that could have been produced within 18 km of San José Mogote (see also Feinman and Nicholas 1987a: Fig. 4.11). While this rise in potential productivity (which was clustered even closer to the site) was in part a function of the expected greater yields of the maize plant, the larger factor was the concentration of potential farmers, whose labor could have been realized or tapped for surplus (Table 10.4). In fact, the grid square that contained San José Mogote (with the greatest population) was the regional center for potential surplus production (Feinman and Nicholas 1987a: 39).

The question then returns systemically to the potential politico-ritual (Harrison 1987) as well as economic (Brunton 1975) gains that may have led households to agglomerate and tie themselves to certain individuals who had greater access to specific desired and/or symbolically laden goods (see Hayden 1978; Paynter and Cole 1980). For example, based on survey collections and selected excavations, there is little question that the highly decorated San José and Guadalupe phase serving bowls, which may have been used for feasting and/or ritual events, were both more diverse and abundant at sites in the Etla arm. Clearly, Oaxacan households were drawn centripetally to (or reprodu-

ced themselves more rapidly in) the vicinity of the region's first sedentary village that contained some of the area's earliest (and most
elaborate) civic-ceremonial features.

While households may have derived economic, defensive, and
politico-religious "benefits" through nucleation, the participation
"costs" for the average household may not have been that high (Drennan, this volume). Intraregional variation in access to goods, domestic
architecture, and burial furniture was more continuous than
dichotomous (or class-like) in nature (Flannery, Marcus, and
Kowalewski 1981: 71). Certain households gained greater access to
venison, shell, magnetite, jade, mica, and nonlocal pottery, yet such
exotic and sumptuary items were not *restricted* to an elite few. Public
buildings were no longer simply the wattle-and-daub structures of prior
times, yet the newly adopted stone masonry and adobe construction
techniques (adopted by 900 B.C.) also would not have required excess-
ively large labor commitments. While some civic-ceremonial and craft
specialists at San José Mogote may have been supported through the
agricultural work of others, the former segment of population does not
appear to have been large. Finally, there is no evidence for the kinds of
large central storage facilities, granaries, or other architectural features
that one might expect if onerous labor/tribute demands were the rule.

The elaboration of political differentiation

During the Rosario phase (600–500 B.C.), San José Mogote decreased
in spatial extent and hence estimated population. Yet, the site
remained the most populous and architecturally elaborate community
in the valley. It also continued as a "magnet" for valley settlements,
despite a weak regional trend toward greater demographic dispersion.
While more minor centers became the foci for smaller population
clusters in the southern and eastern arms of the valley, the great
majority of the regional population remained in Etla.

After 700 B.C. at San José Mogote, both public architecture and
elite residential construction became more elaborate and monumental
– for example, by incorporating huge blocks of limestone that weighed
more than a ton (Flannery and Marcus 1983c: 75–7). In addition,
Monument 3, the region's earliest *danzante*, was positioned in association with public buildings at the site. According to Marcus (1976a),
this carved stone, which predated the display of several hundred such

249

danzantes at later Monte Albán, depicted a slain or sacrificed captive. The differential control of force also is indicated by the inclusion of an adult skeleton, thought to be a sacrificial victim (Flannery and Marcus 1983b: 58–60), under the wall of a high-status residence built on an artificially enhanced mound that previously was the site of a public structure.

Thus, demographic decentralization (see Kowalewski et al. 1989), which occurred with the loss of population at San José Mogote itself, apparently coincided with the expansion in the status, influence, and power of specific households at the site (and perhaps increasing participation "costs" for some commoner households). The highly decorated *gris* serving vessels, still much more abundant at San José Mogote than anywhere else (Kowalewski et al. 1989), now were more evenly distributed across the different arms of the valley. Perhaps the feasts and rituals held most frequently at San José Mogote now also were serving to help integrate a larger segment of the valley population.

Nevertheless, proximity to San José Mogote still had economic advantages as cultural artifacts other than pottery were more abundant on the surfaces of Rosario phase sites in Etla than elsewhere (Kowalewski et al. 1989). A similar pattern was found in the relative proportions of obsidian to the total chipped stone assemblage at three excavated Rosario phase communities. At Fábrica San José, a relatively small community 5 km east of San José Mogote, Drennan (1976b: Table 5) found that obsidian comprised more than twenty-five percent of the total chipped stone associated with household units. At Tierras Largas, a slightly smaller village near the southern edge of the demographic cluster surrounding San José Mogote, Winter (1972: 172) found that the obsidian composed a slightly smaller proportion (twenty percent) of the total in household units. Based on a very small proportion of these units, Winter and Pires-Ferreira (1976) suggest that the obsidian at Tierras Largas may have been pooled during the Middle Formative period as it had been earlier at San José Mogote. Interestingly, at Santo Domingo Tomaltepec, a somewhat larger and more elaborate Rosario phase community (than either Fábrica San José or Tierras Largas) located in the Tlacolula arm, Whalen (1981: 74) estimates that obsidian comprised only 0.05% of the total chipped stone found in household units. Thus, in terms of this particular exotic, the disparity in access between households positioned proxi-

mate and distant from the regional head town was far greater than it was even during the Tierras Largas phase.

Based on a careful analysis of the chipped stone artifacts from a series of excavated Guadalupe and Rosario phase house floors at three Oaxacan settlements (San José Mogote, Fábrica San José, and Huitzo), William Parry (1987: 23–5) argues that, while the quantity of obsidian was variable from house to house, the differences were not due to status differentials. He bases this interpretation on the percentage of obsidian in the chipped stone counts for each structure. Yet, Parry (1987: 108–10) acknowledges that the total quantity of household chipped stone was not independent of status. High-status residences at San José Mogote had considerably more chipped stone than found in the other examined structures, perhaps because these households at San José Mogote were more involved in craft activities. Interestingly, according to a more straightforward measure (quantity of obsidian per structure), the three high-status houses average more than sixteen pieces of obsidian, while the seven low-status houses contain an average of only ten pieces. It would be unwise to overemphasize these differences, given the vagueries of the archaeological record. Yet, Parry (1987: 125–31) also noted that obsidian "lancets," large blades with fine parallel pressure retouch, which were presumably used for ritual bloodletting, were found only at the site of San José Mogote in high-status and civic-ceremonial contexts. Thus at this time in Oaxaca, the use and distribution of obsidian, perhaps one of the more abundant and utilitarian of exotic goods (since some obsidian was used for domestic tasks), may have been associated to a degree with higher status.

Several implications may be drawn from these patterns. First, they add suggestively to the previously discussed issue of why households chose to cluster in Etla when the rest of the region remained much more sparsely settled. Second, they indicate that households in Etla, most probably at San José Mogote where the greatest volume and variety of exotic goods have been found, controlled, or at least dominated, interregional interactions during the Rosario phase.

While the area within an 18 km radius of San José Mogote remained the principal zone of possible surplus production, much greater potential for maize production above subsistence now existed in other areas of the valley (Table 10.4). The correspondence of this trend with aforementioned ceramic evidence for more Rosario phase

valley-wide integration is at least suggestive. While again the greater productivity of the maize plant contributed to the overall 1000-year trend in potential production (a farmer cultivating two hectares of prime valley land in a year with average rainfall now could sustain roughly four people as opposed to three in the Tierras Largas phase), the much more significant variable is the greater number of potential farmers (Table 10.4; Feinman and Nicholas 1987a).

As in earlier phases, there is little evidence for true "pressure" on resources (Feinman and Nicholas 1987a: Table 4.2). Large tracts of good quality farmland remained underutilized or uninhabited in the Valley of Oaxaca (Nicholas et al. 1986). In fact, even in those rare years when the entire Rosario phase "support zone" (for San José Mogote) experienced a dry rainfall year, a small maize surplus still could have been produced. In addition, despite significant organizational shifts, the regional population density remained little changed from the San José through Rosario phases (Table 10.3). Thus, for the pre-Monte Albán era of chiefdom formation and consolidation, there seems little question that the data from the Valley of Oaxaca more closely coincide with Drennan's (1987: 313–14) second evolutionary trajectory.

THE MESOAMERICAN HIGHLANDS: A COMPARATIVE VIEW

In the preceding discussion (see also Drennan 1987: 316–17), political development in the Early and Middle Formative period Valley of Oaxaca was interpreted as related to a series of factors. These included civic-ceremonial differentiation, changing patterns of interregional exchange (as well as local access to exotic goods), and population growth and aggregation which translated into the spatially concentrated capabilities to produce much larger quantities of maize above household subsistence needs. Nevertheless, to evaluate more completely the alternative local demographic-environmental position, comparative research is necessary (see also Kirch 1984).

William T. Sanders (1984a: 277), an advocate of both such a broadly comparative approach and the overriding importance of local factors in social change, has argued that: "Mesoamerica, instead of providing us with a single laboratory case of cultural evolution, can actually provide hundreds of such cases." While I do not concur that

the control of exotic communications and goods can be so easily and necessarily relegated to "negligible" importance, I do agree that the developmental sequences for Mesoamerican regions may be compared and contrasted productively as long as it is recognized that these regional sequences are not *entirely* independent of each other.

In selecting a comparative sample from the Formative period in the Mesoamerican highlands, I have restricted the analysis to regions where a systematic areal survey (with population estimates) is completed. In prehistoric contexts, it is difficult if not impossible to gauge ancient *regional* population parameters in the absence of such studies. Since the examination of these parameters is a primary goal, this criterion for sample restriction seemed reasonable, while also providing a greater degree of comparability.

Five highland regions in addition to the Valley of Oaxaca (Fig. 10.2; Table 10.1) are examined: the Basin of Mexico (Sanders 1965; Parsons 1971; Blanton 1972; Sanders, Parsons, and Santley 1979; Parsons et al. 1982), the Río Amatzinac Valley in eastern Morelos (Hirth 1980, 1987b), the Cuicatlán Cañada (Redmond 1983), the Tamazulapan Valley in the Mixteca Alta (Byland 1980), and Ejutla (Feinman 1985; Feinman and Nicholas 1988), a small valley immediately south of the Valley of Oaxaca. More cursory consideration is given to the Tehuacán Valley (MacNeish et al. 1972; Drennan 1979; Drennan and Nowack 1984) and the Nochixtlán Valley (Spores 1972), where demographic patterns can only be partially and preliminarily reconstructed.

Although significant Formative era excavations have been conducted in most of these seven regions (e.g. Vaillant 1930, 1931, 1935; MacNeish et al. 1972; Spencer 1982; Grove 1987a), relatively few large horizontal exposures of domestic units have been published, and a land use study comparable to Kirkby's (1972) has not been completed. As a consequence, this discussion focuses on comparative settlement patterns and demography.

While seemingly straightforward, consideration must be given to the different procedures employed for estimating past populations in the five survey regions. In eastern Morelos, Tamazulapan, and Ejutla, the procedures employed by the original investigators corresponded with those used for the Valley of Oaxaca. Hence, it was easy to derive the midpoints of presented ranges and achieve roughly comparable figures. Redmond (1983) does not provide a best fit demographic estimate or population range for all Cuicatec sites; however, she does present the

areal size of each settlement. When no other relevant information was available, these data were used to estimate the pre-Hispanic population in a manner directly comparable to that employed elsewhere. In other cases, Redmond also lists observed house mounds and terraces, featu.·es which she uses to construct a second set of population estimates considerably different (often much higher) than those she bases on site area. Where such information was presented, I incorporated it with site-size information, deriving estimates that generally were in the middle of Redmond's (1983: 96) figures.

More troublesome was the Basin of Mexico, where the initial survey technique (Parsons 1971; Blanton 1972) set the standard for all the oth·:r discussed regions. Unfortunately, these conventions were not maintained in the regional summary volume (Sanders, Parsons, and Santley 1979), where the authors decided *not* to express population estimates as initial minimum–maximum ranges. In lieu, data are presented only as the maximum estimates (sometimes plus twenty percent). The comparability problem is complicated by the absence of more detailed reports (such as Parsons 1971; Blanton 1972; Parsons et al. 1982) for much of the surveyed region. Lacking such published studies, information strictly comparable to that presented originally by Parsons (1971) and Blanton (1972) or that used in the other highland regions simply cannot be calculated. A further complication in the Basin of Mexico is that roughly half of the area, including southern portions of the basin known to be key to Early and Middle Formative period occupation, has not been surveyed because of more recent urbanization. Nevertheless, many of the phase-by-phase population estimates presented for the entire basin (Sanders, Parsons, and Santley 1979) combine both areas that have and have not been studied. Lacking the raw site descriptions for all of the areas that have been surveyed, there is little choice but to accept these summary figures as presented. Thus, while I recognize that there is a possible methodological bias which may artificially inflate the demographic figures for the basin above those for other regions, I use them for three reasons:

(1) I am more comfortable following the estimates of the original investigators than manipulating numbers for an area about which I am less familiar;

(2) inflating population estimates for the basin may make some sense since the regional survey was conducted under much

more urban conditions than were encountered in other
regions (hence a greater percentage of ancient sites may
have been covered or destroyed); and
(3) the estimated population densities for the basin are not that
much higher than those for the other regions (Table 10.3).

Settlement pattern comparison indicates that the three largest
regions (Río Amatzinac, the Basin of Mexico, and the Valley of Oaxaca) were in certain ways similar early in the Formative. As in the
Valley of Oaxaca, the first phase in eastern Morelos (Amate), when
sedentary villages were situated across the landscape, coincided with
differences in intraregional size and nonresidential architecture. Like
Tierras Largas-phase San José Mogote, Amate-phase Chalcatzingo was
twice the size of any contemporary community (Hirth 1987b: 351),
and contained the only monumental architecture in the region
thought to pertain to this phase (Grove 1981a; Prindiville and Grove
1987). Both San José Mogote and Chalcatzingo also were situated
proximate to the majority of the rest of the regional populace. Significant size differences also were noted between Basin of Mexico communities of this era (Tolstoy 1975; Tolstoy et al. 1977; Sanders,
Parsons, and Santley 1979: 94–6). While, at present, nondomestic
architecture has not been found at these Early Horizon Basin settlements, the areal difference might be a consequence of the research/ex-
cavation tactics that have been employed in the basin (Grove 1981a:
383).

At this time, no such intraregional settlement size distinctions are
evident in any of the other five regions. Whatever social meaning
might be attached to these areal differences, it seems to have had more
to do with the total size of the regional population than with population density or demographic pressure on resources (Tables 10.2, 10.3).
The population density of Tamazulapan was basically on par with that
in the basin, the Valley of Oaxaca, and eastern Morelos. However, the
three latter regions were all greater in areal scale and had considerably
larger (although still very small) populations. Perhaps these larger
valleys, with more sizeable and stable mating communities (despite
similar population densities), had a demographic advantage over the
inhabitants of adjacent smaller valleys (like Tamazulapan). Either
such mating imbalances (see Wobst 1974, 1975, 1976) or simply the
larger number of interacting communities and households (Johnson

255

1978, 1982, 1983) may have contributed to the beginnings of social or ritual differentiation in these larger, more populous regions (see Friedman and Rowlands 1978; Blanton et al. 1981; Kowalewski et al. 1989).

While the intraregional distinctions were minimal at the outset of the Early Formative era, they rapidly became more marked in the Río Amatzinac Valley as they had in the Valley of Oaxaca. By the end of the Early Formative, Chalcatzingo (like San José Mogote) was clearly a community unlike any other in its respective region in terms of size (twice the extent of the next largest settlement), public construction, and participation in long-distance exchange networks ("Olmec interaction sphere") (Grove 1981, 1987; Flannery 1982). As noted by Flannery (1982), Chalcatzingo also had a "centripetal pull" on other regional settlements (see Hirth 1987b: 353).

Based on the material from the Tlatilco graves (Porter 1953) and other findings, households in the Basin of Mexico also participated in the long-distance exchange sphere at this time. In addition, as in the other two regions, population growth was reasonably rapid (Table 10.5). However, unlike in the Río Amatzinac and Oaxaca Valleys, no single basin community was markedly larger than all others, and there is no evidence for mounded architecture (Sanders, Parsons, and Santley 1979: 96–7; Parsons et al. 1982: 365–7). While several basin communities are estimated to have contained roughly 1,000 people, none of these, to date, has provided clear indications for politico-ritual differentiation. Although as Parsons and others (Parsons et al. 1982: 365) have speculated, something on that order may have existed at Cuicuilco.

Regardless, the three areas that had settlement size and architectural (for Oaxaca and the Río Amatzinac) distinctions early in the Early Formative then also had greater intraregional differences along those same dimensions by the *end* of the period. Interestingly, of the eight areas considered, these also are the only three in which certain households clearly participated in the pan-regional interaction sphere and had access to a range of rare exotic goods (see also Drennan 1983a: 49–50; Drennan and Nowack 1984: 152). Thus, participation in that exchange sphere appears to have been greater where pre-existing/indigenous differences (in community size) already were present (Flannery 1968; Drennan 1976a; Drennan and Nowack 1984: 153). Significantly, as suggested for Oaxaca above, the emergence of a greater degree of politico-ritual differentiation by the end of the Early Forma-

tive is cross-regionally tied both to the differential participation of households in that exchange sphere, as well as to the agglomeration of population around those communities that were more actively involved in exchange and had distinctive civic-ceremonial construction. In such instances, an emerging chief has both increased spatial access to potential surplus production, as well as a means to realize that surplus through exotic goods used either ritually and/or in local exchanges. Here, it is worth noting the agricultural intensification (terracing) evident at Barranca phase Chalcatzingo (Grove 1987b: 420).

The best opportunities for chiefs and other high-status challengers to obtain material rewards for their supporters and to evidence personal resourcefulness and ability lay not in controlling subsistence and utilitarian resources . . . but in establishing access to "scarce" nonutilitarian resources, including gold, pearls, and textiles. The means to acquire these scarce items centered . . . on chiefly participation in various regional and "long distance" exchange systems . . .   (HELMS 1979: 34)

Again, a strong case cannot be made for a strict demographic-resource interpretation. By the end of the Early Formative era, Tamazulapan and possibly Tehuacán (MacNeish et al. 1972: 386–90) had population densities (Table 10.3) on par with the Río Amatzinac, the Valley of Oaxaca, and the basin, and yet there is less evidence for differentiation in the former regions. In Tamazulapan, Byland (1980: 130) estimates that the largest community had only seventy inhabitants and lacked public architecture.

Considering all eight regions, the largest and the densest population (Table 10.2) was in the basin, but political differences may have been less developed there than in the valleys of the Río Amatzinac or Oaxaca. Furthermore, there would seem to be little support for some simple or constant demographic threshold for organizational change in these data. The population (5,000) estimated for the Early Horizon in the Basin of Mexico is significantly higher than those estimated in the Valley of Oaxaca or the Río Amatzinac Valley for the later San José or Barranca phases (or for that matter the Rosario and Cantera phases) respectively. Yet, the degree of political differentiation was evidently greater in the latter two regions. Only later in First Intermediate phase 2 (650–300 B.C.), when the population of the Basin of Mexico is estimated to have reached 80,000, do we find a series of the largest

257

settlements in the region with *definite* civic-ceremonial architecture
(Sanders, Parsons, and Santley 1979: 97).

During the Middle Formative era, the greatest similarities again can
be drawn between the Río Amatzinac and Oaxaca, with Chalcatzingo
becoming more architecturally elaborate (and remaining larger than)
any of the other communities in the former valley. As in the Rosario
phase Valley of Oaxaca, small secondary population clusters were
established away from the major center, but at the same time the
majority of the regional inhabitants remained nucleated in and around
that "central place." At Chalcatzingo in the Cantera phase, long-
distance exchanges of goods, information, and perhaps elite mates
(Grove 1987a) remained partially focused on the lowland Gulf Coast,
while in the Valley of Oaxaca, Middle Formative period preciosity
exchanges became more focused on other highland regions (Pires-
Ferreira 1975).

During the Middle Formative period, changing patterns of highland
exchange may have contributed to the eventual emergence of political
differentiation in several of the smaller valleys. In Tamazulapan and
Cuicatlán during the Late Cruz and Perdido phases respectively (Table
10.1), "central places," large communities with distinctive mounded
architecture, emerged. In both regions, smaller communities clustered
around them. In Cuicatlán, Redmond (1983: 75–7) has shown that
these "special" communities had greater access to exotic goods,
including obsidian and marine shell. In both areas, these shifts
coincided with the development of more distinctive local utilitarian
ceramic traditions, while certain highly decorated bowls showed closer
stylistic ties to outside the region (Byland 1980: 140; Redmond 1983:
63–81). These ceramic shifts parallel what was noted at an earlier date
in the Valley of Oaxaca, and all may relate to the increasing participation of a few select households in extralocal exchanges while regional
boundaries became less permeable for the majority of the populace.

In the Tehuacán Valley, Drennan and Nowack (1984: 154) postu-
late a similar shift in boundary relations at a slightly later date during
the Late Santa Maria phase. Again, it is timed with the emergence of a
"central place" (Quachilco), at which exotic goods were more
abundant than usual (Drennan 1978: 78) and around which other
settlements clustered (MacNeish et al. 1972: 397–8). Even in the
Ejutla Valley, where larger communities with public architecture did
not develop until later (in Monte Albán Late I), the rise of these early

"central places" was marked by population nucleation around them (Feinman 1985; Feinman and Nicholas 1988).

While in these cases, some population growth always coincides with the early stages of political differentiation, the most significant intervening factors do not seem to be pressure on resources or even agricultural risk. In addition, even in instances where the estimated rate of demographic change is rapid, "central places" do not necessarily emerge (Table 10.5). For example, the Early Cruz–Late Cruz phase transition in the Tamazulapan Valley was an episode of relatively rapid demographic growth (0.52 percent), yet a civic-ceremonial hierarchy apparently did not develop until somewhat later.

At higher elevations (the Basin of Mexico, Tamazulapan), where early maize farming may have been the most risky, human populations achieved greater demographic densities during the Early Formative without the emergence of "central places." If risk were the key variable in political change, one might expect the opposite, political changes occurring at lower population densities in those environments where farmers faced greater uncertainty (cf. Sanders 1984a). Likewise, while boundary conditions and the relative freedom of movement clearly influence the political process, I see little support for a strict or simple application of Carneiro's (1970) circumscription hypothesis at this stage of political development. In this sample, political differentiation occurs first in some of the larger valleys (e.g. Oaxaca) and at very low population densities (cf. Sanders and Webster 1978: 297–8).

Although the major focus of this discussion is on political development, several observations concerning long-term demographic change are appropriate. Increasing population was an overall (although not a simple linear) trend in each studied region. Yet, the population sizes, densities, and even rates of change in highland Mesoamerica varied through time and across space (Tables 10.2, 10.3, 10.5). In terms of the effective social-demographic units of ancient highland Mesoamerican society (e.g. the area as a whole, individual highland valleys, specific sites), there is simply no empirical basis (see also Feinman et al. 1985) for modeling population growth as a constant or a given (cf. Logan and Sanders 1976: 33; Sanders and Webster 1978: 297). Here, I am not suggesting that population was necessarily "regulated," but that the size and density of human groups are interrelated with social, economic, environmental, and political factors (and hence by definition at times influenced by them) (e.g. Cowgill 1975).

Nevertheless, in this comparative analysis, certain cross-regional patterns were observed. Often those settlements that either were slightly larger than average, or had special architecture, or had historical precedence at a time when intraregional community differences were minimal, subsequently became the regional "central places." In every area, the development of these nodal places coincided with population concentration around (as well as in) the emergent centers. Furthermore, the emergence of such settlement differences often co-occurred with apparent shifts in extraregional exchange relations and boundary activities, whereby certain households located in the regional centers controlled a larger portion of these formerly more open external contacts. The latter relationship is not totally surprising, since in a study of longer temporal trends in pre-Hispanic Oaxaca (Kowalewski et al. 1983), a strong negative relationship was noted between centralization and boundary permeability.

SUMMARY THOUGHTS AND CONCLUSIONS

The thrust of this analysis is not to eliminate the variables, land and population, from a consideration of sociopolitical change during the Formative era in highland Mexico. Nor is the aim to polarize further the often polemical debate in evolutionary studies between ideological and economic factors. Land, production, population, and labor were important factors in the developmental processes discussed above, but so apparently were changes in the nature of interregional relations and information flows. What this empirical investigation has endeavored to discourage is the notion that the whys, wheres, whens, and hows of sociopolitical change in highland Mexico can be retrodicted simply through the narrow consideration of physical environments, that are artificially presumed to be isolated, and demographic processes, that are assumed to be constant.

Here, consideration has been given both to intraregional processes which fostered population nucleation, and hence the spatial inequities in the amount of surplus that could have been produced, as well as to interregional relationships that led certain households and settlements to control a disproportionate share of exotic goods and presumably information. In examining the latter, the key is not the total volume of

goods and information that was passed between regions but rather the pathways taken and the nature of the things exchanged (Brumfiel and Earle 1987: 4). Nodal households actively participating in interregional exchange would derive an advantage if the total volume of exchange decreased. Hence, it is not surprising that during the Middle Formative period in the Valley of Oaxaca, Parry (1987: 134) noted that the percentage of total chipped stone comprised by obsidian declined from fifteen to ten percent. At the same time, obsidian (particularly certain ritually important items) was distributed more differentially.

It should be clear that my arguments do not hinge on the strict *economic* significance of the rare and symbolically laden goods that were pan-regionally exchanged during the Mesoamerican Formative. Rather, it has been argued that these items (and the information conveyed with them) helped to socially distinguish certain individuals, households, corporate groups, and communities. Yet, greater access to these preciosities (as well as the rituals and the civic-ceremonial activities that they contributed to and the individuals that they marked) apparently was attractive, and the demographic nucleation that occurred around certain nodal communities clearly had important economic implications in terms of labor and agricultural production.

The specific factors which first served to differentiate communities like San José Mogote and Chalcatzingo from neighboring settlements remain somewhat unclear. Yet, through this comparative analysis, the processes surrounding the magnification of those initial differences have become more evident. Thus, even in a specific diachronic case, the factors and mechanisms which promote the beginnings of social inequality and leader–follower relations may not be the same as the conditions which embellish and extend those differences. Clearly then, the examination and comparison of long temporal durations and particular diachronic sequences is essential if we are to understand and account for societal variation and change. Some neo-evolutionists might eschew such a claim as "too-historical," and so by necessity, unscientific and non-evolutionary (e.g. Carneiro 1987). Yet, one need look no further than the paleontological writings of Stephen J. Gould (1986) to see that science and a consideration of history are so far from antithetical that both are indeed essential for an adequate understanding of evolutionary change.

Acknowledgments

I am grateful for the National Science Foundation support given both to the Valley of Oaxaca Settlement Pattern Project (GS-28547, GS-388030, BNS-19640 to Richard E. Blanton; BNS-7914124 to Stephen A. Kowalewski) and the Ejutla Valley Settlement Pattern Project (BNS-84-06229, BNS-85-42668 to Feinman). Both Blanton and Kowalewski, as well as Kent V. Flannery and Joyce Marcus, have been very generous and supportive. The permission and assistance of the Instituto Nacional de Antropología e Historia and the Centro Regional de Oaxaca are recognized with great appreciation. Joaquín García Bárcena and Manuel Esparza have been particularly helpful over the years. Many additional individuals and institutions have supported this research; a toast to you all.

I also would like to thank all of the seminar participants, the staff of the School of American Research, and particularly Timothy K. Earle and Jonathan Haas for one of the most intellectually stimulating yet marvelously comfortable weeks that I have ever spent. In fact, I enjoyed my stay at the School so much that I have returned. I am grateful to Douglas W. Schwartz for the opportunity to revise this manuscript as a Resident Scholar. John E. Clark and Brian Hayden provided valuable comments on an earlier draft. Finally, my greatest appreciation is owed Linda M. Nicholas, who prepared the tables and figures, and assisted in all stages of this research.

11

Pre-Hispanic chiefdom trajectories in Mesoamerica, Central America, and northern South America

ROBERT D. DRENNAN

Archaeologists have developed considerably more sophisticated methods for reconstructing patterns of social, political, and economic organization than they once possessed. Yet the spotty distribution of sophisticated and rigorous archaeological studies requires us to make the most of several classes of data more noted for their conspicuous character than for their ability to reveal prehistoric behavior in subtle detail. In this paper I will attempt to summarize, characterize, and compare the available archaeological data concerning the sequences of development of some prehistoric chiefdoms of Mesoamerica, Central America, and northern South America. I do not pretend to summarize the archaeology of this large area. I have chosen six regions that offer long documented sequences rather than static reconstructions of single periods. How much I say about each region depends in part on how much information is available and in part on how unorthodox my reconstruction of the sequence is. (I have tried to justify more fully my departures from commonly accepted reconstructions than my acceptance of consensus.)

For each sequence I will attempt to discuss the following five aspects of chiefdom development: public works, differences in status or wealth, trade or exchange, warfare, and societal scale. I do *not* intend

this list as a set of criteria which I will seek in the archaeological data in an effort to identify chiefdoms. That task has been undertaken by scholars from Service (1962) and Fried (1967) to C. Renfrew (1973b), Peebles and Kus (1977), Creamer and Haas (1985), and Snarskis (1987). The five categories are simply a convenient way to discuss the evidence from several sequences of chiefdom development.

The six regional sequences demonstrate chiefdom development. Some have preferred to call one or another of these societies "states" or "tribes" or something else. I do not wish to debate this issue. Whatever utility discussions of whether to use the label "chiefdom" or "state" for some society might once have had, it is no longer enlightening to pursue the issue this way (but see Kristiansen, Chapter 2 above). The sequences I will discuss all involve the development of societies that are larger and more complex than autonomous, egalitarian villages, yet not so large or complex as the societies of the Mesoamerican Classic and Postclassic or of the central Andean Middle and Late Horizons. I mean to imply nothing more than this when I say that I will deal with sequences of chiefdom development and that my interest is in comparing these sequences with each other rather than with sequences of state development (cf. Drennan and Uribe 1987b: x–xii). I take here an essentially inductive approach, because we have tended to lose sight of some important aspects of the sequences of social change we are comparing. This chapter, then, has more to do with posing questions than finding answers.

FORMATIVE MESOAMERICA

Southern Gulf Coast

The most spectacular of Mesoamerica's Formative chiefdoms focused on the Olmec centers of the southern Gulf Coast, a hot, humid, forested region of about 100 by 80 km with meandering, often flooded rivers, where sedentary agricultural settlement began soon after 1500 B.C. San Lorenzo, the earliest major center, quickly exceeded small village status, since Coe and Diehl (1980: 105–7, 137, 143) found Bajío phase (1350–1250 B.C.) remains "just about everywhere." A single earth-fill platform 2 m high seems an example of what later became the standard Mesoamerican pattern: open plazas bounded by temple platforms for communal ritual assembly. Artificial fill up to a

depth of 4 m locally was also laid down during the Bajío phase, but it has not been shown to cover more than one small area, so estimates of large work forces moving great quantities of earth are conjectural (e.g. Diehl 1981: 74–5).

San Lorenzo phase materials (1150–900 B.C.) are more abundant, and Coe and Diehl (1980a: 388) estimate population at 1,000. Monumental sculpture was made in basalt brought from sources some 60 km away. Some "altars" weighed as much as 40 metric tons and required a labor force of hundreds working together to be transported (Coe and Diehl 1980a: 296–7, 320). Over sixty-five large sculptures come from San Lorenzo proper, and another ten from nearby. Coe and Diehl (1980a: 29, 57, 71–8) imagine large mound groups that were systematically demolished in later times, but only one 2 m mound is known for the San Lorenzo phase. Monumental sculpture ceased and many, but not all, plazas were abandoned at the end of the San Lorenzo phase (Coe and Diehl 1980a: 294–5). Materials of the ensuing Nacaste phase (900–700 B.C.), however, seem to have been as widely distributed as those of the San Lorenzo phase (Coe and Diehl 1980a: 188), so it is not clear that the site suffered a major population decline until after 600 B.C.

The other investigated Olmec center, La Venta, developed later, between 800 and 400 B.C. (Drucker, Heizer, and Squier 1957). Its public architecture dwarfs that of San Lorenzo; its principal pyramid rises over 33 m above a platform base 73 m by 128 m (Heizer 1961: 44). Before this pyramid lies a symmetrical arrangement of platform mounds and plazas partially enclosed by a "palisade" of natural basalt columns. This complex, some 450 m long, includes a phenomenal array of offerings consisting of ceramics and small jade sculptures, "massive offerings" of perhaps 4,500 metric tons of serpentine blocks, tombs, etc. (Drucker, Heizer, and Squier 1959, Heizer 1961: 44). La Venta has often been described as an empty ceremonial center, but it is now clear that it included significant residential zones as well (González 1988). To call it an "urban settlement" (González 1988: 136), however, is certainly a misleading overcorrection of previous errors.

Monumental stone sculpture extremely similar to that of San Lorenzo in form, content, style, size, and quantity also occurs. Some of the sculpture of San Lorenzo and La Venta is religious in character (e.g. representations of serpents and jaguars and human/animal com-

binations [cf. Joralemon 1971]). The famous colossal heads, however, some over 3 m high, may be portraits of specific individuals (Stirling 1965: 733, Coe 1977: 186, Coe and Diehl 1980: 293, Grove 1981b: 61 and 67), and monuments such as La Venta Stela 2 (Drucker 1952: 174) depict figures like later Maya rulers. Such glorification of individuals suggests strong and effective leadership in their hands. Tomb C at La Venta contained thirty-seven celts of jade and serpentine, three ceramic vessels, two jade earspools, one serpentine figurine, one decorated obsidian core, and 182 other ornamental jade objects (Drucker, Heizer, and Squier 1959: 272–4). Such tombs are known only for La Venta and only for the last of the four construction phases there, but by the end of the Olmec sequence it is clear that substantial differences of status and/or wealth existed.

All attempts to reconstruct regional economies of Formative societies in the southern Gulf Coast have been based on ethnographic analogies (e.g. Drucker 1961, Heizer 1961 and 1962, Coe and Diehl 1980) without direct archaeological support. Maize is generally assumed to have been a major crop (if not the principal staple), but the only direct evidence for this is the presence of *manos* and *metates* (e.g. Coe 1981: 16).

Obsidian was brought to San Lorenzo from at least eight different localities up to 800 km distant in various directions (Cobean et al. 1971), suggesting complicated interlinked networks of trading relationships rather than simply efficient, cost-effective obsidian procurement. Luxury items, such as iron ore mirrors and jade objects, came from largely unknown sources perhaps at a distance of several hundred kilometers. Although jade and obsidian are conspicuous in the archaeological record, and much has been made of the economic significance of the obsidian "trade" (e.g. Cobean et al. 1971: 670–1), the quantities produced and consumed were much too small for them to have been of any direct economic significance (Drennan 1984a and 1984b). The ready movement of such goods, however, and the long-noted sharing of the Olmec art style between many regions of Mesoamerica indicate high levels of communication between peoples separated by distances of several hundred kilometers.

Heizer (1961: 47) calculates 2 million man-days of labor to create the public works at La Venta with a work force between 50 and 3,500 depending on the pacing of the work. The largest estimate implies a regional population of perhaps as much as 15,000, which could easily

have been supported by simple agricultural techniques within about 40 km of the center (Drucker 1961: 69; Heizer 1962: 311). Substantially lower estimates of sustaining population and the area needed to support it are also reasonable. Coe and Diehl's (1980: 297) highest estimate of work crews needed at San Lorenzo is 1,000, requiring a regional population of 4,000 or 5,000, which could have been supported within a few kilometers of San Lorenzo (Coe and Diehl 1980: 147). There is no survey information for the immediate region, but small villages existed during San Lorenzo times in the Chontalpa region some 100 km northeast of San Lorenzo (Sisson 1970: 44–5). During La Venta times there were still small villages in the Chontalpa (about 20 km northeast), although not in any greater numbers than earlier. Prospecting for sites along former river channels within a few kilometers of La Venta has also revealed some small settlements (Rust and Sharer 1988). San Lorenzo and La Venta at their respective peaks, then, were probably centers for societies whose total populations numbered a few thousand people who lived in an area no more than a few dozen kilometers across.

The southern Gulf Coast may also have had other major Formative centers like Tres Zapotes (Drucker 1943) and Laguna de los Cerros (Bove 1978), although probably not all were contemporaneous. These centers are spaced far enough apart that their sustaining areas need not have impinged on one another. Whether there was warfare between Olmec centers is unclear, notwithstanding Coe (Coe 1981: 19, Coe and Diehl 1980: 148 and 152). There is no evidence of fortifications (but see Earle, Chapter 4 above), but the occasional sculpted figure carries what might be a weapon (e.g. La Venta Stela 2 [Drucker 1952: 174]). Cannibalism was practiced (Coe and Diehl 1980: 375–6 and 386), but warfare and cannibalism are not the same thing. By A.D. 1 or earlier the social phenomenon that produced the monumental public works identified with Olmec sites had ended, and the region was increasingly affected by the Classic period states that were developing elsewhere.

Valley of Oaxaca

The Valley of Oaxaca is a pocket of level alluvium at 1500 m above sea level surrounded by steep mountain ridges of lower agricultural potential. Precipitation is highly seasonal – adequate for agriculture in the

rainy season, nonexistent in the dry season. The valley is about 70 km long and includes about 2,000 km². Feinman (Chapter 10 above) discusses its sequence in greater detail.

Sedentary maize-based agricultural occupation began soon after 1500 B.C. A Tierras Largas phase (1350–1150 B.C.) population of a few hundred lived in small, autonomous, egalitarian villages, mostly in the small Etla arm of the valley (Feinman et al. 1985: 338 and 346). At least one of these villages, San José Mogote, which was slightly larger than the others, had a rectangular structure about 4.4 by 5.5 m with a plastered floor and walls made of closely spaced pine posts. It was rebuilt on the same location and to the same plan repeatedly during the phase, and Flannery and Marcus (1976: 211) have identified it as a "public building" and suggested that it was used for some communal ritual.

As the ensuing San José (1150–850 B.C.) and Guadalupe (850–550 B.C.) phases began, San José Mogote grew to a population of about 700, and the entire Valley of Oaxaca contained some 2,000 inhabitants, of whom roughly half were still concentrated in the Etla region (Feinman et al. 1985: 341–2 and 346; Kowalewski, Fisch, and Flannery 1983: 51). Modest status differences are observable in residential architecture with some houses raised on platforms about 1 m high (Flannery and Marcus 1983b: 55; Whalen 1981). Systematic comparisons of artifact assemblages associated with different houses at Fábrica San José (Drennan 1976a) show modest but unmistakable concentrations of such materials as ornaments, decorated ceramics, fine serving bowls, and animal bone (especially deer) in households where burials received more elaborate offerings (up to four ceramic vessels, fifty-four jadeite beads, one jadeite pendant [Drennan 1976a: 248 and 250–1]). Tomb 3 at San José Mogote was formed by lining a grave with flat stone slabs.

Public buildings at San José Mogote and Huitzo were raised on 1 m platforms (Flannery and Marcus 1976a: 211–13, 1983b) and may have been arranged around plazas in the characteristic Mesoamerican fashion. Public buildings at several settlements may indicate competing centers at distances of around 20 km (cf. Flannery and Marcus 1983b: 56). There are, however, no direct archaeological indications of warfare or hostility between these centers, and San José Mogote was much larger than any other community. Two small carved stones from

San José Mogote are the entire known corpus of sculpture (Flannery and Marcus 1983b: 54).

Evidence of specialized production of bone and lithic tools and ornaments occurs at Fábrica San José (Drennan 1976a), San José Mogote, and Tierras Largas (Flannery and Winter 1976). Each village had such specialists, so that little interdependence between villages is indicated. Manufacture of small magnetite mirrors, however, seems restricted to San José Mogote. Up through the San José phase, settlements were located near the valley's best alluvial farmland, the productive potential of which far outstripped the needs of regional population (Feinman et al. 1985: 340). Some Guadalupe phase settlements, however, were situated in less favorable locations with respect to the best alluvial soils. One such community, Fábrica San José, may have specialized in producing salt and possibly hunting deer (Drennan 1976a). All such specialization was a part-time activity of farming households.

Luxury goods, like shell, were brought from other regions, probably in both finished and unfinished form. Obsidian came from sources in different directions and at varying distances apparently through shifting participation in a complicated pattern of separate networks (Pires-Ferreira 1975). At first individual households seem to have procured their obsidian separately; later, more centralized procurement, perhaps by higher status families, is suggested (Winter and Pires-Ferreira 1976). This pattern began at San José Mogote and spread to smaller villages as well by the Guadalupe phase.

Up to this point, then, Valley of Oaxaca societies show evidence of status differences, public works, regional-level leadership, and economic specialization, but all on an extremely modest scale compared, for instance, to the southern Gulf Coast.

The Rosario phase (550–450 B.C.) saw a quantum leap in public works at San José Mogote (Flannery and Marcus 1983b: 57). Earth-fill platforms that were as big as 22 by 28 m by 2 m high and faced with limestone slabs formed plaza groups. One such platform supported an elite residence much more elaborate than the ordinary houses. These public works still fall far short of those of La Venta in terms of labor investment. Monument 3, a stone slab with a relief carving of a contorted naked figure, was placed in a passageway to be stepped on, and probably represented forcible domination by the San José Mogote

rulers (Marcus 1976a: 44–5). Stone-lined tombs were the most elaborate burials, but were emptied in prehistoric times (Flannery and Marcus 1983b: 60). Regional population stayed about the same as in the previous period (Feinman et al. 1985: 346). Whether or not San José Mogote by this time dominated the entire valley, there was no other comparable center in terms of population or public works. The mountainous zone immediately surrounding the valley was apparently unoccupied (Drennan 1983b), and populations were sparse in other valleys in the southern Mexican highlands.

In Monte Albán Ia (450–100 B.C.), San José Mogote's population dropped as the newly founded regional center at Monte Albán grew rapidly to some 5,000 inhabitants (Blanton 1978: 35). Total valley population surged to some 15,000 (Feinman et al. 1985: 346) and expanded into the surrounding mountains as well (Drennan 1983b). Monte Albán surely dominated this entire area extending to distances of at least 40 or 50 km. Public buildings on stone-faced platforms similar to the smaller ones of Rosario phase San José Mogote began to define the site's 150 m by 300 m main plaza (Blanton 1978: 3 and 35, Flannery and Marcus 1976a: 215–16 and 1983d). Over 300 stone slabs, known as *danzantes*, were carved with relief figures like those of San José Mogote Monument 3. They were set up in an impressive display of the exercise of political/military power (cf. Marcus 1976a: 125–7). The richest tomb from this period at Monte Albán was constructed of stone slabs and contained seventy-two ceramic vessels (Acosta 1965: 817; Flannery and Marcus 1983d: 90). Monte Albán Ia carried patterns that emerged during the Rosario phase to an altogether new scale. The centuries that followed the Monte Albán Ia phase saw the development of larger and differently organized societies that extend beyond the realm of the comparisons attempted in this paper.

Basin of Mexico

The Basin of Mexico, at 2200 m above sea level, has a long frost season during the dry winter. Rainfall is adequate for agriculture in the south, marginal in the north. The basin is about 90 km long and includes some 6,000 km^2 (excluding swamps and lakes). Sedentary maize-based agricultural settlement began slightly later than in other parts of Mesoamerica.

The Early Horizon (1150–950 B.C.) saw low population levels, reaching about 5,000 by its end, concentrated in the wettest southern portions of the basin (Sanders, Parsons, and Santley 1979: 94–6 and 183, Tolstoy 1975). There were several villages with populations of a few hundred, but most of the settlements were very small hamlets. Burials with offerings including up to twenty-three (often extremely elaborate) ceramic vessels, figurines, and other ornamental items are known from Tlatilco (Tolstoy et al. 1977: 103, Porter 1953), but there is no evidence of public works or ceremonial architecture. These patterns subsequently intensified (Sanders, Parsons, and Santley 1979: 96–7, 183; Tolstoy 1975) as population grew to some 25,000.

During the First Intermediate Phase 2 (450–200 B.C.) population continued to grow (to more than 75,000) and to expand northward somewhat (Sanders, Parsons, and Santley 1979: 97–8, 183). A half-dozen "regional centers" each held several thousand inhabitants; one, Cuicuilco, probably had more than 5,000. Complexes of platform mounds (up to 5 m in height) supported temple buildings and defined plazas for communal rituals at these centers. Sustaining areas of centers were within 10 km or less. Cuicuilco may have dominated one or more nearby centers, forming a yet larger and more complex socio-political unit. Part-time village specialization may also have occurred (cf. Sanders, Parsons, and Santley 1979: 98; Flannery and Winter 1976: 34–5). Most obsidian came from nearby sources (Pires-Ferreira 1975; Tolstoy et al. 1977: 102); shell and other luxury items came from distant regions.

Population continued to grow in First Intermediate Phase 3 (200 B.C.–A.D. 1) to approximately 145,000 (Sanders, Parsons, and Santley 1979: 98–105; 183). About a dozen regional centers were packed closely together. Two were much larger than the others: Cuicuilco (20,000 inhabitants) and Teotihuacán (20,000 to 40,000). Some seventy percent of the population of the basin lived in one of the regional centers – an extraordinarily "urbanized" population. Teotihuacán represented a substantial expansion of population into the northern reaches of the basin, but the demographic center of gravity was still in the south. The most massive public works of the basin were at Cuicuilco, where the largest pyramid reached its maximum size of about 80 m in diameter and 20 m in height, but Teotihuacán had also embarked on a major program of platform mound construction. It is difficult to imagine that Cuicuilco and Teotihuacán did not dominate

271

at least some of the other regional centers since none lay more than about 30 km away from one of these two.

It is easy to envision considerable competition between centers so closely spaced. Isolated hilltop complexes and some fortifications may suggest hostilities, but regional centers were not ordinarily in defensible locations or fortified. Sanders, Parsons, and Santley (1979: 369–85) and others have argued that this period reflects population pressure and competition between centers over farmland. On the other hand, Brumfiel (1976) argues that settlement spacing does not show evidence of regional population pressure, and many arable portions of the basin remained unexploited. Elsewhere I have suggested (Drennan 1987: 313–14, 318) that this part of the sequence reflects competition over tributary populations rather than over natural resources.

In the succeeding First Intermediate Phase 4, Teotihuacán clearly won out in whatever the competition was. It grew enormously while regional population dropped. The best agricultural land in the south was abandoned as nearly everyone concentrated in and closely around Teotihuacán. By this point the scale and complexity of this single polity place it outside the realm of chiefdoms.

CENTRAL AMERICA

Volcán Barú Region

The Pacific slopes of western Panama are forested and steep, occasionally interrupted by patches of more level fertile soils receiving ample precipitation at elevations above 1200 m (Linares, Sheets, and Rosenthal 1975: 137–40). We have archaeological information for 62 km^2 along the upper course of the Río Chiriquí Viejo (Sheets 1980).

Sedentary maize-based agricultural occupation began at lower elevations about 200 B.C. and spread into higher elevations some 400 years later (Linares 1980a: 94; Linares and Sheets 1980: 54; Linares, Sheets, and Rosenthal 1975: 144; Sheets 1980: 267, 274; Smith 1980: 159–61, 167–8). Bugaba phase settlement at lower elevations focused on three villages, each covering some 50 ha, and two smaller villages (Linares and Sheets 1980: 48–9), all quite close together. At higher elevations another cluster of forty communities ranged from 18 ha down to 1 ha or less. Linares and Sheets (1980: 53–4) estimate population for the excavated Pittí-González site at about one household per

ha of occupied area. On this basis, the entire region held some 2,500 inhabitants.

One of the lower villages, Barriles, yielded stone statues (up to 2.4 m high) of naked individuals carrying others on their shoulders and of figures holding human heads. Some of these statues were parts either of very large corn-grinding *metates* or of chiefly thrones (Linares, Sheets, and Rosenthal 1975; Haberland 1984: 244–5). A raised area about 30 by 50 m lined with stone slabs and boulders has been described as a "ceremonial center," and the largest statues apparently once stood in a row to one side of it (Stirling 1950). Shaft tombs included large sculptured metates as offerings. These manifestations of complex social patterns are late in the sequence at Barriles (Late Bugaba phase [A.D. 400–600]) (Linares, Sheets, and Rosenthal 1975: 142; Linares and Sheets 1980: 54–5; Linares 1980a: 92). Sheets, Rosenthal, and Ranere (1980: 405–9) find debris from ground stone celt manufacture and repair in quantity at seven of the forty-five sites studied – always either the largest sites in the region or the largest sites in their particular subarea (Linares and Sheets 1980: 52).

About A.D. 600 the Volcán Barú erupted and covered much of the landscape with pumice. Higher elevations became uninhabitable, although Barriles continued to develop as a regional center (Linares, Sheets, and Rosenthal 1975: 144; Linares and Sheets 1980: 92; Sheets 1980: 268), possibly for an area extending well beyond the surveyed zone. By A.D. 1000 Barriles ceased to be such a center, and whatever centralized organization it represented was absent from the region for the five centuries until the Spanish Conquest (Haberland 1984: 254).

Central Panama

This vaguely defined region falls within a square roughly 200 km on a side and includes coastal plains with mangrove swamps and open grasslands as well as forested mountains rising up to over 3000 m. Here we focus on the relatively level, dry Pacific lowland zone.

Large sedentary or near-sedentary settlements may date early in the third millennium B.C. at Monagrillo (Ranere and Hansell 1978; Cooke 1984: 273–9). Hansell (1987: 129) reports that La Mula-Sarigua covered 65 ha between 1000 and 200 B.C. As in the Volcán Barú region, a settlement and subsistence shift took place around 200 B.C. as maize-agricultural villages became numerous, especially in major

river floodplains (Cooke 1984: 272, 283–6; Weiland 1984: 33 and 46). At Sitio Sierra, twenty-five burials of about this date contained modest, mostly utilitarian, offerings, providing no evidence of substantial status differences (Cooke 1984: 285, 287). The site, however, covered some 45 ha, suggesting a population at least in the hundreds (Weiland 1984: 40). Burials of El Indio phase (A.D. 200–500) in the Tonosí Valley show somewhat more differentiation with offerings including ornamental items of agate, onyx, serpentine, mica, bone, and *tumbaga*, with individual graves including up to six items (Cooke 1984: 290).

The famous burials of Coclé province, after A.D. 500, provide the most dramatic archaeological evidence of Central American chiefdoms. Settlements of this period seem to have been larger and more numerous than those of preceding times (Weiland 1984: 46). They were spread throughout the lowland plains and shared pottery types and other stylistic features (Linares 1977: 31). At Sitio Conte were burials containing the remains of twenty or more individuals buried at the same time. Offerings included polished stone celts, bone awls, flaked stone projectile points, stingray spines, and sharks' teeth. Helmets, breastplates, headbands, cuffs, rings, earspools, beads, pendants, and other ornaments were fashioned from gold, *tumbaga*, bone, agate, serpentine, and other stones (Lothrop 1937; 1942). The number of ceramic vessels in a single grave could reach one hundred. Some of these items and some of the materials of which they were made were imported from distant regions (such as emeralds and possibly some of the goldwork from Colombia).

Linares (1977: 59–70) interprets the animal iconography of the polychrome pottery in the Sitio Conte graves as rank symbols for chiefs whose status derived from ferocity in warfare. Bundles of spears, *atlatls* (spearthrowers), and the armor-like character of much of the goldwork suggest that many of those buried in the graves were warriors. Certainly physical violence is well documented at Playa Venado, where burials of 369 individuals displayed numerous examples of decapitation (Lothrop 1954). If cultural material at Sitio Conte covers only the 3 ha reported (Linares 1977: 34), the site never had a large residential population, and Linares (1977: 58) argues that it had none during the period of elaborate burials. She suggests that some of the largest graves could be those of a chief, his sons, and warriors all killed in battle (Linares 1977: 75–7).

Elaborate burials at Sitio Conte ended by about A.D. 900, but similar social patterns continued in central Panama. Spanish Conquest period sources speak unanimously of wealthy and powerful chiefs, dedicating seemingly continual effort to the display of personal adornment symbolizing wealth and rank. Warfare on a very local scale was endemic, chiefly succession was almost always in dispute, and burial practices strongly paralleled those evidenced for earlier times at Sitio Conte (cf. Oviedo 1851 (II): 256–60). One early sixteenth-century chief, Natá, resided in a community of forty-five to fifty houses (Oviedo 1851 (II): 212). Cooke reports that the archaeological site corresponding to this settlement covers some 400 ha (Linares 1977: 73), which suggests a population of at least 2,000 by the methods Linares and Sheets (1980: 53–4) applied to Volcán Barú settlements. The town was reported to be a significant exchange center in the early sixteenth century, and Spanish accounts describe large quantities of food stored there (cf. Linares 1977: 73). We do not know whether the highly ranked people of earlier periods who were buried at Sitio Conte lived at such sizeable communities that functioned similarly as regional exchange centers.

NORTHERN SOUTH AMERICA

Alto Magdalena

The Alto Magdalena, an area of about 100 by 50 km in the Andes of southwestern Colombia, ranges from dry, broad, natural alluvial terraces at 600 m above sea level, through humid, steep slopes with occasional patches of fertile rolling land between 1000 and 3000 m, to cold, level, waterlogged *páramo* above 3000 m.

Sedentary agricultural occupation began before 500 B.C., but is poorly documented. The zone is famous for statues depicting a wide variety of human and animal forms. There are naturalistic, larger-than-life anthropomorphic figures with feline fangs (e.g. Duque Gómez 1964: Lámina XV), sometimes holding infants (e.g. Duque Gómez 1964: Lámina XXV; Reichel-Dolmatoff 1972: 45). Sometimes only the heads are represented in stylized form (e.g. Reichel-Dolmatoff 1972: 35). Figures with clubs often flanked larger figures (e.g. Reichel-Dolmatoff 1972: 63) in a warrior-like grouping. Birds, snakes, lizards, crocodiles, frogs, and other animals also appear (e.g.

Reichel-Dolmatoff 1972: 62, 97; Sotomayor and Uribe 1987: 166–8, 301–2). The most comprehensive catalog of this sculpture lists over 500 pieces (Sotomayor and Uribe 1987).

A special concentration of statues occurs within about 5 km of San Agustín, but dozens of scattered localities once sported a few statues. Statues were often associated with a large stone slab tomb (Duque Gómez and Cubillos 1979: 27, 62–3 and 1983: 61, 77), but tomb offerings might be no more than a half-dozen ceramic vessels and some polished stone beads. Gold ornaments occurred, but only rarely (Duque Gómez 1964: 35–214). The tombs and associated statues were covered by earthen mounds up to 25 m in diameter and 4 m high (cf. Cubillos 1980: 47–8, Lámina VII; Duque Gómez and Cubillos 1983: 44–5, 61, 77). Such barrows occurred singly or in small groups. At Alto de los Idolos there were about 10 mounds and an area, perhaps 20 by 50 m, that was leveled artificially by adding fill to the hill slope (Duque Gómez and Cubillos 1979).

These public works are difficult to date. Associated radiocarbon dates (Sotomayor and Uribe 1987: 14–16) from 555 B.C. ± 50 (Duque Gómez 1964: 456–7) to A.D. 690 ± 80 are concentrated in the first few centuries A.D. suggesting some 1,200 or 1,300 years of tomb building and statue carving, gradually increasing to a peak, then tapering off. The activity was sporadic and scattered in the sense that efforts seem focused on one locality for a while, then on another. Particularly when the long time span and scattered nature of the public works are considered, it is difficult to argue that concentrated labor forces on a huge scale were needed.

During the first few centuries A.D., population levels in the Alto Magdalena were probably six or seven times higher than they had been before. Regional population densities may have reached 50 or 100 per km^2 (Drennan 1985: 173–9). The complexes of barrows and statues were not unoccupied ritual centers since residential debris occurs in and around them (e.g. Duque Gómez 1964: 227–32; Reichel-Dolmatoff 1975), but they were not large, densely populated, nucleated settlements either. Although occupation may have tended to congregate in the general vicinity of tomb and statue complexes, settlement was very dispersed, so large zones of occupation represent relatively small numbers of people. Five to ten people per occupied hectare seems reasonable (cf. Drennan 1985: 177).

Taken together, the evidence for this period suggests little stability.

The public works associated with the burials of presumed chiefs seem to skip across the landscape through time. There may have been several contemporaneous, possibly competing, chiefs in different parts of the Alto Magdalena. The domain of a single powerful chief may have encompassed a few thousand people within a radius on the order of 10 km.

After A.D. 700 or 800, population in the region continued to grow, perhaps doubling its previous size (Drennan 1985: 173–9). There is little evidence of public works, although shaft and chamber tomb burials contained offerings of grinding stones, celts, and ceramic vessels. Although such tombs had occurred in earlier periods (e.g. Duque Gómez and Cubillos 1983: 67–9), they were now much more numerous. None comprises such elaborate burial treatment as the earlier barrows, but many more people merited such treatment. This situation continued until the Spanish Conquest in the 1530s.

Residential sites of this latest period consisted of circular houses some 3 to 5 m in diameter (Duque Gómez 1964: 234 and 237, Duque Gómez and Cubillos 1981; Llanos and Durán 1983). A residential terrace dating to the earlier period of barrows and statues has been tested at Barranquilla Alta, and, although no actual house remains were encountered, it suggests a similar residential pattern (Drennan 1985: 129–35). A round structure some 9 m in diameter has been interpreted by Duque Gómez and Cubillos (1981) as a ceremonial house. Carbonized remains of maize, beans, and wild fruits have been encountered for this late period (Duque Gómez 1964: 237, Lámina XXII; Duque Gómez and Cubillos 1981; Llanos and Durán 1983), and pollen of maize, quinoa, beans, potatoes, sweet potatoes, manioc, and coca documents crops grown from about A.D. 1 (Drennan, Herrera, and Piñeros 1989).

The likeliest imports to the Alto Magdalena are the gold ornaments which were present, but rare, in the tombs. After A.D. 500 gold ornaments were major items of long-distance trade in northern South America and Central America, and even reached Mesoamerica (e.g. Bray 1974; Helms 1979). Obsidian was also present, but quite rare in all periods, and may have originated within the Alto Magdalena. The region seems, then, surprisingly unconnected to long-distance exchange, even of luxury items, throughout its sequence. The period of barrows and statues, when there were certainly chiefs of some wealth and power, may have been too early for much gold trade. The

small amount of gold in later times, like the absence of elaborate tombs, may suggest chiefs of less significance than their predecessors, a judgment in which the early Spanish accounts seem to concur.

COMPARISONS

Making comparisons between Mesoamerica, Central America, and northern South America is not a new idea. Such comparisons are explicit or implicit in the entire history of archaeology in Central America and northern South America. Indeed, the usual name for that area (which I have thus far studiously avoided) is the "Intermediate Area," implying that its prime characteristic is its lack of cultural evolutionary success between Mesoamerica and the central Andes. One recent effort at summary and comparison (also spawned by a School of American Research Advanced Seminar) begins thus: "Why did lower Central American societies and cultures develop the way that they did? Or, to put it another way, why did lower Central America not develop more along the lines of Mesoamerica or Peru?" (Willey 1984: 375).

Beginning comparisons in this way tends to frame them in rather static terms; it leads to comparing the largest and most complex societies in Mesoamerica (or Peru) with the largest and most complex societies in Central America or northern South America. In short, it leads to comparing chiefdoms to states. This may or may not be a useful thing to do. If it is, it is surely much more meaningful to compare the early chiefdoms of Mesoamerica to the later states that, in one sense or another, developed from them. If it is important to compare chiefdoms to states (just *any* chiefdoms to *any* states), then we should probably follow in the cultural evolutionary, comparative ethnography footsteps of Lewis Henry Morgan (as, indeed, several recent scholars have [e.g. Service 1962, 1975; Johnson and Earle 1987]). If we insist on pursuing the difficult, time-consuming, expensive, and relatively unreliable means of archaeology to reconstruct prehistoric societies, then we simply must take advantage of the one major benefit to be derived: the possibility of studying long, continuous sequences of change in which the societies that occur at various points are "genetically" related to each other.

As soon as we turn to the subject of long, continuous sequences of change we are also led to change the geographic focus of our com-

278

parison. Such sequences are not to be found at the level of areas the size of Mesoamerica or lower Central America or northern South America. Meaningful sequences of social change (at least for the kind of societies we are studying) are to be found at the level of much smaller regions – regions on a scale of one or a very few of the social units we wish to study. In all six sequences discussed here populations of a few thousand people developed in areas of a few thousand km^2 or less. (The Volcán Barú region was an unusually small study area, probably encompassing only part of a meaningful sociopolitical entity, and the Basin of Mexico had larger populations divided into more sociopolitical units than the other regions.) Comparisons placed on such a basis have been made before, with enlightening results (e.g. Sanders and Webster 1978 or Blanton et al. 1981, for Mesoamerica, or Kirch 1984, for Polynesia), and several of the other chapters in this volume take such an approach. Elsewhere I have argued that this approach is particularly productive and important to the study of chiefdoms as opposed to other kinds of societies (Drennan and Uribe 1987b: vii–ix).

Warfare and long-distance exchange

Of the several categories of evidence discussed above, warfare is the one for which the implications of the six sequences are clearest. Warfare is an extremely common feature of ethnographically described chiefdoms. Carneiro (1970) has served as a rallying point for those who see this supposedly endemic warfare as having major developmental implications. In the six sequences discussed here, it is most dramatically represented in central Panama in sixteenth-century sources and earlier at Sitio Conte and Playa Venado. At least some warfare may be suggested by sculpture in the Alto Magdalena. The case is more equivocal in the Volcán Barú region, at least for the period when Barriles was a thriving center or earlier. Warfare is still harder to find clear evidence of in any of the three Mesoamerican sequences discussed. None of the six shows systematic patterns of fortification in any period. Absence of fortifications does not, of course, mean absence of warfare, but it forces us to think what warfare may have been about. Whatever warfare did occur in the six sequences discussed here was undoubtedly not about control of land as Carneiro (1970) would have us believe, but about status rivalry, as the cumulative effect of Spanish

Conquest period accounts of Intermediate Area chiefdoms makes clear. Warfare was not so much between corporate groups of people as between chiefs and their henchmen. It had to do with establishing pecking orders between chiefs and, at least as much as any other factor, with succession at the death of a chief (Earle 1978: 162–5, 180).

Despite the idea that chiefly positions were inherited, considerable politicking was clearly necessary for a young man to take possession of his birthright. Those who seek to apply Carneiro's "Theory of the Origin of the State" to the emergence of chiefdoms have confused the politics of birth with the birth of politics in placing warfare in a pivotal developmental role. However important warfare may have been in playing the chiefly game, it was not important in the processes that wrote the rules. The development of chiefdoms cannot be understood simply by studying the ways in which chiefs in developed chiefdoms seek to maintain and increase their power, any more than the development of presidential government in the United States can be understood simply by studying how and why Ronald Reagan won the presidency in 1980. In none of the six sequences is there any evidence of warfare early on in chiefdom development. Without exception, the best evidence of warfare comes relatively late in a sequence and might, therefore, have played some role in the transition to statehood where that happened (as Carneiro originally suggested), but that is a subject beyond the scope of this volume. This may well not be the case in all sequences of chiefdom development; for example, Steponaitis suggested at the seminar that Mississippian chiefdoms at their peak had a pacifying effect on local warfare.

A similar conclusion can be reached concerning trade or exchange at long distance (i.e. several hundred kilometers). At such distances, exchange of food staples is out of the question, given the pre-Hispanic technology of transport (Drennan 1984a, 1984b). The items imported from distant regions in the six sequences came in small quantities and were almost always luxury goods – things like jadeite, gold, emeralds, and mother of pearl. Displays of such items had important social and ideological implications (cf. Flannery 1968; Drennan 1976b; Linares 1977; Helms 1979), but their role in chiefdoms was analogous to that of warfare. In some regions (the Alto Magdalena and the Volcán Barú region seem notable exceptions), display of imported items was one strategy chiefs could turn to in status competition, but it had little to do with the emergence of chiefdoms. The two places where such items

were most conspicuously represented were Sitio Conte and La Venta. In both instances, chiefdoms were already well developed, and the displays of imported goods were of symbolic, rather than economic (cf. Drennan 1984a), importance. Such goods played little role in mobilizing resources. Rather they represented a major way in which resources, once mobilized by elites, were expended. Even in the case of the best candidate for a utilitarian imported good, obsidian, quantities were too small to make the trade or exchange itself an activity of economic significance (cf. Drennan 1984a). Trade or exchange at long distance, then, provided the plumes of the chiefly peacock, not its basic diet.

Although the distinction between fundamental economic significance and conspicuous consumption of luxury goods may, at first, sound like the useful distinction made by D'Altroy and Earle (1985) between staple finance and wealth finance, it is not the same. D'Altroy and Earle were concerned with how much easier "wealth" items are to use essentially as money than staples are. My point here is that, although some of the same kinds of "wealth" items were used in chiefdoms in these six sequences, they were not used in any way resembling money. Their use, in short, can in no way be considered finance.

Local economy, public works, status, and wealth

In the six sequences, chiefdoms were certainly or probably built on a subsistence system focused on maize agriculture. It has, of course, been frequently suggested that maize, because of its storability, its possibilities for intensive production, its - protein content, its seasonality, or other characteristics, spawned the development of complex societies in the Intermediate Area (e.g. Reichel-Dolmatoff 1973, 1987: 136–8; Roosevelt 1980; Snarskis 1984, 1987; etc.). Clearly more is involved than simply the availability of maize for cultivation, however, since many regions in the New World where maize was cultivated did not develop complex patterns of social organization, and since some regions (the southern Gulf Coast, the Volcán Barú region, the Alto Magdalena) saw the development of chiefdoms followed by a disappearance or diminution of complexity despite continued maize cultivation. Maize agriculture may simply have played the permissive role of making possible (but not necessary) regional populations of a

size and density without which significant complexity cannot exist.

Another approach to local economies is through craft specialization and exchange. This aspect is best documented in the Valley of Oaxaca sequence, where part-time specialized households existed quite early in the sequence. This would seem to have little to do with the popular scenario in which different villages specialize in different products and the central tendencies of chiefdom organization emerge in the context of the distribution (or redistribution) of those products. The Valley of Oaxaca does not fit this pattern because, until late in the sequence of chiefdom development, specialization was not on a village basis. Rather, each village contained the specialists it required. The advantages of proximity to craft specialists would, however, certainly provide one reason for the existence of a large community like San José Mogote. The development of craft specialization within villages would also encourage more nucleated settlements. In this regard, the Valley of Oaxaca, the Basin of Mexico, and the southern Gulf Coast seem to stand out from the Volcán Barú region, central Panama, and the Alto Magdalena. Settlements in the three Mesoamerican regions customarily have settlement densities (*not* regional population densities) of thirty per ha or more (Drennan 1988). Those of the other three regions are not as firmly documented but fairly widespread consensus among archaeologists working there points toward settlement densities of around five per ha. If these differences in settlement densities do reflect different degrees of craft specialization, then the three Mesoamerican sequences are characterized from the earliest periods considered here by more integrated local economies, that is, by greater economic interdependence between families. The three sequences from the Intermediate Area, by contrast, show greater economic redundancy and autonomy of family units who, in consequence, did not tend to locate in such close proximity even within the larger settlement units. In making this suggestion, I do not, of course, intend to imply that local specialization and exchange did not occur in the three sequences of the Intermediate Area. It certainly did, and some evidence to that effect is cited above at least for the latter part of the Volcán Barú and central Panama sequences. The question, however, is one of relative intensity.

Public works are also of greatest significance for their role in the local economy. The scale of public works is certainly one measure of the extent to which leaders can control the expenditure of human

effort. In this regard the southern Gulf Coast and the Alto Magdalena stand out for the large scale of their public works from fairly early in their sequences. Central Panama could be added to this category on the grounds that the elaborateness of burials such as those from Sitio Conte qualifies them as public works. The Basin of Mexico and the Valley of Oaxaca are surprising for the small scale of their public works until close to the end of the chiefdom sequence. (Both, of course, went on to substantially larger-scale public works programs in the context of much larger and more complex societies.)

Turning from the scale of public works to the nature of public works reveals a different contrast. In central Panama and in the Alto Magdalena, public works were single-mindedly oriented to important individuals, especially their burials. The Volcán Barú case may be similar in this regard, although it is not as well documented. In the Valley of Oaxaca and the Basin of Mexico, however, public works focused on creating spaces for communal ritual. The southern Gulf Coast is more like the other two Mesoamerican regions in that plaza and mound group construction was a major element, but tombs (at least by the end of the sequence at La Venta) and monumental portrait sculpture were also substantial. Here we arrive at the category of status and wealth differences as well. In central Panama, in the Alto Magdalena, and perhaps in the Volcán Barú region, there is evidence of quite substantial and conspicuous status differentiation. Status differences in the Valley of Oaxaca and the Basin of Mexico were much more modest, and the southern Gulf Coast is in some ways intermediate with the late development of elaborate tombs. It is hard to avoid the conclusion that a large portion of the resources mobilized in the local economies in central Panama and the Alto Magdalena went into competition over status dominance, focused heavily on the person of the chief. While such competition surely occurred in the Valley of Oaxaca and the Basin of Mexico, in neither region did it consume nearly such a large portion of whatever the chiefly equivalent of the gross domestic product is. (Real data on which to base a reconstruction of local economy in the southern Gulf Coast would be exceedingly interesting in this connection.) This distinction parallels that drawn by C. Renfrew (1974) between "individualizing" and "group-oriented" chiefdoms, but Renfrew's tendency to see individualizing chiefdoms as somehow more advanced and grading off into states is not supported by the sequences included here.

Different trajectories

The trajectories of chiefdom development in the Valley of Oaxaca and the Basin of Mexico, then, are similar in several respects. Both show mobilization of resources toward public works programs designed to create communal ritual space. Societies in both sequences show modest internal differentiation in regard to wealth and status. And both show some sign of early internal economic differentiation and interdependence. The trajectories of chiefdom development in central Panama and the Alto Magdalena, on the other hand, mobilized resources toward fierce status competition focused on the persons of chiefs. Internal wealth and status differences were strongly marked. And local economies may have been based on family units of considerable redundancy and independence. The trajectory of the Volcán Barú region is more difficult to reconstruct, because data are scarcer, but it seems rather more like those of central Panama and the Alto Magdalena. In the southern Gulf Coast, public works programs aimed both at creating communal ritual space and at glorifying high-status persons. Data on the nature of the local economy are lacking.

Such differences between sequences of chiefdom development in different regions have implications for some more general issues about what chiefdoms are and how they develop. One implication is that chiefdoms vary in more important ways than just that some are small and incipient, others large and highly developed, indeed very nearly states. Despite the fact that sociopolitical entities in these six sequences arrived at similar overall demographic levels, it is quite true that chiefdoms vary substantially in size. Overall population size and other demographic variables, however, do not correlate well with other variables differentiating "highly developed" from "not so highly developed" chiefdoms. Indeed, demographic variables that ought to correlate well with each other, if degree of development were the major difference between chiefdoms, do not do so (Drennan 1987). There are a number of important ways that chiefdoms differ from each other, aside from being more or less developed.

Another implication is that the two trajectories of development most clearly differentiated in these six sequences (those of the Valley of Oaxaca and the Basin of Mexico on the one hand and of central Panama and the Alto Magdalena on the other) diverged very early on.

Within the first two or three centuries of sedentary agricultural living, there were signs that rather different courses of development were being followed. It is impossible not to notice that the sequences of the Valley of Oaxaca and the Basin of Mexico are the two that I cut off at a point when much larger and more complex societies emerged, rather than pursuing them to the time of the Spanish Conquest. The more integrated local economies and the tradition of mobilizing resources to create spaces for communal ritual would certainly seem, on the surface of things, to provide a sounder footing for the development of the institutions around which those later states were organized than would the internal economic independence and fiercely personalized status rivalry of central Panama and the Alto Magdalena. Clearly, there is a sense in which the trajectories of the Valley of Oaxaca and the Basin of Mexico were aimed at state development from the establishment of sedentary agriculture and in which those of central Panama and the Alto Magdalena were not.

What this early divergence implies is that efforts to understand the differences between sequences of state development and sequences that lack state development cannot be directed exclusively at those points in the sequences where states emerge. They must also be directed to much earlier points where divergences begin. The same must be said of much more multifaceted differences between chiefdom trajectories. With reference to the first implication noted above, there are more than just two kinds of chiefdoms, those that are headed towards becoming states and those that are not. The clearest differences to emerge among the six sequences discussed here contrast two Mesoamerican sequences with two Intermediate Area sequences, but it would be erroneous to extend this observation to the conclusion that Mesoamerica as a whole contrasted with the Intermediate Area in this way. Indeed, the southern Gulf Coast sequence does not fit comfortably with the other two Mesoamerican sequences in this regard. There are also differences between Intermediate Area sequences that are masked by concentrating on a general characterization of the Intermediate Area. (Drolet [1984: 130] lists some, for example.) Moreover, the Valley of Oaxaca and Basin of Mexico sequences differ from one another as well. Competition between a dozen or more closely packed chiefdoms of similar scale has often been seen as important in the Basin of Mexico, while one center overshadowed all others from the

beginning of the sequence in the Valley of Oaxaca. Seeking to understand such differences offers more potential for understanding processes of social change than does sweeping them under the rug.

It is not my intention to suggest that each developmental sequence is unique and can only be understood in terms of its historical particulars. My point is rather that at least some of the factors responsible for even the most spectacular differences in sequences of complex society development began to operate much earlier on in those sequences than we are accustomed to think. We cannot fully understand why there is such a major political transformation in the Valley of Oaxaca or the Basin of Mexico toward the end of the Formative in contrast to the apparent reversal of developmental trends in the southern Gulf Coast or the Alto Magdalena unless we understand how chiefdoms in the southern Gulf Coast and the Alto Magdalena came so quickly to their heavy focus on individual status rivalry in contrast to the minimal status differences of the first millennium of complex society in Oaxaca or Mexico.

Finally, although it has not been my purpose to advance a model to account for the different trajectories observed, I would like to elaborate on the implications of these comparisons for the model advanced by Sanders and Webster (1978) since their conclusions from a similar comparison parallel those of this study in some respects. Sanders and Webster argue that trajectories like those of the Valley of Oaxaca and the Basin of Mexico (that is, those with minimal status differentiation for a substantial period followed by rapid state development) are formed by environments that offer a high degree of resource diversity as well as a high degree of risk to agriculture. Trajectories like that of the southern Gulf Coast, on the other hand, (that is, those involving rapid chiefdom development and then collapse without the emergence of states) are formed by environments that offer little resource diversity and low levels of risk to agriculture. The Alto Magdalena and central Panama (and possibly the Volcán Barú region) would have to be classified as the same kind of trajectory as the southern Gulf Coast on the basis of the features emphasized by Sanders and Webster. None of the three regions, however, can be categorized as low diversity (cf. Linares 1977: 10–11, 1980b: 7–11; Cooke 1984: 265; Botero 1985). While the Alto Magdalena, and probably the Volcán Barú region, would be classified as of low agricultural risk by Sanders and Webster's standards, central Panama would not (Linares 1977: 10–11). However

it is that we finally account for differences and similarities such as those observed in these sequences, they seem not to be simply the effect of differing environmental variables such as agricultural risk and diversity.

References

Acosta, Jorge R. (1965) "Preclassic and classic architecture of Oaxaca." In *Handbook of Middle American Indians*, Vol. 3: *Archaeology of southern Mesoamerica*, Part 2, ed. by R. Wauchope and G. R. Willey, 814–36. Austin: University of Texas Press.

Adams, R.McC. (1966) *The evolution of urban society*. Chicago: Aldine.
   (1970) "The study of ancient Mesopotamian settlement patterns and the problem of urban origins." *Sumer* 25: 111–23.

Adamson, A.M. (1936) *Marquesan insects: environment*. B. P. Bishop Museum Bulletin 139. Honolulu.
   (1939) *Review of the fauna of the Marquesas Islands and discussion of its origin*. B. P. Bishop Museum Bulletin 159. Honolulu.

Adcock, Sir Frank and D. J. Moseley (1975) *Diplomacy in ancient Greece*. London: Thames and Hudson.

Alexander, Lawrence S. (1982) "Phase I archaeological reconnaissance of the Oliver Lock and Dam Project Area, Tuscaloosa, Alabama." *Report of Investigations* 33. University of Alabama Office of Archaeological Research.

Andrewes, Antony (1967) *Greek society*. Harmondsworth: Penguin Books.

Arribas, A. and F. Molina (1982) "Los Millares: neue Ausgrabungen in der kupferzeitlichen Siedlung (1978–1981)." *Madrider Mitteilungen* 23: 9–32.

Athens, J. S. (1983) "Prehistoric pondfield agriculture in Hawaii: archaeological investigations at the Hanalei National Wildlife Refuge, Kaua'i."

References

Typescript report in Department of Anthropology, B. P. Bishop Museum, Honolulu.

Baier, Stephen (1980) "Long-term structural change in the economy of central Niger." In *West African culture dynamics: archaeological and historical perspectives*, ed. by B. K. Swartz, Jr. and R. E. Dumett, 587–602. The Hague: Mouton.

Baier, Stephen and Paul Lovejoy (1977) "Gradations in servility at the desert's edge." In *Slavery in Africa: anthropological and historical perspectives*, ed. by S. Miers and I. Kopytoff, 391–411. Madison: University of Wisconsin Press.

Bailey, Anne and J. R. Llobera (1981) *The Asiatic mode of production*. London: Routledge and Kegan.

Balcer, J. M. (1974) "The Mycenaean dam at Tiryns." *American Journal of Archaeology* 78: 141–9.

Bargatzky, Thomas (1984) "Culture, environment, and the ills of adaptation-alism." *Current Anthropology* 25: 399–415.

Barker, G. and D. Webley (1978) "Causewayed camps and early Neolithic economies in central southern England." *Proceedings of the Prehistoric Society* 44: 161–86.

Barrett, John (in press) "Time and tradition: the rituals of everyday life." In *Proceedings of the British–Scandinavian Bronze Age Colloquium*. Stockholm: National Museum of Antiquities.

Barrett, J. C. and R. Bradley (1980) "Later Bronze Age settlement in southern Wessex and Cranborne Chase." In *Settlement and society in the British later Bronze Age*, ed. by J. Barrett and R. Bradley, 181–208. BAR British Series 83. Oxford.

Barth, Fredrik (1973) "A general perspective on nomad–sedentary relations in the Middle East." In *The desert and the sown: nomads in the wider society*, ed. by C. Nelson, 11–21. Berkeley: University of California Press.

Barth, Heinrich (1857–9) *Travels and discoveries in north and central Africa*, 3 vols. New York: Harper.

Bartonek, Antonín (1974) "The place of the Dorians in the Late Helladic world." In *Bronze Age migrations in the Aegean*, ed. by J. A. Crossland and A. Birchall. Park Ridge, N.J.: Noyes Press.

(1983) "The Linear B texts and their quantitative evaluation." In *Res Mycenae*, ed. by A. Heubeck and G. Neumann, 15–27. Göttingen: Vandenhoeck and Ruprecht.

Bary, Erwin de (1898) *Le dernier rapport d'un européen sur Ghat et les Touaregs de l'Air (Journal de voyage d'Erwin de Bary, 1876–1877)*, Vol. 3, transl. by Henri Schirmer. Paris: Librairie Fischbacker.

Bass, G. F. (1987) "Oldest known shipwreck reveals splendors of the Bronze Age." *National Geographic* 172: 692–733.

Battuta, Ibn (1968) (Origin. 1929) *Travels in Asia and Africa 1325–1354*. Transl. and selected by H.A.R. Gibb. New York: Augustus M. Kelley.

References

Bellwood, P. (1972) "A settlement pattern survey, Hanatekua Valley, Hiva Oa, Marquesas Islands." *Pacific Anthropological Records* 17. Honolulu.

Benhazera, Maurice (1908) *Six mois chez les Touaregs du Ahaggar*. Alger: Jourdan.

Bennett, E. L., Jr. (1956) "The landholders of Pylos." *American Journal of Archaeology* 60: 103–33.

Bennett, W. C. (1931) *Archaeology of Kauai*. B. P. Bishop Museum Bulletin 80. Honolulu.

Bernus, Edmond (1981) *Touaregs Nigeriens: unite culturelle et diversite d'un peuple pasteur*. Paris: Office de la Recherche Scientifique et Technique Outre-Mer.

Bernus, Suzanne and Pierre Gouletquer (1976) "Du cuivre au sel: Recherches ethno-archéologiques sur la region d'Azelich (campagne 1973–75)." *JSA XLVI* (1976): 7–68.

Bintliff, J. L. (1977) *Natural environment and human settlement in prehistoric Greece*. BAR International Series 28. Oxford.

(1982) "Settlement patterns, land tenure and social structure: a diachronic model." In *Ranking, resource and exchange: aspects of the archaeology of early European society*, ed. by C. Renfrew and S. Shennan, 106–12. Cambridge University Press.

Blake, Michael (1987) "Paso de la Amada: an early Formative chiefdom in Chiapas." Paper presented at the 86th Annual Meeting of the American Anthropological Association, Chicago, Illinois.

Blanton, Richard E. (1972) "Prehistoric settlement patterns of the Ixtapalapa Peninsula region, Mexico." Department of Anthropology, Occasional Papers in Anthropology, No. 6. University Park: Pennsylvania State University.

(1978) *Monte Albán: settlement patterns at the ancient Zapotec capital*. New York: Academic Press.

Blanton, Richard E., Stephen A. Kowalewski, Gary Feinman, and Jill Appel (1981) *Ancient Mesoamerica: a comparison of change in three regions*. Cambridge University Press.

(1982) *Monte Albán's hinterland, part I: the prehistoric settlement patterns of the central and southern parts of the Valley of Oaxaca, Mexico*. Memoirs of the Museum of Anthropology, No. 15. Ann Arbor: University of Michigan.

Bockisch, G. and H. Geiss (1974) "Beginn und Entwicklung der mykenischen Staaten." In *Beiträge zur Enstehung des Staates*, ed. by J. Hermann and I. Sellnow, 104–22. Berlin: Akademie Verlag.

Bonte, Pierre (1975) "Le Problème de l'Etat chez les Touareg Kel Gress." In *Etudes sur les sociétés de pasteurs nomades*, Vol. 3: *Classes sociales et état dans les sociétés de pasteurs nomades*, ed. by P. Bonte et al., 42–62. Centre d'études et de Recherches Marxistes, No. 121. Paris.

(1977) "Non-stratified social formations among pastoral nomads." In *The evolution of social systems*, ed. by J. Friedman and M. Rowlands, 173–200. London: Duckworth.

290

References

(1979) "Pastoral production, territorial organisation and kinship in segmentary lineage societies." In *Social and ecological systems*, ed. by P. C. Burnham and R. F. Ellen, 203–34. A.S.A. monographs, No. 18. New York: Academic Press.

Boserup, Ester (1965) *The conditions of agricultural growth*. Chicago: Aldine.

Botero, Pedro José (1985) "Soilscapes." In *Regional archaeology in the Valle de la Plata, Colombia: a preliminary report on the 1984 season of the Proyecto Arqueológico Valle de la Plata*, ed. by D. R. Drennan, 41–80. Museum of Anthropology, University of Michigan, Technical Reports, No. 16. Ann Arbor.

Boutroz, Labiib (1981) *Phoenician sport: its influence on the origin of the Olympic games*. Amsterdam: J. C. Gieben.

Bove, Frederick J. (1978) "Laguna de los Cerros: an Olmec central place." *Journal of New World Archaeology* 2 (3): 1–56.

Boville, E. W. (1968) *The golden trade of the Moors*. Oxford University Press.

Bozeman, Adda B. (1960) *Politics and culture in international history*. Princeton University Press.

Bozeman, Tandy K. (1981) "Moundville phase sites in the Black Warrior Valley, Alabama: preliminary results of the U.M.M.A. survey." *Southeastern Archaeological Conference Bulletin* 24: 84–6.

(1982) "Moundville phase communities in the Black Warrior River Valley, Alabama." Unpublished Ph.D. dissertation, Department of Anthropology, University of California, Santa Barbara. Ann Arbor: University Microfilm.

Bradley, Richard (1972) "Prehistorians and pastoralists in Neolithic and Bronze Age England." *World Archaeology* 4: 192–204.

(1978a) *The prehistoric settlement of Britain*. London: Routledge and Kegan Paul.

(1978b) "Colonisation and land use in the Late Neolithic and Early Bronze Age." In *The effect of man on the landscape: the lowland zone*, ed. by S. Limbrey and J. G. Evans, 95–102. Council for British Archaeology research report, No. 21. London.

(1981a) "From ritual to romance – ceremonial enclosures and hillforts." In *Hillfort studies*, ed. by G. Guilbert, 20–7. Leicester University Press.

(1981b) "Economic growth and social change: two examples from prehistoric Europe." In *Economic archaeology*, ed. by A. Sheridan and G. Bailey, 231–8. BAR International Series 96. Oxford.

(1982) "The destruction of wealth in later prehistory." *Man* 17: 108–22.

(1984) *The social foundations of prehistoric Britain: themes and variations in the archaeology of power*. London: Longman Archaeology Series.

(1986a) "The Bronze Age in the Oxford area – its local and regional significance." In *The archaeology of the Oxford region*, ed. by G. Briggs, J. Cook, and T. Rowley, 38–48. Oxford University Department for External Studies.

(1986b) "The Dorset cursus: the archaeology of the enigma." Gr. 12 Council on British Archaeology. Wessex Lecture III.

References

(1987a) "Time regained – the creation of continuity." *Journal of the British Archaeological Association* 140: 1–17.

(1987b) "Flint technology and the character of Neolithic settlement." In *Lithic analysis and later British prehistory,* ed. by A. Brown and M. Edmonds, 181–6. BAR British Series 162. Oxford.

(1987c) "Stages in the chronological development of hoards and votive deposits." *Proceedings of the Prehistoric Society* 53: 351–62.

(1988) "Hoarding, recycling and the consumption of prehistoric metalwork: technological change in Western Europe." *World Archaeology* 20 (2): 249–60.

Bradley, Richard and Robert Chapman (1986) "The nature and development of long-distance relations in later Neolithic Britain and Ireland." In *Peer polity interaction and sociopolitical change,* ed. by C. Renfrew and J. Cherry, 127–36. Cambridge University Press.

Bradley, R. and J. Gardiner (1984) *Neolithic studies: a review of some current research.* BAR British Series 133. Oxford.

Bradley, Richard and Ken Gordon (1988) "Human skulls from the River Thames and their significance." *Antiquity* 62 (236): 503–9.

Bradley, Richard and Robin Holgate (1984) "The Neolithic sequence in the upper Thames valley." In *Neolithic studies,* ed. by R. Bradley and J. Gardiner, 107–58. BAR British Series 133. Oxford.

Bradley, R. and I. Hodder (1979) "British prehistory: an integrated view." *Man* 14: 93–104.

Brain, Jeffrey P. (1978) "Late prehistoric settlement patterning in the Yazoo Basin and Natchez Bluffs regions of the Lower Mississippi Valley." In *Mississippian settlement patterns,* ed. by B. D. Smith, 331–68. New York: Academic Press.

Branigan, K. (1983) "Craft specialization in Minoan Crete." In *Minoan society: proceedings of the Cambridge colloquium 1981,* ed. by O. Krzyskowska and L. Nixon, 23–32. Bristol Classical Press.

Braun, David P. (1986) "Midwestern Hopewellian exchange and supralocal interaction." In *Peer polity and socio-political change,* ed. by C. Renfrew and J. F. Cherry, 117–26. Cambridge University Press.

Bray, Warwick (1974) "The organization of the metal trade." In *El Dorado: the gold of ancient Colombia from El Museo del Oro, Banco de la República, Bogotá, Colombia,* 41–54. Greenwich, Conn.: New York Graphic Society.

Brown, F. (1931) *Flora of southeastern Polynesia, I. Monocotyledons.* B. P. Bishop Museum Bulletin 84. Honolulu.

(1935) *Flora of southeastern Polynesia, II. Dicotyledons.* B. P. Bishop Museum Bulletin 130. Honolulu.

Brumfiel, Elizabeth (1976) "Regional growth in the eastern Valley of Mexico: a test of the 'population pressure' hypothesis." In *The early Mesoamerican village,* ed. by K. V. Flannery, 234–50. New York: Academic Press.

Brumfiel, Elizabeth M. and Timothy K. Earle (1987) "Specialization, exchange, and complex societies: an introduction." In *Specialization,*

exchange, and complex societies, ed. by E. Brumfiel and T. Earle, 1–9. Cambridge University Press.

Brunton, Ron (1975) "Why do the Trobriands have chiefs?" *Man* 10: 544–58.

Burgess C. (1980) *The age of Stonehenge*. London: Dent.

Burgess, Colin, Peter Topping, Claude Mordant, and Margaret Maddison (1988) *Enclosures and defences in the Neolithic of Western Europe*. BAR International Series 403. Oxford.

Burke, Peter (1986) "City-states." In *States in history*, ed. by J. A. Hall, 137–53. Oxford: Basil Blackwell Ltd.

Burn, A. R. (1984) *Persia and the Greeks*. 2nd edn. London: Duckworth.

Burnham, Philip (1979) "Spatial mobility and political centralization in pastoral societies." In *Pastoral production and society*, ed. by L'Equipe écologie et anthropologie des sociétés pastorales, 349–60. Cambridge University Press.

Byland, Bruce E. (1980) "Political and economic evolution in the Tamazulapan Valley, Mixteca Alta, Oaxaca, Mexico: a regional approach." Ph.D. dissertation, Department of Anthropology, Pennsylvania State University. Ann Arbor: University Microfilms.

Byock, J. L. (1988) *Medieval Iceland: society, sagas, and power*. Berkeley: University of California Press.

Caddell, Gloria M. (1981) "Plant resources, archaeological plant remains, and prehistoric plant use patterns in the central Tombigbee River valley." In *Biocultural studies in the Gainesville Lake area*, ed. by G. M. Caddell, A. Woodrick, and M. C. Hill, 1–90. Archaeological Investigations in the Gainesville Lake Area of the Tennessee–Tombigbee Waterway, vol. 4. Report of Investigations 14. University of Alabama Office of Archaeological Research.

(1983) "Floral remains from the Lubbub Creek Archaeological Locality." In *Studies of material remains from the Lubbub Creek Archaeological Locality*, ed. by C. S. Peebles, 194–271. Prehistoric Agricultural Communities in West Central Alabama, Vol. 2. Mobile, Ala.: U.S. Army Corps of Engineers, Mobile District.

Cahiers du Pacifique (1978) "Les Iles Marquies: geomorphologie, climatologie, faune et flore." *Cahiers du Pacifique* no. 21. Paris: Fondation Singer–Polignac.

Carneiro, Robert L. (1961) "Slash and burn cultivation among the Kuikuru and its implications for cultural development in the Amazon Basin." *Antropológica*, no. 11. Philadelphia: University Museum, University of Pennsylvania.

(1970) "A theory of the origin of the state." *Science* 169: 733–8.

(1977) "Comment on B. Price, 'Shifts in production and organization: a cluster-interaction model.'" *Current Anthropology* 18: 222–3.

(1981) "The chiefdom as precursor of the state." In *The transition to statehood in the New World*, ed. by G. Jones and R. Kautz, 37–79. Cambridge University Press.

(1987) "Cross-currents in the theory of state formation." *American Ethnologist* 14: 756–70.

Cartledge, P. A. (1977) "Hoplites and heroes: Sparta's contribution to the techniques of ancient warfare." *Journal of Hellenic Studies* 47: 11–28.

Cashden, E. (1983) "Territoriality among human foragers: ecological models and an application to four Bushman groups." *Current Anthropology* 24: 47–66.

Caso, Alfonso (1965) "Existió un imperio Olmeco?" *Memoria del Colegio Nacional* 5 (3): 3–52. Mexico.

Catt, John (1978) "The contribution of loess to soils in lowland Britain." In *The effect of man on the landscape: the lowland zone*, ed. by S. Limbrey and J. S. Evans, 12–20. Council for British Archaeology, research report No. 21. London.

Chadwick, John (1976) *The Mycenaean world*. Cambridge University Press.

Chapman, R. W. (1981) "Archaeological theory and communal burial in prehistoric Europe." In *Pattern of the past: studies in honour of David Clarke*, ed. by I. Hodder, G. Isaac, and N. Hammond, 387–441. Cambridge University Press.

(1984) "Early metallurgy in Iberia and the Western Mediterranean: innovation, adoption, and production." In *The Deya conference of prehistory: early settlement in the Western Mediterranean islands and their peripheral areas*, ed. by W.H. Waldren, et al., 1139–65. BAR International Series 229. Oxford.

Cherry, J. F. (1984) "The emergence of the state in the prehistoric Aegean." *Proceedings of the Cambridge Philological Society* n.s. 130: 18–48.

(1986) "Polities and palaces: some problems in Minoan state formation." In *Peer polity interaction and socio-political change*, ed. by C. Renfrew and J. F. Cherry, 19–45. Cambridge University Press.

Childe, V. G. (1951) *Man makes himself*. New York: Mentor Books.
(1954) *What happened in history*. Harmondsworth: Penguin Books.

Chubb, L. J. (1930) *Geology of the Marquesas Islands*. B. P. Bishop Museum Bulletin 68. Honolulu.

Claessen, H. J. M. (1978) "The early state: a structural approach." In *The early state*, ed. by H. J. M. Claessen and P. Skalník, 533–96. The Hague: Mouton Publishers.

(1981) "Reaching for the moon? Some problems and prospects of cultural evolutionism." In *Archaeological approaches to the study of complexity*, ed. by S. van der Leeuw, 14–37. Amsterdam: University of Amsterdam.

Claessen, Henri J. M. and Peter Skalník (1978) "The early state: models and reality." In *The early state*, ed. by H. J. M. Claessen and P. Skalník, 3–30. The Hague: Mouton Publishers.

Clark, John E., Michael Blake, Pedro Guzzy, Marta Cuevas, and Tamara Salcedo (1987) *Final report to the Instituto Nacional de Antropología e Historia of the early Preclassic Pacific coastal project*. Provo, UT: New World Archaeological Foundation, Brigham Young University.

Clough, Timothy and William Cummins (1979) *Stone axe studies*. London: Council for British Archaeology.

References

Cobean, R., M. D. Coe, E. Perry, Jr., K. Turekian, and D. Kharkar (1971) "Obsidian trade at San Lorenzo Tenochtilán, Mexico." *Science* 174: 666–71.

Coe, Michael D (1965a) *The jaguar's children: Pre-classic central Mexico.* New York: New York Museum of Primitive Art.

(1965b) "The Olmec style and its distribution." In *Handbook of Middle American Indians*, Vol. 3: *Archaeology of southern Mesoamerica*, Part 2, ed. by G. Willey, 739–75. Austin: University of Texas Press.

(1977) "Olmec and Maya: a study in relationships." In *The origins of Maya civilization*, ed. by R. E. W. Adams, 183–96. Albuquerque: University of New Mexico Press.

(1981) "Gift of the river: ecology of the San Lorenzo Olmec." In *The Olmec and their neighbours: essays in memory of Matthew W. Stirling*, ed. by E. P. Benson, 15–20. Washington, D.C.: Dumbarton Oaks Research Library and Collection.

Coe, Michael D. and Richard A. Diehl (1980) *In the land of the Olmec*, Vol. 1: *The archaeology of San Lorenzo Tenochtitlán*, Vol. 2: *The people of the river*. Austin: University of Texas Press.

Cohen, Ronald (1978) "State origins: a reappraisal." In *The early state*, ed. by H. J. M. Claessen and P. Skalník, 30–76. The Hague: Mouton Publishers.

Cole, Gloria, Mary C. Hill, and H. Blaine Ensor (1982) "Bioarchaeological comparisons of the Late Miller III and Summerville I phases in the Gainesville Lake area." In *Archaeology of the Gainesville Lake area: synthesis*, ed. by N. J. Jenkins, 187–258. Archaeological Investigations in the Gainesville Lake Area of the Tennessee–Tombigbee Waterway, Vol. 5. Report of Investigations 23. University of Alabama Office of Archaeological Research.

Coles, J. M. and A. F. Harding (1979) *The Bronze Age in Europe*. London: Methuen.

Collier, G. (1975) *Fields of the Tzotzil*. Austin: University of Texas Press.

Collis, John (1984) *Oppida: earliest towns north of the Alps*. Sheffield University, Department of Prehistory and Archaeology.

Conner, W. Robert (1984) *Thucydides*. Princeton University Press.

Cooke, Richard (1984) "Archaeological research in central and eastern Panama: a review of some problems." In *The archaeology of lower Central America*, ed. by F. W. Lange and D. Z. Stone, 263–302. Albuquerque: University of New Mexico Press.

Cordy, R. (1974) "Cultural adaptation and evolution in Hawaii: a suggested new sequence." *Journal of the Polynesian Society* 83: 180–91.

(1981) *A study of prehistoric social change in the Hawaiian Islands*. New York: Academic Press.

Cowgill, George L. (1975) "On causes and consequences of ancient and modern population changes." *American Anthropologist* 77: 505–25.

Cox, P. (1980) "Masi and tanu 'eli: ancient Polynesian technologies for the preservation and concealment of food." *Pacific Tropical Botanical Garden Bulletin* 10: 81–93.

Creamer, Winifred and Jonathan Haas (1985) "Tribe versus chiefdom in lower Central America." *American Antiquity* 50: 738–54.

Cubillos, Julio César (1980) *Arqueología de San Agustín: El Estrecho, El Parador, y Mesita C. Bogotá.* Publicacion de la Fundación de Investigaciones Arqueológicas Nacionales del Banco de la República. Bogotá.

Cunliffe, Barry W. (1978a) *Iron Age communities in Britain.* 2nd edition. London: Routledge and Kegan Paul.

(1978b) "Settlement and population in the British Iron Age: some facts, figures and fantasies." In *Lowland Iron Age communities in Europe,* ed. by B. Cunliffe and T. Rowley, 3–24. BAR International Series, Supplementary 48. Oxford.

(1984a) *Danebury: an Iron Age hillfort in Hampshire.* London: Council for British Archaeology.

(1984b) "Iron Age Wessex: continuity and change." In *Aspects of the Iron Age in central southern Britain,* ed. by B. Cunliffe and D. Miles, 12–45. Oxford University Committee on Archaeology.

Cunliffe, Barry and Trevor Rowley, eds. (1978) *Lowland Iron Age Communities in Europe.* BAR International Series 48. Oxford.

Curren, Caleb (1984) *The Protohistoric period in central Alabama.* Camden, Ala.: Alabama Tombigbee Regional Commission.

(1987) "The route of the Soto army through Alabama." De Soto Working Paper 3. University, Ala.: State Museum of Natural History.

Dahl, Gudrun and Anders Hjort (1976) *Having herds.* Stockholm Studies in Social Anthropology, No. 2. Stockholm University. Stockholm.

D'Altroy, Terrence and Timothy Earle (1985) "Staple finance, wealth finance, and storage in the Inca political economy." *Current Anthropology* 26 (2): 187–206.

Davidson, J. (1985) *The prehistory of New Zealand.* Auckland: Longman Paul.

Davies, J. K. (1978) *Democracy and Classical Greece.* London: Fontana/Collins.

Davis, K. and W. E. Moore (1966) "Some principles of social stratification." In *Class, status, and power: social stratification in comparative perspective,* ed. by R. Bendix and S. M. Lipset, 47–53. New York: Free Press.

DeJarnette, David L. and Christopher S. Peebles (1970) "The development of Alabama archaeology: the Snow's Bend site." *Journal of Alabama Archaeology* 16: 77–119.

Dening, G., ed. (1974) *The Marquesan Journal of Edward Robarts, 1797–1824.* Honolulu: University Press of Hawaii.

(1980) *Islands and beaches: discourse on a silent land, Marquesas 1774–1880.* Honolulu: University Press of Hawaii.

Dent, John (1983) "Weapons, wounds and war in the Iron Age." *Archaeological Journal* 140: 120–8.

DePratter, Chester (1983) "Late prehistoric and early historic chiefdoms in the southeastern United States." Ph.D. dissertation, Department of

References

Anthropology and Linguistics, University of Georgia, Athens. Ann Arbor: University Microfilms.

Desborough, V. R. d'A. (1964) *The last Myceneans and their successors: an archaeological survey c. 1200–c. 1000 B.C.* Oxford University Press.

Dickens, Roy S., Jr. (1976) *Cherokee prehistory.* Knoxville: University of Tennessee Press.

Diehl, Richard A. (1981) "Olmec architecture: a comparison of San Lorenzo and La Venta." In *The Olmec and their neighbors: essays in memory of Matthew W. Stirling,* ed. by E. P. Benson, 69–82. Washington, D.C.: Dumbarton Oaks Research Library and Collection.

Doyle, Michael W. (1986) *Empires.* Ithaca, N.Y.: Cornell University Press.

Drennan, Robert D. (1976a) "Religion and socal evolution in Formative Mesoamerica." In *The early Mesoamerican village,* ed. by K. V. Flannery, 345–68. New York: Academic Press.

(1976b) *Fábrica San José and middle Formative society in the Valley of Oaxaca.* Memoirs of the Museum of Anthropology, University of Michigan, No. 8. Ann Arbor: University of Michigan.

(1978) *Excavations at Quachilco: a report on the 1977 season of the Palo Blanco project in the Tehuacán Valley.* Technical Reports of the Museum of Anthropology, No. 7. Ann Arbor: University of Michigan.

(1979) *Prehistoric social, political, and economic development in the area of the Tehuacán Valley: some results of the Palo Blanco project.* Technical Reports of the Museum of Anthropology, no. 11. Ann Arbor: University of Michigan.

(1983a) "Ritual and ceremonial development at the early village level." In *The cloud people: divergent evolution of the Zapotec and Mixtec civilizations,* ed. by K. V. Flannery and J. Marcus, 46–50. New York: Academic Press.

(1983b) "Monte Albán I and II settlement in the mountain survey zone between the valleys of Oaxaca and Nochixtlán." In *The cloud people: divergent evolution of the Zapotec and Mixtec civilizations,* ed. by K.V. Flannery and J. Marcus, 110–11. New York: Academic Press.

(1984a) "Long-distance movement of goods in the Mesoamerican Formative and Classic." *American Antiquity* 49: 27–43.

(1984b) "Long distance transport in prehispanic Mesoamerica." *American Anthropologist* 86: 105–12.

(1985) "Archaeological survey and excavation." In *Regional archaeology in the Valle de la Plata, Columbia: a preliminary report on the 1984 season of the Proyecto Arqueológico Valle de la Plata,* ed. by R. D. Drennan, 117–80. Museum of Anthropology, University of Michigan, Technical Reports No. 16. Ann Arbor.

(1987) "Regional demography in chiefdoms." In *Chiefdoms in the Americas,* ed. by R. D. Drennan and C. A. Uribe, 307–24. Lanham, Md.: University Press of America.

(1988) "Household location and compact versus dispersed settlement in

Prehispanic Mesoamerica," in *Household and community in the Mesoamerican past: case studies in the Maya area and Oaxaca*, ed. by R. R. Wilk and W. Ashmore, 273–94. Albuquerque: University of New Mexico Press.

Drennan, Robert D. and Kent V. Flannery (1983) "The growth of site hierarchies in the Valley of Oaxaca: part II." In *The cloud people: divergent evolution of the Zapotec and Mixtec civilizations*, ed. by K. V. Flannery and J. Marcus, 65–71. New York: Academic Press.

Drennan, Robert D., Luisa Fernanda Herrera, and Fernando Piñeros (1989) "Environment and human occupation." In *Prehispanic chiefdoms in the Valle de la Plata*, Vol. 1: *The environmental context of human habitation*, ed. by Luisa Fernanda Herrera, Robert D. Drennan, and Carlos A. Uribe. University of Pittsburgh Memoirs in Latin American Archaeology, No. 2. Pittsburgh.

Drennan, Robert D. and J. A. Nowack (1984) "Exchange and sociopolitical development in the Techacán Valley." In *Trade and exchange in early Mesoamerica*, by K. Hirth, 147–56. Albuquerque: University of New Mexico Press.

Drennan, Robert D. and Carlos A. Uribe (1987a) *Chiefdoms in the Americas*. Lanham, MD: University Press of America.

(1987b) "Introduction." In *Chiefdoms in the Americas*, by R. D. Drennan and C.A. Uribe, vii–xii. Landham, MD: University Press of America.

(1987c) "Central America." In *Chiefdoms in the Americas*, by R. Drennan and C. Uribe, 59–62. Lanham, MD: University Press of America.

Drolet, Robert P. (1984) "Community life in a late phase agricultural village, southeastern Costa Rica." In *Recent developments in Isthmian archaeology: advances in the prehistory of lower Central America*, by F. W. Lange, 123–52. BAR International Series 212. Oxford.

Drucker, Philip (1943) "Ceramic sequences at Tres Zapotes, Veracruz, Mexico." Smithsonian Institution, Bureau of American Ethnology, Bulletin 140. Washington, D.C.

(1952) "La Venta, Tabasco: a study of Olmec ceramics and art." Smithsonian Institution, Bureau of American Ethnology, Bulletin 153. Washington, D.C.

(1961) "The La Venta Olmec support area." *Kroeber Anthropological Society Papers* 25: 59–73.

(1981) "On the nature of Olmec polity." In *The Olmec and their neighbors: essays in memory of Matthew W. Stirling*, by E. P. Benson, 29–48. Washington, D.C.: Dumbarton Oaks Research Library and Collection.

Drucker, Philip, Robert F. Heiser, and Robert J. Squier (1957) "Radiocarbon dates from La Venta, Tabasco." *Science* 126: 72–3.

(1959) "Excavations at La Venta, Tabasco, 1955." Smithsonian Institution, Bureau of American Ethnology, Bulletin No. 170. Washington, D.C.

Duque Gómez, Luis (1964) *Exploraciones arqueológicas en San Agustín*.

References

Revista Colombiana de Antropología, Suplemento No. 1. Bogotá: Imprenta Nacional.

Duque Gómez, Luis and Julio César Cubillos (1979) *Arqueología de San Agustín: Alto de los Idolos, montículos y tumbas.* Bogotá: Fundación de Investigaciones Arqueológicas Nacionales del Banco de la República.

(1981) *Arqueología de San Agustín: La Estación.* Bogotá: Fundación de Investigaciones Arqueológicas Nacionales del Banco de la República.

(1983) *Arqueología de San Agustín: exploraciones y trabajos de reconstrucción en las Mesita A Y B.* Bogotá: Fundación de Investigaciones Arqueológicas Nacionales del Banco de la República.

Duveyrier, Henri (1863) *Notes sur les Touaregs et leur pays.* Paris: impr. de L. Martinet.

(1864) *Exploration du Sahara. Les Touaregs du Nord.* Paris: Challanel ainé.

Dye, T. (1982) "The causes and consequences of a decline in the prehistoric Marquesan fishing industry." Paper presented at the Pacific Science Congress, Dunedin, New Zealand, 1982.

Earle, Timothy K. (1977) "A reappraisal of redistribution: complex Hawaiian chiefdoms." In *Exchange systems in prehistory*, ed. by T. K. Earle and J. Ericson, 213–32. New York: Academic Press.

(1978) *Economic and social organization of a complex chiefdom: the Halelea district, Kaua'i, Hawaii.* Museum of Anthropology, University of Michigan, Anthropological Papers, Vol. 63. Ann Arbor: University of Michigan.

(1980) "Prehistoric irrigation in the Hawaiian Islands; an evaluation of evolutionary significance." *Archaeology and Physical Anthropology in Oceania* 15: 1–28.

(1982) "The ecology and politics of primitive valuables." In *Culture and ecology: eclectic perspectives*, by J. Kennedy and R. Edgerton, 65–83. Special Publication 15. Washington, D.C.: American Anthropological Association.

(1984) "Introduction." In *On the evolution of complex societies: essays in honor of Harry Hoijer 1982*, ed. by T. Earle, 1–5. Malibu: Undena Publications.

(1987a) "Chiefdoms in archaeological and ethnohistorical perspective." *Annual Review of Anthropology* 16: 279–308.

(1987b) "The economic bases of chiefdoms." Paper presented at the center for research in the Humanities, University of Copenhagen, spring 1987.

(1989) "The evolution of chiefdoms." *Current Anthropology* 30: 84–8.

Edmonds, Mark and Julian Thomas (1987) "The archers: an everyday story of countryfolk." In *Lithic analysis and later British prehistory*, ed. by A. Brown and M. Edmonds, 187–99. BAR British Series 162. Oxford.

Ekholm, Kajsa (1977) "External exchange and the transformation of central African social systems." In *The evolution of social systems*, ed. by J. Friedman and M. J. Rowlands, 115–36. London: Duckworth.

(1980) "On the limitations of civilization: the structure and dynamics of global systems." *Dialectical Anthropology* 5: 155–66.

(1981) "On the structure and dynamics of global systems." In *The anthropology of pre-capitalist societies*, ed. by J. S. Kahn and J. R. Llobera, 241–61. London: The Macmillan Press.

Ekholm, Kajsa and Jonathan Friedman (1979) "'Capital,' imperialism, and exploitation in ancient world systems." In *Power and propaganda. A symposium on ancient empires*, ed. by M. T. Larsen. Mesopotamia, Studies in Assyriology No. 7, 41–58. Copenhagen: Akademisk Forlag.

(1980) "Towards a global anthropology." In *History and Underdevelopment. Essays on Underdevelopment and European Expansion in Asia and Africa*, ed. by L. Blussé, H. L. Wesseling, and G. D. Winius, 61–76. Paris: Leiden Centre for History of European Expansion and Edition de la Maison Sciences de l'Homme.

Ellison, Ann (1980) "Deverel–Rimbury urn cemeteries: the evidence for social organisation." In *Settlement and society in the British Later Bronze Age*, ed. by J. Barrett and R. Bradley, 115–26. BAR British Series 83 (i). Oxford.

(1981) "Towards a socioeconomic model for the Middle Bronze Age in southern England." In *Pattern of the past*, ed. by I. Hodder, G. Isaac, and N. Hammond, 413–38. Cambridge University Press.

Engels, F. (1972) (Orig. 1884.) "The origin of the family, private property and the state." In *Selected works in one volume*, by K. Marx and F. Engels, 455–593. New York: International Publishers.

(1977) "Familiens, privatejendommens og statens oprindelse." (Danish translation of 4th edition from 1891 of "The origin of family, private property and the state" with a new large preface by Engels.) Copenhagen: Politisk Revy.

Evans, J. G. (1975) *The environment of early man in the British Isles*. London: Elek.

Feinman, Gary M. (1985) "Investigations in a near-periphery: regional settlement pattern survey in the Ejutla Valley, Oaxaca, Mexico." *Mexicon* 7: 60–8.

Feinman, Gary M., S. A. Kowalewski, L. Finsten, R. E. Blanton, and L. Nicholas (1985) "Long-term demographic change: a perspective from the Valley of Oaxaca, Mexico." *Journal of Field Archaeology* 12: 333–62.

Feinman, Gary M. and Jill Neitzel (1984) *Too many types: an overview of sedentary prestate societies in the Americas*. Advances in Archaeological Method and Theory, Vol. 7, ed. by M. Shiffer, 39–102. New York: Academic Press.

Feinman, Gary M. and Linda M. Nicholas (1987a) "Labor, surplus, and production: a regional analysis of Formative Oaxacan socio-economic change." In *Coasts, plains and deserts: essays in honor of Reynold J. Ruppé*, ed. by S. Gaines. Anthropological Research papers, No. 38, 27–50. Temple: Arizona State University.

(1987b) "Labor, production and surplus in Formative Oaxaca: a regional

References

analysis." Paper presented at the 10th Annual Meeting of the Midwest Mesoamericanist Conference, University of Illinois, Urbana.

(1988) "The prehispanic settlement of the Ejutla Valley, Mexico: a preliminary perspective." *Mexican* 10: 5–13.

Fine, John V. A. (1983) *The ancient Greeks: a critical history.* Cambridge: Harvard University Press.

Finley, Moses I. (1957) "The Mycenaean tablets and economic history." *Economic History Review* 10: 128–41.

(1973) *The ancient economy.* Berkeley: University of California Press.

(1981) *Early Greece: the Bronze and Archaic Ages.* Rev. edition New York: W. W. Norton Co.

Finley, Moses I. and H. W. Pleket (1976) *The Olympic games: the first thousand years.* London: Chatto and Windus.

Flannery, Kent V. (1968) "The Olmec and the Valley of Oaxaca: a model for inter-regional interaction in Formative times." In *Dumbarton Oaks conference on the Olmec*, ed. by E. P. Benson, 79–110. Washington, D.C.: Dumbarton Oaks Research Library and Collection.

(1972) "The cultural evolution of civilizations." *Annual Review of Ecology and Systematics* 3: 399–426.

(1976a) *The early Mesoamerican village.* New York: Academic Press.

(1976b) "Contextual analysis of ritual paraphernalia from Formative Oaxaca." In *The early Mesoamerican village*, ed. by K. V. Flannery, 333–45. New York: Academic Press.

(1982) "Review of *In the land of the Olmec: the archaeology of San Lorenzo Tenochtitlán*, Vol. 1, by M. Coe and R. Diehl, and *In the Land of the Olmec: the people of the river*, Vol. 2, by M. Coe and R. Diehl." *American Anthropologist* 84: 442–7.

(1983) "Precolumbian farming in the valleys of Oaxaca, Nochixtla'n, Tehuaca'n and Cuicatla'n: a comparative study." In *The cloud people: divergent evolution of the Zapotec and Mixtec civilization*, ed. by K. V. Flannery and J. Marcus, 323–39. New York: Academic Press.

Flannery, Kent V., Anne V. T. Kirkby, Michael J. Kirkby, and Aubrey W. Williams, Jr. (1967) "Farming systems and political growth in ancient Oaxaca." *Science* 158: 445–53.

Flannery, Kent V. and Joyce Marcus (1976a) "Evolution of the public building in Formative Oaxaca." In *Cultural change and continuity: essays in honor of James Bennett Griffin*, ed. by C. E. Cleland, 205–21. New York: Academic Press.

(1976b) "Formative Oaxaca and the Zapotec cosmos." *American Scientist* 64: 374–83.

(1983a) "*The cloud people: divergent evolution of the Zapotec and Mixtec civilizations.* New York: Academic Press.

(1983b) "The growth of site hierarchies in the Valley of Oaxaca, part I." In *The cloud people: divergent evolution of the Zapotec and Mixtec civilizations*, ed. by K. V. Flannery and J. Marcus, 53–64. New York: Academic Press.

(1983c) "The Rosario phase and the origins of Monte Albán I." In *The*

cloud people: divergent evolution of the Zapotec and Mixtec civilizations, ed. by K.V. Flannery and J. Marcus, 74–7. New York: Academic Press.

(1983d) "The earliest public building, tombs, and monuments at Monte Albán, with notes on the internal chronology of Period I." In *The cloud people: divergent evolution of the Zapotec and Mixtec civilizations*, ed. by K. V. Flannery and J. Marcus, 87–91. New York: Academic Press.

Flannery, Kent V., Joyce Marcus, and Stephen A. Kowalewski (1981) "The Preceramic and Formative of the Valley of Oaxaca." In *Supplement to the handbook of Middle American Indians*, Vol. 1: *Archaeology*, ed. by J. Sabloff, 48–93. Austin: University of Texas Press.

Flannery, Kent V. and Marcus C. Winter (1976) "Analyzing household activities." In *The early Mesoamerican village*, ed. by K. V. Flannery, 34–48. New York: Academic Press.

Fleiss, Peter J. (1966) *Thucydides and the politics of bipolarity*. Baton Rouge, LA: Louisiana University Press.

Fleming, A. (1971) "Territorial patterns in Bronze Age Wessex." *Proceedings of the Prehistoric Society* 37: 138–66.

(1973) "Tombs for the living." *Man* 8: 177–93.

(1982) "Social boundaries and land boundaries." In *Ranking, resources and exchange*, ed. by C. Renfrew and S. Shennan, 52–5. Cambridge University Press.

(1989) "The genesis of coaxial field systems." In *What's new? a closer look at the process of innovation*, ed. by S. E. van der Leeuw and R. Torrence. One world archaeology No. 14, 63–81. London: Unwin Hyman.

Forbes, H. A. (1976) "'We have a little of everything': the ecological basis of some agricultural practices in Methana, Trizinia." *Annals of the New York Academy of Sciences* 268: 236–50.

Ford, James A. (1936) *Analysis of Indian village site collections from Louisiana and Mississippi*. Anthropological Study 2. New Orleans: Department of Conservation, Louisiana Geological Survey.

Forrest, W. G. (1978) *The emergence of Greek democracy: the character of Greek politics, 800–400 B.C.* London: Weidenfeld and Nicolson.

(1980) *A history of Sparta*. 2nd edn. London: Duckworth.

Foster, B. R. (1987) "The late bronze age palace economy: a view from the East." In *The function of the Minoan palaces*, ed. by R. Hägg and N. Marinatos. Proceedings of the fourth international symposium at the Swedish Institute in Athens, June 10–16, 1984, 11–16. Stockholm: Skrifter utgivna av Sevenska Institutet i Athen, 4°, XXXV.

Foster, E. D. (1977) "An administrative department at Knossos concerned with perfumery and offerings." *Minos* 16: 19–51.

Foucauld, (Père) Charles de (1925–30) *Poesies touaregues, dialecte de l'Ahaggar*. Paris: Leroux, Vol. 1: 1925; Vol. 2: 1930.

(1951–2) *Dictionnaire Touaregeg-Francasi; Dialecte de l'Ahaggar*. Paris: Imprimerie Nationale de France.

Foureau, Fernand (1902) *D'Alger au Congo par le Tchad: Mission saharienne Foureau-Lamy*. Paris: Masson.

References

Fowler, Melvin D. (1978) "Cahokia and the American Bottoms: settlement archaeology." In *Mississippian settlement patterns*, ed. by B. D. Smith, 455–78. New York: Academic Press.

Frankenstein, Susan and Michael J. Rowlands (1978) "The internal structure and regional context of early Iron Age society in southwestern Germany." *University of London Institute of Archaeology Bulletin* 15: 73–112.

Fraser, G. M. (1972) *The steel bonnets*. New York: Alfred A. Knopf.

Fried, Morton H. (1960) "On the evolution and social stratification of the states." In *Culture in History*, ed. by S. Diamond, 713–31. New York: Columbia University Press.

(1967) *The evolution of political society: an essay in political economy*. New York: Random House.

(1978) "The state, the chicken, and the egg, or what came first." In *Origins of the State: the anthropology of political evolution*, ed. by R. Cohen and E. R. Service, 35–48. Philadelphia: Institute for the Study of Human Issues.

Friedman, Jonathan (1975a) "Religion as economy and economy as religion." *Ethnos* 1.4.

(1975b) "Tribes, states and transformations." In *Marxist analyses and social anthropology*, ed. by M. Bloch, 161–202. London and New York: Malaby Press.

(1976) "Evolutionary models in anthropology." Unpublished manuscript in possession of author.

(1979) *System, structure, and contradiction in the evolution of "Asiatic" social formations*. Copenhagen: National Museum Press.

(1982) "Catastrophe and continuity in social evolution." In *Theory and explanation in archaeology*, ed. by C. Renfrew, M. J. Rowlands, and B. Segraves, 175–96. New York: Academic Press.

Friedman, J. and M. J. Rowlands (1977) "Notes towards an epigenetic model of the evolution of 'civilization.'" In *The evolution of social systems*, ed. by J. Friedman and M.J. Rowlands, 201–76. London: Duckworth.

Fuglestad, Finn (1983) A *history of Niger, 1850–1960*. African Studies No. 41. Cambridge University Press.

Gailey, Christine W. and Thomas C. Patterson (1987) "Power relations and state formation." In *Power relations and state formation*, ed. by T. C. Patterson and C. W. Gailey, 1–26. Washington, D.C.: American Anthropological Association.

Gamble, C. (1981) "Social control and the economy." In *Economic archaeology: towards an integration of ecological and social approaches*, ed. by A. Sheridan and G. Bailey, 215–29. BAR International Series 96. Oxford.

(1982) "Animal husbandry, population and urbanization." In *An island polity: the archaeology of exploitation in Melos*, ed. by C. Renfrew and M. Wagstaff, 161–71. Cambridge University Press.

Gast, Marceau (1976) *Les Kel Rela: Historique et essai d'analyse du groupe de*

commandement des Kel Ahaggar. Revue de l'occident Musulman et de la Méditerranée No. 21, 47–65. Aix-en-Provence: Centre Nationale de la Recherche Scientifique et des Universités d'Aix–Marseille.

Gent, Henry (1983) "Centralised storage in later prehistoric Britain." *Proceedings of the Prehistoric Society* 49: 243–67.

Gibson, D. Blair (1988) "Agro-pastoralism and regional social organization in early Ireland." In *Tribe and polity,* ed. by D. B. Gibson and M. Geselowitz, 41–68. New York: Plenum Press.

Gilman, A. (1976) "Bronze Age dynamics in southeast Spain." *Dialectical Anthropology* 1: 307–19.

(1981) "The development of social stratification in Bronze Age Europe." *Current Anthropology* 22 (1): 1–24.

(1987a) "Unequal development in Copper Age Iberia." In *Specialization, exchange, and complex societies,* ed. by E. M. Brumfiel and T. K. Earle, 22–9. Cambridge University Press.

(1987b) "Regadío y conflicto en sociedades acéfalas." *Boletín del Seminario de Arte y Arqueología,* Universidad de Valladolid 53: 59–72.

Gilman, A. and J. B. Thornes (1985) *Land use and prehistory in south-east Spain.* London: George Allen and Unwin.

Goad, Sharon I. (1978) "Exchange networks in the prehistoric southeastern United States." Ph.D. dissertation, Department of Anthropology, University of Georgia, Athens. Ann Arbor: University Microfilm.

Godelier, Maurice (1977) "Economy and religion: an evolutionary optical illusion." In *The evolution of social systems,* ed. by J. Friedman and M. Rowlands. London: Duckworth.

Goldman, I. (1970) *Ancient Polynesian Society.* University of Chicago Press.

González, Lauck, Rebecca (1988) "Proyecto arqueológico La Venta." *Arqueología* 4: 121–65. Mexico, DF: Dirección de Monumentos Prehispánicos, Instituto Nacional de Antropología e Historia.

Goody, J. (1971) *Technology, tradition and the state in Africa.* Oxford University Press.

Gould, Stephen Jay (1986) "Evolution and the triumph of homology, or why history matters." *American Scientist* 74: 60–9.

Green, H. Stephen (1980) *The flint arrowheads of the British Isles.* BAR British series 75. Oxford.

Green, R. C. (1979) "Lapita." In *The prehistory of Polynesia,* ed. by J. Jenning, 27–60. Cambridge: Harvard University Press.

(1980) *Makaha before A.D. 1880: Makaha Valley Historical Project Report* 5. Pacific Anthropological Records 31. Honolulu.

(1986) "Some basic components of the Ancestral Polynesian settlement system: building blocks for more complex Polynesian societies." In *Island Societies: archaeological approaches to evolution and transformation,* ed. by P. V. Kirch, 42–9. Cambridge University Press.

Grove, David C. (1981a) "The Formative period and the evolution of complex culture." In *Supplement to the handbook of Middle American*

References

Indians, Vol. 1, ed. by J. Sabloff, 373–90. Austin: University of Texas Press.

(1981b) "Olmec monuments: mutilation as a clue to meaning." In *The Olmec and their neighbors: essays in memory of Matthew W. Stirling,* ed. by E. P. Benson, 49–68. Washington, D.C.: Dumbarton Oaks Research Library and Collections.

(1987a) *Ancient Chalcatzingo.* Austin: University of Texas Press.

(1987b) "Comments on the site and its organization." In *Ancient Chalcatzingo,* ed. by D. Grove, 420–33. Austin: University of Texas Press.

(1987c) "'Torches,' 'knuckledusters' and the legitimization of Formative period rulership." *Mexicon* 9: 60–5.

Haas, Jonathan (1982) *The evolution of the prehistoric state.* New York: Columbia University Press.

Haas, Jonathan, Sheila Pozorski, and Thomas Pozorski (1987) *The origins and development of the Andean state.* Cambridge University Press.

Haberland, Wolfgang (1984) "The archaeology of Greater Chiriquí." In *The archaeology of lower Central America,* ed. by F. W. Lange and D. Z. Stone, 233–53. Albuquerque: University of New Mexico Press.

Halstead, P. and J. O'Shea (1982) "A friend in need is a friend indeed: social storage and the origins of social ranking." In *Ranking, resource and exchange: aspects of the archaeology of early European society,* ed. by C. Renfrew and S. Shennan, 92–9. Cambridge University Press.

Hammond, N. G. L. (1986) *A history of Greece to 322 B.C.* 3rd edn. Oxford University Press.

Handy, E. S. C. (1923) *The native culture of the Marquesas.* B. P. Bishop Museum Bulletin 9. Honolulu.

Handy, W.C. (1922) *Tattooing in the Marquesas.* B. P. Bishop Museum Bulletin 1. Honolulu.

Hansell, Patricia (1987) "The Formative in central Pacific Panama: La Mula-Sarigua." In *Chiefdoms in the Americas,* ed. by R. D. Drennan and C. A. Uribe, 119–39. Lanham, MD: University Press of America.

Hardin, Margaret (1981) "The identification of individual style on Moundville Engraved vessels: a preliminary note." *Southeastern Archaeological Conference Bulletin* 24: 108–10.

Harrison, R. J. and A. Gilman (1977) "Trade in the second and third millennia B.C. between the Maghreb and Iberia." In *Ancient Europe and the Mediterranean: studies presented in honour of Hugh O. Hencken,* ed. by V. Markotic, 90–104. Warminster, Wilts.: Aris and Philips.

Harrison, Simon (1987) "Cultural efflorescence and political evolution on the Sepik River." *American Ethnologist* 14: 491–507.

Haselgrove, Colin (1982) "Wealth, prestige and power: the dynamics of political centralisation in south-east England." In *Ranking, resources and exchange,* ed. by C. Renfrew and S. Shennan, 79–88. Cambridge University Press.

References

Hayden, Brian (1978) "Bigger is better?: factors determining Ontario Iroquois site sizes." *Canadian Journal of Archaeology* 2: 107–15.

Hedeager, Lotte (1987a) "Empire, frontier and the barbarian hinterland: Rome and northern Europe from A.D. 1 – 400." In *Centre and periphery in the ancient world*, ed. by M. Rowlands, M. T. Larsen, and K. Kristiansen, 125–40. Cambridge University Press.

(1987b) In press.

(1988) "Danernes land. Fra ca. ar 200 f.Kr. – ca. 700 e.Kr." *Danmarkshistorie*, Vol. 2, by Olaf Olsen (ed.). Copenhagen: Gyldendal and Politikens.

Hedeager, Lotte and Kristian Kristiansen (1988) "Oldtid o. 4000 f.Kr.–1000 e.Kr." In *Det Danske Landbrugs historie*, Vol. 1, by Claus Bjørn (ed.). Copenhagen: Landbohistorisk Selskab.

Heizer, Robert F. (1961) "Inferences on the nature of Olmec society based upon data from the La Venta site." *Kroeber Anthropological Society Papers* 25: 43–57.

(1962) "The possible sociopolitical structure of the La Venta Olmecs." In *Proceedings of the 34th International Congress of Americanists, Vienna, 1960*. Vienna: Verlag Ferdinand Berger, Horn.

Helms, Mary W. (1979) *Ancient Panama: chiefs in search of power*. Austin: University of Texas Press.

(1986) "Esoteric knowledge, geographical distance and the elaboration of leadership status: dynamics of resource control." Paper prepared for the Conference on Ecology and Cultural Evolution in the Tropics, Ann Arbor, Michigan.

(1988a) "Thoughts on public symbols and distant domains relevant to the chiefdoms of lower Central America." In *Wealth and hierarchy in lower Central America*, ed. by F. Lange. Dumbarton Oaks Research Library and Collections, Washington D.C. in press.

(1988b) *Ulysses Sail. An ethnographic odyssey of power, knowledge, and geographical distance*. Princeton University Press.

Herman, Gabriel (1987) *Ritualized friendship and the Greek city*. Cambridge University Press.

Hernando Gonzalo, A. (1987) "Evolución cultural diferencial del Calcolítico entre las zonas áridas y húmedas del sureste Español?" *Trabajos de Prehistoria* 44: 171–200.

Herrera, Luisa Fernanda (1987) "Transformaciones del medio ambiente natural en el Valle de la Plata." Report to the Fundación de Investigaciones Arqueológicas Nacionales de Colombia. Ms. in possession of author.

Herrmann, Joachim (1982) "Militärische Demokratie und die Übergangsperiode zur Klassengesellschaft." *Ethnographisch-Archäologische Zeitschrift* 23.

Herskovits, M. J. (1952) *Economic anthropology*. New York: Knopf.

Hirth, Kenneth G. (1980) *Eastern Morelos and Teotihuacán: a settlement survey*. Vanderbilt University Publications in Anthropology, No. 25. Nashville: Vanderbilt University.

References

(1987a) "Interregional exchange as elite behavior." Paper presented at the 86th Annual Meeting of the American Anthropological Association, Chicago, Illinois.

(1987b) "Formative period settlement patterns in the Río Amatzinas Valley." In *Ancient Chalcatzingo*, ed. by D. Grove, 343–67. Austin: University of Texas Press.

Hodder, Ian (1986) *Reading the past. Current approaches to interpretation in archaeology.* Cambridge University Press.

Hodder, I. and C. Orton (1976) *Spatial analysis in archaeology.* Cambridge University Press.

Hodges, Richard (1982) "The evolution of gateway communities: their socioeconomic implications." In *Ranking resources and exchange. Aspects of the archaeology of early European society,* ed. by C. Renfrew and S. Shennan, 117–23. Cambridge University Press.

Hommon, R. J. (1976) "The formation of primitive states in pre-contact Hawaii." Unpublished doctoral dissertation, Department of Anthropology, University of Arizona. Ann Arbor: University Microfilm.

(1980) "Multiple resource nomination form for Kaho'olawe archaeological sites." *National Register of Historic Sites,* Washington, D.C.

(1986) "Social evolution in ancient Hawai'i." In *Island Societies: archaeological approaches to evolution and transformation,* ed. by P. V. Kirch, Kirch, 55–68. Cambridge University Press.

Hooker, J. T. (1982) "The end of Pylos and the Linear B evidence." *Studi Micenei ed Egeo–Anatolici* 23: 209–17.

Hopper, R. J. (1976) *The early Greeks.* New York: Barnes Nobles.

Hornblower, S. and M. C. Greenstock (1984) *The Athenian empire.* 3rd edn. London Association of Classical Teachers.

Hudson, Charles (1988) "A Spanish-Coosa alliance in sixteenth-century north Georgia." *The Georgia Historical Quarterly* 72 (4): 559–626.

(1989) "Critique of Little and Curren's reconstruction of De Soto's route through Alabama." De Soto Working Paper 12. University, AL: State Museum of Natural History.

Hudson, Charles, Marvin T. Smith, and Chester B. DePratter (1987) "The Hernando de Soto expedition: from Mabila to the Mississippi River." Ms. in possession of the author.

Hudson, Charles, Marvin T. Smith, David Halley, Richard Polhemus, and Chester B. DePratter (1985) "Coosa: a chiefdom in the sixteenth century southeastern United States." *American Antiquity* 50 (4): 723–37.

Hudson, Charles, Marvin T. Smith, Chester B. DePratter, and Emilia Kelley (1989) "The Tristán de Luna expedition, 1559–1561." *Southeastern Archaeology* 8 (1): 31–45.

Iakovidis, S. (1982) "The Mycenaean bronze industry." In *Early metallurgy in Cyprus, 4000–500 B.C.,* by J.D. Muhly, R. Maddin, and V. Karageorghis, 213–30. Nicosia: Pierides Foundation.

Irons, William (1979) "Political stratification among pastoral nomads." In *Pastoral production and society,* ed. by Equipe écologie et anthropologie des sociétés pastorales. Cambridge University Press.

307

Jeffrey, L. H. (1976) *Archaic Greece: the city-states c. 700–500 B.C.* Earnest Benn Ltd.

Jenkins, Ned J. and Jerry J. Nielsen (1974) *Archaeological salvage investigations at the West Jefferson Steam Plant site, Jefferson County, Alabama.* University, AL: University of Alabama Department of Anthropology.

Jennings, J., ed. (1979) *The prehistory of Polynesia.* Cambridge: Harvard University Press.

Jensen, Jørgen (1981) "Et rigdomscenter fra yngre bronzealder pa Sjaelland (A Late Bronze Age centre of wealth on Zealand)." *Aerbøger for Nordisk Oldkyndighed og Historie* 1981: 48–96.

(1987) "Bronze Age research in Denmark 1970–85." *Journal of Danish Archaeology* 6: 155–74.

Johannessen, Sissel (1984) "Paleoethnobotany." In *American Bottom archaeology*, by C. J. Bareis and James W. Porter, 197–214. Urbana: University of Illinois Press.

Johnson, Allen W. and Timothy Earle (1987) *The evolution of human societies: from foraging group to agrarian state.* Stanford University Press.

Johnson, Gregory A. (1978) "Information sources and the development of decision-making organizations." In *Social archaeology: beyond subsistence and dating*, by C. Redman, M. Berman, E. Curtis, W. Langhorne, N. Veraggi, and J. Wanser, 87–112. New York: Academic Press.

(1982) "Organizational structure and scalar stress." In *Theory and explanation in archaeology: the Southhampton conference*, ed. by C. Renfrew, M. Rowland, and B. Segraves, 389–421. New York: Academic Press.

(1983) "Decision-making organization and pastoral nomad camp size." *Human Ecology* 11: 175–99.

(in press) "Dynamics of southwestern prehistory: far outside – looking in." In *Dynamics of southwestern prehistory*, ed. by D. Schwartz. Santa Fe: School of American Research.

Jones, A. H. M. (1957) *Athenian democracy.* Oxford: Basil Blackwell Ltd.

Jones, Walter B. (1939) "Geology of the Tennessee Valley region of Alabama." In *An archaeological survey of Wheeler Basin on the Tennessee River in northern Alabama*, ed. by W. S. Webb, 9–20. Bulletin 122. Washington, D.C.: Bureau of American Ethnology.

Joralemon, Peter David (1971) *A study of Olmec iconography.* Dumbarton Oaks studies in Pre-Columbian Art and Archaeology, No. 7. Washington, D.C.

Keeley, Helen (1984) *Environmental archaeology: a regional review*, Vol. 1. London: Department of the Environment.

(1987) *Environmental archaeology: a regional review*, Vol. 2. London: Historic Buildings and Monuments Commission.

Keenan, Jeremy (1977a) "Power and wealth are cousins: descent, class and marital strategies among the Kel Ahaggar (2 parts)." *Africa* 47 (3): 242–52 and 47 (4): 333–43.

References

(1977b) *The Tuareg: people of Ahaggar.* New York: St. Martin's Press.

Kellum-Ottino, M. (1971) *Archéologie d'une vallée des iles Marquises.* Publications de la Société des Océanistes 26. Paris.

Killen, J. T. (1964) "The wool industry of Crete in the Late Bronze Age." *Annual of the British School at Athens* 59: 1–15.

(1984) "The textile industries at Pylos and Knossos." In *Pylos comes alive: industry and administration in a Mycenaean palace,* 49–63. New York: Fordham University, Lincoln Center.

Kinnes, Ian (1979) *Round barrows and ring ditches in the British Neolithic.* London: British Museum.

Kirch, Patrick V. (1973) "Prehistoric subsistence patterns in the northern Marquesas Islands, French Polynesia." *Archaeology and Physical Anthropology in Oceania* 8: 24–40.

(1982) "Advances in Polynesian prehistory: three decades in review." *Advances in World Archaeology* 1: 51–97.

(1984) *The evolution of the Polynesian chiefdoms.* Cambridge University Press.

(1985a) *Feathered gods and fishhooks: an introduction to Hawaiian archaeology and prehistory.* Honolulu: University of Hawaii Press.

(1985b) "Intensive agriculture in prehistoric Hawai'i: the wet and the dry." In *Prehistoric intensive agriculture in the tropics,* ed. by I. S. Farrington, 435–54. BAR International Series 232. Oxford.

(1986a) *Island societies: archaeological approaches to evolution and transformation.* Cambridge University Press.

(1986b) "Rethinking east Polynesian prehistory." *Journal of the Polynesian Society* 95: 9–40.

(1987) "Lapita and Oceanic cultural origins: excavations in the Mussau Islands, Bismarck Archipelago, 1985." *Journal of Field Archaeology* 14: 163–80.

(1988) "Long-distance exchange and island colonization: the Lapita case." *Norwegian Archaeological Review* 21: 103–17.

Kirch, P. V. and R. C. Green (1987) "History, phylogeny, and evolution in Polynesia." *Current Anthropology* 28: 431–56.

Kirch, P. V. and M. Kelly (1975) *Prehistory and ecology in a windward Hawaiian valley: Halawa valley, Molokai.* Pacific Anthropological Records 24. Honolulu.

Kirkby, Anne V.T. (1973) *The use of land and water resources in the past and present Valley of Oaxaca, Mexico.* Memoirs of the Museum of Anthropology, No. 5. Ann Arbor: University of Michigan.

Knight, Vernon J., Jr. (1981) "Mississippian ritual." Ph.D. dissertation, Department of Anthropology, University of Florida, Gainesville. Ann Arbor: University Microfilms.

(1982) "Document and literature review." In *Phase I archaeological reconnaissance of the Oliver Lock and Dam Project Area, Tuscaloosa, Alabama,* ed. by L. S. Alexander, 27–102. Report of Investigations 33. University of Alabama Office of Archaeological Research.

References

(1989) "Mississippian social organization." Paper presented at the annual meeting of the Society for American Archaeology, Atlanta, Georgia.

Kocher, A. E. and A. L. Goodman (1918) *Soil Survey of Hinds County, Mississippi*. Washington, D.C.: U.S. Department of Agriculture.

Kohler, Timothy A., and Eric Blinman (1987) "Solving mixture problems in archaeology: analysis of ceramic materials for dating and demographic reconstruction." *Journal of Anthropological Archaeology* 6: 1–28.

Kopcke, G. (1987) "The Cretan palaces and trade." In *The function of the Minoan palaces*, ed. by R. Hägg and N. Marinatos. Proceedings of the fourth international symposium at the Swedish Institute in Athens, June 10–16, 1984, 255–9. Stockholm: Skrifter utgivna av Sevenska Institutet i Athen, 4°, XXXV.

Kowalewski, Stephen A. (1980) "Population-resource balances in period I of Oaxaca, Mexico." *American Antiquity* 45: 151–65.

(1982) "Population and agricultural potential: Early I through V." In *Monte Albán's hinterland*, Part I: *The prehispanic settlement patterns of the central and southern parts of the Valley of Oaxaca, Mexico*, ed. by R. Blanton, S. Kowalewski, G. Feinman, and J. Appel. Memoirs of the Museum of Anthropology, No. 15, 149–80. Ann Arbor: University of Michigan.

Kowalewski, Stephen A., Richard E. Blanton, Gary Feinman, and Laura Finsten (1983) "Boundaries, scale, and internal organization." *Journal of Anthropological Archaeology* 2: 32–56.

Kowalewski, Stephen A., Gary Feinman, Laura Finsten, and Richard E. Blanton (1989) *Monte Albán's hinterland*, Part II: *The prehispanic settlement patterns of Tlacolula, Etla, and Ocotlán, the Valley of Oaxaca, Mexico*. Museum of Anthropology. Ann Arbor: University of Michigan.

Kowalewski, Stephen A., Eva Fisch, and Kent V. Flannery (1983) "San José and Guadalupe phase settlement patterns in the Valley of Oaxaca." In *The cloud people: divergent evolution of the Zapotec and Mixtec civilizations*, ed. by K. V. Flannery and J. Marcus, 50–3. New York: Academic Press.

Krader, Lawrence (1979) "The origin of the state among the nomads of Asia." In *Pastoral production and society*, ed. by Equipe écologie et anthropologie des sociétés pastorales. Cambridge University Press.

Kristiansen, Kristian (1978) "The consumption of wealth in Bronze Age Denmark. A study in the dynamics of economic processes in tribe societies." In *New directions in Scandinavian archaeology*, ed. by K. Kristiansen and C. Paluda-Muller, 158–91. Copenhagen: National Museum Press.

(1982) "The formation of tribal systems in later European prehistory: northern Europe 4000–500 B.C." In *Theory and explanation in archaeology: the Southampton conference*, ed. by C. Renfrew, M. Rowlands, and B. Seagrave, 241–80. New York: Academic Press.

(1984) "Ideology and material culture: an archaeological perspective." In *Marxist perspectives in archaeology*, by M. Spriggs, 72–100. Cambridge University Press.

310

References

(1987a) "From stone to bronze: the evolution of social complexity in northern Europe, 2300–1200 B.C." In *Specialization, exchange and complex society*, ed. by E. Brumfiel and T. Earle, 30–51. Cambridge University Press.

(1987b) "Center and periphery in Bronze Age Scandinavia." In *Centre and periphery in ancient world systems*, ed. by M. Rowlands, M. T. Larsen, and K. Kristiansen, 74–86. Cambridge University Press.

Krupp, E. C. (1983) *Echoes of the ancient skies: the astronomy of lost civilizations*. New York: Harper and Row.

Krzyszkowska, O. (1983) "Wealth and prosperity in pre-palatial Crete: the case of ivory." In *Minoan society: proceedings of the Cambridge Colloquium 1981*, ed. by O. Krzyszkowska and L. Nixon, 163–9. Bristol Classical Press.

Kuhns, Richard (1962) *The house, the city and the judge: the growth of moral awareness in the "Oresteia."* Indianapolis: Bobbs-Merrill.

Ladd, E. J. (1973) *Makaha Valley Historical Project Interim Report 3*. Pacific Anthropological Records 19. Honolulu.

Larsen, J. A. O. (1968) *Greek federal states*. Oxford University Press.

Larsson, Thomas (1986) *The Bronze Age metalwork in southern Sweden: aspects of social and spatial organization 1800–500 B.C.* Archaeology and Environment 6. University of Umea.

Leacock, E. B. (1972) (Orig. 1884) "Introduction". In *The origin of the family, private property and the state*, by F. Engels, 7–67. New York: International Publishers.

Lee, R. (1979) *The !Kung San*. Cambridge University Press.

Lees, Susan H. (1973) *Sociopolitical aspects of canal irrigation in the Valley of Oaxaca*. Memoirs of the Museum of Anthropology, no. 6. Ann Arbor: University of Michigan.

Levy, Janet (1982) *Social and religious organisation in Bronze Age Denmark. An analysis of ritual hoard finds*. BAR International Series 124. Oxford.

Lewthwaite, J. (1983) "Why did civilization not emerge more often? A comparative approach to the development of Minoan Crete." In *Minoan society: proceedings of the Cambridge colloquium 1981*, ed. by O. Krzyszkowska and L. Nixon, 171–83. Bristol: Bristol Classical Press.

Lhote, Henri (1955) *Les Touaregs du Hoggar (Ahaggar)*. 2nd edn. Paris: Payot.

Lightfoot, Kent G. (1979) "Food redistribution among prehistoric Pueblo groups." *Kiva* 44: 319–39.

(1984) *Prehistoric political dynamics: a case study from the American Southwest*. DeKalb: Northern Illinois University Press.

Linares, Olga F. (1977) *Ecology and the arts in ancient Panama: on the development of social rank and symbolism in the central provinces*. Dumbarton Oaks Studies on Pre-Columbian Art and Archaeology, No. 17. Washington, D.C.

(1980a) "The ceramic record: time and place." In *Adaptive radiations in prehistoric Panama*, by O. F. Linares and A. J. Ranere. Peabody Museum Monographs, No. 5, 81–117. Cambridge: Harvard University.

(1980b) "Introduction." In *Adaptive radiations in prehistoric Panama*, ed. by O. F. Linares and A. J. Ranere. Peabody Museum Monographs, No. 5, 7–14. Cambridge: Harvard University.

Linares, Olga F. and Payson D. Sheets (1980) "Highland agricultural villages in the Volcán Barú region." In *Adaptive radiations in prehistoric Panama*, ed. by O. F. Linares and A. J. Ranere. Peabody Museum Monographs, No. 5, 44–55. Cambridge: Harvard University.

Linares, Olga F., Payson D. Sheets, and E. Jane Rosenthal (1975) "Prehistoric agriculture on tropical highlands." *Science* 187: 137–46.

Linton, R. (1925) *Archaeology of the Marquesas Islands*. B. P. Bishop Museum Bulletin 23. Honolulu.

Llanos Vargas, Hector and Anabella Durán de Gómez (1983) *Asentamientos prehispánicos del Quinchana, San Agustín*. Bogotá: Fundación de Investigaciones Arqueológicas Nacionales del Banco de la República.

Logan, Michael H., and William T. Sanders (1976) "The model." In *The Valley of Mexico: studies in prehispanic ecology and society*, ed. by E. Wolf, 31–58. Albuquerque: University of New Mexico Press.

Lorenz, Karl G. (1986) "Archaeological testing in the uplands of Holmes County, Mississippi." Ms. on file, Department of Anthropology, University of Illinois, Urbana, Champaign.

Lothrop, Samuel Kirkland (1937) *Coclé: an archaeological study of central Panama*, Part 1. Memoirs of the Peabody Museum of Archaeology and Ethnology, Vol. 7. Cambridge: Harvard University.

(1942) *Coclé: an archaeological study of central Panama*, Part 2. Memoirs of the Peabody Museum of Archaeology and Ethnology, Vol. 7. Cambridge: Harvard University.

(1954) "Suicide, sacrifice, and mutilations in burials at Venado Beach, Panama." *American Antiquity* 19: 226–34.

Lowe, Eugene N. (1919) *Mississippi: its geology, geography, soil, and mineral resources*. Bulletin 14. Jackson: Mississippi State Geological Survey.

Lowie, R. (1947) *Primitive society*. New York: Boni and Liveright.

Lull, V. (1983) *La "cultura" de El Argar*. Madrid: Akal Editor.

(1984) "A new assessment of Argaric society and culture." In *The Deya conference of prehistory: early settlement in the Western Mediterranean islands and their peripheral areas*, ed. by W. H. Waldren et al., 1197–238. BAR International Series 229. Oxford.

Lynott, Mark J., Thomas W. Boutton, James E. Price, and Dwight E. Nelson (1986) "Stable carbon isotopic evidence for maize agriculture in southeast Missouri and northeast Arkansas." *American Antiquity* 51: 51–65.

MacNeish, Richard S., Frederick A. Peterson, and Kent V. Flannery (1970) *The prehistory of the Tehuacán Valley*, Vol. 2: *Non-ceramic artifacts*. Austin: University of Texas Press.

MacNeish, Richard S., Melvin L. Fowler, Angel Garcia Cook, Frederick A. Peterson, Antoinette Nelken-Terner, and James A. Neely (1972) *The prehistory of the Tehuacán Valley*, Vol. 5: *Excavations and reconnaissance*. Austin: University of Texas Press.

References

Mair, Lucy (1977) *African kingdoms*. Oxford: Clarendon Press.

Malinowski, B. (1935) *Coral gardens and their magic*. London: Allen and Unwin.

Mann, Michael (1986a) "The autonomous power of the state: its origins, mechanisms and results." In *States in history*, ed. by John A. Hall, 106–36. Oxford: Basil Blackwell Ltd.

(1986b) *The sources of social power: a history of power from the beginning to A.D. 1760*, Vol. 1. Cambridge University Press.

Marcus, Joyce (1976a) "The origin of Mesoamerican writing." *Annual Review of Anthropology* 5: 35–67.

(1976b) "The iconography of militarism at Monte Albán and neighboring sites in the Valley of Oaxaca." In *Origins of religious art and iconography in Preclassic Mesoamerica*, ed. by H. B. Nicholson, 123–40. UCLA Latin American Center and the Ethnic Arts Council of Los Angeles.

(1983) "The Espiridioón complex and the origins of the Oaxacan Formative." In *The cloud people: divergent evolution of the Zapotec and Mixtec civilizations*, ed. by K. V. Flannery and J. Marcus, 42–3. New York: Academic Press.

(in press) "Zapotec chiefdoms and the nature of Formative religions." In *The Olmec and the development of Formative Mesoamerican civilization*, ed. by R. Sharer and D. Grove. Cambridge University Press.

Marx, K. (1967a) (Orig. 1867.) *Capital: a critique of political economy*, Vol. 1: *The process of capitalist production*. New York: International Publishers.

(1967b) (Orig. 1894.) *Capital: a critique of political economy*, Vol. 3: *The process of capitalist production as a whole*. New York: International Publishers.

Marx, K. and F. Engels (1965) (Origin. 1846.) "The German ideology." In *Pre-capitalist economic formations*, ed. by E. Hobsbawn, 121–39. New York: International Publishers.

Mathers, C. (1984a) "Beyond the grave: the context and wider implications of mortuary practice in south-eastern Spain." In *Papers in Iberian archaeology*, ed. by T. F. C. Blagg, R. F. J. Jones, and S. J. Keay, 13–46. BAR International Series 193. Oxford.

(1984b) "'Linear regression', inflation and prestige competition: second millennium transformations in southeast Spain." In *The Deya conference of prehistory: early settlement in the Western Mediterranean islands and their peripheral areas*, ed. by W. H. Waldren et al., 1167–96. BAR International Series 229. Oxford.

Mercer, Roger (1980) *Hambledon Hill – a Neolithic landscape*. Edinburgh University Press.

Michals, Lauren (1981) "The exploitation of fauna during the Moundville I phase at Moundville." *Southeastern Archaeological Conference Bulletin* 24: 91–3.

(1987) "Faunal remains." In *The Mill Creek site, 1Tu265, Black Warrior River, Alabama*, ed. by T.S. Mistovich, 171–82. Report of Investigations 54. University of Alabama Office of Archaeological Research.

References

Mistovich, Tim S. (1987) *The Mill Creek site. 1Tu265, Black Warrior River, Alabama.* Report of Investigations 54. University of Alabama Office of Archaeological Research.

(1988) "Early Mississippian in the Black Warrior Valley: the pace of transition." *Southeastern Archaeological* 7 (1): 21–38.

Molina González, F. (1983) *Prehistoria de Granada.* Granada: Editorial Don Quijote.

Moñita García, R., M. Corral Cañón, M. A. Díaz Hernández, M. R. Colmenarejo Hernández, and M. M. Sánchez García-Arista (1986) "Espacios de habitación y funerarios en el S.E. durante el Calcolítico." *Arqueología Espacial* 8: 139–56.

Moore, Clarence B. (1905) "Certain aborginial remains of the Black Warrior River." *Journal of the Academy of Natural Sciences of Philadelphia* 13: 125–244.

(1907) "Moundville revisited." *Journal of the Academy of Natural Sciences of Philadelphia* 13: 337–405.

Morgan, H. L. (1877) *Ancient society; or researches in the lines of human progress from savagery; through barbarism to civilization.* New York: H. Holt and Co.

Morris, Ian (1987) *Burial and ancient society: the rise of the Greek city-state.* Cambridge University Press.

Murdock, George Peter (1959) *Africa: its peoples and their culture history.* New York: McGraw-Hill Book Company, Inc.

Murphy, Robert F. (1967) "Tuareg kinship." *American Anthropologist* 69: 163–70.

Murphy, Robert F. and Julian H. Steward (1956) "Tappers and trappers: Parallel processes in acculturation." *Economic Development and Cultural Change* 4: 335–55.

Murray, Oswyn (1980) *Early Greece.* London: Fontana Press.

Musset, Lucien (1975) *The Germanic invasions: the making of Europe A.D. 400–600.* Translated by Edward and Columba James. The Pennsylvania University Press.

Neitzel, Robert S. (1968) "Archaeological, historic and natural resources of the Big Black River basin, Mississippi." In *Big Black River, Mississippi: comprehensive basin study,* Appendix G. Richmond, VA: National Park Service, Southeast Region.

Nicholas, Linda M. (1989) "Prehispanic land use in Oaxaca." In *Monte Albán's hinterland,* Part II: *The prehispanic settlement patterns of Tlacolula, Etla, and Ocotlán, the Valley of Oaxaca, Mexico,* ed. by S. Kowalewski, G. Feinman, L. Finsten, and R. Blanton. Museum of Anthropology. Ann Arbor: University of Michigan.

Nicholas, Linda, Gary Feinman, Stephen A. Kowalewski, Richard E. Blanton, and Laura Finsten (1986) "Prehispanic colonization of the Valley of Oaxaca, Mexico." *Human Ecology* 14: 131–62.

Nicolaisen, Johannes (1963) *Ecology and culture of the pastoral Tuareg.* Copenhagen: National Museum.

References

Nielsen, Jerry J., John W. O'Hear, and Charles W. Moorehead (1973) *An archaeological survey of Hale and Greene counties, Alabama*. University of Alabama Museums.

North, D. C. (1981) *Structure and change in economic history*. New York: Norton.

Oberg, K. (1955) "Types of social structure among the lowland tribes of South and Central America." *American Anthropologist* 57: 472–87.

O'Hear, John W. (1975) "Site 1Je32: community organization in the West Jefferson phase." Unpublished Master's thesis, Department of Anthropology, University of Alabama, Tuscaloosa.

Ottino, P. (1985) "Archéologie des iles Marquises: contribution à la connaissance de l'ile de Ua Pou." Thèse de 3ème Cycle en Ethnologie Préhistorique, Université de Paris (Sorbonne).

Oviedo y Valdés, Gonzalo Fernández de (1851) *Historia genral y natural de las indias, islas, y tierra-firme del mar océano*, 2 vols. Managua: Banco de América, 1977.

Palmer, R. (1984) *Danebury, an Iron Age hillfort in Hampshire: an aerial photographic interpretation of its environment*. London: Royal Commission on Historic Monuments (England).

Parry, William J. (1987) *Chipped stone tools in Formative Oaxaca, Mexico: their procurement, production and use*. Memoirs of the Museum of Anthropology, No. 20. Ann Arbor: University of Michigan.

Parsons, Jeffrey R. (1971) *Prehistoric settlement patterns in the Texcoco region, Mexico*. Memoirs of the Museum of Anthropology, No. 3. Ann Arbor: University of Michigan.

Parsons, Jeffrey R., Elizabeth Brumfiel, Mary H. Parsons, and David J. Wilson (1982) *Prehispanic settlement patterns in the southern Valley of Mexico: the Chalco–Xochimilco region*. Memoirs of the Museum of Anthropology, No. 14. Ann Arbor: University of Michigan.

Paynter, Robert, and John W. Cole (1980) "Ethnographic overproduction, tribal political economy, and the Kapauku of Irian Jaya." In *Beyond the myths of culture*, ed. by E. Ross, 61–99. New York: Academic Press.

Peebles, Christopher S. (1971) "Moundville and surrounding sites: some structural considerations of Mortuary practices II." In *Approaches to the social dimensions of mortuary practices*, ed. by James A. Brown, 68–91. Memoir 25. Society for American Archaeology.

(1974) "Moundville: the organization of a prehistoric community and culture." Ph.D. dissertation, Department of Anthropology, University of California, Santa Barbara. Ann Arbor: University Microfilms.

(1978) "Determinants of settlement size and location in the Moundville phase." In *Mississippian settlement patterns*, by B. D. Smith, 369–416. New York: Academic Press.

(1979) "Excavations at Moundville, 1905–1951." Microfiche edition. Ann Arbor: University of Michigan Press.

(1983) "Moundville: late prehistoric sociopolitical organization in the southeastern United States." In *The development of political organiza-*

tion in native North America, ed. by E. Tooker, 183–98. The American Ethnological Society.

(1986) "Paradise lost, strayed, and stolen: prehistoric social devolution in the Southeast." In *The burden of being civilized: an anthropological perspective on the discontents of civilization*, ed. by M. Richardson and M. Webb, 24–40. Southern Anthropological Society Proceedings 18. Athens: University of Georgia Press.

(1987a) "Moundville from A.D. 100 to 1500 as seen from A.D. 1840 to 1895." In *Chiefdoms in the Americas*, ed. by Robert D. Drennan and Carlos A. Uribe, 21–41. Lanham, MD: University Press of America.

(1987b) "The rise and fall of the Mississippian in western Alabama: the Moundville and Summerville phases, A.D. 1000 to 1600." *Mississippi Archaeology* 22 (1): 1–31.

Peebles, Christopher S. and Susan M. Kus (1977) "Some archaeological correlates of ranked societies." *American Antiquity* 42 (3): 421–48.

Peebles, Christopher S. and Margaret J. Schoeninger (1981) "Notes on the relationship between social status and diet at Moundville." *Southeastern Archaeological Conference Bulletin* 24: 96–7.

Peebles, Christopher S., Margaret J. Schoeninger, Vincas P. Steponaitis, and C. Margaret Scarry (1981) "A precious bequest: contemporary research with WPA-CCC collections from Moundville, Alabama." In *The research potential of anthropological museum collections*, ed. by A. Cantwell, J. B. Griffin, and N. A. Rothschild, 433–47. Annals of the New York Academy of Sciences 376. New York.

Pérez de Barradas, José (1943) *Arqueología agustiniana: excavaciones arqueológicas realizadas de Marzo a Diciembre 1937*. Bogotá: Imprenta Nacional.

Piperno, Dolores P. and Karen Husum Clary (1984) "Early plant use and cultivation in the Santa María Basin, Panama: data from phytoliths and pollen." In *Recent developments in Isthmian archaeology: advances in the prehistory of lower Central America*, ed. by F. W. Lange, 85–122. BAR International Series 212. Oxford.

Pires-Ferreira, Jane W. (1975) *Formative Mesoamerican exchange networks with special reference to the Valley of Oaxaca*. Memoirs of the Museum of Anthropology, University of Michigan, No. 7. Ann Arbor.

Plog, Stephen (1976) "Measurement of prehistoric interaction between communities." In *The early Mesoamerican village*, ed. by K. V. Flannery, 255–72. New York: Academic Press.

Podolefsky, A. (1987) "Population density, land tenure, and law in the New Guinea Highlands." *American Anthropologist* 89: 581–95.

Polanyi, K. (1944) *The great transformation*. New York: Farrar and Rinehart.

Pope, Melody K. (1989) "Microtools from the Black Warrior Valley: technology, use, and context." Unpublished Master's thesis, Department of Anthropology, State University of New York, Binghamton.

Porter, Muriel N. (1953) *Tlatilco and the Pre-classic cultures of the New*

References

World. Viking Fund Publications in Anthropology, No. 19. New York: Wenner-Gren Foundation for Anthropological Research.

Powell, Mary Lucas (1988) *Status and health in prehistory*. Washington, D.C.: Smithsonian Institution Press.

Price, B. (1978) "Secondary state formation: an explanatory model." In *The origin of the state*, ed. by R. Carneiro and E. Service, 161–86. Philadelphia: ISHI.

Prindiville, Mary and David C. Grove (1987) "The settlement and its architecture." In *Ancient Chalcatzingo*, ed. by D. Grove, 63–81. New York: Academic Press.

Randsborg, Klavs (1974) "Social stratification in Early Bronze Age Denmark: a study in the regulation of cultural systems." *Praehistorische Zeitschrift*, Vol. 49.

(1982) "Rank, rights and resources: an archaeological perspective from Denmark." In *Ranking, resource and exchange: aspects of the archaeology of early European Society*, ed. by C. Renfrew and S. Shennan, 132–9. Cambridge University Press.

Ranere, Anthony J. and Patricia Hansell (1978) "Early subsistence patterns along the Pacific coast of central Panama." In *Prehistoric coastal adaptations: the economy and ecology of maritime Middle America*, ed. by B. J. Stark and B. Voorhies, 43–59. New York: Academic Press.

Rappaport, R. (1967) *Pigs for the ancestors*. New Haven: Yale University Press.

Redmond, Elsa M. (1983) *A fuego y sangre: early Zapotec imperialism in the Cuicatlán Cañada, Oaxaca*. Memoirs of the Museum of Anthropology, No. 16. Ann Arbor: University of Michigan.

Reichel-Dolmatoff, Gerardo (1972) *San Agustín: a culture of Colombia*. New York: Praeger.

(1973) "The agricultural basis of the sub-Andean chiefdoms of Colombia." In *Peoples and cultures of native South America*, ed. by D. R. Gross, 28–38. Garden City, NY: Doubleday and Natural History Press.

(1975) *Contribuciones al conocimiento de la estratigrafía cerámica de San Agustín, Colombia*. Bogotá: Biblioteca Banco Popular.

(1987) *Arqueología de Colombia: un texto introductorio*. Bogotá: Fundación Segunda Expedición Botanica.

Renfrew, Colin (1972) *The emergence of civilisation: the Cyclades and the Aegean in the third millennium B.C.* London: Methuen.

(1973a) *Before civilization: the radiocarbon revolution and prehistoric Europe*. London: Jonathan Cape.

(1973b) "Monuments, mobilisation, and social organisation in Neolithic Wessex." In *The explanation of culture change: models in prehistory*, ed. by C. Renfrew, 539–58. London: Duckworth.

(1974) "Beyond a subsistence economy: the evolution of social organisation in prehistoric Europe." In *Reconstructing complex societies: an archaeological colloquium*, ed. by C. B. Moore, 69–95. Supplement to the

bulletin of the American Schools of Oriental Research, No. 20. Ann Arbor.

(1982a) "Socio-economic change in ranked society." In *Ranking, resources and exchange,* ed. by C. Renfrew and S. Shennan, 1–9. Cambridge University Press.

(1982b) "Prehistoric exchange." In *An island polity: the archaeology of exploitation in Melos,* ed. by C. Renfrew and M. Wagstaff, 222–7. Cambridge University Press.

(1986a) "Introduction: peer polity interaction and socio-political change." In *Peer polity interaction and socio-political change,* ed. by C. Renfrew and J. F. Cherry, 1–18. Cambridge University Press.

(1986b) "Epilogue and prospect." In *Peer polity interaction and socio-political change,* ed. by C. Renfrew and J. F. Cherry, 153–8. Cambridge University Press.

Renfrew, Colin and John Cherry, eds. (1986) *Peer polity interaction and socio-political change.* Cambridge University Press.

Renfrew, J. M. (1982) "Early agriculture in Melos." In *An island polity: the archaeology of exploitation in Melos,* ed. by C. Renfrew and M. Wagstaff, 156–60. Cambridge University Press.

Rhodes, P. J. (1985) *The Athenian empire.* Oxford University Press.

Richards, Julian (1984) "The development of the Neolithic landscape in the environs of Stonehenge." In *Neolithic studies,* ed. by R. Bradley and J. Gardiner. 177–87. BAR British Series 133. Oxford.

Rick, J. (1987) "Dates as data: an examination of the Peruvian preceramic record." *American Antiquity* 52: 55–73.

Robinson, Mark and George Lambrick (1984) "Holocene alluviation and hydrology in the Upper Thames Basin." *Nature* 308: 809–14.

Robkin, A.L.H. (1979) "The agricultural year, the commodity SA and the linen industry of Mycenaean Pylos." *American Journal of Archaeology* 83: 469–74.

Rolett, B. V. (1986) "Turtles, priests, and the afterworld: a study in the iconographic interpretation of Polynesian petroglyphs." In *Island Societies: archaeological approaches to evolution and transformation,* ed. by P. V. Kirch, 78–87. Cambridge University Press.

(1987) "A millennium of changing subsistence and ecology in the Marquesas Islands, French Polynesia." Paper presented at the American Anthropological Association Annual Meeting, Chicago.

(1989) "Hanamiai: changing subsistence and ecology in the prehistory of Tahuata (Marquesas Islands, French Polynesia)." Unpublished Ph.D. dissertation. New Haven: Yale University.

Roosevelt, Anna Curtenius (1980) *Parmana: prehistoric maize and manioc subsistence along the Amazon and Orinoco.* New York: Academic Press.

Root, Dolores (1983) "Information exchange and the spatial configurations of egalitarian societies." In *Archaeological hammers and theories,* by J. Moore and A. Keene, 193–219. New York: Academic Press.

Roscoe, P. B. (1988) "From big-men to the state: a processual approach to circumscription theory." *American Behavioral Scientist* 31: 472–83.

References

Rosendahl, P. H. (1972) "Aboriginal agriculture and residential patterns in upland Lapakahi, Hawaii." Unpublished Ph.D. dissertation, Department of Anthropology, University of Hawaii. Ann Arbor: University Microfilm.

Rowlands, Michael (1987) "Centre and periphery: a review of a concept." In *Centre and periphery in the ancient world*, ed. by M. Rowlands, M. T. Larsen, and K. Kristiansen, 1–12. Cambridge University Press.

Rowlands, Michael, Mogens Larsen, and Kristian Kristiansen (1987) *Centre and periphery in the ancient world*. Cambridge University Press.

Rønne, Preben (1987) "Stiluariationer i aeldre bronzealder." *Aarbøger for Nordok Old Kyndighed oy Historie* 1986: 71–124.

Rucker, Marc D. (1976) *Archaeological investigations at Pocahontas Mound A, Hinds County, Mississippi.* Archaeological Excavation Report 3. Jackson: Mississippi State Highway Department.

Rust, William F. and Robert J. Sharer (1988) "Olmec settlement data from La Venta, Tabasco, Mexico." *Science* 242: 102–4.

Sáenz, Candelario (1986) "They have eaten our grandfather! The special status of Air Twareg Smiths." Ph.D. dissertation, Columbia University, New York City. Ann Arbor: University Microfilm.

(n.d.) "Clienthood and Tribute among Twareg of the Air."

Sahlins, M. D. (1958) *Social stratification in Polynesia.* Seattle: University of Washington Press.

(1972) *Stone age economics.* Chicago: Aldine.

(1976) *Culture and practical reason.* University of Chicago Press.

Ste. Croix, G. E. M. de (1981) *The class struggle in the ancient Greek world from the Archaic Age to the Arab conquests.* London: Duckworth.

(1985) "Class in Marx's conception of history, ancient and modern." *Monthly Review* 36 (10): 20–46.

Salmon, J. (1977) "Political hoplites?" *Journal of Hellenic Studies* 97: 84–101.

Sandars, N. K. (1985) *The Sea Peoples: warriors of the ancient Mediterranean.* London: Thames and Hudson.

Sanders, William T. (1965) "The cultural ecology of the Teotihuacán Valley." Ms., Department of Sociology and Anthropology. University Park: Pennsylvania State University.

(1972) "Population, agricultural history and societal evolution in Mesoamerica." In *Population growth: anthropological implications*, ed. by B. Spooner, 101–53. Cambridge: M.I.T. Press.

(1984a) "Formative exchange systems: comments." In *Trade and exchange in early Mesoamerica*, ed. by K. Hirth, 275–9. Albuquerque: University of New Mexico Press.

(1984b) "Pre-industrial demography and social evolution." In *On the evolution of complex societies: essays in honor of Harry Hoijer 1982*, ed. by T. Earle, 7–39. Malibu: Undena Publications.

Sanders, William T., Jeffrey R. Parsons, and Robert S. Santley (1979) *The Basin of Mexico: ecological processes in the evolution of a civilization.* New York: Academic Press.

319

References

Sanders, William T. and Barbara Price (1968) *Mesoamerica: the evolution of a civilization*. New York: Random House.

Sanders, William T. and David Webster (1978) "Unilinealism, multilinealism, and the evolution of complex societies." In *Social archaeology: beyond subsistence and dating*, ed. by C. L. Redman, M. J. Berman, E. V. Curtin, W. T. Langhorne, Jr., N. M. Versaggi, and J. C. Wanser, 249–302. New York: Academic Press.

Sandford, Stephen (1983) *Management of pastoral development in the third world*. England: John Wiley and Sons.

Scarry, C. Margaret (1981) "The University of Michigan Moundville excavations: 1978–1979." *Southeastern Archaeological Conference Bulletin* 24: 87–90.

(1986) "Change in plant procurement and production during the emergence of the Moundville chiefdom." Ph.D. dissertation, Department of Anthropology, University of Michigan, Ann Arbor. Ann Arbor: University Microfilms.

(1988) "Variability in Mississippian crop production strategies." Paper presented at the annual meeting of the Society for American Archaeology, Phoenix, Arizona.

Scott, Susan L. (1983) "Analysis, synthesis, and interpretation of faunal remains from the Lubbub Creek archaeological locality." In *Prehistoric agricultural communities in west-central Alabama*, ed. by Christopher S. Peebles, 272–379. Report submitted to Interagency Archeological Services, Atlanta, by the University of Michigan, Ann Arbor.

Service, Elman R. (1962) *Primitive social organization: an evolutionary perspective*. New York: Random House.

(1972) *Primitive social organization. An evolutionary perspective*. 2nd edn. New York: Random House.

(1975) *Origins of the state and civilization: the process of cultural evolution*. New York: Norton.

Shanks, Michael and Chris Tilley (1987) *Social theory and archaeology*. Cambridge: Polity Press.

Shaffer, John G. and Vincas P. Steponaitis (1982) "James A. Ford's and Moreau B. Chambers's mound excavations in the Big Black River drainage, Mississippi: a preliminary descriptive report." Ms. in possession of Vincas P. Steponaitis.

(1983) "Burial mounds from the Big Black drainage in Mississippi: some new interpretations." Paper presented at the annual meeting of the Southeastern Archaeological Conference, Columbia, South Carolina.

Sheahan, G. M. Jr (1955) "The Marquesas of the South Seas: a study in change." M.Litt. Thesis, University of Cambridge.

Sheets, Payson D. (1980) "The Volcán Barú region: a site survey." In *Adaptive radiations in prehistoric Panama*, by O. F. Linares and A. J. Ranere. Peabody Museum Monographs, No. 5, 267–75. Cambridge: Harvard University.

Sheets, Payson D., E. Jane Rosenthal, and Anthony J. Ranere (1980) "Stone

References

tools from Volcán Barú." In *Adaptive radiations in prehistoric Panama*, by O. F. Linares and A. J. Ranere. Peabody Museum Monographs, No. 5, 404–28. Cambridge: Harvard University.

Sheldon, Craig T. (1974) "The Mississippian-historic transition in central Alabama." Ph.D. dissertation, Department of Anthropology, University of Oregon, Eugene. Ann Arbor: University Microfilms.

Shelmerdine, C. W. (1981) "Nichoria in context: a major town in the Pylos Kingdom." *American Journal of Archaeology* 85: 319–25.

(1985) *The perfume industry of Mycenaean Pylos*. Goteborg: Paul Astroms Forlag.

Shennan, S. (1986a) "Central Europe in the third millennium B.C.: an evolutionary trajectory for the beginning of the European Bronze Age." *Journal of Anthropological Archaeology* 5 (2): 115–46.

(1986b) "Interaction and change in third millennium B.C. western and central Europe." In *Peer polity interaction and socio-political change*, ed. by C. Renfrew and J. F. Cherry, 137–48. Cambridge University Press.

(1987) "Trends in the study of later European prehistory." *Annual Review of Anthropology* 16: 365–82.

Sherratt, A. G. (1981) "Plough and pastoralism: aspects of the secondary products revolution." In *Pattern of the past: studies in honour of David Clarke*, ed. by I. Hodder, G. Isaac, and N. Hammond, 261–305. Cambridge University Press.

(1984) "Social Evolution: Europe in the late Neolithic and Copper Ages." In *European social evolution*, ed. by J. Bintliff, 123–34. Bradford: University Press.

Simpson, R. H. (1981) *Mycenaean Greece*. Park Ridge, NJ: Noyes Press.

Sinoto, Y. H. (1966) "A tentative cultural sequence in the northern Marquesas Islands, French Polynesia." *Journal of the Polynesian Society* 75: 287–303.

(1979) "The Marquesas." In *The prehistory of Polynesia*, ed. by J. Jennings, 110–34. Harvard University Press.

Sisson, Edward B. (1970) "Settlement patterns and land use in the northwestern Chontalpa, Tabasco, Mexico: a progress report." *Cerámica de Cultural Maya et al* 6: 41–54. Philadelphia: Dept. of Anthropology, Temple University.

Skjolsvold, A. (1972) *Excavations of a habitation cave, Hanapetéo, Hiva Oa, Marquesas Islands*. Pacific Anthropological Records 16. Honolulu.

Smith, Bruce D. (1978) "Variation in Mississippian settlement patterns." In *Mississippian settlement patterns*, ed. by B. D. Smith, 479–503. New York: Academic Press.

(1986) "The archaeology of the southeastern United States: from Dalton to de Soto, 10,500–500 B. P." In *Advances in world archaeology*, Vol. 5, ed. by F. Wendorf and A. Close, 1–92. Orlando, FL: Academic Press.

Smith, C. Earle (1980) "Plant remains from the Chiriquí sites and ancient vegetational patterns." In *Adaptive radiations in prehistoric Panama*, by

O. F. Linares and A. J. Ranere. Peabody Museum Monographs, No. 5, 151–74. Cambridge: Harvard University.

Smith, I. F. (1965) *Windmill Hill and Avebury: excavations by Alexander Keiller*, 1925–1939. London: Oxford University Press.

Smith, Michael E. (1987) "Household possessions and wealth in agrarian states." *Journal of Anthropological Archaeology* 6: 297–335.

Smith, R. W. (1984) "The ecology of Neolithic farming systems as exemplified by the Avebury region of Wiltshire." *Proc. Prehist. Soc.* 50: 99–120.

Smith, T. R. (1987) *Mycenaean trade and interaction in the West Central Mediterranean, 1600–1000 B.C.* Oxford: BAR International Series 371.

Snarskis, Michael J. (1984) "Prehistoric microsettlement patterns in the Central Highlands–Atlantic Watershed of Costa Rica." In *Recent developments in Isthmian archaeology: advances in the prehistory of lower Central America*, ed. by R. W. Lange, 153–78. BAR International Series 212. Oxford.

(1987) "The archeological evidence for chiefdoms in eastern and central Costa Rica." In *Chiefdoms in the Americas*, ed. by R. D. Drennan and C. A. Uribe, 105–18. Lanham, MD: University Press of America.

Snodgrass, Anthony (1965) "The hoplite reform and history." *Journal of Hellenic Studies* 85: 110–22.

(1971) *The dark age of Greece*. Edinburgh: Edinburgh University Press.

(1980) *Archaic Greece*. London: J. M. Dent Sons.

Sofri, Gianni (1975) *Det asiatiska producktionssattet. En marxistisk stridsfraga*. Stockholm: Bokforlaget Prisma. (Swedish translation from the Italian: *Il modo di produzione asiatico*, 1969).

Sørensen, Marie Louise S. (1989) "Material order and cultural classification: the role of bronze objects in the transition from Bronze Age to Iron Age in Scandinavia." In *The archaeology of contextual meanings*, ed. by I. Hodder, 90–101. Cambridge University Press.

Sotomayor, María Lucía and María Victoria Uribe (1987) *Estatuaria del Macizo Colombiano*. Bogotá: Instituto Nacional de Antropología.

Sourvinou-Inwood, Christiane (1974) "Movements of populations in Attica at the end of the Mycenaean period." In *Bronze Age migrations in the Aegean*, by J. A. Crossland and A. Birchall. Park Ridge, NJ: Noyes Press.

Spencer, Charles S. (1982) *The Cuicatlán Cañada and Monte Albán*. New York: Academic Press.

(1987) "Rethinking the chiefdom." In *Chiefdoms in the Americas*, ed. by R. D. Drennan and C. A. Uribe, 369–90. Lanham, MD: University Press of America.

Spores, Ronald (1972) *An archaeological settlement survey of the Nochixtlán Valley, Oaxaca*. Publications in Anthropology, No. 1. Vanderbilt University, Nashville.

Startin, D. W. A. (1976) "Mathematics and manpower in archaeological explanation." Unpublished MA thesis, University of Oxford.

References

(1982) "Prehistoric earthmoving." In *Settlement patterns in the Oxford region*, ed. by H. J. Chase and A. Whittle, 153–6. Oxford University Press.

Startin, D. W. A. and Richard Bradley (1981) "Some notes on work organization and society in Neolithic Wessex." In *Astronomy and society during the period 400–1500 B.C.*, ed. by C. Ruggles and A. Whittle, 289–96. BAR British Series 88. Oxford.

Steadman, D. (1989) "Extinction of birds in Eastern Polynesia: a review of the record and comparison with other Pacific island groups." *Journal of Archaeological Science* 10: 177–205.

von den Steinen, K. (1925) *Die Marquesaner und ihre Kunst*, Vol. 1: *Tatuierung*, Berlin.

(1928) *Die Marquesaner und ihre Kunst*, Vol. 2: *Plastik*; Vol. 3: *Die Sammlungen*. Berlin.

Steponaitis, Vincas (1978) "Locational theory and complex chiefdoms: a Mississippian example." In *Mississippian settlement patterns*, ed. by B. Smith, 417–53. New York: Academic Press.

(1983a) *Ceramics, chronology, and community patterns: an archaeological study at Moundville*. New York: Academic Press.

(1983b) "The Smithsonian Institution's investigations at Moundville in 1869 and 1882." *Midcontinental Journal of Archaeology* 8: 127–60.

(1986a) "Prehistoric archaeology in the southeastern United States, 1970–1985." *Annual Review of Anthropology* 15: 363–404.

(1986b) "The University of Alabama Excavations at 1Tu50, a Moundville I phase center in the Black Warrior Valley." Paper presented at the Annual Meeting of the Southeastern Archaeological Conference, Nashville, Tennessee.

Steward, Julian (1955) *Theory of culture change*. Urbana: University of Illinois Press.

Stirling, Matthew W. (1943) *Stone monuments of southern Mexico*. Smithsonian Institution, Bureau of American Ethnology, Bulletin 138. Washington, D.C.

(1950) "Exploring ancient Panama by helicopter." *The National Geographic Magazine* 97: 227–46.

(1965) "Monumental sculpture of southern Veracruz and Tabasco." In *Handbook of Middle American Indians*, Vol. 3: *Archaeology of southern Mesoamerica*, Part 2, ed. by R. Wauchope and G. R. Willey, 716–38. Austin: University of Texas Press.

Stopford, Jennie (1987) "Danebury: an alternative view." *Scottish Archaeological Review* 4: 70–5.

Stuiver, M. and Reimer, D. (1986) "A computer program for radiocarbon age calibration." *Radiocarbon* 28 (2B): 1022–30.

Suggs, R. C. (1961) "The archaeology of Nuku Hiva, Marquesas Islands, French Polynesia." *Anthropological Papers, American Museum of Natural History* 49: 1–205.

References

Tharp, W. E., E. H. Smies, and G. W. Musgrave (1920) *Soil survey of Madison County, Mississippi.* Washington, D.C.: U.S. Department of Agriculture.

Thomas, J. (1987) "Relations of production and social change in the Neolithic of north-west Europe." *Man* 22: 405–30.

Thomas, N.J. (1986) "Social and cultural dynamics in early Marquesan history." Unpublished Ph.D. dissertation, Australian National University, Canberra.

Thomson, R. (1978) *The Marquesas Islands: their description and early history by R. D. Craig.* Laie: Brigham Young University (Hawaii) Press.

Thorpe, Ian (1984) "Ritual, power, and ideology – a reconstruction of earlier Neolithic rituals in Wessex." In *Neolithic studies. A review of some current research,* ed. by R. Bradley and J. Gardiner, 41–60. Oxford: BAR British Series 133.

Thorpe, I. J. and Colin Richards (1984) "The decline of ritual authority and the introduction of beakers into Britain." In *Neolithic studies. A review of some current research,* ed. by R. Bradley and J. Gardiner, 67–86. Oxford: BAR British series 133.

Thrane, Henrik (1984) *Lusehøj ved voldtofte – en sydvestfynsk storhøj fra yngre Broncealder.* Fynske studier XIII. Odense.

Todd, Malcolm (1981) *Roman Britain.* Brighton: Harvester Press.

Tolstoy, Paul (1975) "Settlement and population trends in the Basin of Mexico (Ixtapaluca and Zacatenco phases)." *Journal of Field Archaeology* 2: 331–49.

(1978) "Western Mesoamerica before A.D. 900." In *Chronologies in New World archeology,* ed. by R. E. Taylor and C. W. Meighan, 241–84. New York: Academic Press.

Tolstoy, Paul, Suzanne K. Fish, Martin W. Boskenbaum, and Kathryn B. Vaughn (1977) "Early sedentary communities of the Basin of Mexico." *Journal of Field Archaeology* 4: 91–106.

Tolstoy, Paul and Louise I. Paradis (1971) "Early and middle Preclassic culture in the Basin of Mexico." In *Observations on the emergence of civilization in Mesoamerica,* ed. by R. Heizer and J. Graham. Contributions of the University of California Archaeological Research Facility, No. 11, 7–28. Berkeley: University of California.

Torrance, R. (1982) "The obsidian quarries and their use." In *An island polity: the archaeology of exploitation in Melos,* ed. by C. Renfrew and M. Wagstaff, 193–221. Cambridge University Press.

Tuggle, H. D. and M. J. Tomonari-Tuggle (1980) "Prehistoric agriculture in Kohala, Hawaii." *Journal of Field Archaeology* 7: 297–312.

Upham, Steadman (1987) "A theoretical consideration of Middle Range Societies." In *Chiefdoms in the Americas,* ed. by R. D. Drennan and C. A. Uribe, 345–68. Lanham, MD: University Press of America.

Vaillant, George C. (1930) *Excavations at Zacatenco.* Anthropological Papers of the American Museum of Natural History, Vol. 32, Part 1. New York: American Museum Press.

References

(1931) *Excavations at Ticomán*. Anthropological Papers of the American Museum of Natural History, Vol. 32, Parts 1 and 2. New York: American Museum Press.

(1935) *Excavations at El Arbolillo*. Anthropological Papers of the American Museum of Natural History, Vol. 35, Part 2. New York: American Museum Press.

Van der Leeuw, Sander E. (1981) "Preliminary report on the analysis of Moundville phase ceramic technology." *Southeastern Archaeological Conference Bulletin* 24: 105–8.

Vermeule, Emily (1964) *Greece in the Bronze Age*. University of Chicago Press.

Wait, Gerald (1985) *Ritual and religion in Iron Age Britain*. BAR British Series 149 (i). Oxford.

Wall, Julia (1987) "The role of daggers in Early Bronze Age Britain: the evidence of wear analysis." *Oxford Journal of Archaeology* 6: 115–18.

Wallace-Hadrill, J. M. (1971) *Early Germanic kinship in England and on the Continent*. Oxford Press.

Walthall, John A. (1981) *Galena and aboriginal trade in eastern North America*. Illinois State Museum Scientific Papers 17.

Walthall, John A. and Ben Coblentz (1977) "An archaeological survey of the Big Sandy Bottoms in the Black Warrior Valley." Ms. on file, Mound State Monument, Moundville, Alabama.

Webb, Malcolm C. (1975) "The flag follows trade: an essay on the necessary interaction of military and commercial factors in state formation." In *Ancient civilization and trade*, ed. by J. A. Sabloff and C. C. Lamberg-Karlovsky, 155–210. Albuquerque: University of New Mexico Press.

(1987) "Broader perspectives on Andean state origins." In *The origin and development of the Andean state*, ed. by J. Haas, S. Pozorski and T. Pozorski, 161–7. Cambridge University Press.

Weiland, Doris (1984) "Prehistoric settlement patterns in the Santa María drainage of central Panama: a preliminary analysis." In *Recent developments in Isthmian archaeology: advances in the prehistory of lower Central America*, ed. by F. W. Lange, 31–54. Oxford: BAR International Series 212.

Welch, Paul D. (1981) "The West Jefferson phase: Terminal Woodland tribal society in west central Alabama." *Southeastern Archaeological Conference Bulletin* 24: 81–3.

(1985) "Mississippian emergence in west central Alabama." In *The Mississippian emergence*, ed. by B. D. Smith. Washington, D. C.: Smithsonian Institution Press.

(1986) "Models of chiefdom economy: prehistoric Moundville as a case study." Ph.D. dissertation, Department of Anthropology, University of Michigan, Ann Arbor. Ann Arbor: University Microfilms.

Welinder, Stig (1976) *Ekonomiska processer i forhistorisk expansion*. Lund: Acta Archaeologica Lundensia, Ser. in 8 Minore, No. 7.

Whalen, Michael E. (1981) *Excavations at Santo Domingo Tomaltepec:*

evolution of a Formative community in the Valley of Oaxaca, Mexico. Memoirs of the Museum of Anthropology, University of Michigan, No. 12. Ann Arbor.

Whitelaw, T. M. (1983) "The settlement at Fournou Korifi, Myrtos, and aspects of Early Minoan social organization." In *Minoan society: proceedings of the Cambridge colloquium 1981,* ed. by O. Krzyszkowska and L. Nixon, 323–45. Bristol Classical Press.

Wickham, Chris (1985) "The uniqueness of the East." *The Journal of Peasant Studies* 12 (2 and 3): 166–96.

Wight, Martin (1977) *Systems of states, edited with introduction by Hedley Bull.* England: Leicester University Press.

Willey, Gordon R. (1984) "A summary of the archaeology of lower Central America." In *The archaeology of lower Central America,* ed. by F. W. Lange and D. Z. Stone, 341–78. Albuquerque: University of New Mexico Press.

Williams, Stephen and Jeffrey P. Brain (1983) "Excavations at the Lake George site, Yazoo County, Mississippi, 1958–1960." Papers of the Peabody Museum of Archaeology and Ethnology, Vol. 74. Cambridge: Harvard University.

Wimberly, Stephen (1956) "A review of Moundville pottery." *Southeastern Archaeological Conference Newsletter* 5 (1): 17–20.

Winter, Marcus C. (1972) "Tierras Largas: a Formative community in the Valley of Oaxaca, Mexico." Ph.D. dissertation, Department of Anthropology, University of Arizona. Ann Arbor: University Microfilms.

(1984) "Exchange in formative highland Oaxaca." In *Trade and exchange in early Mesoamerica,* ed. by K. Hirth, 306–10. Albuquerque: University of New Mexico Press.

Winter, Marcus C. and Jane W. Pires-Ferreira (1976) "Distribution of obsidian among households in two Oaxacan villages." In *The early Mesoamerican village,* ed. by K. V. Flannery, 306–10. New York: Academic Press.

Wittfogel, K. (1957) *Oriental despotism.* New Haven: Yale.

Wobst, H. Martin (1974) "Boundary conditions for Paleolithic social systems: a simulation approach." *American Antiquity* 39: 147–79.

(1975) "The demography of finite populations and the origins of the incest taboo." *Memoirs of the Society of American Archaeology* 30: 75–81.

(1976) "Locational relationships in Paleolithic society." *Journal of Human Evolution* 5: 49–58.

Wolf, E. R. (1981) "The mills of inequality: a Marxian approach." In *Social inequality: comparative and developmental approaches,* ed. by G. D. Berreman, 41–57. New York: Academic Press.

(1982) *Europe and the people without history.* Berkeley: University of California Press.

Woodrick, Anne (1981) "An analysis of the faunal remains from the Gainesville Lake area." In *Biocultural Studies in the Gainesville lake*

References

area, ed. by Gloria M. Caddell, Anne Woodrick, and Mary C. Hill, 91–168. *Archaeological Investigations in the Gainesville Lake Area of the Tennessee–Tombigbee Waterway*, Vol. 4. Report of Investigations 14. University, AL: University of Alabama Office of Archaeological Research.

Worley, Barbara A. (1987) "Property and gender relations among Twareg nomads." *Nomadic Peoples* 23: 31–5.

(1988) "Bed posts and broad swords: Twareg women's work parties and the dialectics of sexual conflict." In *Dialectics and gender: anthropological approaches*, ed. by R. R. Randolph et al., 273–87. Boulder: Westview Press.

(n.d.) "Livestock, vassals, slaves, and drum: the property of women and gender relations among Twareg nomads." Ph.D. dissertation, Columbia University.

Wright, Henry T. (1984) "Prestate political formations." In *On the evolution of complex societies: essays in honor of Harry Hoijer 1982*, ed. by T. Earle, 41–77. Malibu: Undena Publications.

Yarnell, Richard A. and M. Jean Black (1985) "Temporal trends indicated by a survey of Archaic and Woodland plant food remains from southeastern North America." *Southeastern Archaeology* 4 (2): 93–106.

Yellen, J. E. and H. Harpending (1972) "Hunting-gatherer populations and archaeological inference." *World Archaeology* 4: 244–53.

Yen, D.E. (1974) *The sweet potato and Oceania: an essay in ethnobotany*. B.P. Bishop Museum Bulletin 236. Honolulu.

(1975) "Indigenous food processing in Oceania." In *Gastronomy: the anthropology of food and food habits*, ed. by M. Arnott, 147–68. Chicago: Aldine.

Zeiltin, Robert N. (1979) "Prehistoric long-distance exchange on the southern Isthmus of Tehuantepec, Mexico." Ph.D. dissertation, Department of Anthropology, Yale University. Ann Arbor: University Microfilms.

Index

Index

Index

Index

Gross burial mound (Pocahontas), 219, 220 (Table), 221, 223 (Table), 224 (Fig.)
group-oriented chiefdoms, 3, 8, 22–3, 92, 283
Guadalupe phase (Valley of Oaxaca), 244, 245, 248, 251, 268, 269
guest-friendship (*xenia*), 176–7, 181, 189, 192 -
Gulf Coast societies, 208, 231, 247, 258, 264–7, 281–6 *passim*

Haas, J., 147, 150, 170, 178
Hadj Iata (Twareg), 107
haka'iki (Marquesan hereditary chiefs), 125, 126, 131, 132, 140–4 *passim*
Halawa Valley (Hawaii), 76, 78, 79
Hambledon Hill causewayed camp, 86 (map), 87, 88, 89
Hammond, N. G. L., 187, 188
Hampshire, monuments, 84, 93
Hanamiai site (Marquesas), 134
Handy, E. S. C., 124, 126, 137
Hane (Marquesas), 132
Hawaii, island of, 75, 79
Hawaiian chiefdoms, 74–80, 98, 124, 131; agriculture, 76–7, 144; compared with Marquesas, 143–5; land tenure, 12, 79–80; monuments, 77–9, 80, 96; population, 76–7, 133, 144; settlement patterns, 77; *see also* irrigation systems
health, status-related distinctions in, 202, 203
Hedeager, L., 32
heiau shrines (Hawaii), 78, 79, 145
Heizer, R. F., 266
Hellas/Hellene, 175
Hellenic League, 187
Helms, M. W., 247–8, 257
henge monuments, 54, 57, 68, 96; labor investment, 53, 66, 93 (Table); location, 85, 90 (map), 91, 92
hereditary leadership, 148, 158, 176–7, 182, 247, 280; see also *haka'iki*
Herman, G., 181
Hernando Gonzalo, A., 153
Herodotus, 185
Herrmann, J., 19
Hesiod, 174
Hilalian Arabs, 106
hill forts, 12, 48, 61, 62, 69, 93–4; 98; chiefly redistribution role, 46, 80; food storage role, 47, 57, 60, 93; labor investment, 59, 65–6, 94
hilltop settlements (Wessex), 57, 59, 87
Hippias, 185
Hirth, K. G., 232

Hivaoa island (Marquesas), 122
Hjort, A., 103–4
hoards: nordic Bronze Age, 29 (Fig.), 30, 31; nordic Iron Age, 32, 34, 35, 36
Homer, 167, 174, 177, 185
Hommon, R. J., 76
Hopewellian, 26
hoplites, 180–1, 183, 185, 186
household unit, 13, 73–4, 241, 242; craft specialization within, 205, 214, 269, 282; Greek (*oikos*), 171, 175, 176, 185
Huitzo (Valley of Oaxaca), 245, 251, 268
hunter gatherers, property rights among, 72–3
Hylleis, 175

Ibergalan, the, 101
Ibn Battuta, 110, 111, 113
Ibutkutan (Twaregs), 116
ideology/ideological control: relationship to economic factors in evolutionary theory, 8–10, 39, 40, 44–5, 62–3, 70, 98, 260; role in emergence of city-states, 172–3, 174, 192; role in operation of British chiefdoms, 46, 55, 58, 62, 64, 65, 69; as source of chiefly power, 1, 6–9, 171–2, 214
Ifadeyan Twaregs, 108
Igdalan Twaregs, 111
Ighalgawan, Mt., 113, 114
Ighalgawan warrior aristocracy, 100, 101, 113, 114, 116
Ihaggaran see Ahaggar region
Ikherkheran Twaregs, 116
imajaghan (Twareg warrior aristocrats), 103, 105, 107–8, 109, 112, 113, 114, 115, 118
Imanan Twaregs, 108, 109–10, 111
Imanan Valley, 101, 113
imghad, see client class, Twareg
Impressed Ware complex, 151
In Abangharit, 101, 113, 114
In Azoua, 113, 114
In Azzouza, 113
individualizing chiefdoms, 3, 22, 23 (Fig.), 92, 283
information monopoly, 38, 260–1
interaction networks, *see* exchange; regional interaction
"Intermediate Area," 278, 280, 281, 282, 285; *see also* Central American societies; South America, northern
international style and ideology, 7, 10, 14, 28, 31, 39; *see also* exotic wealth objects
Ionians, 174, 175, 191
Ireland, Iron Age, 102, 105
Iron Age: Ireland, 102, 105; northern

Index

Macedon, 187, 188, 191

Maiden Castle, 86 (map), 88

maize agriculture: in Central America and northern South America, 272, 273–4, 277, 281–2; in Formative Mesoamerica, 237–9, 242–4, 248, 251–2, 268, 270; Mississippian, 193, 195, 203–4, 213–17 *passim*; relationship between productivity and demographic change, 237–9, 242–4, 248, 251–2

Makaha Valley, Oahu (Hawaii), 78

Makashiki ceremonies (Hawaii), 78

Malinowski, B., 2

Mallia, 164

mana (supernatural efficacy, Polynesia), 130, 140, 142

managerial explanations of development of social complexity, 130, 146–7, 148, 213

Mangaia island (Polynesia), 124

Mangareva island (Polynesia), 124

Mann, M., 38, 173, 176, 177, 180, 186

Mantaro Valley, 6

Mararaba, 113

Marcus, J., 245, 249, 268

Marden, 90 (map), 91

Marquesas, 121–45; agriculture/subsistence, 128–9, 134–7, 141, 144; compared with Hawaii, 143–5; competition between social groups, 9, 121, 131–2, 135, 139, 141, 142–3, 144, 145; environment (*see also* drought), 4, 122–3, 134–5, 144; exchange relationships, 140–1; population, 4, 5, 124, 133, 141, 142; settlement patterns and monumental architecture, 78, 131, 133, 137–40, 141, 144–5; sociopolitical structure and evolution, 125–7, 140–5; warfare, 126, 131, 132, 139, 142

Marx, Karl, 20, 72, 147, 148, 149, 155

Marxist interpretations, 148, 149–51, 155, 178

mata'eina'a (Polynesian descent group), 124, 125, 126, 131, 143

materialist interpretations of chiefdoms, 44–5, 70; *see also* economic factors

Mau'i island (Hawaii), 75

Maumbury Rings, 91

ma'ae (Marquesan temples), 139

meat consumption, 68, 69, 85, 96; elite, 57, 202

Mediterranean: exchange relationships, 6, 7, 161–2, 164, 166–7; social complexity in later prehistory, 148–68

Megara, 182, 188

Melanesia, 120

Melos, 160

Melville, Herman, 124

Mendaña, Alvaro de, 122

Mesoamerica, 8, 9, 11, 14, 231–6, 252–3, 263–4, 278–9; burial 244, 264, 266, 268, 270, 283; exchange relationships, 232, 242, 245–9 *passim*, 251, 252–3, 256–8 *passim*, 260–1, 266, 269; monumental architecture (*see also* Oaxaca Valley), 231, 255, 257, 258, 264–5, 271, 283; warfare, 267, 270, 272, 279–80; *see also* Gulf Coast societies; Mesoamerican highlands

Mesoamerican highlands, 7, 78, 231–6, 252–61; agriculture, 237–8, 239, 242–4, 251–2, 257; ceramics, 239, 241, 247, 248, 250, 258; chronology, 234 (Table); craft production, 247, 249, 251; population, 4, 232, 237–46 *passim*, 248, 250, 252–5, 257–60, 268, 270, 272; *see also* Basin of Mexico; Cuicatlán Cañada; Ejutla Valley; Morelos; Oaxaca Valley; Tamazulapan Valley

Mesopotamia, 169, 173, 185

Messenia, 178, 183, 186

metallurgy, 30, 42, 153, 167; and development of stratification, 154–6; *see also* Aegean; bronze metallurgy; metals

metals, 10; role in British prehistory, 54, 57–8, 59, 61, 62, 66–9 *passim*, 97; role in nordic prehistory, 28, 29–30, 31, 35–6, 38; *see also* metallurgy

metates, 266, 273

Mexico, *see* Basin of Mexico; Mesoamerican highlands

Micronesia, 120

Middle Formative period, 250, 252, 254, 258, 261

Miletus, 187

militärische Demokratie, 17, 19, 117, 158; *see also* "Germanic mode of production"

military might, *see* warfare

Millaran (southeastern Spain), 152, 157, 159, 160, 161, 162

Minoan civilization, 6, 159, 163–4, 173; wealth finance system, 161–2, 164–7 *passim*

Mississippian societies, 7, 8, 77, 193–4, 224–7, 280; agriculture, 193, 195, 203–4, 213–17 *passim*; ceramics, 208, 209, 217, 222; ceremonial centers/monuments, 195, 197–200, 214, 217, 218–21; craft production, 205–6, 213, 214, 226, 227; exchange relationships, 208–12, 214, 215, 222, 225–6; political centralization, 193, 194, 203, 212, 213–15, 225, 226–7; *see also* Moundville region; Pocahontas region

Mitylene, 188

Index

Index

Index

Index

Printed in the United Kingdom
by Lightning Source UK Ltd.
107833UKS00002B/34-36